高等院校市场营销专业系列教材

市场营销学
(双语版)
Marketing

陈丽燕　刘永丹　龙　凤　主编

清华大学出版社
北京

内容简介

本书依据国家教育部高等学校本科专业教材编写的基本要求,从中国市场营销活动的实际情况与高等院校经管类人才的培养目标及特点出发,使用中英双语介绍市场营销学的基本理论与政策,系统地阐述了市场营销学的基本原理、基本方法及营销策略,并尽力融入实用性、前沿性、中国化的新内容。使读者在掌握市场营销基本原理和方法的同时,把握市场营销发展的趋势,掌握相关专业知识的英文表达,从而提高专业能力和英文水平。

本书可作为高等院校市场营销专业的教材,也可供从事涉外市场营销工作的人士参考。

本书封面贴有清华大学出版社防伪标签,无标签者不得销售。

版权所有,侵权必究。举报:010-62782989,beiqinquan@tup.tsinghua.edu.cn。

图书在版编目(CIP)数据

市场营销学:双语版:英、汉/陈丽燕,刘永丹,龙凤主编. —北京:清华大学出版社,2016
(2024.1重印)
(高等院校市场营销专业系列教材)
ISBN 978-7-302-44312-4

Ⅰ.①市… Ⅱ.①陈… ②刘… ③龙… Ⅲ.①市场营销学—双语教学—高等学校—教材—英、汉 Ⅳ.①F713.50

中国版本图书馆 CIP 数据核字(2016)第 164311 号

责任编辑:李玉萍 张新元
装帧设计:刘孝琼
责任校对:吴春华
责任印制:杨 艳

出版发行:清华大学出版社
网 址:https://www.tup.com.cn,https://www.wqxuetang.com
地 址:北京清华大学学研大厦 A 座 邮 编:100084
社 总 机:010-83470000 邮 购:010-62786544
投稿与读者服务:010-62776969,c-service@tup.tsinghua.edu.cn
质量反馈:010-62772015,zhiliang@tup.tsinghua.edu.cn
课件下载:https://www.tup.com.cn,010-62791865

印 装 者:三河市铭诚印务有限公司
经 销:全国新华书店
开 本:185mm×260mm 印 张:19.75 字 数:477 千字
版 次:2016 年 9 月第 1 版 印 次:2024 年 1 月第 9 次印刷
定 价:59.50 元

产品编号:052411-03

前言
Preface

　　伴随着中国融入世界经济发展的大潮，国内出现了大量的涉外企业，而同时国际上越来越多的跨国公司也进入中国的市场，这些企业的经营发展需要大量既懂营销专业知识又擅长在英语环境下沟通的专门人才。在这样的人才需求背景下，很多院校积极推进双语教学工作，以适应社会的需要。随着双语教学的不断深入，市场营销课程已成为高等院校双语教学改革试点中的亮点和热点。然而，教材建设却明显滞后，相关专业的学生缺乏专门、适用的教材，严重制约了学生岗位职业能力的发展。为了能够培养出复合型、应用型、涉外型的市场营销的专门人才，编写适合高等院校学生使用的教材对进一步提高高等院校市场营销专业双语教学的质量有着十分重要的意义。

　　本书在比较分析现存双语教材的种类和特点的基础上，通过探索双语教材选择和使用的标准，为双语教学提供理论支持。本书以市场营销基础知识为主体，以涉外市场营销专业培养目标为编写方向，以市场营销学为支撑，强调英语与市场营销学的融合。教材立意新颖，具有很强的针对性、实用性、适用性。

　　市场营销学是一门建立在经济科学、行为科学和现代管理理论基础之上的应用科学。它主要研究市场营销活动及其规律性，具有综合性、边缘性的特点，属于管理学范畴。课程的核心内容就是研究在买方市场条件下，卖方如何从顾客的需要出发制定企业发展战略、组织企业市场营销活动，从而在满足顾客需求的前提下，使企业在激烈竞争的市场环境中获得生存和发展。而企业必须依靠掌握营销理论和技巧的市场营销专业人员才能实现目标。不仅如此，在市场经济条件下，市场营销理论、方法和技巧不仅广泛应用于企业和各种非营利性组织，而且逐渐应用于微观和宏观各个层次，涉及社会经济生活的各个方面。它是工商管理类各专业的核心课程，也是经济学类各专业的基础课程。

　　本书总体框架由黑龙江外国语学院陈丽燕负责设计。全书共有10章，参与编写的成员分工如下：第3、4、5、6、7章汉语稿由陈丽燕编写；第9、10章汉语稿和第1、7、8、9、10章英语稿由黑龙江外国语学院刘永丹编写；第8章汉语稿和第2、3、4、5、6章英语稿由黑龙江外国语学院龙凤编写；第1章汉语稿由东北林业大学工程技术学院王巍编写；第2章汉语稿由黑龙江外国语学院刘音编写。此外，陈福明教授和外籍专家Lucy Qi负责了全书的审校工作，他们的认真审校使英文书稿更加地道流畅。在此特别感谢老师们的辛勤劳动。

　　本书在编写过程中，借鉴了国内外营销学者大量的最新的研究成果，特别是吸纳了一些国内最近出版的教材中的新内容与新观点。在此，谨向这些同行师友们致以深深的谢意。

　　本书是对市场营销双语教学教材建设的一个探索，书中缺点、疏漏和不妥之处在所难免，如广大师生和读者能来信、来电批评指正，使本教材日趋完善，编者将不胜感谢。

编　者

目 录
Contents

第一章 认识市场营销活动 What Is Marketing ··············· 1
第一节 市场与市场营销概述 An Overview of Market and Marketing ··············· 1
一、市场 Market ··············· 1
二、市场营销 Marketing ··············· 6
第二节 市场营销观念 Marketing Concept ··············· 9
一、如何理解市场营销观念 How to Understand Marketing Concept ··············· 9
二、市场营销观念的演进 Evolution of Marketing Concept ··············· 10
本章小结 Summary ··············· 20
思考题 Questions ··············· 21

第二章 市场营销调研 Marketing Research ··············· 22
第一节 市场营销调研概述 An Overview of Marketing Research ··············· 22
一、市场营销调研的含义和类型 Definition and Classifications of Marketing Research ··············· 22
二、市场营销调研的内容 Contents of Marketing Research ··············· 24
第二节 市场营销调研的基本程序 Basic Procedures of Marketing Research ··············· 27
一、调研准备阶段 Preparation Stage ··············· 27
二、调研实施阶段 Implementation Stage ··············· 30
三、调研资料整理、分析与报告撰写阶段 Data Collation, Analysis and Report Writing Stage ··············· 31
第三节 市场营销调研的方法 Marketing Research Methods ··············· 32
一、按调研对象划分 According to Research Subjects ··············· 33
二、按获得信息的方式划分 According to Ways of Obtaining Information ··············· 37
本章小结 Summary ··············· 40
思考题 Questions ··············· 40

第三章 分析市场营销环境 Analyzing Marketing Environment ··············· 42
第一节 认知市场营销环境 Understanding Marketing Environment ··············· 42
一、市场营销环境的含义及其构成 Meaning and Composition of Marketing Environment ··············· 42
二、市场营销环境的特点 Characteristics of Marketing Environment ··············· 44
三、企业营销与营销环境的互动 Interaction Between Enterprise Marketing and Marketing Environment ··············· 45
第二节 分析微观营销环境 Analyzing Micro-environment ··············· 47
一、企业内部条件 Enterprise's Internal Conditions ··············· 47

二、供应商 Suppliers ……47

三、营销中间商 Marketing Intermediaries ……48

四、目标顾客 Target Customers ……49

五、竞争者 Competitors ……49

六、公众 The Public ……50

第三节 分析宏观营销环境 Analyzing Macro-environment ……52

一、人口环境 Population Environment ……53

二、社会文化环境 Social Culture Environment ……57

三、经济环境 Economic Environment ……62

四、科技环境 Science and Technology Environment ……66

五、政治法律环境 Political and Legal Environment ……67

六、自然环境 Natural Environment ……69

本章小结 Summary ……71

思考题 Questions ……71

第四章 市场购买行为分析 Analyzing Market Purchase Behavior ……73

第一节 消费者市场及其购买行为分析 Consumer Market and Consumer Purchasing Behavior ……73

一、消费者市场的概念及购买模式 Concept of Consumer Market and Purchasing Patterns ……73

二、影响消费者购买行为的因素 Factors influencing Consumer Purchase Behavior ……75

三、消费者购买行为的类型 Types of Consumer Purchase Behavior ……87

四、消费者购买行为决策过程 Decision-making Process of Consumer Purchase Behavior ……90

第二节 组织市场及其购买行为分析 Institutional Markets and Institution Purchase Behavior ……94

一、组织市场的概念及类型 Concept and Types of Institutional Markets ……94

二、组织市场购买行为 Purchase Behavior of Institutional Market ……96

本章小结 Summary ……107

思考题 Questions ……108

第五章 目标市场选择及市场定位策略 Strategies for Target Market Selection and Market Positioning ……109

第一节 市场细分 Market Segmentation ……109

一、市场细分的含义 Concept of Market Segmentation ……109

二、有效市场细分的要求 Requirements of Effective Market Segmentation ……111

三、市场细分的程序 Procedures of Market Segmentation ……111

四、市场细分的依据 Basis of Market Segmentation ……112

五、市场细分的方法 Methods of Market Segmentation ……118

第二节 选择目标市场 Selecting Target Market ……119

一、目标市场及目标市场选择的含义 Meaning of Target Market and Target Market Selection ……119

二、目标市场选择的标准 Criteria of Target Market Selection ……120

三、目标市场的选择策略 Strategies for Target Market Selection ……122

四、目标市场的营销策略 Marketing Strategies for Target Market ······ 123
　　五、影响目标市场选择的因素 Factors Influencing Target Market Selection ······ 127
第三节　市场定位 Market Positioning ······ 130
　　一、市场定位的含义 Meaning of Market Positioning ······ 130
　　二、市场定位的作用 Functions of Market Positioning ······ 131
　　三、市场定位的步骤 Steps of Market Positioning ······ 132
　　四、市场定位的方法 Methods of Market Positioning ······ 135
　　五、市场定位策略 Strategies for Market Positioning ······ 138
本章小结 Summary ······ 140
思考题 Questions ······ 141

第六章　产品策略 Product Strategies ······ 143

第一节　产品概述 Overview of Products ······ 143
　　一、产品的含义 Concept of Product ······ 143
　　二、产品整体概念 Total Product Concept ······ 144
　　三、产品的分类 Categories of Product ······ 147
第二节　产品生命周期策略 Product Life Cycle Strategies ······ 152
　　一、产品生命周期的概念 Concept of Product Life Cycle ······ 152
　　二、产品生命周期各阶段的特点及营销策略 Characteristics and Marketing Strategies at Every Stage of the Product Life Cycle ······ 154
第三节　产品品牌与包装策略 Branding and Packaging Strategies ······ 164
　　一、品牌策略 Branding Strategy ······ 164
　　二、包装策略 Packaging Strategies ······ 169
第四节　产品组合策略 Product Mix Strategies ······ 173
　　一、产品组合及其相关概念 Product Mix and Related Concepts ······ 173
　　二、产品组合策略的分类 Categories of Product Mix Strategies ······ 176
第五节　新产品开发策略 New-Product Development Strategies ······ 182
　　一、新产品的概念及类型 Concept and Types of New Products ······ 182
　　二、新产品开发的策略 Strategies of New-product Development ······ 184
本章小结 Summary ······ 185
思考题 Questions ······ 186

第七章　价格策略 Pricing Strategies ······ 187

第一节　定价的程序与方法 Pricing Procedures and Methods ······ 187
　　一、定价程序 Pricing Procedures ······ 187
　　二、定价方法 Pricing Approaches ······ 192
第二节　定价的基本策略 Pricing Strategies ······ 199
　　一、产品组合定价策略 Portfolio Pricing Strategies ······ 199
　　二、新产品定价策略 New Product Pricing Strategies ······ 201

三、心理定价策略 Psychological Pricing Strategies · 203
　　四、地理定价策略 Geographical Pricing Strategies · 204
　　五、折扣定价策略 Discount Pricing Strategies · 206
　　六、差别定价策略 Segmentation Pricing Strategies · 208
　　七、价格调整策略 Price Adjustment Strategies · 209
本章小结 Summary · 211
思考题 Questions · 212

第八章　分销渠道策略 Distribution Channel Strategies · 213

第一节　分销渠道的职能及类型 Functions and Types of Distribution Channels · 213
　　一、分销渠道的概念 Definition of Distribution Channels · 213
　　二、分销渠道的职能 Functions of Distribution Channels · 214
　　三、分销渠道的类型 Types of Distribution Channels · 215
第二节　选择分销渠道策略 Selecting Strategies for Distribution Channels · 218
　　一、影响分销渠道策略设计的因素 Factors Influencing the Design of Channel Strategies · 218
　　二、分销渠道选择的策略 Strategy for Selecting Distribution Channels · 222
第三节　批发商与零售商的分销策略 Wholesaling and Retailing Distribution Strategies · 227
　　一、批发商的分销策略 Wholesaling Distribution Strategies · 227
　　二、零售商的分销策略 Retailing Distribution Strategies · 229
第四节　分销渠道管理策略 Channel Management Strategies · 232
　　一、渠道管理的内容 Contents of Channel Management · 232
　　二、渠道管理的策略 Channel Management Strategies · 233
本章小结 Summary · 236
思考题 Questions · 237

第九章　促销策略 Promotion Strategies · 238

第一节　促销与促销组合策略 Promotion and Promotion Mix Strategies · 238
　　一、促销的含义 Meaning of Promotion · 238
　　二、促销的作用 Effects of Promotion · 240
　　三、促销组合策略 Strategies of Promotion Mix · 242
第二节　人员推销策略 Personal Selling Strategies · 250
　　一、人员推销的含义及特点 Meaning and Characteristics of Personal Selling · 250
　　二、人员推销的任务 Assignments of Personal Selling · 252
　　三、人员推销策略的含义及内容 Meaning and Contents of Personal Selling Strategies · 253
　　四、人员推销的形式策略 Form Strategy of Personal Selling · 253
　　五、人员推销的基本策略 Basic Strategies of Personal Selling · 255
　　六、人员推销的工作流程策略 Working Procedure Strategy of Personal Selling · 256
　　七、人员推销的管理策略 Management Strategies of Personal Selling · 258
第三节　广告策略 Advertising Strategies · 265

一、广告的含义及类型 The Meaning and Types of Advertisement ……… 265

　　二、广告策略的概念及其程序 The Concept and Other Procedures of Ads ……… 268

第四节　公共关系策略 Public Relation Strategies ……… 278

　　一、公共关系的概念及特征 Concept and Essential Characteristics of Public Relations ……… 278

　　二、公共关系策略 Public Relations Strategy ……… 280

第五节　营业推广策略 Sales promotion Strategies ……… 284

　　一、营业推广的概念 The Concept of Sales Promotion ……… 284

　　二、营业推广策略的含义 The Meaning of Sales Promotion Strategies ……… 284

　　三、营业推广策略的类型及活动方式 The Types of Sales Promotion Strategies and the Ways of Activities ……… 285

　　四、营业推广策略实施程序 The Implementation Procedures of Sales Promotion Strategies ……… 289

本章小结 Summary ……… 290

思考题 Questions ……… 291

第十章　营销素养和社会责任 Marketing Ethics and Social Responsibility ……… 292

第一节　加强营销素养 Reinforce Marketing Ethics ……… 292

　　一、营销人员必备的营销素养 Salesmen's Requisite Marketing Ethics ……… 292

　　二、营销人员提高业务素养的途径 Ways of Promoting Salesmen's Professional Quality ……… 296

第二节　实施对社会负责的市场营销 Marketing with Social Responsibility ……… 297

　　一、社会对于营销的批评 Social Criticism of Marketing ……… 297

　　二、营销中的社会责任 Social Responsibility in Marketing ……… 298

　　三、实施对社会负责的营销 Implement the Marketing Responsible for the Society ……… 300

本章小结 Summary ……… 302

思考题 Questions ……… 302

参考文献 ……… 303

第一章 认识市场营销活动
What Is Marketing

【学习目标】

1. 市场的概念及市场分类；
2. 市场营销的核心概念；
3. 市场营销观念的演进。

Learning Objectives

1. Concept and types of markets;
2. Core concepts of marketing;
3. Evolution of marketing concepts.

市场营销不是企业经营活动的某一方面，它始于产品生产之前，并一直延续到产品售出以后，贯穿于企业经营活动的全过程。它是企业在占领市场、扩大销售、实现预期目标的过程中所进行的一系列商务活动。企业的成功并不是取决于生产而是取决于顾客，因此，树立现代市场营销观念、正确认识市场营销活动是成功开展营销活动的前提和基础。

Marketing is not an aspect of business activities. It begins before production and extends to after-sales, which is a whole process of business operations. Marketing is a series of business activities in the process of occupying market, expanding sales, and achieving objectives. An enterprise's success does not depend on production but on the customer, therefore, correct understanding of marketing concepts and marketing campaigns is the basis of successful implementation of marketing activities.

第一节 市场与市场营销概述
An Overview of Market and Marketing

一、市场 Market

(一)市场的概念 Concept of Market

市场是社会生产分工、商品生产与商品交换的产物，属商品经济的范畴。哪里存在商品交换，哪里就有市场。市场的含义是随着商品经济的发展而不断延伸的。

Market is the result of social production division, commodity production and commodities exchange. It belongs to the scope of commodity economy. Where there exists commodity exchange, there is market. The meaning of market extends with the development of commodity economy.

美国著名营销学家菲利普·科特勒认为："市场是指某种产品的实际购买者和潜在购买者的集合。这些购买者有某种欲望或需要，并且能够通过交换得到满足。因而，市场规模取决于具有这种需要及支付能力、并且愿意进行交换的人的数量。"

Philip Kotler, the famous American marketing expert, believes that the market is a collection of actual and potential buyers of certain products. These buyers have certain desire or needs, which can be met through exchange. Thus, market scale depends on the number of people who have the needs and payment abilities and are willing to be engaged in the trade.

市场是人口、购买力、购买欲望三要素的集合体。

Market is an aggregate of population, purchasing power and purchasing desire.

其中，人口指的是对产品有现实和潜在需要的人，是构成市场的最基本的要素。购买力是顾客支付货币、购买商品或服务的能力。购买力是构成市场的重要因素，有支付能力的需求才促成有意义的市场。购买欲望是顾客购买商品的动机、愿望或要求，是顾客把潜在购买力变成现实购买力的重要条件。市场的三个要素相互制约，缺一不可，只有三者结合起来，才能构成现实的市场，才能决定市场的规模和容量。

Population is the people with actual and potential needs, who constitute the most basic element of market. Purchasing power is the ability to pay and to buy goods or services. It is an important factor of market, and demand with ability to pay constitutes a meaningful market. Purchasing desire is the motivation, will or demand of customers to purchase goods and is an important condition to turn customers' potential purchasing power into reality. These three elements of market are indispensable and restrain each other. Only the combination of the three can constitute a real market, and determine the size and capacity of the market.

(二)市场的分类 Types of Market

市场按不同的标准可以划分为各种不同的类型。不同的市场类型，有其不同的交换内容及其具体的需求与特点。

Market can be divided into various types by different standards. Different markets have different exchange contents, specific needs and characteristics.

1. 按竞争程度划分 Divided by Competition Degree

按照竞争程度划分，市场有完全竞争市场、完全垄断市场、垄断竞争市场和寡头垄断市场。

Based on competition degree, there are fully competitive market, monopoly market, monopolistic competition market, and oligopoly market.

完全竞争市场是指竞争不受任何干扰的市场，它意味着市场中产品价格稳定，产品质量相同，要素转移自由，信息传递迅速。理想的完全竞争市场实际上是不存在的。在现实生活中，农产品市场比较接近完全竞争市场的情况。

Fully competitive market is the one without any interference which means stable price, same quality free factors and quick information transfer. Ideal fully competitive market does not exist in reality and agricultural market is similar to it in real life.

完全垄断市场是指整个产业只有一家企业，它的产品没有任何替代品，其他企业无法进入该产业。完全垄断企业能够操纵整个产业的产品和价格，该企业就是代表产业。形成完全垄断的原因主要有自然垄断、原料控制、专利权和政府特许。

Monopoly market refers to that there is only one enterprise in an industry. There are no substitutes for its products; other enterprises cannot enter the field. The monopoly enterprise is on behalf of the industry, and it is able to manipulate the entire industry's product and price. Full monopoly is mainly due to natural monopoly, raw material control, patents, and government concessions.

垄断竞争市场是介于完全竞争市场和完全垄断市场之间的市场。垄断竞争市场的主要特点是：一切同类商品之间存在差别，市场上有很多同类企业，企业进入市场比较容易，比如一般日用工业品。垄断竞争对消费者的满足程度最高，在一定的价格水平下消费者对商品的选择余地较大，它是目前经济生活中普遍存在的市场结构。

Monopolistic competition market is a market between fully competitive market and monopoly market. Its main features are as follows: there are differences among all the goods of the same kind; there are many similar enterprises and it's easy for them to enter the market, such as general industrial products for daily use. Monopolistic competition, in which consumers have greater choice at a certain price level, gives consumers the maximum level of satisfaction and is the prevailing market structure in current economic life.

寡头垄断市场是指一种产品在拥有大量消费者或用户的情况下，由少数几家大企业控制绝大部分的商品生产经营量，剩下的一小部分产品量则由众多的小企业去生产经营。产生这种市场的主要原因是资源的有限性、技术的先进性、资本规模的集中性以及规模经济效益所形成的排他性，诸如钢铁、石油、航空等领域。

Oligopoly market refers to the market where a kind of product owns a large number of consumers or users and a few big enterprises control the most production of the goods, leaving a small amount produced by a large number of small enterprises. This is due to limited resources, advanced technology, centralized capital and exclusivity formed by Scale Economies Effect in such business lines as steel, oil, aviation, etc.

2. 按流通区域划分 Divided by Circulation Regions

按商品流通区域划分，市场可分为国内市场和国际市场。

Based on circulation regions, there are domestic and international markets.

国内市场，是指在一国范围内可使商品和劳务发生转移的区域市场。国内市场的发展与繁荣，不仅能够促进本国经济的发展，而且能为发展对外贸易、进入国际市场提供牢固的基础与条件。国内市场又可分为省区市场、城乡市场等。

Domestic markets refer to the regional markets within a country for the transfer of goods and services. Development of domestic markets can not only promote economy but also provide solid foundation and favorable conditions for developing foreign trade and entering international markets. Domestic markets can be divided into province markets, urban and rural markets, etc.

国际市场，是指越出本国国境与其他国家进行贸易活动所形成的多国间市场。国别市场、贸易集团区域市场、洲别市场等都属于国际市场。

International markets are the multinational ones which are beyond one country's border with trading activities taking place in different countries. Country markets, markets for trading blocs and continent markets all belong to international markets.

3. 按产品形态划分 Divided by Product Forms

市场按产品形态划分，可分为有形产品市场与无形产品市场。

Based on product forms, there are tangible product market and intangible product market.

有形产品市场是指具有物质形态的商品市场，它包括工业品商品市场与农产品商品市场。工业品商品市场可分为轻工商品市场、机械商品市场、零配件商品市场、生产设施商品市场等市场；农产品商品市场可分为种植类、养殖类、林产类等商品市场。

Tangible product market is for commodities with physical forms, including those for industrial goods and agricultural goods. The markets for light industry goods, machinery, spare parts and production facilities all belongs to industrial goods market, while agricultural goods market includes those for cultivation, aquaculture and forestry products.

无形产品市场是指不提供有形的物质产品，而通过交换提供各种形式的服务，用以满足非物质消费需求的市场。在无形产品市场中，又可分为劳务市场、服务市场、信息市场等市场。

Intangible product market is the one where there is no tangible products exchange but the exchange of various services to meet the demand for non-material consumption. The markets for labor, services and information all belong to intangible product markets.

4. 按产品用途划分 Divided by Product Uses

市场按产品用途划分，可分为消费者市场与生产者市场，实际上也就是生活消费品市场与生产消费品市场。

Based on product uses, there are consumer market and industry market, which are actually markets for consumer goods and industrial goods.

消费者市场是指居民生活消费品的商品市场，可分为食品市场、日用工业品市场、服装市场、家具市场等生活消费品市场。

Consumer market is for consumer goods, which includes food market, daily-use industrial products market, clothing market, furniture market, etc.

生产者市场是指生产者所需的各种生产资料的商品市场。生产者市场包括原材料、生产工具、生产设施、肥料、种子等生产消费品商品市场。

Industry market is for various means of production needed by producers, including markets for raw materials, production tools, production facilities, fertilizer and seeds, etc.

5. 按生产要素划分 Divided by Production Factors

市场按产品生产过程中所需的基本生产要素划分，可分为物质产品市场、资金市场、劳动力市场、科技市场、信息市场、服务市场、房地产市场等要素市场。

Based on production factors required in the production process, there are markets for material products, capital, labor, science and technology, information, services and real estate, etc.

物质产品市场是指生产活动所需的原材料、生产工具、生产设施等生产资料商品市场。

Material product market is for raw materials, production tools, production facilities and so on.

资金市场是指进行生产经营活动所需资金的交易市场，可分为资金借贷市场、证券市场、股票市场等资金市场。

Capital market is for funds needed in production and business activities, which includes capital lending, securities, stocks and other financial markets.

劳动力市场是指进行生产活动所需劳动力的交易市场，可分为零用工市场、人才市场等。

Labor market is for labor exchange required in production activities. They can be markets for flexible employment and human resources market, etc.

科技市场是指进行生产活动所需科学技术的交易市场，可分为科技成果转让市场、科技成果出租市场等。

Science and technology market is for technology exchange needed in production activities, including transfer and rental markets for scientific and technological achievements.

信息市场是指进行生产经营活动所需各种信息的交易市场，可分为科技信息市场、商品供求信息市场、竞争者信息市场、社会经济发展信息市场以及网络信息市场等。

Information market is for information exchange, which is required in production and business activities, including markets for technology information, commodity supply and demand, competitors, socio-economic development, network and so on.

服务市场是指进行生产经营活动所需各种服务的交易市场，可分为中介服务市场、代理服务市场、承包服务市场等服务市场，还可按服务行业划分为餐旅、洗染、维修、医疗以及劳务等服务市场。

Service market is for service exchange that are needed in production and business activities. It can be divided into intermediary services, agency services and contracting services. According to service sectors, there are service markets for hospitality, laundry, maintenance, medical treatment, labor and other services.

6. 按购买者的购买目的和用途来划分 Divided by Buyers' Aims and Purposes

按照顾客购买目的或用途的不同，市场可分为消费者市场和组织市场两大类。

Based on buyers' aims or purposes, there are consumer market and organization market.

消费者市场是指个人或家庭为了生活消费而购买产品和服务的市场。

Consumer market is market where individuals and households can buy goods and services for personal consumption.

组织市场是指以某种组织为购买单位的购买者去购买所需产品与服务而构成的市场。

组织市场又包括生产者市场、中间商市场、非营利组织市场和政府市场。

Organization market is market where an organization buys goods and services as a purchasing unit. Organization market includes industry market, reseller market, non-profit organization market and government market.

总之，市场有各种不同的类型。认识不同的市场类型，有利于生产者与消费者准确地选择市场，进行业务范围定位，进而进行产品定位，找到最有利的市场空间。

In brief, market has a variety of types. Understanding different markets helps producers and consumers to choose appropriate markets, locate business scopes and find the most favorable market space based on a good product positioning.

二、市场营销 Marketing

(一)市场营销的概念 Concepts of Marketing

菲利普·科特勒认为，市场营销是通过创造和交换产品及价值，从而使个人或群体满足欲望和需要的社会过程和管理过程。它包含两种含义：作为动词，指企业的具体活动或行为，这时称为市场营销或市场经营；作为名词，指研究企业的市场营销活动或行为的学科，称为市场营销学、营销学或市场学等。

Philip Kotler believes that marketing is a social and managerial process by which products and value are created and exchanged to satisfy the wants and needs of individuals and groups. Marketing can be understood as actions—companies' actual activities and behaviors, which is also called Market Management. Marketing can also be understood as a noun—the study of companies' marketing activities and behaviors, which is also called Marketing Discipline.

(二)市场营销的核心概念 Core Concepts of Marketing

1. 需要、欲望及需求 Needs, Wants and Demands

1) 需要 Needs

需要是一种感觉缺失的状态。它包括生理需要和心理需要。对食物、衣服、房屋等的需要属生理需要；对安全、归属感、尊重和自我实现等的需要属心理需要。市场营销者不能创造这些需要，而只能适应它们。

Human needs are states of felt deprivation, which include basic physical needs and psychological needs. The former includes needs for food, clothing, housing, etc. The latter includes needs for safety, belongingness, esteem, self-actualization, etc. Marketers are not able to create such needs but adapt to them.

2) 欲望 Wants

欲望是从需要派生出的一种形式，是文化和个性形成的人类特定需要。不同背景下的消费者欲望不同，如饥饿的美国人可能想要一个汉堡包，中国人可能需要米饭。人的欲望受社会因素及机构因素，诸如职业、团体、家庭、教会等影响。

Wants are the form derived form human needs, which are specific needs shaped by cultures and individual personalities. Consumers with different background have different wants. A hungry

American, for example, probably wants a hamburger while a Chinese may want rice. Wants are influenced by social and organizational factors, such as occupations, groups, families and churches.

3) 需求 Demands

指有支付能力和购买某种物品的意愿。消费者的需要在有购买力作后盾时就成为需求。许多人想购买奥迪牌轿车,但只有具有支付能力的人才能购买。

Demands refer to buying power and the willing to buy something. When backed by buying power, wants become demands. Many people want to buy an Audi, but only those who are able to pay can buy such cars.

2. 产品及相关的效用、价值和满足 Products and Related Utility, Value and Satisfaction

1) 产品 Product

产品是指用来满足顾客需求和欲望的商品、服务、信息和体验的组合。产品包括有形产品和无形产品。有形产品是向市场提供的实体和服务的可识别的形象表现,通常表现为产品质量、式样、品牌以及服务设施、环境等。无形产品或服务是通过其他载体,诸如人、地、活动、组织和观念等来提供的。当我们感到疲劳时,可以到音乐厅欣赏歌星唱歌(人),可以到公园去游玩(地),可以到室外散步(活动),可以参加俱乐部活动(组织)或者接受一种新的意识(观念)。

Product is the combination of goods, services, information and experiences that satisfy the demands or wants of customers. There are tangible and intangible products. Tangible products are physical objects or recognizable forms of services supplied in market, such as quality, style, brand, service equipments or environment, etc. Intangible products provide services through other carriers such as people, places, activities, organizations, ideas, etc. When we feel tired, we could go to concert halls to enjoy singers' singing (people), go to the park (place), walk in the open (activity), participate in clubs (organization) or accept a new notion (idea).

2) 效用、价值和满意 Utility, Value and Satisfaction

消费者对产品的选择,是基于他们对满足其需要的每种产品的效用的评估。效用是消费者对满足其需要的产品的全部效能的估价。那么,如何确定产品的全部效能呢?例如某消费者到某地去的交通工具,可以是自行车、摩托车、汽车、飞机等。这些可供选择的产品构成了产品的选择组合。假设某消费者有不同的需求——快速、安全、舒适及价廉,这些就构成了其需求组合。每种产品能满足其不同的需要。

How consumers choose products depends on their evaluation of the utility from each product that satisfies them. Utility is consumers' evaluation of the whole effectiveness from the product that satisfies them. Then, how to determine the whole effectiveness? For example, if consumer chooses transport means to some place, the options can be a bicycle, a motorcycle, an automobile, an aircraft, etc., which constitute a combination of selection. Suppose a consumer has different needs—speed, safety, comfort and cost saving, which is his selection combination. Each product can meet his different need.

顾客通常会面对能满足其需要的一系列产品和服务。怎样从这些市场供给中加以选择呢?顾客对各种各样的市场供给传递的价值和满意度形成期望并据此购买。

Consumers usually face a broad array of products and services that might satisfy a given need. How do they choose among these many market offerings? Customers have expectations about the value and satisfaction that various market offerings will deliver and buy accordingly.

3. 交换、交易和关系 Exchange, Transaction and Relationship

1) 交换 Exchange

产品只有通过交换才使市场营销产生。只有通过等价交换，买卖双方彼此获得所需的产品，才产生市场营销。很显然，交换是市场营销的核心概念。

Only through product exchange can marketing come into being. Through equivalent exchange, both buyers and sellers get the products they need and so marketing comes about. Obviously, exchange is the core concept in marketing.

2) 交易 Transaction

如果双方通过谈判并达成协议，交易便发生，交易是交换的基本组成部分。交易是指是以货币为媒介的买卖双方价值的交换。

When an agreement has been reached through negotiation, there occurs a transaction. Transaction is an essential component of exchange. Transaction means value exchange between a buyer and a seller, with currency as a medium.

交易涉及几个方面，即两件有价值的物品，双方同意的条件、时间、地点，还有来维护和迫使交易双方执行承诺的法律制度。

Transactions involve the following aspects—two pieces of goods with value, agreed conditions, time, place and legal system that maintains the implementation of the two parties' commitments.

3) 关系 Relationship

精明能干的市场营销者都会重视同顾客、分销商等建立长期、信任和互利的关系。而这些关系要靠不断承诺及为对方提供高质量产品、良好服务及公平价格来实现，靠双方加强经济、技术及社会联系来实现。关系营销可以减少交易费用和时间，最好的交易是使协商成为惯例化。

Capable marketers think it important to establish long-term, trusting and mutually beneficial relationships with customers and distributors. These relationships depend on constant commitments and supply of high quality products, good services and fair prices. The relationships also depend on the economical, technical and social ties between two parties. Relationship marketing can reduce transaction cost and time, and the best transaction is the one that makes consultation practices.

4. 市场、市场营销及市场营销者 Market, Marketing and Marketer

1) 市场 Market

市场是由有特定需求或欲求并且可以通过交换来满足其需求满足的潜在顾客所组成的。一般说来，市场是买卖双方进行交换的场所。从市场营销学的角度来看，卖方组成行业，买方组成市场。行业和市场构成了一个简单的市场营销系统。

Markets are made up of potential customers who have specific needs or wants and may meet their needs or wants through exchange. In general, markets are places where buyers and sellers trade. From the view of marketing principle, sellers make up the industries and buyers make up the markets. Industries and markets constitute a simple marketing system.

2) 市场营销及市场营销者 Marketing and Marketer

市场营销是指与市场有关的人类活动，即为满足消费者需求和欲望而利用市场来实现潜在交换的活动，是一种社会的和管理的过程。

Marketing means human activities related to markets, i.e., activities that aim to meet the needs and wants of consumers and realize potential exchange through markets, which is a social and managerial process.

市场营销者则是从事市场营销活动的人。市场营销者既可以是卖方，也可以是买方。作为买方，他力图在市场上推销自己，以获取卖方的青睐，这样买方就是在进行市场营销。当买卖双方都在积极寻求交换时，他们都可称为市场营销者，并称这种营销为互惠的市场营销。

Marketers are people engaged in marketing activities. Marketers can be sellers or buyers. As a buyer, a marketer tries to market himself to obtain sellers' favor, which is the marketing made by the buyer. When the buyer and the seller are actively seeking exchange, they both can be marketers, and the marketing they are performing is called reciprocal marketing.

第二节 市场营销观念
Marketing Concept

市场营销作为一种有意识的经营活动，是在一定的经营思想指导下进行的。这种思想是企业营销的导向，是一种观念。市场营销指导思想的正确与否，对企业经营的成败兴衰具有决定性的意义。

As conscious activities, marketing is carried out under certain guidance of business ideas. Enterprises' marketing is orientated by those ideas or notions. Whether the marketing idea is correct or not is of great significance to a enterprise's success or failure.

企业的经营思想是在一定的经济基础上产生的，并随着经济的发展和市场形势的变化而发展变化。在西方市场经济高度发达的社会里，企业营销管理的指导思想大体上有五种，即生产观念、产品观念、推销观念、市场营销观念和社会市场营销观念。

Enterprises' business ideas come about on certain economic basis and develop as economy and market situations develop and change. In the western society where market economy has highly developed, generally, guiding ideas in marketing management can be divided into five types: production concept, product concept, selling concept, marketing concept and social marketing concept.

一、如何理解市场营销观念 How to Understand Marketing Concept

市场营销观念是企业在从事生产和营销活动时所依据的指导思想和行为准则。它体现了人们对市场环境、企业在市场运行中所处的地位以及企业与市场的相互关系等基本问题的认识、看法和根本态度，是企业所奉行的一种经营哲学或理念。

Marketing Concept is the enterprise's guiding ideology and behavior standards in production and marketing activities. It reflects people's knowledge, opinions and basic attitude on marketing environment, enterprise status in marketing operations and relationship between enterprises and markets. It is a kind of management philosophy or idea that enterprises follow.

市场营销观念作为一种指导思想和经营理念，是企业一切经营活动的出发点。它支配着企业营销实践的各个方面，包括从事市场营销活动的目的、组织市场营销活动的重点、应建立的市场营销组织结构和管理体制，以及采取的市场营销策略、方法和手段等。奉行正确的营销观念是企业组织市场营销实践的核心和关键所在。

As guiding ideology and business ideas, marketing concept is the starting point of all the business activities of enterprises. It dominates all aspects of marketing practices, including the purposes and focuses of marketing activities, the organization structure and management system that should be built, the marketing strategies, methods and techniques, etc. Following the right marketing concept is the key of enterprises' marketing practices.

二、市场营销观念的演进 Evolution of Marketing Concept

企业营销管理的指导思想大体上有以下几种营销观念：以企业为中心的营销观念、以消费者为中心的营销观念、以社会长远利益为中心的营销观念以及其他现代市场营销的新观念。

There are the following marketing concepts as guiding ideas in marketing management—enterprises as the center, consumers as the center, long-term social interests as the center and other new modern marketing ideas.

(一)以企业为中心的市场营销观念 Enterprise-centered Marketing Concept

在早期的企业经营活动中，企业的市场营销观念，多称为经营观念。其基本特征是以企业为中心，以利润为导向。这是由于当时产品在市场上主要表现为供不应求，企业在销售方面基本上不成问题，企业间的竞争主要表现为以成本为基础的价格竞争。以企业为中心的市场营销观念按其发展顺序来看主要有以下三种。

In early business activities, enterprises' marketing concept is kind of business concept, with enterprises as the center driven by profit. Enterprises had no problem with sales because demand exceeded supply at that time. The competition among enterprises is mainly price competition based on costs. According to the order of development, there are three types of enterprise-centered marketing concept.

1. 生产观念 Production Concept

生产观念是指企业的一切经营活动以生产为中心的"以产定销"。生产观念的假设前提是消费者可以接受任何买得到和买得起的商品，因而企业的主要任务就是努力提高效率、降低成本、扩大生产。

With production concept, all the business activities of an enterprise focus on production-basing sales on production. The premise of this concept is that consumers can accept any goods available and affordable, so the main task of enterprises is to improve efficiency, reduce costs and expand production.

这是一种传统的、古老的经营思想，20世纪20年代以前在西方发达国家占支配地位。当时由于生产效率不高，许多商品的供应还不能充分满足市场的需要。例如，在20世纪20年代初，美国汽车大王亨利·福特的经营哲学就是千方百计地增加T型车的产量，降低成本和价格，以更多地占领市场，获得规模经济效益。至于消费者对汽车颜色等方面的爱好，则不予考虑，他的T型车只有黑色的。

It is an ancient and traditional management thought dominant before 1920s in the western developed countries. Due to low production efficiency, supplies of many commodities could not fully meet the market needs. The business philosophy of Henry Ford, the American automobile magnate, for example, was to try every means to increase the production of Model T cars, reduce costs and prices so as to occupy more market and gain scale economic benefit. Consumers' preference for color or other aspects would not be considered and Model T cars had the only color of black.

生产观念在两种情况下适用：一是商品需求超过供给，卖方竞争较弱，买方争购，选择余地不多；二是产品成本和售价太高，只有提高生产效率，降低成本，从而降低售价，才能扩大销路。

Production concept applies in two cases: ① Demand exceeds supply when selling competition is weak and buyers compete to buy for there is few choices; ② Production cost and price are too high, and the market can be expanded only through improving production efficiency and reducing costs and price.

生产观念容易导致企业形成"营销近视"。主要是因为它们过度集中于自身运作，而失去了对真正目标——满足顾客需求和建立顾客关系——的了解。

Production concept tends to lead to "marketing myopia", because enterprises concentrate on their own operations so much that they ignore their real goal—to meet customers' demands and build customer relationships.

2. 产品观念 Product Concept

产品观念认为，消费者最喜欢那些高质量、多功能和有特色的产品。因而，企业应该集中力量改进产品，使之日臻完善。

Product Concept holds that consumers like the products of high quality, multi-function and distinctive features. Therefore, enterprises should focus on improving their products towards perfection.

许多经理认为，顾客欣赏精心制造的产品，他们能够鉴别产品的质量和功能，并愿花较多的钱买质量上乘的产品。然而，由于产品观念的奉行，曾使许多企业患有"营销近视症"。这些企业将自己的注意力集中在现有产品上，即集中主要的技术、资源进行产品的研究和大规模生产，而看不到消费者需求的不断发展变化，以及对产品提出的新要求，不能随顾客需求变化以及市场形势的发展去及早地预测和顺应这种变化，树立新的市场营销观念和策略，最终导致企业经营的挫折和失败。

Many managers think that customers appreciate carefully manufactured products, and they can compare qualities and functions, willing to spend more money on products of better quality. The Product Concept, however, has caused many enterprises' "marketing myopia". Those enterprises focused their attention on existing products, devoting technology and resources to product research and mass production. They could not see the changes in consumers' demands and new requirements, neither could they forecast nor make advantage of those changes, which finally led to business failures and setbacks.

生产观念和产品观念都属于以生产为中心的经营思想，其区别只在于：前者注重以量取胜，后者注重以质取胜，二者都没有把市场需要放在首位。

Both production and product concepts belong to production-centered business ideas. The difference lies in that the former pays attention to amount and the latter to quality. Neither of them put market in the first place.

3. 推销观念 Selling Concept

20 世纪 20 年代末，西方国家的市场发生了重大的变化，特别是 1929 年开始的资本主义世界大危机，使产品严重供过于求，销售困难，竞争加剧。企业担心的已不是生产问题而是销售问题。于是，推销技术特别受到企业的重视，推销观念也就成为工商企业主要的指导思想。

At the end of 1920s, great changes took place in western markets. Especially in the world capitalist crisis, which began in 1929, there appeared supply excess, sales difficulties and fierce competition. What worried the enterprises was not production but sales. Accordingly, selling techniques were emphasized and Selling Concept became enterprises' guiding ideology.

推销观念是假设企业若不大力刺激顾客的兴趣，顾客就不会购买或不会大量购买它的产品。因此，企业必须建立专门的推销机构，大力施展推销和促销技术。

Selling Concept is based on the assumption that if an enterprise is not to stimulate customers, customers will not buy its products or buy in bulk. Therefore, the enterprise must establish special selling agencies, and display their marketing and promotion techniques fully.

大多数企业在生产能力过剩时都遵循推销观念，它们的目标是售出所制造的产品而非市场需要的产品。由于这种观念强调销售交易而非与顾客建立长期的互惠关系，因此会带来市场风险。

Most enterprises follow the selling concept in excess production and their goal is to sell their products rather than meet the needs of the market. Such concept emphasizes transactions, not long-term business relationship of mutual benefit, which would cause marketing risks.

（二）以消费者为中心的市场营销观念 Consumer-centered Marketing Concept

以消费者为中心的市场营销思想统称为市场营销观念。市场营销观念是商品经济发展史上的一种全新的经营哲学，它是第二次世界大战后在美国新的市场形势下形成的，相继盛行于美国、日本、西欧以及其他经济发达国家。

The marketing thought focusing on consumers is called Marketing Concept, which is a new business philosophy and was formed in the new market situation in America after WWII. Later on, it became popular in USA, Japan, Western European and other developed countries.

1. 市场营销观念的含义 Meaning of Marketing Concept

所谓市场营销观念，是一种以顾客需要和欲望为导向的经营哲学，它把企业的生产经营活动看作一个不断满足顾客需要的过程，而不仅仅是制造或销售某种产品的过程。在市场营销观念下，重视顾客的关注点和顾客价值才是销售和获利之路。

The so-called Marketing Concept is a customer-oriented business philosophy. It regards production activities not only as a manufacturing or selling process, but also as a process of constantly meeting customers' needs. Under the guidance of Marketing Concept, focusing on customers' concern and customer value is the right way of selling and gaining profit.

市场营销观念的形成和在实践的广泛运用，对西方企业改善经营起了重要作用，取得了重大成就，如美国的P&G、IBM、麦当劳等公司都是运用市场营销观念取得成功的范例。因此，在西方，有人把这一经营思想的变革同产业革命相提并论，称之为"市场营销革命"，甚至还有人说这是企业经营思想方面的"哥白尼日心说"。虽然这未免夸大其词，但这一经营思想的重要性及其影响之大，由此可见一斑。不过，近年来也有人提出，不应过分夸大市场营销革命的作用而忽视技术革命和新产品开发的作用，因为新产品毕竟是占领市场的物质基础。

The formation of Marketing Concept and its appliance in practice play an important role in western companies' operation and have made significant achievements, such as P&G, IBM, McDonald's and other companies. Some in western countries equated this revolution in business thoughts with the Industrial Revolution, calling it "Marketing Revolution", and some even say it is "Copernicus's Heliocentric Theory" in business management ideas. Although this would be exaggerated, the importance of this business idea and its influence can be gauged. In recent years, however, some people have pointed out that the marketing revolution could not be exaggerated, and the role of technical revolution and the development of new products should not be ignored as new products which are the material bases for occupying the market.

2. 市场营销观念与推销观念的区别 Difference Between Marketing Concept and Selling Concept

市场营销观念取代传统观念，是企业经营思想上的深刻变革，是一次根本性的转变。

It is a profound and fundamental change in business philosophy that Marketing Concept has replaced traditional attitudes.

如图1-1所示，推销观念以企业现有产品为出发点，要求大力推销与促销，以实现有利销售。而市场营销观念则注重买方需求，以目标顾客及其需求、欲望为出发点，通过融合和协调影响消费者满意程度的营销活动，来赢得顾客的满意，从而获得利润。从本质上说，市场营销观念是一种对顾客的需求和欲望的导向。这种导向以使顾客产生满意感而实施的企业综合营销努力为基础，表明了对消费者主权论的信奉，即究竟应该生产什么的决定权不在企业手中，也不在政府手里，而是在消费者手中。

企业应该生产消费者所需要的东西，这样才能使消费者利益最大化，企业也能赚取利润。

As is shown in Figure 1-1, with Selling Concept, the company focuses on existing products to realize beneficial sales through selling and promotion. Marketing Concept focuses on the buyer's demand. It holds that companies, starting from the target customers and their wants, can gain and maintain customers' satisfaction therefore, to gain profit by integrating and coordinating these marketing activities, which will affect customers' satisfaction. In essence, Marketing Concept is an orientation of customer needs and desires. Such orientation is based on enterprises' all-round marketing efforts which aim to make customers satisfied. Such orientation also indicates a belief in consumer sovereignty, which means it is the customers, neither the enterprise nor the government, that decide what to produce.

Enterprises should produce what consumers need, so as to maximize the interests of consumers and profit of their own.

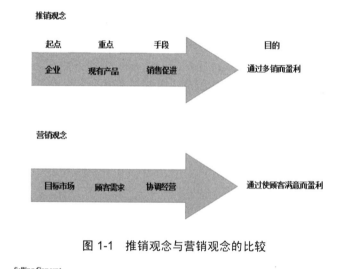

图 1-1　推销观念与营销观念的比较

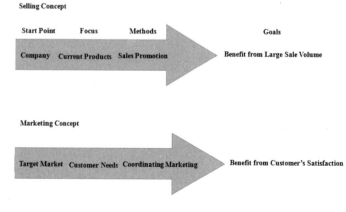

Figure 1-1　Comparing Selling Concept and Marketing Concept

(三)以社会长远利益为中心的社会市场营销观念 Social Marketing Concept Focusing on Long-term Social Interest

20世纪70年代以来，西方国家市场环境发生了许多变化，如能源短缺，通货膨胀，失业增加，消费者保护运动盛行，等等。在这种背景下，人们纷纷对单纯的市场营销观念提出了怀疑和指责，认为市场营销观念没有真正付诸实践，即使在某些企业里真正确立了市场营销观念，但它们忽视了满足消费者个人需求同社会长远利益之间的矛盾，从而造成了资源大量浪费和环境污染等社会弊端。

Since 1970s, many changes have taken place in the market environment of western countries, such as energy shortages, inflation, unemployment, consumer protection campaign and so on. In such context, Marketing Concept was doubted and accused for people believe that Marketing Concept has not really been put into practice, and even in some enterprises where Marketing Concept has been really established, the contradiction between consumers' needs and long-term social interests is neglected, which resulted in substantial waste of resources, environmental pollution and other social problems.

所谓社会市场营销观念，就是不仅要满足消费者的需要和欲望并由此获得企业的利润，而且要符合消费者自身和整个社会的长远利益。要正确处理消费者欲望、企业利润和社会整体利益之间的矛盾，统筹兼顾，求得三者之间的平衡与协调。不少公司通过采用和实践社会营销观念，获得了可观的销售量和利润。

The so-called Social Marketing Concept, is not only to meet the needs and desires of consumers and thus get the profits, but also is in line with long-term interests of both customer and society. It requires good coordination and balance between consumer desires, enterprise profit and the whole society interest should be coordinated and balanced well. Many enterprises have achieved good sales and profit through Social Marketing Concept.

(四)现代市场营销观念的新发展 New Developments in Modern Marketing Concept

1. 大市场营销观念 Mega Marketing Concept

美国著名市场营销大师菲利普·科特勒，针对现代世界经济迈向区域化和全球化，企业之间的竞争范围早已超越本土，形成了无国界竞争的态势，提出了"大市场营销"观念。他指出，企业为了进入特定的市场，并在那里从事业务经营，在策略上应协调运用经济的、心理的、政治的、公共关系等手段，以获得外国或地方各方面的合作与支持，从而达到预期的目的。大市场营销战略在"4P"的基础上加上"2P"，即权力(Power)和公共关系(Public relations)，从而把营销理论进一步扩展。

The American famous marketing master, Philip Kotler, put forward the "Mega Marketing" concept under the background of economic regionalization and globalization, and the situation that the competition between enterprises has already been beyond the local and internationalized. He pointed out that enterprises should adopt a comprehensive strategy of economics, psychology, politics, public relations and other means to win support and cooperation from abroad or any other regions thus to realize the intended goal. 2Ps (Power and Public Relations) should be added to the Mega Marketing strategy on the basis of 4Ps, which further expands marketing theories.

大市场营销观念相比市场营销观念有所发展，主要体现在以下几方面：一是处理企业与外部环境的关系上，变市场营销的顺从和适应为采取适当的措施，积极主动地去影响。二是在市场营销目标上，市场营销观念认为重点是通过深入的市场调研，满足目标市场的需求，而大市场营销观念认为，企业应采用一切营销手段打开和进入某目标市场。三是在营销手段上，大市场营销观念在市场营销观念常用的"4P"基础上再加上政治权力和公共关系"2P"。

Compared with Marketing Concept, Mega Marketing Concept has developed in the following aspects: on the relationship between enterprises and external environment, obedience and adaptation should be changed into active measures and influence; on marketing objectives, Marketing Concept holds that, the key point is to satisfy target market through further market research, and Mega Marketing Concept holds that the enterprise should employ any marketing methods to enter target market; on marketing tools, Mega Marketing Concept has extra 2Ps on the basis of 4Ps, the commonly used marketing concept.

2. 绿色市场营销观念 Green Marketing Concept

绿色市场营销观念是指企业在绿色消费需求的推动下，保护环境，充分利用环境资源和绿色资源，研发绿色产品，把日常生活中的废品和大自然的绿色资源变为消费品，从而满足消费者需求的企业营销理念。它是以消费者的绿色消费需求为基础，综合利用各种资源进行企业的整体营销过程。这种绿色市场营销观念有利于社会环境，有利于人们的健康，是现代人比较推崇的营销观念。企业的绿色市场营销观念不仅有利于企业的长远的发展，而且有利于社会和人们的健康生活。

With Green Marketing Concept, enterprises, driven by the demand for green consumption, protect environment, make full use of environmental resources and green resources, develop green products, and change domestic wastes and natural green resources into consumption goods to meet consumers' needs. This concept is a marketing process of comprehensive utilization of various resources based on green consumption. The Green Marketing Concept is conducive to social environment and people's health and is favored by modern people. The Green Marketing Concept is not only conducive to the long-term development of enterprises, but also to the society and people's healthy life.

进入20世纪90年代以来，绿色消费已成为一种新的消费趋势，并将成为21世纪的消费主流。企业要生存和发展下去，就要向消费者提供安全卫生的产品。企业选择的生产技术要尽量减少生产过程对环境的不利影响，保护环境。

Since 1990s, green consumption has been a new trend and will become the mainstream in the 21st century. Enterprises need to provide safe and sanitary products in order to survive and develop. Enterprises also need to use the technology that can minimize the adverse effects to the environment in the production process and protect the environment.

绿色市场营销观念是以消费者的绿色需求为基础,是环保意识与市场营销观念的融合。企业在注重经济效益的同时,应比以往更注意生态效益和社会效益。绿色市场营销观念是对市场营销观念的进一步补充和发展。

Green Marketing Concept is a combination of environmental awareness and marketing concept based on the green consumption demand. Besides economic benefits, enterprises should pay more attention to ecological and social benefits than ever before. Green Marketing Concept is development and complement to Marketing Concept.

3. 整合营销观念 Integrated Marketing Concept

1990 年,美国市场营销专家罗伯特·F.劳特朋提出了整合营销概念,认为企业的全部活动都要以营销为主轴。他重新调整了营销要素,用"4C"——顾客欲望与需求(Consumer)、满足欲望与需求的成本(Cost)、购买的方便性(Convenience)以及沟通与传播(Communication)取代了传统的"4P"——产品(Product)、价格(Price)、通路(Passage)和促销(Promotion)。

Robert F. Lauterborn, an American marketing expert, put forward Integrated Marketing Concept in 1990, which holds that all the enterprises' activities should focus on marketing. He adjusted marketing elements, using 4Cs—customer, cost, convenience and communication, instead of 4Ps—product, price, passage and promotion.

美国西北大学舒尔茨教授 1993 年出版的《整合营销传播》一书,从理论上确立了整合营销传播的思想。整合营销传播(IMC)兴起于商品经济最发达的美国。其内涵是:"以消费者为核心重组企业行为和市场行为,综合使用各种形式的传播方式,以统一的目标和统一的传播形象传递一致的产品信息,实现与消费者的双向沟通,迅速树立产品品牌在消费者心目中的地位,建立品牌与消费者长期密切的关系,更有效地达到广告传播和产品营销的目的。"

Professor Schultz in Northwestern University published *Integrated Marketing Communication* in 1993. The book set up the thinking of integrated marketing communication from a theoretical point of view. Integrated Marketing Communication, IMC, initiated in the USA, with the most developed commodity economy. The IMC connotation is to restructure enterprise behavior and marketing behavior with consumers as the core, to employ various forms of transmission comprehensively, to deliver consistent product information through unified goals and images, to realize the two-way communication with consumers, to set up quickly the status of the product brand in consumers, to establish a close long-term relationship between brands and consumers and to achieve more effective advertising and marketing.

将旧的推销观念与市场营销观念、整合营销观念比较可以发现:市场营销与整合营销的出发点和营销中心是一致的,但满足需求的营销手段和营销目的却不同。

Comparing Selling Concept, Marketing Concept and Integrated Marketing Communication, we find that the starting point and marketing center of the latter two are consistent, but the means of marketing to meet the demands and goals of marketing are different.

4. 服务营销观念 Service Marketing Concept

说到服务营销观念，则不能不提到服务营销。在20世纪70年代，全球经济在第二次世界大战结束后的几十年中得到了飞速发展，人民生活水平不断提高，服务业也由此得到了迅速发展。营销理论界对服务营销的特性开始予以越来越多的关注。1981年布姆斯和比特纳建议在传统市场营销理论"4P"的基础上增加三个"服务性的P"，即人、过程和物质环境。

When it comes to the Concept of Service Marketing, service marketing must be talked about. In early 1970s, world economy developed rapidly after WWII. People's living standards improved gradually, which also led to the development of service industry. Marketing theories paid more and more attention to the features of service marketing. In 1981, Booms and Bitner proposed that "3 service Ps" should be added to the traditional 4Ps theory—People, Process and Physical Evidence.

"7P"的核心在于它揭示了员工的参与对整个营销活动的重要意义，企业应关注为用户提供服务的全过程，通过互动沟通了解客户在此过程中的感受，使客户成为服务营销过程的参与者，从而及时改进自己的服务来满足客户的期望。企业营销也应重视内部各部门之间分工与合作过程的管理，因为营销是一个由各部门协作、全体员工共同参与的活动，而部门之间的有效分工与合作是营销活动实现的根本保证。

The core of 7Ps is that it reveals the significance of staff's involvement in marketing activities. Enterprises, during the whole service process, should understand customers' feelings via interactive communication and make customers participate in process of service marketing. Then, the enterprise can improve its service and meet customers' expectation. The enterprise should also pay attention to the management on labor division and cooperation between internal departments, because marketing involves cooperation among departments and all staff and effective labor division and cooperation among departments are the fundamental guarantee for marketing achievements.

那么"7P"是否只适合服务业呢？正如《商业银行基层网点服务营销策略探讨》一文中引用中南财经政法大学企业管理博士王成慧所说的话："服务营销'7P'虽然是针对服务业的特殊性而提出的，但其理论价值和实践上的指导意义却不仅仅限于服务营销的范畴，它对整个营销理论乃至企业理论的发展都有启迪。""7P"的后三个P正是正在兴起的服务营销观念的体现。

Is the 7Ps framework only suitable for the service industry? Wang Chenghui, PhD of Business Management in Zhongnan University of Economics and Law once said in the essay *Research on Service Marketing Strategies in Commercial Bank Outlets at the Grassroots Level* "Although the 7Ps framework is proposed on the basis of special nature of service industry, its theoretical value and practical guidance are not limited to the areas of service marketing. It has enlightened all the marketing theories and even enterprise theories." The latter three of 7Ps reflect the emerging concept of service marketing.

5. 网络营销观念 Network Marketing Concept

网络营销观念产生于 20 世纪 90 年代，发展于 20 世纪末至今。网络营销产生和发展的背景主要有三个方面，即网络信息技术的发展，消费者价值观的改变，激烈的商业竞争。

The Concept of Network Marketing (CNM) started in 1990s and developed in the late 20th century. The background of CNM lies in three aspects: the development of network and information technology, change of consumer value and intense commercial competition.

网络营销方式能够根据网络本身的特点和网络顾客的需求，将产品说明、促销方法、顾客意见调查、产品广告、公共关系、顾客服务等各种营销活动组合在一起，进行有针对性的联络和沟通。网络营销的优势在于它突破了时间和空间的限制，能够快捷准确地捕获顾客信息，从而对目标顾客和销售的产品进行跟踪，使之更加接近于目标顾客的需要。

Network Marketing is able to combine product introduction, promotion methods, customer surveys, advertising, public relations, customer service and other marketing activities and make targeted liaison and communication. The advantage of network marketing is that it could break through limitation of time and space, capture customer information quickly and accurately, and thus track the target customers and sell products so as to meet customers' needs better.

6. 关系营销观念 Relationship Marketing Concept

关系营销是自 20 世纪 70 年代起，由北欧的一些学者提出并发展起来的，以建立、维护、促进、改善和调整"关系"为核心，对传统的营销观念进行革新的理论。20 世纪 80 年代以来，关系营销得到了更大的发展，在企业界得到了较为广泛的应用，在理论上也得到了更为深入的探讨，影响越来越大，被克里斯丁·葛罗斯誉为"20 世纪 90 年代及未来的营销理论"。

Relationship Marketing was proposed and developed by some Northern European scholars in the 1970s, which is an innovated marketing theory focusing on establishing maintaining stimulating, improving and adjusting "relationship". Relationship Marketing has been developed much more since 1980s and has been widely applied in business. It was also studied further from theoretical views and became more and more influential. Professor Christian Gronroos regards it as "the marketing theory of 1990s and the future".

关系营销是管理"关系"的一系列活动所构成的一个社会性过程，重点在于利益各方的相互交流，并形成一种稳定、相互信任的关系。关系营销的最终实现要靠产品或价值的成熟、顺利、高质量的交换，关系营销的一系列活动都是为了达到一定的营销目标。从实践意义上讲，关系营销已经完全突破了简单的企业与消费者之间的关系，延伸到有直接或间接联系的供应商、中间商、政府职能部门、个人及社会团体等各方面。

Relationship Marketing is a social process formed by a series of relationship management activities. Its emphasis lies in mutual communication between parties and stable relationship with mutual trust. The final realization of relationship marketing depends on mature, smooth and high-quality exchange. The series of activities of relationship marketing aim to reach marketing goals. On a practical level, relationship marketing has completely broken through the simple relationship between enterprises and consumers. It has extended to suppliers, intermediaries, government departments, individuals and other social organizations that are directly or indirectly linked to the enterprises.

在关系营销观念下，好的企业不仅需要质量可靠、功能先进的产品，更需要在公众面前展示出良好的企业形象，而这种形象的塑造，在很大程度上取决于企业与公众之间的关系。树立关系营销观念，企业能够更好地适应复杂的营销环境，从而保持营销工作的主动性。关系营销观念倡导的不是以现有利益为中心的关系，而是建立一种兼顾各方利益的稳定的合作关系。

Guiding by relationship Marketing Concept, a good enterprise not only need products of reliable quality and advanced functions, but also should demonstrate good corporate image in front of the public, which mainly depends on the relationship between the enterprise and the public. The enterprise with Relationship Marketing Concept is able to cope with complex marketing environment and maintain the initiative position in marketing. This concept does not advocate the relationship focusing on current interests, but establish a stable cooperation relationship that balances all parties' benefits.

从市场营销观念的演变过程可以发现，市场营销观念的核心是正确处理企业、顾客和社会三者之间的利益关系。市场营销观念是随着市场营销环境和营销实践的变化而发展变化的，不断会有新的观念被提出和使用。

From the evolution process of marketing concepts, it can be found that the core of marketing concepts is to handle well the relationship of enterprises, customers and society. Marketing concept develop with the change of marketing environment and marketing practices and new concepts will be proposed and applied constantly.

本 章 小 结
Summary

菲利普·科特勒认为："市场是指某种产品的实际购买者和潜在购买者的集合。这些购买者有某种欲望或需要，并且能够通过交换得到满足。因而，市场规模取决于具有这种需要及支付能力，并且愿意进行交换的人的数量。"市场是人口、购买力、购买欲望三要素的集合体。市场按不同的标准可以划分为各种不同的类型。不同的市场类型有其不同的交换内容及具体的需求与特点。

Philip Kotler believes that market is the combination of actual and potential buyers of certain product. The buyers have some wants or needs which can be satisfied through exchange. Market is a collection of three elements—population purchasing power and purchasing desire.

Market can be categorized into different types according to different standards, and different types have different exchange contents, specific requirements and characteristics.

市场营销是通过创造和交换产品及价值，从而使个人或群体满足欲望和需要的社会过程和管理过程。市场营销的核心概念包括需要、欲望、需求，效用、价值和满足(Utility，Value，Satisfaction)，交换、交易和关系，市场、市场营销及市场营销者。

Marketing is a social and management process during which products and value are created and exchanged to meet the wants and needs of individuals and groups. The core concepts in marketing include needs, desires, wants, utility, value, satisfaction, exchange, transaction, relationship, market, marketing and marketers.

市场营销观念包括以企业为中心的营销观念、以消费者为中心的营销观念和以社会长远利益为中心的营销观念及现代营销观念的新发展等。企业要根据自己的实际情况，去贯彻市场营销观念，从而取胜于国内外市场。

Marketing Concepts include concepts with enterprises as the center, consumers as the center, long-term interests of society as the center and other new developments of modern marketing concepts. Enterprises should implement proper marketing concepts according to actual situation to win market both at home and abroad.

思 考 题
Questions

1. 什么是市场？市场的类型有哪些？

What is market and what are the types of market?

2. 市场营销的含义及核心概念是什么？

What are the meaning and core definitions of marketing?

3. 举例说明以企业为中心的营销观念类型。

Give examples of enterprise-centered marketing concept.

4. 现代市场营销观念的新发展有哪些？

What are the new developments of modern marketing concepts?

第二章 市场营销调研
Marketing Research

【学习目标】
1. 市场营销调研的含义和类型;
2. 市场营销调研的内容;
3. 市场营销调研的基本程序;
4. 市场营销调研的常用方法。

Learning Objectives

1. Definition and classifications of marketing research;
2. Contents of marketing research;
3. Basic procedures of marketing research;
4. Methods of marketing research.

企业的营销活动是在不断变化的环境中进行的。在技术不断发展、市场结构趋于多样化、市场竞争激烈的今天,受错综复杂的环境因素的影响,呈现在企业面前的市场需求往往变化多端。因此,企业要想做好营销工作,必须重视市场调研,并能够在此基础上对事物发展做出预测。市场调研是企业加强管理、做好计划的基础,只有市场调研搞好了,才能使企业在瞬息万变的市场中得以快速发展。

It is known that all marketing activities of enterprises are conducted in a dynamic environment. Nowadays, with the influence of complicated environmental elements such as continuous development of technology, various structures of market and severe competition, market demands are changeable and unpredictable. Therefore if enterprises want to get successful marketing, they must focus on marketing research and forecast products' development accordingly. Marketing research is the foundation of enhanced management and good plans for an enterprise. Only full-scale marketing research can let an enterprise develop rapidly in such kind of economic environment.

第一节 市场营销调研概述
An Overview of Marketing Research

一、市场营销调研的含义和类型 Definition and Classifications of Marketing Research

(一)市场营销调研的含义 Definition of Marketing Research

市场营销调研于1910年首先在美国出现,第二次世界大战后逐渐推广到世界各国。市场营销调研是指以进行科学的营销管理和营销决策为目的，运用科学的方法对有关信息进行有计划、有步骤、系统的收集、整理、分析和报告的过程。

In 1910, the first marketing research was carried out in America and then it spread all over the world after World War II. Marketing research is a set of processes in which relevant information is collected, sorted, analyzed and reported in a purposeful, systematical, and scientific way to achieve scientific marketing management and marketing decisions.

市场营销调研在企业制定营销规划、确定企业发展方向、制定企业的市场营销组合策略等方面有着极其重要的作用。在营销决策的执行过程中，具有检验与矫正功能的市场营销调研能够为调整营销计划、改进和评估各种营销策略提供依据。

Marketing research plays an important role in making marketing plans, setting development directions and making marketing mix strategies for companies. In the process of carrying out marketing decisions, marketing research, which has functions of checking and correcting, can provide proofs to adjust marketing plans, improve and assess various marketing strategies.

(二)市场营销调研的类型 Classifications of Marketing Research

市场营销调研可按不同标准进行分类，最常见的是按调研方法与调研目的进行分类。

Marketing research can be classified by various criteria, and is usually classified according to research methods and purposes.

1. 按调研方法分类 According to Marketing Research Methods

(1) 定性调研。定性调研是根据研究者的认识和经验，确定研究对象是否具有某种性质，或确定某一现象变化的过程和原因的调研方法。

Qualitative research is a method of marketing research based on researchers' recognition and experience to examine whether a research target has certain natures or to determine processes of and reasons behind a certain phenomenon.

(2) 定量调研。定量调研就是对一定数量的有代表性的样本进行标准化的问卷访问，然后对调查的数据进行计算机的录入、整理和分析，并撰写总结报告的方法。

Quantitative research is applied to giving standardized questionnaires, then investigation data are input, sorted out and analyzed on computer to form a final report based on representative samples.

2. 按调研目的分类 According to Purposes of Marketing Research

(1) 探测性调研。探测性调研是指花费尽量少的成本和时间，对环境进行初始调研，以便确定问题及与这些问题相关的变量的总体特性的一种调研方法。探测性调研虽然有时也规定大致的调研方向和步骤，但是一般没有一个固定的计划。探测性调研主要用于帮助澄清或辨明一个问题，而不是寻求问题的解决办法。它往往是在大规模的正式调研之前开展的小规模定性研究，其研究目的只是对营销问题的本质作一个初步的评估，以便为进一步的研究确定范围和方向。

Exploratory research is to carry out fundamental research on environment with the least cost and time in order to locate the problem and overall characteristics of variables associated with the problem. Though exploratory research regulates general marketing directions and steps sometimes, it usually doesn't have a fixed plan. What exploratory research does is to clarify or recognize a problem, rather than work out solutions. It is usually a small-scale qualitative research, which happens before the large-scale formal research, in order to make a basic evaluation of the nature of the marketing problem and then determine the scope and direction for further study.

(2) 描述性调研。描述性调研是指通过详细的调查和分析，对市场营销活动的某个特定方面进行客观的描述，以说明它的性质和特征。描述性调研是营销调研中使用最多的一种类型，与探测性调研相比，它研究的问题更加具体，数据收集的具体目标更明确，而且通常在事先已形成了具体的研究假设。

Descriptive research is to describe a particular aspect of marketing activities through detailed investigation and analyses to show its nature and characteristics. This research method is one of the most frequently used types in marketing research. Compared with exploratory research, the problem it studies is more concrete and the goal of data collection is much clearer. In addition, its specific research hypotheses have formed in advance.

(3) 因果性调研。因果性调研是指调查一个变量是否会引起或决定另一个变量变化的一种调研方法，目的是识别变量间的因果关系。这种调研方法是以实验为基础的调研，因此，又被称为实验调研。以实验为基础的调研与以访问或观察为基础的调研有着根本的区别。在访问和观察的情况下，调研人员是一个被动的数据收集者，他们只是询问人们一些问题或是观察他们在干什么。

Causal research is used to investigate whether a variable can cause or determine the change of another variable. The purpose is to clarify causal connection between the two variables. This method of research bases on experiment and is also called experimental research, which is totally different from the research based on interviews or observation. In the situation of interviews or observation, researchers collect data passively and they only ask people questions or observe what interviewees do.

(4) 预测性调研。预测性调研是指专门为了预测未来一定时期内某一环节因素的变动趋势及其对企业市场营销活动的影响而进行的市场调研，例如，对市场上消费者对某种产品需求量变化趋势的调研、某产品供给量变化趋势的调研等。

Forecasting research is used to predict the trend of a certain factor in a future period, and its influence on enterprises' marketing activities, such as researches on changes of certain product demands product supplies etc.

二、市场营销调研的内容 Contents of Marketing Research

常见的营销调研的主要有以下几个方面的内容。

The contents of marketing research have the following main aspects.

1. 宏观环境调研 Research on Macro-environment

主要是调研企业经营所面临的外部宏观环境，包括政治、法律、经济、技术、人口、文化和自然环境，它们是独立于企业以外的不可控的因素，只有在了解的基础上去适应它们，才能取得经营成功。

It mainly researches into the external macro-environment faced by enterprises in operation, including politics, law, economics, technology, population, culture and natural environment, which are uncontrollable factors and independent from enterprises. Only adapting on the basis of understanding can an enterprise get operational success.

2. 企业竞争调研　Research on Enterprise Competition

在任何市场上销售产品，企业都面临着竞争。市场上从事同类商品生产经营的企业之间存在现实的或潜在的竞争。同一市场上同类企业数量的多少，决定了竞争强度的不同。

All enterprises face competition while selling products. There is real or potential competitions between enterprises producing the same kind of products. In the same market, the quantity of similar enterprises determines the competition intensity.

企业调研竞争环境，目的是认识市场状况和市场竞争强度，并根据本企业的优势制定正确的竞争策略。通过竞争环境调研，企业可以了解竞争对手优势，取长补短，扬长避短，与竞争者在目标市场选择、产品档次、价格和服务策略上有所差别，与竞争对手形成良好的互补经营结构。

The purpose for making research an enterprise of on competitive environment is to recognize the market situation and competition intensity so as to develop proper competitive strategies according to the advantages of the enterprise. Through this research, the enterprise can know its competitors' merits, complement each other, develop strong points and avoid weak points and choose different target market, product classes, prices and service tactics from the competitors to form a good complementary business structure.

3. 消费者行为调研 Consumer Behavior Research

消费者行为调研涉及八个方面的信息：购买者是谁(Who)，购买什么(What)，为什么购买(Why)，何时购买(When)，何地购买(Where)，购买信息来自何处(Where)，购买金额是多少(How Much)以及如何购买(How)。了解消费者的购买行为是营销管理的一项基础性工作，由此得到的信息是市场细分以及市场定位等战略决策的依据，也为市场研究提供基础数据。

Consumer behavior research involves information from eight aspects: Who are consumers (who)? What to buy (what)? Why to buy (why)? When to buy (when)? Where to buy (where)? Where do they get purchasing information (where)? How much do they pay (how much)? And how to buy (how)? It is fundamental to understand consumers' purchasing behavior for marketing management. Information obtained from analyzing consumers' behavior is the proof for strategies and tactics of marketing segmentation and market positioning, and it also provides basic data for marketing research.

4. 市场调研 Market Research

市场调研主要包括市场占有率、市场容量和市场变化趋势的调研。市场占有率能够反映本企业在市场上的地位和竞争力。市场容量是指市场对某种商品或服务在一定期间内需求量的最大限度。市场容量受价格与购买力的影响。市场变化趋势通过销售趋势反映出来。销售趋势的变化有稳定形态、升降倾向形态、季节形态和抛物线形态等。

Market research mainly includes researches an market share, market capacity and tendency of market change. Market share could reveal on enterprise's status and competitiveness in market. Market capacity, which is influenced by price and purchasing power, refers to the maximum tolerance of market demand for certain goods or services within a certain period. The tendency of market change can be reflected by sales trend. Sales trend can be stable, up and down, seasonal, parabolic, etc.

5. 产品调研 Product Research

产品调研包括对新产品的开发和测试以及现有产品的研发、诊断和改造等内容的调研。调研者要了解消费者对产品使用(试用)的感受，并针对产品外观、功能、包装、设计、价格等各个属性分别进行评价，这就需要了解消费者对各种属性组合的偏好。通过定量分析，调研者能够找出产品属性间的最佳组合，并估计产品的预期市场占有率与产品的市场份额。

Product research is carried out on developing and testing new product, and the development, diagnosis and transformation of existing product. Researchers should know the consumer's feeling of product use (trial), and then evaluate elements such as product appearance, function, packaging, design, price, etc. In order to do this, researchers need to know consumers' preference of different element combination. Through quantitative analysis, they can find out the best combination of product elements and estimate expected market share of products.

6. 价格调研 Research on Price

价格调研有助于做出正确的定价决策，使企业了解市场供求状况和影响价格的主要因素及这些因素的发展趋势。

Price research can help to make correct pricing decisions, and allow the enterprise to understand the situation of market supply and demand, main factors affecting price, and tendency of these factors.

7. 促销调研 Research on Promotion

促销调研是指对各种促销方式效果进行的调研，其中最常用的是广告调研，它包括为广告创作而进行的广告创意调研、为选择媒体而进行的广告媒体调研、为评价广告效果而进行的广告跟踪调研等。除了广告调研之外，对其他的促销方式(如人员推销、营销推广等)的效果也可以进行调研。如一家企业就聘请调研者对其三种不同形式的优惠券的促销效果进行测试：他们将不同的优惠券邮寄给三组消费者，并跟踪这三组消费者的兑付率，最后用统计，计算出兑付率的差异，并确定出最有效的优惠券形式。

Promotion research refers to research on various ways and effects of promotion. One of the most commonly used researches is on advertisement, which includes research on Ad creativity for advertising production, research on Ad media for selecting the means of media, and Ad tracking for assessing Ad effect, etc. Besides advertising research, more researches can be carried out into other ways of promotion, such as personal selling, marketing promotion, etc. For example, a company asks researchers to test on the promotion effect of three different forms of vouchers: they mail different vouchers to three groups of consumers, follow up their utilization rand, then calculate difference of utilization rate by statistical method, and finally determine the most effective type of voucher.

第二节 市场营销调研的基本程序
Basic Procedures of Marketing Research

建立一套系统科学的工作程序是市场调研得以顺利进行、工作效率和质量得以提高的重要保证。典型的市场营销调研过程分为以下三个阶段：调研准备阶段，调研实施阶段和调研资料整理、分析与报告撰写阶段。

Establishing a set of systematic and scientific working procedures is an important guarantee of smooth market research with efficiency and good quality. Typical process of marketing research is composed of the following three stages: preparation stage, implementation stage and the stage of data collection, and analysis and report writing.

一、调研准备阶段 Preparation Stage

市场调研的准备阶段是市场调研工作的开始。准备工作是否充分，对后续的实际调研工作的开展和调研质量的好坏影响很大。它具体包括以下几方面。

Preparation stage is the beginning of marketing research work. Whether preparation is sufficient or not has strong impact on actual research and research quality. It includes the following aspects.

(一)确定调研目标 Determining Research Objectives

确定调研目标就是指确定为什么进行市场调研以及调研的主题是什么。通过调研目标的确定，企业能得到一些与调研问题相关的具体信息。确定所要研究及解决的问题是调研活动的开始，它的正确界定可以为整个调研过程提供保证和方向。企业总会面临这样或那样的问题，市场调研的目标应是本企业当前亟须解决的问题。

Determining research objectives is to find out the reasons to do marketing research and the theme of the research. Having determined research objectives, the enterprise can get some specific information about research. It is the beginning of the research activity to decide what issues to be researched into and what problems to be solved. The right objectives can provide guarantee and direction for the whole research process. Enterprises always face various problems, and the objective of market research should be the urgent issue to be dealt with for enterprises.

调研目标的确定需要制定者具有很好的洞察力和创造力，对于暂时无法确定的调研目标，可以先进行一般性的初步调研。初步调研可以为确定的调研问题指出行动方向或缩小调研范围。

To fix research objective, the decision maker needs to have good insight and creativity. If it is unable to determine the research objective temporarily, preliminary research work can be done. Preliminary research can point out the direction for determined objective or narrow research scope.

(二)制订调研方案和调研计划 Making Research Scheme and Plan

调研方案是营销调研中重要的指导性文件，是对调研的具体设计，包括确定调研的目的和要求、调研对象、调研内容、调研方法和抽样方法等。调研计划是对某项调研的组织领导、人员配备、完成时间、工作进度、费用预算等的预先安排，目的是使调研工作有计划、有秩序地进行，以保证调研计划的实施。大型市场调研需要调研方案和调研计划，小型市场调研可以合二为一，统一制订调研计划。调研计划必须包含以下内容。

Research scheme is an important guiding document for marketing research, and it is the specific design of research, including research purposes and requirements, research target, research content, research methods and sampling methods, etc. Research plan is an advanced arrangement of a certain research for leadership, staffing, finishing time, working speed, expense budget, etc. Its purpose is to make the research carried out in an orderly way to ensure the implementation of the research plan. Large market research involves both research scheme and plan. Small marketing research, however, can combine the two into one research plan. Marketing research plan must contain the following content.

(1) 确定调研目的。说明本次调研的背景，所要研究的问题和备选的各种可能决策，该项调研结果可能带来的社会效益或经济效益等。

Determining research purposes. It is to show the research background, research issues, possible alternative decisions, the social or economical benefit brought by investigation results, etc.

(2) 确定调研时间、地点、范围、对象。

Determining research time, place, scope and target.

(3) 确定调研内容。这是整个计划的基础。例如，某公司打算向市场推出家用电脑，在研究这种产品是否能很快达到一定的销售规模时，需要收集以下信息：有多少家庭的收入和储蓄水平已足以支付购买家用电脑的费用？人们购买家用电脑的主要目的是什么？哪部分人群对购买家用电脑更可能感兴趣？有多少人近期有购买家用电脑的打算？有哪些因素可能阻止人们的购买决心？

Determining research content. It is the basis of the whole plan. For example, if a company plans to launch a home computer to the market, it should collect the following information to study whether it can reach a certain sales scale quickly: How many families can afford home computers according to the level of their incomes and savings? What is the main purpose of buying the home computer? What kinds of people are more interested in home computers? How many people have a recent plan to buy home computers? What are the factors that may prevent people from their purchasing determination?

(4) 确定资料来源。调研资料主要分为原始资料和二手资料两大类。一般来说，专业调查人员应掌握主要二手资料的提供源，以尽可能利用二手资料，因为获得二手资料相对来说较容易且快捷，特别是互联网的发展为企业收集二手资料提供了极大的方便。不过，在正式的营销调研中，收集一手资料往往必不可少，这是因为，一手资料对解决特定的问题针对性更强，而二手资料往往存在时效性和准确性等方面的问题。实际上，营销调研的核心之一，就是如何有效地收集到必要、充分、可靠的一手资料。

Determining sources of data. Research data are mainly divided into two categories: the original data and the second-hand data. In general, professional investigators should obtain the main source of secondary data in order to use the second-hand data as much as possible, because it is easier, faster and more convenient to obtain second-hand data especially with the help of Internet development. In a formal marketing research, however, first-hand data is often essential. This is because first-hand data can solve specific problems to the point, while second-hand data, very often, is not timely or accurate enough. In fact, one of the marketing research cores is how to collect necessary, sufficient and reliable first-hand data effectively.

(5) 确定调研方法。调研方法是收集资料的方法，可供选择的方法有文案调研法和实地调研法。其中，实地调研法又有访问法、观察法、实验法等。

Determining research methods. Research method is to collect data. There are available methods such as document research method and spot research method. The latter includes methods of interview, observation, experiment, etc.

(6) 确定抽样计划。这一计划要解决下述三个问题：谁是抽样对象，调查样本有多大，样本应如何挑选出来。常见的抽样方法有随机抽样和非随机抽样两大类。随机抽样包括简单随机抽样、分层抽样、分群抽样和地区抽样等几种具体方法；非随机抽样包括任意抽样、判断抽样和配额抽样等几种具体方法。这些方法各有其利弊，需根据实际情况加以权衡后选择使用。

Determining sampling plan. The plan should solve the following three questions: who are the sampling target, how many they are and how to pick them out. Two commonly used sampling methods are random sampling and non-random sampling. Random sampling includes simple random sampling, stratified sampling, cluster sampling and area sampling; non-random sampling includes convenience sampling, judgmental sampling and quota sampling. All these methods have their advantages and disadvantages. We should choose the suitable ones after careful consideration.

(7) 确定调研工具。在收集原始数据时，有两类可供选择的调研工具：一是调研问卷；二是某些设备工具，如录音机、照相机、摄像机以及交通流量计数器等。其中最常用的是问卷，问卷由一组需由被调查者回答的问题组成。如果决定了使用问卷，还有一个问卷的准确、系统的设计问题，例如，怎样将开放式(被调查者用自己的话回答)、封闭式(被调查者在列出的几个答案中做出选择)和程度测量式三种基本类型的问题结合使用，怎样排列问题顺序，怎样防止误解和遗漏等问题。

Determining research tools. There are two types of research tools to collect raw data: one is questionnaire and the other is some device tools, such as recorders, cameras, video cameras, as well as traffic flow counter, etc. One of the most commonly used tools is questionnaire, which is composed of a group of questions to be answered by participants. If questionnaire is used, there is a problem about whether the questionnaire is designed accurately and systematically. For example, how to arrange the three basic types of questions such as open-ended questions (requiring participants to answer in their own words), close-ended questions (answerable by checking one of several predetermined answers) and level measuring questions, how to arrange the order of the questions, and how to prevent misunderstanding and omissions.

(8) 确定调研人员。重点是考虑参加市场调研的人员应具备的条件。

Determining researchers. It focuses on what qualifications the researchers should have.

(9) 确定调研的进度和经费预算。一般需要列出完成每一步骤所需要的周期和起止时间。调研经费的多少要考虑企业的承受能力和资料本身价值的大小，同时应尽可能考虑全面，在有效的前提下力求费用最省。

Determining research schedule and budget. Generally it is necessary to list the required time by each step and starting and ending time. While doing research budget, researchers should consider the enterprise's financial ability and the value of the data itself. Meanwhile, overall consideration is needed. Researchers should strive for the least expense on the premise of effectiveness.

二、调研实施阶段 Implementation Stage

计划被批准后，就要按计划规定的时间、方法着手进行信息的收集工作，具体包括建立相应的调查组织，训练调查人员，准备调查工具，展开实地调查等。

Once the plan is approved, researchers will start to collect information with certain methods in stipulated time, to set up a survey organization, to train investigators, to prepare survey tools, to conduct fieldwork and so on.

(一)调研人员的培训与管理 Researchers' Training and Management

对调研人员进行培训，能够让调研人员理解调研计划、掌握调研技术和与调研目标有关的经济知识、设计有针对性的问卷等。

Training for researchers can help them understand the research plan and master research techniques and economic knowledge related to the research objectives, so that they are able to design targeted questionnaires.

调研人员的管理是指对调研人员的调研工作进展情况进行及时的检查监督。主要是看他们收集的资料是否符合调研要求，发现问题及时纠正，或令其重新调研；还可以采取抽样复查的方法，验证所收集资料的准确性。

Management of researchers refers to timely checking and supervision on research progress. The goal of this stage is to assess whether the information collected conforms to the requirements of the research. If there is any problem, they can correct it in time, or do the research again. The method of sampling check can also be adopted to verify the accuracy of the data collected.

(二)实施调研 Implementation of Research

调研人员按计划规定的时间、地点及方法，实地收集有关资料，不仅要收集二手资料，也要收集原始资料。调研的质量取决于调研人员的素质、责任心和组织管理的科学性。

Researchers should gather fieldwork information, not only second-hand data but also primary information, according to planned time, place and method stipulated. The quality of research depends on researchers' quality, responsibility sense and scientific organization and management.

三、调研资料整理、分析与报告撰写阶段 Data Collation, Analysis and Report Writing Stage

在调研资料的整理、分析与报告撰写阶段，市场调研人员要对问卷资料进行统计处理，并由市场分析人员对数据结果进行分析，最后由研究者撰写市场调研报告。

At the stages of data collation, analysis and report writing, market investigators should process questionnaire data statistically, and then market analysts analyze the result data, and finally researchers write the marketing research report.

(一)分类整理调研资料 Sorting Out Data

通过调查收集来的信息资料必须经过分析和处理后才能使用。分析整理工作的步骤如下：第一，检查资料是否齐全；第二，对资料进行编辑加工，去粗取精，找出误差，剔除前后矛盾；第三，对资料进行分类，包括画图、制表等；第四，运用统计模型和其他数学模型对数据进行处理，充分发掘现有数据的应用价值，建立相关信息之间的内在联系。

The data collected through investigation must be analyzed and processed before being adopted. The sorting procedures are as follows: first, to check whether the data is complete; second, to edit and process the data, refine the information, find out error and eliminate inconsistence; third, to classify the data, including drawing graphs, making lists, etc.; fourth, to process the data with statistical model or other mathematical models, to fully explore the application value of the existing data and to set up intrinsic link between relevant data.

(二)提出研究报告 Presenting Research Report

市场调研的最后一个程序就是提出调研报告，作为企业领导决策的参考。

The last step of marketing research is to present a research report as references for corporate leaders to make decisions.

市场调研报告的内容一般应包括以下内容。

Content of the report usually contains the following.

(1) 引言，说明调研的目的、对象、范围、方法、时间、地点等。即对市场调研的原因、目的、意义等进行简要说明，提出本报告所要解决的问题。

The first part is introduction, which presents the research purpose, target, scope, method, time and place, etc. It is a brief description of the cause, goal, significance of the marketing research and the problem to be solved.

(2) 摘要，简明扼要地介绍本次调研的过程以及调研方法等，同时简明概括整个研究的结论和建议。

The second is summary, which introduces the research process and research method, etc., and summarizes the research conclusion and recommendation briefly.

(3) 资料分析，分为统计分析和理论分析。统计分析着重对调研的内容进行描述，要求有序地摆出经过整理且有效的调研资料，并做出简述，解决"是什么"的问题；理论分析就是依据资料数据，运用科学的研究方法，系统地展开分析，回答"为什么"的问题。

The third is the part of data analysis, which includes statistical analysis and theoretical analysis. The statistical analysis focuses on the description of research content. It requires orderly listing of the processed and effective data and brief statement to answer the question of "What". The theoretical analysis, which is based on the data, is to use scientific research methods to make systematical analysis to answer the question of "Why".

(4) 提出建议，即依据前文的分析，提出具有可行性的解决问题的建议，或做出预测，回答"怎么办"的问题。

The fourth is proposal part, that is, on the basis of the above analysis, to put forward practical suggestions, or make prediction to answer the question of "How".

(5) 附件，包括样本分配、数据图表、问卷附件、访问记录和参考资料目录等。

The fifth is appendices, including sample distribution, data graphics, questionnaire attached, interview recordings and list of reference materials, etc.

报告提出后，调研人员还需跟踪了解该报告所提的建议是否被决策者采纳。如果采纳了，采纳后的实际效果如何，是否需要提出进一步的补充和修正意见等。如果没有被采纳，要找出原因是什么。

After proposing the report, researchers should follow up to confirm whether suggestions in the report are adopted by decision makers. If suggestions are adopted, they should observe their actual effect, and decide whether to propose further complement and amendment advice. If suggestions are not adopted, they should figure out the reasons.

第三节　市场营销调研的方法
Marketing Research Methods

市场调研的方法，是指市场调研人员在实际调研过程中收集信息资料所采取的具体方法。市场营销调研的方法很多，按照不同的标准可以分为各种不同的分类。企业在进行市场营销调研时，应根据调研的目的与调研的对象，选用适宜的市场营销调研方法。

Marketing research methods refer to specific methods used by researchers in the process of actual research to gather information. There are many marketing research methods, which have a variety of different classifications according to different standards. While doing marketing research, enterprises should select appropriate marketing research methods according to research purpose and research target.

一、按调研对象划分 According to Research Subjects

在开展调研活动时，调研者可以对调研对象进行普查、典型调查，也可以采用抽样调查的方法。

While conducting research activities, researchers can use census or typical survey, and they can also adopt the method of sampling survey.

1. 普查法(Census Method)

它是指调查调研对象总体中的个体信息的方法，以准确了解营销过程中某个过程或方面的全部情况。此种调查方法取得的资料全面、精确，有很高的实用价值，但是普查耗费的人力、物力较多，组织工作量大，调查时间长，企业一般很少采用这种方法。

Census method refers to investigating each individual of overall survey subjects in order to understand certain marketing process or aspect thoroughly. Data obtained thereby are comprehensive, accurate and very practical. This method, however, takes more manpower and material resources, and the organizing workload is big and survey time is long, so enterprises seldom use this method.

2. 典型调查法(Typical survey method)

它是指对市场中的典型单位和具有代表性的消费者进行深入调研，以了解全部单位及消费者需求的一种市场调研方法。通过典型调查，可以了解市场营销活动中的一般现象。它也是了解营销现象之间的内在的、必然的联系，研究寻找解决企业营销问题的一个很好的途径。此种调查方法可以节省人力、财力，能较快地取得所需资料。但是它的难度在于能否科学地选择典型调查对象。调研者应避免选择那种极端的类型作为调查对象。

Typical survey means carrying out a deep investigation and research into typical unit and representative sample of consumers in the market in order to find out the demand of all units and consumers. Through typical survey, general phenomenon in marketing activities can be known. It is also a good way to comprehend the inherent and inevitable connections between various marketing phenomena, so as to find a way to solve the problem of enterprise marketing. This method can help save manpower and financial resources and obtain needed information quickly. But the point is whether typical survey subject can be chosen scientifically. Researchers should avoid choosing extreme types as survey subjects.

3. 抽样调查法(Sampling Survey Method)

它是指根据概率分布的随机原则，即被调查者都有同等被抽取的可能性的原则，从被调查者的总体中，按照一定的规则抽取一定数量的样本进行调查，以推断出市场需求总量和平均水平的调查。抽样调查法常被用于确定的调研对象。事实证明，一个相对较小但精心选择的样本能准确地反映出总体的特征,而且在调研成本上也是可以接受的。可供选择的抽样方法的种类如图 2-1 所示。

Based on random principle of probability distribution, i.e., the respondents have the same possibility to be chosen, the sampling survey is used to choose a number of samples from the whole respondents according to certain rules, and then deduce the total and average market demand. The sampling survey method is often used to fix research target. It has been proved that a relatively small but carefully chosen sample can reflect the overall characteristics accurately, and the research cost is acceptable. The available sampling survey methods are shown as Figure 2-1.

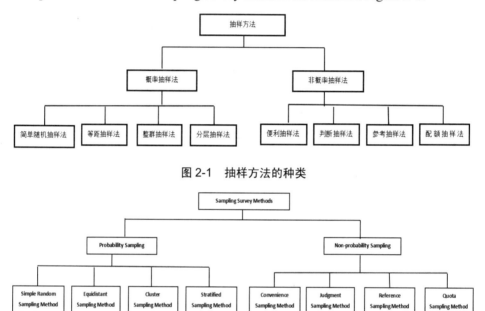

图 2-1 抽样方法的种类

Figure 2-1 Types of Sampling Survey Methods

(1) 概率抽样法。在概率抽样中,总体的每一个单位都有一个已知的、非零的机会被选入样本中,每一个单位被选中的机会可能并不相等,但是被选中的概率却是已知的,而这个概率是由选择样本元素的具体程序决定的。概率抽样的最大优点是可以估算出抽样误差,即可以知道推断出的总体特征与实际特征之间的误差,但概率抽样法比非概率抽样法要花费更多的时间和成本。

Probability sampling method. In probability sampling, each unit has a known, non-zero chance of being selected as sample. Though the chosen opportunity of each unit may not be equal, the chosen probability is known, and this probability is determined by specific procedures of selecting sample elements. The biggest advantage of this method is that sampling deviation can be estimated, that is to say, the deviation between the deduced overall characteristics and actual characteristics can be inferred, but probability sampling method takes more time and cost than non-probability method.

① 简单随机抽样法。它是按随机原则直接从总体 N 个单位中抽取 n 个单位作样本,这种抽样方式能使总体中每一个单位有同等机会被抽中,这种方式是抽样中最基本、最简单的方式。简单随机抽样满足了概率抽样的一切必要要求,能够得到具有有效代表性的样

本，但是，它必须以一个完整的总体元素列表为依据，这在实际调研活动中并不容易做到。

The method of simple random sampling. It chooses n units randomly from the total N units as samples. This sampling method, which is the most basic and simplest, can make each unit chosen with equal opportunities. Simple random sampling can meet all necessary requirements of the probability sampling and is able to get valid and representative sample. However, it must be based on a complete overall list of elements, which is not easy in actual research activities.

② 等距抽样法。它是指在总体列表中，先随意选择一个起点，然后按照一个固定的间隔逐一选择起点之后的元素，直到达到预定的样本容量。例如，在一个容量为40的总体中选取一个容量为5的样本，则样本距离为8，我们首先随意确定一个起点，比如从第10个元素开始，则被选入样本中的元素应该是：第10个、第18个、第26个、第34个和第2个。等距抽样比简单随机抽样所花费的时间和费用都会更少，而且也可以抽取出具有较大代表性的样本，所以比简单随机抽样更为流行。但是，它和简单随机抽样一样，需要一个完整的总体元素列表。此外，如果在元素列表中存在自然的周期性，等距抽样可能会产生严重误差。

Equidistant sampling method. It is used to choose a tart point randomly from the whole list, and then select elements at regular intervals until the expected sample size is reached. For example, if 5 samples are to be chosen from the total 40, the interval should be 8. We first randomly determine a starting point, starting from the tenth element for example, then the chosen elements should be the 10th, 18th, 26th, 34th and 2nd. Equidistant sampling will take less time and cost than simple random sampling. It is also able to extract very representative samples. That is why it is used more often than simple random sampling. But, like simple random sampling, it needs a complete list of elements as a whole. In addition, if natural cyclicity exists in the list of elements, equidistant sampling may generate serious deviation.

③ 分层抽样法。它是首先将总体分成相互独立的、完全的子集，然后再按照独立的随机抽样方法在各个子集中抽取一定数量的元素去构成所需的样本。所谓的独立的、完全的子集，是指总体中的每一个元素都要被分配到其中的一个子集中去，而且还能被重复分配。分层抽样会花费更多的成本，但是这一缺陷可以通过较低的误差率来得到弥补。

Stratified sampling method. When applying this method, the whole (or Superset) will be divided into independent and complete subset. Then according to the method of random sampling, a certain number of elements will be chosen from each subset to form the required sample. The so-called independent and complete subset means that each element of the total has to be put into one of the subsets, and can be distributed repeatedly. Stratified sampling method will spend more, but the defect can be remedied by low deviation rate.

④ 整群抽样法。以上谈到的各种抽样方法都是按照一定的方法，一个一个地从总体的元素中抽取样本。整群抽样中的样本则是一组一组地从总体中被抽取出来。因此，整群抽样法也需要经过以下两个步骤：首先是将总体分成相互独立的完全的子集，然后按照随机抽样的方法抽选子集来构成样本。子集被称为群，在有些时候，调研者对抽取出来的群中的全部元素都要进行观察，而有的时候还要从被选中的群中再次随机抽出部分元素来对它们进行观察。整群抽样与分层抽样都是要将总体分成相互独立的完全的子集，但是后者是

从每个子集中都抽取一定的样本，前者则是只抽取部分子集，对子集中的全部元素或部分元素进行观察。

Cluster sampling method. The above mentioned sampling methods are to draw sample elements one by one from the total. With the cluster sampling method, the sample is extracted from the whole group by group. As a result, the cluster sampling method is to follow two steps: to divide the whole into independent and complete subsets, and then constitute samples with selected subsets. Subset is known as a group. In some cases, researchers need to observe all elements extracted from the group, and sometimes even pick up some elements again at random from the selected group for observing. Both cluster sampling method and stratified sampling method are to divide the whole into independent and complete subsets. The latter is to choose some samples from each subset, but the former is to choose some subsets to observe all or part of the elements of the chosen subsets.

(2) 非概率抽样法。任何不满足概率抽样要求的抽样都被归为非概率抽样。由于无法了解总体中的元素被抽入样本中的概率，所以评估非概率抽样的总体质量有很大的困难。但是，由于非概率抽样法所花费的时间和费用都相对较低，而且合理运用非概率抽样方法也可能产生极具代表性的样本，所以，这一方法仍然在实际中得到广泛运用。常用的非概率抽样方法主要有便利抽样、判断抽样、参考抽样和配额抽样。

Non-probability sampling method. Any sample which does not meet the requirements of probability sampling is classified as non-probability sampling. Because it's unable to know the probability of the elements in the whole being chosen as samples, it's difficult to evaluate the overall quality of non-probability sampling. However, non-probability sampling method takes less time and cost, and the reasonable utility of non-probability sampling will generate a representative sample. So this method is still widely used in practice. The often used non-probability sampling methods include convenience sampling, judgment sampling, reference sampling and quota sampling.

① 便利抽样法。它是指运用最方便的方式来取得样本。例如，直接选用自己公司的雇员来进行新产品的使用测试。显然这种抽样方法很难保证调研结果的准确性，但调研人员有时出于成本原因仍然会使用这种方法。一般来说，这种方式只适用于对调研精度要求不高的探测性调研。

Convenience sampling method. It refers to using the most convenient way to obtain samples, for example, selecting the firm's own employees to test new products. Obviously it is difficult to guarantee the accuracy of the results, but researchers still use this method sometimes for the sake of cost. Generally speaking, this method is only suitable for exploratory research with low requirement of accuracy.

② 判断抽样法。它是调研人员依靠自己的主观判断来选择样本。由于其主观判断往往是建立在历史数据或是个人经验的基础上，所以，在这种抽样方法下，调研结果的质量会受到调研人员素质的影响。

Judgment sampling method. It means that researchers select samples relying on their own subjective judgment. The judgment is often based on historical data or personal experience, so with this kind of sampling method, the quality of research results will be affected by researchers' personnel quality.

③ 参考抽样法。它是指调研人员要求初始被调查者推荐其他样本人群以供选择。这样做会使样本容量随着调查的进行而逐步增加，因此，这种方法又被称为"滚雪球法"。当调研人员所要调查的总体人群很难寻找时，往往会选用参考抽样的方法。这样虽可以节约不少调查费用，但会因样本可能会具有较高的同质性而使调研质量受到影响。

Reference sampling method. It refers to that researchers ask initial respondents to recommend other people for choice. This method will make the sample size gradually increase as the research progresses. As a result, it is also known as "Snowball Method". When it's hard to find the sample population, researchers often choose reference sampling method. This method saves some research cost, but the research result may be influenced by the high homogeneity of the samples.

④ 配额抽样法。它类似于概率抽样的分层抽样方法。它首先对总体进行分类，并根据主观标准在每一小类中按一定的比例选取元素构成样本。这种方法虽可以在一定程度上改善调研质量，但由于对样本的选择仍然依赖于个人主观的判断，所以，样本的代表性多会有偏差。

Quota sampling method. It is similar to stratified sampling. It is to classify the whole population first, and then, according to subjective criteria, select elements from each small class to form samples. Although this method can improve research quality to a certain extent, the representativeness of samples would have some deviation because the choosing samples still depends on subjective judgment.

二、按获得信息的方式划分 According to Ways of Obtaining Information

1. 文案调查法(Desk Research Survey)

文案调查法是指通过搜集各种历史和现实资料，从中获取与调查有关的信息，并进行分析整理的调查方法。它是获得二手资料的重要渠道。该调查法是搜集已经加工过的二手资料，以搜集文献性信息资料为主。其优点是资料搜集过程简易、经济便利，调查方法机动灵活，但是也存在搜集和整理工作较为烦琐、历史性的信息存在一定的时滞性、可靠性不高的缺点。文案调查法具体可以采用以下方式：参考文献查找法、检索工具查找法、咨询法、收听法、购买法、委托法、汇编法等。

By collecting all kinds of historical and current data, the desk research survey is to obtain, analyze and sort out relevant information. It is an important source to obtain second-hand data. Researchers use this method to collect second-hand data which have been processed, mainly to collect documentary data. The advantage of this method lies in that the data gathering process is simple, economic and convenient and it is also a flexible method. It has its disadvantages too, for example, the collecting and sorting work is quite laborious; historical information has a time lag and low reliability. The desk research can be done in the following ways: literature research, research tools, consultation, listening, purchase, entrusting, compilation, etc.

2. 观察法(Observation Method)

观察法又称实地观察法。它是调查员通过直接跟踪，记录所感兴趣的人和事物的行为轨迹，来获得所需资料的一种方法。有经验的调研人员可通过观察法方便地得到某些在其他场合很难得到的信息，并能排除被调查对象的紧张心理或主观因素的影响。观察法具有及时性、方式灵活多样、获得资料相对真实可靠的优点。但是观察者往往受时空条件的影响，很难深入了解被调查者内心世界的活动，所以应用观察法时须扬长避短，尽量降低观察误差。

Observation method, also called field observation method. Through direct tracking, the researcher records the behaviors of interesting people and happenings to obtain the required information. With this method, experienced researchers can get information easily, which is probably difficult to obtain in other places, and can eliminate respondents' nervousness or the influence of subjective factors. Observation method is timely, flexible, and the data obtained thereby is relatively reliable. But since observers are often restricted by time and space conditions, it is difficult to understand respondents' activities of inner world. So while applying the observation method, researchers should develop its strong points and avoid its weak points so as to reduce observation error as much as possible.

3. 询问法(Inquiry Method)

它是调研人员通过与被调查者进行直接或间接的接触，向被调查者了解市场供需情况的一种方法。它是最常见的方法，更适合于描述性调查。询问法在具体做法上又有如下多种形式：邮寄问卷，电话询问和直接面谈。邮寄问卷形式，就是将设计好的问卷邮寄给被调查者，请他们填好后寄回。这种方法的优点是询问面广，被调查者有充分的时间回答问题；缺点是时间周期长，问卷回收率低。随着互联网的发展，通过电子邮件向被调查者发送电子调查问卷成了一种可行的方式，它比发送传统邮件快得多，反应率也高得多。电话询问形式，是以电话为媒介进行询问，由被调查者直接回答的一种询问方法。这种方法可立即得到所需信息，且提问灵活，成本也低；但交谈时间有限，调研人员很难提较复杂的问题，还可能因消费者受到打扰而引起反感。直接面谈形式，即调研人员与被调查人员面对面的直接交谈的形式。根据每次面谈的地点和人数的多少，又可分为上门采访、商场现场采访、个别询问、集体询问、座谈会等形式。其优点是，在面谈中调研人员可充分地提问题，被调查者也能充分发表自己的意见；缺点主要是成本太高、能访问的人数有限，故更适合探测性调查。在直接面谈中，还有一种做法是调研人员携带问卷访问被调查者，并帮助被调查者填写问卷，这种方式可弥补邮寄问卷回收率低、被调查者不理解问卷而导致回答不准确的问题，还可避免因访问中提问太随意而难以对结果进行统计性分析。

It's a method with which researchers can get an understanding of market supply and demand situation from respondents through direct or indirect contact with them. It is the most commonly used method, more suitable for a descriptive survey. Inquiry method has a variety of forms such as mail questionnaires, telephone enquiring and direct interview. Mailing questionnaire is to mail the designed questionnaires to participants and ask them to fill in and send back. The advantage of this approach is that it has a wide coverage and respondents have plenty of time to answer the questions. But it takes a long period and the response rate is low. With the development of Internet, sending e-mail questionnaires to respondents has become a feasible way. It is much faster than sending traditional mails and the response rate is much higher.

Telephone enquiring is to telephone the respondents and they answer questions directly. This method can get the required information immediately, questions can be flexible, and the cost is low. Its shortcoming is that interview time is limited and it is difficult to propose more complex questions. It may also cause antipathy of consumers who are not willing to be disturbed.

Face-to-face contact means that researchers have a direct face-to-face conversation with respondents. According to interview time and place and number of interviewees, there are on-site interviews, mall-spot interviews, individual inquiries, collective inquiries, symposia, etc. Its advantage is that the researchers can ask the respondents questions closely in the interviews and the respondents can also express their opinions fully. However, the cost is too high and the number of respondents is limited. So it's more suitable for exploratory research. In a face-to-face interview, the researcher would also carry questionnaires to visit respondents, and help the respondents to fill in questionnaires. This way can make up for the low rate of mailing questionnaire response, and the respondents' misunderstanding of the questions, which leads to inaccurate answers. This method can also avoid casual questions during interviews, which may lead to results difficult to be statistically analyzed.

4. 实验法(Experimental Method)

实验法是最科学、最适合因果型调查的方法。研究包装、广告或价格对产品销量的影响等多运用此类方法。运用实验法，需挑选被实验者组成若干相互对照的小组，给予不同的条件；同时，对其他变量加以控制；然后观察不同条件下所得结果的差异是否具有统计学上的意义，以找出因果关系。采用实验法的难点在于它耗费很高，并且很难保持外部环境中所有因素不变。

Experimental method is the most scientific method and most suitable for causal research. This method is usually used in research on packaging, advertising or price impact on product sales. This method is used to choose subjects to form several mutual contrast groups, and each group is given different conditions. At the same time, researchers should control the other variables, and then researchers observe whether the differences of results obtained under different conditions, which have statistical significance so as to find out the cause and effect relationship. Its difficulty lies in that it is costly and difficult to keep all factors in the external environment unchanged.

5. 网上调查法(Online Survey)

网上调查法是当代极为重要的调查手段之一，是企业利用互联网搜集和掌握市场信息的一种重要调查方法。网上调查法是通过网络有计划、系统地搜集、调查、记录、整理和分析相关市场信息，为客观地测定及评价当前市场及潜在市场提供依据的调查方法。网上调查广泛地应用于产品消费、社会民意民情、广告效果、企业生产经营情况等方面的调查。网上调查方法分为直接方式和间接方式两种。其中直接调查方式又有网络访谈法、邮件调查法、站点法、随机 IP 法；间接调查方式可以利用 E-mail、公告栏、搜索引擎等搜集资料。

Online survey is one of the contemporary critical means of research, and it is an important method for enterprises to collect data and keep informed of market information. Online survey is to search for, investigate, record, sort out and analyze relevant market information in a well-planned and systematical way. Therefore, it can provide basis for objective measurement and evaluation of current and potential market. Online survey is widely used in research on product consumption, public opinions, advertisement effect, enterprises' production and operation and so on. There are direct and indirect online survey methods. Direct online survey involves online-interview, mail survey, site method, random IP method, etc. Indirect online survey refers to using internet tools to collect data such as E-mail, bulletin boards, search engines and so on.

本章小结
Summary

市场营销调研是针对组织特定的营销问题，采用科学的研究方法，系统地、客观地收集、整理、分析、解释有关市场营销各方面的信息，为营销管理者制定、评估和改进营销决策提供依据的一项营销活动。其内容主要包括宏观环境调研、企业竞争调研、消费者行为调研、市场调研、产品调研、价格调研、促销调研七个方面。进行市场营销调研需要遵循科学的程序和步骤，例如，确定问题和目标、制定调研计划、收集调研信息、分析调研信息、撰写调研报告、评估调研成果。在开展调研活动时，可以对调研对象进行普查、典型调查，也可以采用抽样调查的方法。按获得信息资料的方式不同，可以采取文案调查法、观察法、询问法、实验法、网上调查法等。

Focusing on enterprise's specific marketing issue, marketing research is a process in which relevant information is collected, arranged, analyzed and explained systematically and objectively with scientific methods. Marketing research aims to provide basis for marketing managers to make, evaluate and improve marketing decisions. Its content involves macro environment research, enterprise competition research, consumer behavior research, market research, product research, price research and promotion research. Marketing research needs to follow scientific procedures and steps, such as identifying problems and target, making research plan, collecting research information, analyzing research information, writing a research report and evaluating research results. While conducting research activities, there are research methods such as census, typical survey and sampling methods. According to different ways of obtaining data, there are desk research, observation method, enquiry method, experimental method, online survey , etc.

思 考 题
Questions

1. 解释以下概念：市场营销调研、探测性调研、描述性调研、因果性调研、询问法、观察法、实验法。

Explain the following concepts: marketing research, exploratory research, descriptive research, causal research, inquiry method, observation method and experimental method.

2. 简述市场营销调研的内容。

Briefly describe the content of marketing research.

3. 市场营销调研的基本程序有哪些？

What are the basic processes of marketing research?

4. 市场营销调研的方法有哪些？

What are methods used in marketing research?

第三章 分析市场营销环境
Analyzing Marketing Environment

【学习目标】
1. 市场营销环境的含义和特点；
2. 企业营销与营销环境的互动；
3. 微观营销环境的构成要素及其对企业营销活动的影响；
4. 宏观营销环境的构成要素及其对企业营销活动的影响。

Learning Objectives
1. Definition and features of marketing environment;
2. Interaction between enterprise marketing and marketing environment;
3. Components of micro-environment and its impact on enterprise marketing activities;
4. Components of macro-environment and its impact on enterprise marketing activities.

企业的市场营销活动既要受内部条件的制约，也要受外部条件的制约，为了实现营销目标，企业必须认真分析和研究市场营销环境的变化，把握环境变化的趋势，并努力谋求企业外部市场环境与企业内部条件和营销活动之间的动态平衡。研究市场营销环境，是企业制定营销策略的前提。

Enterprises' marketing activities are restricted not only by internal conditions, but also by external conditions. In order to achieve the marketing goal, an enterprise must carefully analyze and study the change of marketing environment, and try to seek the dynamic equilibrium between marketing activities and internal and external environment and condition. Research on marketing environment is the premise of the enterprise developing marketing strategy.

第一节 认知市场营销环境
Understanding Marketing Environment

一、市场营销环境的含义及其构成 Meaning and Composition of Marketing Environment

(一)市场营销环境的含义 Meaning of Marketing Environment

环境，是指事物外界的情况和条件。这里所说的外部条件，不是指整个的外界事物，而是指那些与企业营销活动有关的因素的集合。任何企业都如同生物有机体一样，总是生存于一定的环境之中，企业的营销活动不可能脱离周围环境而孤立地进行。企业的市场营销环境，是指与企业市场营销有关的，影响产品的供给与需求的各种外界条件和因素的集合。这些外部条件影响着企业的发展以及维持良好的目标客户关系的能力，是企业营销活动的基础。

Environment refers to the outside situation and condition. The external condition here mentioned does not involve the whole external things, but means a collection of factors related to enterprise marketing activities. Every enterprise just like an organism, always lives in a certain environment. Enterprise marketing activities can't be carried out in isolation out of the environment. Enterprise marketing environment refers to the collection of various external condition and factors, which are related to the enterprise marketing and influence product supply and demand. The external condition affects the enterprise's development and ability to maintain good relationship with target customers, and it is the foundation of enterprise marketing activities.

(二)市场营销环境的构成 Composition of Marketing Environment

根据营销环境对企业营销活动发生影响的方式和程度，可以将市场营销环境分为两大类：即微观环境和宏观环境。微观环境，是指企业内部条件、供应商、目标顾客、竞争者、营销渠道等对企业营销活动有直接影响的诸因素；宏观环境，是指一个国家或地区的政治、法律、人口、经济、社会文化、自然、科学技术等影响企业营销活动的不可控的宏观因素。

Marketing environment can be divided into two categories according to its influence on enterprise marketing activities: micro-environment and macro-environment. Micro-environment refers to the enterprise's internal conditions, suppliers, target customers, competitors, marketing channels and other factors which have a direct effect on marketing activities; Macro-environment refers to a country's or a region's politics, law, population, economy, social culture, nature, science and technology and other uncontrollable macro-factors which can influence enterprise marketing activities.

宏观环境与微观环境是市场营销系统中的不同层次，所有的微观环境因素都受宏观环境的制约，而微观环境因素对宏观环境也有影响。企业的营销活动就是在这种外界环境互相联系和作用的基础上进行的。企业的市场营销环境因素及其相互关系如图3-1所示。

Macro-environment and micro-environment are the different levels in the marketing system. All the micro-environment factors are restricted by macro-environment, while the factors of micro-environment may also influence macro-environment. On the basis of external environment's connection and interaction, enterprise marketing activities are carried out. The marketing environment factors and their mutual relations are as shown in Figure 3-1.

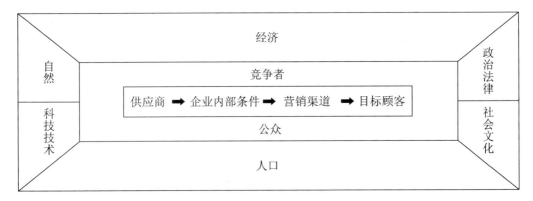

图 3-1 市场营销环境构成

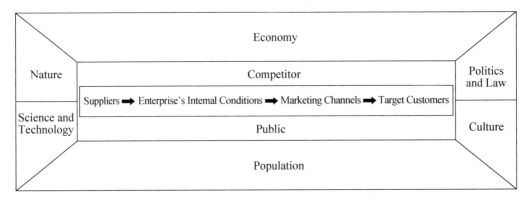

Figure 3-1 Composition Marketing Environment

二、市场营销环境的特点 Characteristics of Marketing Environment

市场营销环境是一个多因素、多层次而且不断变化的集合体，是企业营销活动的基础和条件。其特点主要表现在以下四个方面。

Marketing environment is a multi-factor, multi-level and constantly changing collection, and is the foundation and conditions of the enterprise marketing activities. Its characteristics are mainly displayed in the following four aspects.

(一)客观性 Objectivity

企业市场营销环境不以某个营销组织或个人的意志为转移，它有自己的运行规律和发展特点。营销环境对企业营销活动的影响具有强制性和不可控制性的特点。企业的营销活动只能主动地适应和利用客观环境，而不能改变或违背它。

Enterprise marketing environment has its own rules and development characteristics, not changing with the will of a marketing organization or an individual. Marketing environment's influence on the enterprise marketing activities is forcible and uncontrollable. Enterprise's marketing activities can only actively adapt to and take advantage of the objective environment, but cannot change or disobey it.

(二)差异性 Difference

市场营销环境的差异性不仅表现在不同企业受不同环境的影响，而且同样一种环境因素的变化对不同企业的影响也不相同。在不同的国家或地区之间，宏观环境存在着广泛的差异；不同的企业之间，其微观环境也千差万别。

Difference of marketing environment is shown not only in that different enterprises are affected by different environments, but also in that the change of the same environmental factor would have different influences on various enterprises. The macro-environment varies widely among different countries or regions; the micro-environment among different enterprises is different, too.

(三)关联性 Relevance

市场营销环境不是由某个单一的因素决定的，而是要受一系列相关因素的影响。关联性表明市场营销环境各因素都不是孤立的，而是互相联系、相互渗透、相互作用的。例如，商品的价格不但受市场供求关系的影响，而且还受到财政税收政策的影响。

Marketing environment is not determined by a single factor, but by a series of related factors. Relevance indicates that the factors of marketing environment are not isolated, but interrelated, mutual-penetrating and interacted. For example, prices of goods are not only affected by market supply and demand, but also by fiscal and tax policies.

(四)变化性 Variability

构成企业营销环境的因素是多方面的，每一个因素又都随着社会经济的发展而不断变化。营销环境的变化性主要表现在以下三个方面：一是由于相关性影响，某一环境因素的变化会导致另一环境随之变化；二是每个环境内部的子因素变化也会导致其他环境因素的变化；三是各因素在不同的形势下，对企业活动影响大小不一，例如，随着网络化、全球化、信息化的出现，尤其是电子商务的产生和发展使营销的内、外部环境发生了深刻的变化。

Many factors constitute the enterprise marketing environment, and each factor is changing with the development of social economy. The variability of marketing environment mainly displays in the following three aspects: ① Because of the influence of relevance, the change of one environmental factor will lead to the change of another environment. ② Each sub factor within the environment can also cause the change of other factors. ③ In different situation, factors have different impact on business activities. For example, with the emergence of network, globalization, informatization, especially the emergence and development of electronic commerce, profound changes have taken place in internal and external marketing environment.

三、企业营销与营销环境的互动 Interaction Between Enterprise Marketing and Marketing Environment

企业的微观营销环境影响着企业服务其目标顾客的能力。企业与其供应商、营销中介机构、顾客、竞争者和公众都在一个充满力量和趋势的宏观环境中运作，这些力量和趋势创造机会，也带来威胁。这些力量是"不可控"的，但企业必须对其进行监测和做出反应。

The micro-environment of enterprise influences its ability to serve target customers. Enterprises and their suppliers, marketing intermediaries, customers, competitors and the public are in a macro-environment full of forces and trends. These forces and trends can create opportunities, but also cause threat. The forces are "out of control" but the enterprise must monitor and respond to these forces.

企业的外部营销环境的变化常常对企业形成新的制约条件，甚至威胁企业的生存。由于这种变化是不以企业的意志为转移的客观规律，企业除了适应制约条件以外，没有更多的能力改变外在客观的环境。对于这类制约条件，企业并非通过临时性的措施就能解决，而是必须通过对营销战略进行调整，改革营销方式才能适应。有所作为的营销者应当在外部环境的制约中寻找企业发展的新契机，而不是被动地适应外部环境。

Changes in the external marketing environment of an enterprise often form new restrictions to the enterprise and even threaten the enterprise's existence. Since this change is objective and not changing with the enterprise's will, the enterprise has to adapt to restricting conditions, not able to change the external objective environment very much. The enterprise can not get rid of these restricting conditions through temporary measures. Adjustment of marketing strategies and marketing methods would probably help. Successful marketers are those who can find new opportunities for enterprise development in the restriction of the external environment, rather than passively adapt to the external environment.

企业在接受营销环境制约的同时，也反作用于营销环境。一方面企业可以发挥组织成员的智慧并运用各种可控因素作用于外部营销环境，影响并引导外部环境朝着对自己有利的方向转化。这里最重要的是改善微观环境。例如，企业能够通过开发新产品来创造需要，诱发消费者的潜在需求，形成新的流行热潮。另一方面，企业也应认识到外部营销环境的变化在形成制约条件的同时，也为企业创造了新的发展机会，那样，就能够开辟新的市场而获得发展。

When the enterprise accepts the restriction of marketing environment, it also reacts back to the marketing environment. On the one hand, the enterprise can exert team members' wisdom and use all kinds of controllable factors to react on the external marketing environment. The enterprise could influence and guide the external environment towards a favorable direction. It's most important to improve the micro-environment. For example, enterprises can create a need when developing a new product to create potential demand and form a new fashion. On the other hand, enterprises should realize that changes in the external marketing environment could bring restrictions, and at the same time they also create new development opportunities for the enterprise. In that case, the enterprise will be able to open up new markets for further development.

第二节 分析微观营销环境
Analyzing Micro-environment

微观营销环境因素一般由六个要素构成，即企业内部条件、供应商、营销中间商、目标顾客、竞争者和公众。如图 3-2 所示。

Micro-environment generally consists of six factors: enterprise's internal conditions, suppliers, marketing intermediaries, target customers, competitors and the public, as shown in Figure 3-2.

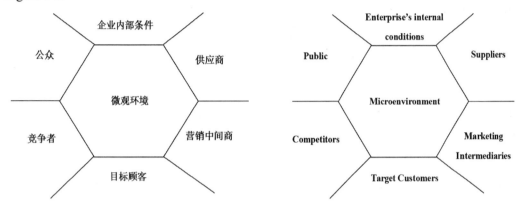

图 3-2 微观营销环境因素　　　　　Figure 3-2　Factors in Micromarketing Environment

一、企业内部条件 Enterprise's Internal Conditions

企业开展市场营销活动时，必须注意各部门如生产、采购、新产品研究与开发、财务管理、市场营销等部门间的协调。因为正是这些部门构成了企业的内部微观环境因素，它们的状况对营销决策的制定与实施具有重大影响。市场营销部门在制定和实施营销目标与计划时，要充分考虑企业内部的环境力量，去努力争取高层管理部门和其他职能部门的理解和支持。

When an enterprise carries out marketing activities, it must pay attention to the coordination among various departments, such as the departments of production, purchasing, research and development of new products, financial management, and marketing department and so on. Because it is these departments that constitute the internal micro-environment of the enterprise, their status has a significant influence on marketing decision making and implementation. When the marketing department sets marketing goals and implements marketing plans, it should fully consider the internal environment of the enterprise to strive for understanding and support from top management and other functional departments.

二、供应商 Suppliers

供应商，是向企业及其竞争者提供生产经营所需资源的企业或个人，包括提供原材料、零部件、设备、能源、劳务、资金及其他用品等。供应商对企业营销活动有实质性的影响，主要表现在：首先，资源供应的可靠性，即资源供应的保证程度，供应商对企业供货的稳定性和及时，是企业营销活动顺利进行的前提；其次，供应资源的价格及其变动趋势直接影响着企业产品的成本、价格和利润；最后，供应资源的质量水平直接影响着产品的质量。企业对供应商的影响力要有足够的认识，要重视与供应商的合作和采购工作。其主要策略是采取一体化经营策略和多渠道采购策略，以增强企业营销工作的主动性。

Suppliers are enterprises or individuals who provide resources for production and operation for the enterprise and its competitors, including raw materials, spare parts, equipment, energy, labor, capital, and other supplies, etc. The supplier has substantial impact on enterprise marketing activities in the following aspects: first, the reliability of the resource supply, that is, to what degree the supplier can guarantee resource supply. Stable and timely supply is the condition of carrying out enterprise marketing activities smoothly. Second, the price of resources and its change trend directly affect the cost and price of the product and profit of the enterprise. Last, the quality of supplied resources directly affects the quality of the product. The enterprise should realize fully the significance of the supplier's influence and pay attention to the cooperation with suppliers and procurement work. Its main strategy is to adopt integration strategy and multi-channel procurement strategy to enhance the initiative of the enterprise in marketing work.

三、营销中间商 Marketing Intermediaries

营销中间商，是协助企业促销和分销其产品给最终购买者的所有中介机构，包括商人中间商、代理中间商、辅助中间商等。商人中间商从生产者手里购进商品，然后转卖给其他经营者或消费者，他们对其经营的商品拥有所有权，如批发商、零售商；代理中间商替生产者寻找买主，帮助推销商品，对其经营的商品没有所有权，如经纪人、制造商的代理商等；辅助中间商不直接经营商品，但对商品经营起促进、服务作用，如物流配送公司(运输、仓储)、市场营销服务机构(广告、咨询、调研)以及财务中介机构(银行、信托、保险等)。这些组织或个人都是营销所不可缺少的中间环节，大多数企业的营销活动都需要他们的协助才能顺利进行。企业在营销过程中，必须处理好同这些中介机构的合作关系。

Marketing intermediaries refer to all the intermediaries who assist the enterprise in promotion and distribution of the products, such as merchant middlemen, agent middlemen, assistant middlemen, etc. Merchant middlemen purchase goods from producers, and then sell them to other businessmen or consumers. They take title to the goods, such as wholesalers and retailers. Agent middlemen look for buyers for producers and help to sell goods, and take no title to the goods, such as brokers, manufacturers' representatives, etc. Assistant middlemen do not directly deal with the goods, but give promotion and service to the business, such as logistics distribution company (transport, storage), marketing service agencies (advertising, consulting, research) and financial intermediaries (banks, trust, insurance, etc.). These organizations or individuals are essential to marketing, and most of the enterprise marketing activities require their assistance in order to run smoothly. During the marketing process, enterprises must keep

第三章 分析市场营销环境
Analyzing Marketing Environment

good cooperative relations with these agencies.

四、目标顾客 Target Customers

顾客是企业服务的对象，也是产品销售的目标市场，是营销活动的出发点和归宿。目标市场包括消费者市场、生产者市场、中间商市场、政府市场、非营利组织及国际市场等。各类市场都有其独特的顾客，要求企业以不同的方式提供相应的产品和服务，从而影响企业营销决策的制定和服务能力的形成。企业的一切营销活动都应以满足顾客的需要为中心。因此，顾客是企业最重要的环境因素。

Customers are the enterprise's service object, and also the target market of product sales. They are the starting point and the ultimate aim of the marketing activities. Target market includes consumer market, producer market, intermediary market, government market, nonprofit organizations and international market, etc. All kinds of market have their unique customers, which require enterprises to provide products and services in different ways. Enterprises' decisions and service ability are thereby affected. All enterprise marketing activities should focus on the needs of customers. Therefore, customers are enterprises' most important environmental factor.

五、竞争者 Competitors

企业不能独占市场，它们都会面对形形色色的竞争对手。在竞争性的市场上，除来自本行业的竞争外，还有来自代用品生产者、潜在加入者、原材料供应者和购买者等多种力量的竞争。从消费需求的角度看，竞争者可以分为以下几种类型：一是欲望竞争者。它是指针对消费者想要满足的各种目前愿望而竞争。例如，房地产公司与汽车制造商为争夺顾客而展开竞争。顾客现有的钱如用于汽车购买则不能用于房子购买，汽车制造商与房地产公司实际上是针对购买者当前所要满足的各种愿望展开争夺。二是一般竞争者。它是指能帮助购买者满足某种愿望的各种方法。例如，汽车、摩托车或自行车都能满足消费者对交通工具的需要，消费者通常只会选择其中一种。这属于较大范围的行业内部竞争。三是产品形式竞争者。它是指能满足购买者的某种愿望的各种型号产品的提供者。例如，自行车既有普通轻便车，又有性能更优良的山地车。四是品牌竞争者。它是指能满足购买者的某种愿望的同种产品的其他品牌的提供者。如轿车中的"奔驰""宝马"以及"别克"等品牌之间的竞争。企业通过分析消费者如何做出购买决策，了解什么是主要竞争者，必须在满足消费者需要和欲望方面比竞争对手做得更好。只有知己知彼、扬长避短，才能在顾客心目中强有力地确定其所提供产品的地位，以获取战略优势，在市场竞争中取胜。

Enterprises cannot monopolize the market, and they will face all kinds of competition. In the competitive market, besides the competition from the industry, there is other competition from substitute producers, potential entrants, raw material suppliers and buyers, etc. From the perspective of consumption demand, competitors can be divided into the following several types: the first is desire competitors. It means to compete for all kinds of desire that consumers want to meet, for example, the competition between real estate companies and automobile manufacturers.

If a consumer spends his money in hand for a car, then he can not buy a house with the money. Carmakers and real estate agencies compete for buyers' various desires at present. The second is general competitors. It refers to the competitors supplying a variety of ways to satisfy the purchaser's desires. For example, an automobile, a motorcycle or a bicycle can meet the needs of consumers for transportation, but usually consumers only choose one of them. It belongs to the wider range of industry internal competition. The third is about product competition. It refers to the competitors supplying product of various models, which can satisfy the buyer's some sort of desire. For example, there are ordinary light-weight bicycles and mountain bicycles with more excellent performance and they are all bicycles. The fourth is brand competitors. It refers to the competitive suppliers of other brands of the same product, which can satisfy the buyer's certain desire. For example, there is competition among car brands "Mercedes Benz" "BMW" and "Buick". Through the analysis of how consumers make purchase decisions, the enterprise can know who are the main competitors, and must do better than its competitors in meeting the needs and desires of the consumers. Only by knowing the competitors and knowing itself, fostering strengths and circumventing weaknesses, can the company determine its product's status and get strategic advantage in order to win in market competition.

六、公众 The Public

公众，是指对企业实现营销目标的能力具有实际或潜在影响力的团体或个人。公众的态度会协助或妨碍企业营销活动的正常开展。公司要花一定时间去观察公众的态度、预测他们的动向，并采取积极措施维持和公众之间的良好关系。

The public refers to the groups or individuals who have real or potential influence on the enterprise's ability to realize its marketing target. Public attitudes can assist or hinder normal development of enterprise marketing activities. Enterprises should spend certain time to observe the public attitude, predict its trends, and take active measures to maintain good relations with the public.

企业公众的类型很多，主要有以下七种。

For the enterprise, the public mainly has the following seven categories.

(1) 金融公众。包括银行、投资公司、证券经济商、股东等，它们对企业的融资能力有重要的影响。

The financial public includes banks, investment companies, securities businesses, shareholders, and so on. They have important influence on the enterprise's financial ability.

(2) 媒介公众。指那些刊载和播送新闻、特写及社论的机构，包括电视台、电台、报纸、杂志等大众媒体。他们主要通过社会舆论来影响其他公众对企业的态度。特别是主流媒体的报道，对企业影响极大。

The public media refers to those organizations that publish and broadcast news, feature stories and editorials, including television, radio, newspapers, magazines and other mass media.

These media could influence other public attitudes to the enterprise through social opinions. Especially the reports from mainstream media have great impact on enterprises.

(3) 政府公众。包括负责管理企业行为的各种有关政府机构。企业管理人员在制订营销计划时必须认真研究与考虑政府各项政策与措施的发展变化。

The government public includes various government departments that are responsible for managing enterprise behaviors. While making the marketing plan, the enterprise management personnel must study and consider fully the development and change of government policies and measures.

(4) 市民行动公众。包括消费者利益保护组织、环境保护组织、少数民族团体等。企业的营销活动可能受到它们的质询。

The citizens' action public includes protection organizations on behalf of consumer interests, environment protection groups, minor ethnic groups, etc. Enterprise's marketing activities could be questioned by them.

(5) 地方公众。包括企业所在地区附近的社区居民群众、地方官员等。每个企业都要同当地的公众团体，如邻里居民和社区组织等保持联系，积极参加社区活动、回答质询和向值得支持的事业提供资助。

The local public includes community residents and local officials in the neighborhood of the enterprise, etc. Every enterprise should keep in touch with local public organizations, such as the neighborhood residents and community organizations, take an active part in community activities, answer questions and provide support to worthy businesses.

(6) 一般公众。指与企业经营活动无关的一般消费者。虽然一般公众并不是有组织地对企业采取行动，然而一般公众对企业的印象却影响着现实消费者对该企业及其产品的看法。

The general public refers to general consumers who have nothing to do with the business activities. Although the general public is not organized to take action to the enterprise, the general public's impression of the enterprise influences the real consumers' opinions of the enterprise and its products.

(7) 企业内部公众。包括生产一线的职工、职能部门员工以及中高层管理人员、董事会成员等。企业应经常向员工通报有关情况，介绍企业发展计划，发动员工出谋划策，关心职工福利，奖励有功人员，增强内部凝聚力。当企业雇员对自己的企业感到满意的时候，他们的态度就会感染企业以外的公众，从而有利于塑造良好的企业形象。

The enterprise internal public includes workers on the line, department staff and senior management personnel and members of the board, etc. Enterprises should often introduce relevant report and business development plans to the staff, encourage employee's ideas, be concerned about employee benefits, reward meritorious staff, and strengthen internal cohesion. When employees are satisfied with their enterprise, their attitudes can infect the public outside of the enterprise, therefore it is good for the corporate image.

第三节 分析宏观营销环境
Analyzing Macro-environment

宏观营销环境因素主要包括人口、经济、自然、科学技术、政治法律和社会文化以及其他一些企业不可控制的环境因素。这些因素及其发展变化的状况对企业的营销活动产生间接的影响和制约,企业及微观环境的参与者无不处在宏观环境之中。其宏观环境因素如图 3-3 所示。

Macro-environment factors include population, economy, nature, science and technology, politics, law and social culture, and some other uncontrollable environmental factors. These factors and the development status have indirect influence and restriction on the enterprise marketing activities. Enterprises and the participants of micro-environment are all in macro-environment. The macro-environment factors are as shown in Figure 3-3.

图 3-3 宏观环境因素

Figure 3-3 Macromarketing Environment

第三章 分析市场营销环境
Analyzing Marketing Environment

一、人口环境 Population Environment

市场是由有购买欲望且有购买力的人构成的，所以，人口是构成市场的第一位因素。人口的数量决定消费者的数量，消费者数量的多少又在一定程度上决定市场的潜在容量。除了人口数量，人口的其他指标，如人口结构、人口分布等，都会影响企业的市场营销活动。因此，人口环境对营销者而言是至关重要的。

Market is made of people who have purchase desire and purchase power, so population is the first factor in a market. Population size can determine the number of consumers, and the number of consumers can determine potential capacity of market to a certain extent. Besides the size of population, other population index can also have an effect on marketing activities, such as population structure, population distribution, etc. Therefore, population environment is crucial for marketers.

(一)人口数量及其变化趋势 Population and Its Trend

人口数量是决定市场规模和潜量的一个基本要素，因此，按人口数目可大略推算出市场规模。人口对市场的影响更多地表现在维持人们生存所必需的基本生活资料上面。某一市场范围内的总人口基本上反映了该消费市场生活消费品的需要量。在其他经济和心理条件不变的情况下，总人口越多，市场容量就越大，企业营销的市场就越广阔。

Population is one of the basic elements which determine market size and potential. Therefore, the size of the market can be estimated according to the number of population. Population's influences on market are mainly reflected in the aspect of basic consumer goods. The total population within a market could reflect the demand for consumption goods. In the condition of invariable economy and psychology, the more population is, the greater the market capacity will be, and the broader the market for enterprise is.

中国是世界上人口最大的国家。2015 年末，中国人口约为 13.74 亿。随着社会主义市场经济的发展，人民收入不断提高，中国已被视为世界最大的潜在市场.

China is a country with the largest population in the world. At the end of 2015, there are about 1.374 billion Chinese people. With the development of the socialist market economy, Chinese people's income is increasing, and China has been regarded as the world's largest potential market.

目前，世界人口环境正发生明显的变化，主要趋势是：①全球人口持续增长。截至 2013 年 1 月 4 日，全世界人口将可能达到 70.57 亿，按目前的年增长率预测，2050 年将达到 79 亿～119 亿。②美国等发达国家人口出生率下降，而发展中国家人口出生率上升。90%的新增人口在发展中国家，使得这些国家人均所得的增加以及需求层次的升级受到影响。

At present, the environment of world population is changing significantly. The trend is: ①the world's population continues to grow. By January 4, 2013, the world's population reached 7.057 billion, according to the current annual growth rate, in 2050 it will be between 7.9 and 11.9 billion. ②The birth rate in the United States and other developed countries declines, while it rises in developing countries. Ninety percent of new population will be in developing countries, which will affect the increase of per capita income and upgrade of demand.

企业既要看到目前的人口数量,还要注意人口增长率,要把握人口变化的趋势,去预测市场容量。

Enterprise should not only notice the current population, but also pay attention to population growth, to grasp the trend of population change and to predict market capacity.

(二)人口结构及其变化趋势 Population Structure and Its Change Trend.

人口结构主要包括人口的年龄结构、性别结构、家庭结构、城乡结构、文化结构以及民族结构。

Population structure mainly includes the population's age structure, gender structure, family structure, urban and rural structure, cultural structure and national structure.

1. 年龄结构及其变化趋势 Age Structure and Its Change Trend

不同年龄的消费者对商品的需求不一样。老年人、中年人、青年人与儿童等的需要是大不相同的。企业应针对人口的结构特点开展营销活动。

Consumers of different ages demand different goods. The elderly, the middle-aged, young people and children's needs are very different. Marketing activities should be undertaken by enterprises in accordance with the features of population structure.

随着社会经济的发展、科学技术的进步、物质文化水平的提高和医疗条件的改善,人口的平均寿命大大延长。人口年龄结构呈现以下趋势:①许多国家人口老龄化加速。人类寿命延长,死亡率下降,人口老龄化是当今世界发展的必然趋势。我国2004年的人口统计数据表明,中国65岁以上人口占总人口的比重为8.58%,比1990年增加了3.01%;15~64岁人口负担老年系数为11.9%,也比1990年增加了3.55%。据联合国预测,到2030年全世界60岁以上的老人将比1990年增加两倍,占全世界人口总数的比例将由1990年的9%上升到16%;同时,由于女性的平均寿命普遍高于男性,因此,未来的老年人中妇女要占多数。随着老年人口的绝对数和相对数的增加,银色产业市场日渐形成并迅速扩大,诸如保健用品、营养品、老年人生活必需品等市场将会兴旺;同时,社会保障体系和公共服务体系的压力加大。②出生率下降引起市场需求变化。美国等发达国家的人口出生率下降,出生婴儿和学龄前儿童数量减少,从而给儿童食品、童装、玩具等生产经营者带来威胁,但同时也使青年夫妇有更多的闲暇时间用于游泳、娱乐和在外用餐。

With the development of social economy, the progress of science and technology, the enhancement of material and cultural level and the improvement of medical conditions, people's average life expectancy has greatly extended. The age structure of population presents the following trends: ① many countries' ageing population accelerates. Prolongation of human life, declination of death rate and population aging are the inevitable trend of the world today. The population statistics of China shows that in 2004, the proportion of China's population aged 65 occupied 8.58% of the whole population, increasing 3.01% than in 1990; the elderly dependency rate taken by people aged 15 to 64 was 11.9%, with a 3.55% increase over 1990. According to the forecast of United Nations, by the year of 2030, people over the age of 60 all over the world will be twice more than the population in 1990, and the proportion in the total world's population will rise from 9% in 1990 to 16%. At the same time, because the average life expectancy of women is generally longer than men, the majority of old people in the future are women. With the increase of absolute quantity and relative quantity of population of older people, the silver industry market has formed and expanded rapidly. The markets of health care products, nutrition products, the elderly daily necessities will be prosperous. Meanwhile, pressure of the social security system and public service system will be heavier. ② The falling birth rate affects the change of market demand. In the developed countries, such as the United States of America, the birth rate is declining, and the number of infants and preschooler is also declining, which poses a threat to producers of children's food, clothes, toys and other children's products. But for young couples, they have more free time for swimming, entertainment, and dining out.

2. 性别结构及其变化趋势 Gender Structure and Its Change Trend

由于男女性别上的差异，往往导致消费需求、购买习惯与行为有很大的差别，反映到市场上就会出现男性用品市场和女性用品市场。例如，生产烟酒的企业主要以男性为目标市场；由于女性多操持家务，大多数日用消费品由女性采购，因此，不仅妇女用品可设专业商店销售，很多家庭用品和儿童用品也都纳入妇女市场。同时，妇女就业率的上升也扩大了高档服饰市场的规模。

Due to gender differences, there are huge differences between men and women on consumers' demands, buying habits and behaviors, which result in two kinds of markets: markets for men and for women. For example, alcohol and tobacco production enterprises mainly consider the male as their target market; Women generally do more housework, and most consumer goods are purchased by women. Therefore, not only can women products be sold in professional stores, a lot of household items and children products are also included in women's market. At the same time, the increase of women's employment has expanded the size of high-grade garment market as well.

3. 家庭结构及其变化趋势 Family Structure and Its Change Trend

家庭包括家庭数量、家庭人口、家庭生命周期、家庭居住环境等。家庭是社会的细胞，也是商品采购和消费的基本单位。一个市场的家庭结构对市场消费需求的潜量和需求结构都有十分重要的影响。例如，家庭数目多，对家具、家电的需求量必然就大。

Family includes family number, family size, family life cycle and family living environment, etc. Family is the cell of the society, also the basic unit of commodity purchase and consumption. The family structure of a market has a very important influence on the quantity and structure of consumption demand. More family numbers will definitely have greater demand for furniture, appliances, and so on.

随着社会经济、文化和观念的变化，各国家庭的特征也在发生变化，非家庭户有增加的趋势。应注意这一变化会引起消费结构的变化，例如，单身家庭和单亲家庭数量的增加、家庭人数的减少、家庭规模的小型化发展，会使小型炊具市场越来越大，同时必然带动对较小的公寓，便宜且较小的家具、陈设以及分量较小的包装食品的需求量的上升。

With the change of social economy, culture and ideology, family characteristics are changing, and the non-household has a tendency to increase. It should be noticed that this change will cause changes in consumption structure. For example, the increase of single families and single-parent families, the decrease of family members and the miniaturization of family size all can make the market of small cooker bigger and bigger. At the same time, the demand for smaller apartments, cheap and small furniture, furnishings, as well as small packaged food will rise accordingly.

4. 城乡结构及其变化趋势 Urban and Rural Structure and Its Change Trend

我国的人口绝大部分在农村，农村人口约占总人口的 80%。这种客观因素决定了企业在国内市场中应当以农民为主要营销对象，市场开拓的重点也应放在农村。

Most of China's population is in the countryside, and the rural population accounts for about 80% of the total population. This objective factor decides that enterprises in the domestic market should take farmers as the main target of marketing, and marketing activities should also focus on the rural areas.

改革开放以来我国每年农转非人口约 1000 万，人口从农村向城市迁移，加大了城市化的进程。

Urbanized population has reached about 10 million each year in China since the policy of reform and opening up, and the population migrates from the country to the city, which increases the process of urbanization.

5. 文化结构及其变化趋势 Cultural Structure and Its Change Trend

人口的教育程度不同，对市场需求会表现出不同的倾向。随着高等教育规模的扩大，人口的受教育程度普遍提高，收入水平也逐步增加。

Because of different education levels of people, market demand will show different tendencies. With the expansion of higher education, there is a general improvement of education level and income level also gradually increases.

6. 民族结构及其变化趋势 National Structure and Its Change Trend

我国除了汉族以外，还有 50 多个少数民族。近年来汉族人口增速大大减缓，少数民族人口增速仍然很高。2005 年 1%人口抽样调查发现：在全国人口中，汉族人口为 118295 万人，占总人口的 90.56%；各少数民族人口为 12333 万人，占总人口的 9.44%。与第五次全国人口普查相比，汉族人口增加了 2355 万人，增长了 2.03%；各少数民族人口增加了 1690 万人，增长了 15.88%。民族不同，其生活习性、文化传统也不相同。反映到市场上，就是各民族的市场需求存在着很大的差异。

In addition to the Han nationality in China, there are more than 50 ethnic minorities. The increase of Han population has greatly slowed down and the population of ethnic minorities increases fast in recent years. A sampling survey of 1% population in 2005 found that: in the nation's population, the Han population reached 1.18295 billion, accounting for 90.56% of the whole population; ethnic minorities' population was 123.33 million, accounting for 9.44% of the total population. Compared with the fifth national population census, the Han population increased by 23.55 million, up to 2.03%; the ethnic population increased by 16.9 million, up to 15.88%. Different ethnic minorities have different life habits and cultural traditions, and therefore they have different market demands from each other.

(三) 人口的地理分布及地区间的人口流动性 Geographical Distribution of Population and Population Mobility Among Regions

人口分布是指人口在不同的地理区域的密集程度。由于农村与城市、东部与西部、南方与北方、热带与寒带、山区与平原等不同区域的自然条件、经济发展水平、市场开放程度以及社会文化传统和社会经济结构与人口政策等因素的不同，分布在不同区域的人口具有不同的需求特点和消费习惯。例如，在食品消费结构和口味方面，我国南方人以大米为主食，北方人以面粉为主食。由于各区域在消费需求方面存在显著的区别，要求企业提供不同的产品和服务。

Population distribution refers to population intensity in different geographical regions. Different areas, such as the rural and urban, the east and west, the north and south, tropical and cold areas, have different natural conditions, economic development levels, market openness, social cultural traditions, social and economic structure and population policy. Therefore, people in different parts have different demand and consumption habits. For example, in terms of food consumption structure and taste, southerners prefer rice as the main food, but the northern people like flour. Due to the significant difference in consumption demand of different parts, enterprises should be able to provide different products and services.

在市场经济条件下，经济落后地区向经济发达地区、一般地区向开发开放地区的人口迁移规模和速度都在增长，会出现地区间的人口的大量流动。因此，企业营销者应密切注意人口流动的客观规律，适时采取相应的对策。

In the condition of market economy, there is population migration from under-developed and common areas to developed and open areas, and the migration scale and speed are growing. Therefore, marketers should pay close attention to the population flow, and take countermeasures in time.

二、社会文化环境 Social Culture Environment

社会文化是人类在社会历史发展过程中所创造的物质财富和精神财富的总和。它体现了一个国家或地区的社会文明程度，是人类知识、信仰、艺术、道德、习俗及后天所获得的一切能力和习惯的复合整体。从市场营销学研究的角度来看，社会文化环境包括物质文化、语言文字、教育水平、宗教信仰、价值观、审美观、社会组织和风俗习惯等。

Social culture is the sum of material and spiritual wealth created in the process of human social and historical development. It embodies the social civilization degree of a country or a region, and it is the compound of human knowledge, belief, art, morals, customs and all ability and habits received after birth. From the perspective of marketing research, it includes material culture, language, education level, religious belief, values, aesthetics, social organization, customs and habits, etc.

(一)物质文化 Material Culture

一个社会的物质文化是指以产品和技术为标志的该社会的物质生产水平，以及受物质生产制约的该社会的人们的消费观念和消费水平。营销人员对物质文化的评估主要是经济基础设施的状况，其中包括运输、动力交通、通讯，金融基本条件如银行、信托公司和其他金融机构，行业以及相关行业的生产工艺能力与水平，行业中技术密集程度。这些方面会间接地影响企业的经营水平，进而影响企业的营销活动。

Material culture refers to the social material production level of a society symbolized by product and technology, and people's consumption concept and consumption level limited by material production. Marketers evaluate material culture mainly from the aspect of economic infrastructure, including transportation, traffic, communication; basic financial conditions such as banks, trust companies and other financial institutions; production technology ability and level in the industry and related industry; technology intensive degree in an industry. These aspects indirectly affect the enterprise marketing level, thus influence enterprise marketing activities.

(二)语言文字 Language

语言文字是人类交流的工具，它是文化的核心组成部分之一。世界上不同的国家拥有各自不同的语言，仅官方语言大约就有100多种，而且许多国家有几种语言。以美国这个移民国家为例，英语是官方语言，在英语以外，美国本土使用较多的语言有西班牙语、法语、意大利语、汉语、波兰语、韩语、日语等二十多种，从而形成了独特的美国文化和高度复杂的社会形态。同时在国际市场营销活动中，营销者在使用语言文字时，还应当注意一种特殊的语言——"身体"语言。因此，企业在开展市场营销尤其是国际市场营销活动时，为使营销活动顺利进行，应尽量了解国际市场的文化背景，掌握不同语言文字的差异。

Language is a tool for human communication, and it is one of the core parts of culture. Different countries have their own language in the world. There are about 100 kinds of official languages, and many countries have several languages. Take the immigration country, the United States of America, for example, English is the official language. Besides English, the most commonly used languages in the United States are over twenty, such as Spanish, French, Italian, Chinese, Polish, Korean, Japanese and so on, which have formed the unique American culture and the highly complicated social form. At the same time in international marketing activities, marketers should also pay attention to a special kind of language—"body" language. When enterprises hold marketing activities, especially international marketing activities, they should fully understand the cultural background of international market, to master language differences in order to promote marketing activities smoothly.

(三)教育水平 Education Level

教育包括知识、技能、理想和观念的学习、培训和传播。教育水平是指消费者受教育的程度。一个国家、一个地区的教育水平与经济发展水平往往是一致的。不同的文化修养表现出不同的审美观，使购买商品的选择原则和方式不同。一般来讲，教育水平高的地区，消费者对商品的鉴别力强，容易接受广告宣传和接受新产品，购买的理性程度高。因此，在进行产品设计和制订产品策略时，应考虑当地的教育水平，使产品的复杂程度、技术性能与之相适应。

Education includes study, training and spread of knowledge, skills and ideals. Education level refers to the education degree of consumers. The education level of a country or a region is often consistent with the economic development level. Different cultures show different aesthetic views, which cause people to purchase goods in different ways. Generally speaking, in an area of higher education, consumers have a strong discriminating power in choosing goods. They are easy to accept advertising and new products, and they are very rational while purchasing. Therefore, when designing products and devising product strategies, enterprises should consider the local education level, and make product's complexity and technical performance adapt to the education level.

(四)宗教信仰 Religious Belief

宗教是反映人们对客观世界认识的一种社会意识形态，是文化的又一重要组成部分。世界上的主要宗教有佛教、基督教、伊斯兰教、印度教等。不同的宗教信仰有不同的文化倾向和戒律，从而影响人们认识事物的方式、价值观念和行为准则，进而影响着人们的消费行为，带来特殊的市场需求。因此，对营销者来说，就必须研究各种宗教信仰，在尊重人们信仰的前提下，用恰当的营销策略满足不同宗教信仰的人们的需要。

Religion is a social ideology reflecting people's understanding of the objective world, and is another important part of culture. The world's main religions are Buddhism, Christianity, Islam, and Hinduism and so on. Different religions have different cultural tendencies and precepts, which influences the ways of people's thinking, values and codes of conduct. It also influences people's consumption behavior and brings special market demand. For marketers, therefore, they have to research all kinds of religious belief. On the premise of respecting people's faith, marketers should meet the needs of people having different religions with appropriate marketing strategies.

(五)价值观念 Values

价值观念是指人们对客观事物的评价标准，即个人对他人或周围事务的看法、思维，是个人思维判断的结果。由于不同文化背景下的价值观各不相同，因此人们对于同一文化现象的认识、感受和理解也就不同。价值观念包括人们对时间、财富和物质享受、新事物和冒险等的态度等。

Values are the criteria of evaluating objective things, referring to personal views and thinking about others or surrounding things, and they are the result of individual judgment. Due to different values in different cultural background, the understanding and feelings of people for the same cultural phenomenon are different, too. Values include attitudes to time, wealth, material comforts, new things and adventures, etc.

1. 对待时间的价值观念 Time Value

在经济高度发达的西方工业化国家，人们的生活节奏普遍较快。他们对时间价值的观念很强烈，视时间为生命与金钱。所以他们对于节省劳动、节省时间的商品和服务的需求强烈，邮购、网上购物、快餐、速溶咖啡等服务以及家务劳动社会化和机械化等会受到欢迎。而在经济较落后的发展中国家，人们的时间观念通常较差，他们更喜欢物美价廉、适用性强和经久耐用的商品等。

In the highly developed western countries, people generally have faster pace of life. They have strong sense of time, regarding time as money and life. So they have a strong demand for products and services which can save labor and time. Such services as mail order, online shopping, fast foods, instant coffee, the socialization of housework and mechanization will be welcomed. In countries of under-developed economy, people usually have weak sense of time. They prefer cheap products with high quality, applicability, durability, and so on.

2. 对待财富和物质享受的态度 Attitudes Towards Wealth and Material Comforts

提倡"节俭观"的地区的人们对高消费商品和服务(包括信用消费)等会起到抑制作用；相比之下，而崇尚"享受观"的地区会直接影响到新产品和新的消费方式潮流的更替速度、奢侈商品和高档名牌商品的销售规模等众多方面。

People in the area advocating "frugality" will have a conservative attitude on the consumption of luxury products and services (including credit consumption). In contrast, the concept of "enjoy" will directly influence the change speed of new products and new ways of consumption, and also influence the sales scale of luxury products and famous-brand products.

3. 对待新事物的态度 Attitudes To New Things

不同国家和地区具有各自的民族性和传统性，消费者对传统文化和外来文化的态度是截然不同的。例如，韩国人的消费观的一个重要表现为"身土不二"，他们十分重视自己的民族文化，提倡消费国产货抵御外国商品。在韩国，国民开的车大多数是国产车，如现代、起亚等；奔驰、宝马的车主经常受到他人的歧视。

Different countries and regions have their own nationality and tradition, and the consumers' attitudes towards traditional culture and foreign culture are very different. For example, one manifestation of the South Koreans' consumption view is only buying goods produced in their own country. They attach great importance to their own national culture, and advocate the consumption of domestic goods instead of foreign goods. In South Korea, most people drive cars made in korea, such as HYUNDAI, KIA, etc. The owners of Mercedes and BMW are often discriminated by the others.

4. 对待冒险的态度 Attitudes to Risk

年轻国度的人们，如美国人，富有冒险精神。一方面，对冒险性娱乐活动有大量需求，像登山探险、蹦极、攀岩等玩乐活动，从而刺激了与冒险相关的产业的发展；另一方面在消费观念上,他们对新产品和新的消费方式等感到好奇,敢于尝试新事物而东方有些国家则相反。如印度,消费者的消费观念比较保守,对原使用的商品忠诚度很高,很少有消费者冒险放弃原使用的商品去尝试新的替代产品或新的品牌。因此,新品牌的替代产品或新升级的产品在这些不具备冒险精神的地区很难打开市场。

People in young countries, such as Americans, are always adventurous. On the one hand, they have a high demand for adventurous entertainment, like mountaineering adventure, bungee, rock climbing, which stimulate the development of the industry related to risk. On the other hand, in terms of consumption concept, they are curious about new products and new ways of consumption, and they are brave to try new things. However, some countries in the East are totally different. Take India for example. In India, people's consumption concept is more conservative and they have very high loyalty to the products they have used before. Few consumers would like to risk abandoning the original products they are familiar with to try a new alternative product or a new brand. Therefore, the new brand of the alternative product or new upgrade product may hardly occupy the market in the regions without adventurous spirit.

因此,对于不同的价值观念,企业营销人员应采取不同的策略。企业在制定促销策略时应把产品与目标市场的文化传统联系起来。

Therefore, for different values, marketers should adopt different strategies. Enterprises should relate the product to the culture of target market while making marketing strategy.

(六)风俗习惯 Customs

风俗习惯是人类社会代代相传的思想和行为规范,也是消费者的一种消费形式。它在饮食、服饰、居住、婚丧、信仰、节日、人际关系等方面都表现出独特的心理特征、伦理道德、行为方式和生活习惯。不同的国家、不同的民族有不同的风俗习惯,对消费者的消费嗜好、消费模式、消费行为等具有重要的影响。例如,在我国,春节前是购物高峰;而在西方国家,每逢圣诞节来临,人们就购买圣诞树、礼品、食品,欢度圣诞节。禁忌是风俗习惯的一种特殊的表现形式,如我国壮族禁食牛肉,土家族禁食狗肉;德国人忌用核桃,认为核桃是不祥之物等等。企业营销者必须了解各地的风俗习惯,根据不同地区、不同民族的风俗习惯有针对性地开展营销活动。

Customs is the thought and behavior norm of human society passed from generation to generation. It is also a form of consumption. In the aspect of food, clothing, housing, diet, religion, festival, interpersonal relationships, etc., customs can show unique psychological characteristics, ethics, behavior patterns and life habits. Different countries and different nationalities have different customs and habits, which has important influence on consumers' preference, consumption patterns and consumption behavior. For example, the time before Spring Festival is the shopping peak in China; whereas in western countries, when Christmas is coming, people always buy Christmas trees, gifts, and food for celebrating Christmas. Taboo is a special manifestation of customs and habits. For example, in our country, the minority of Zhuang doesn't eat beef; Tujia people don't eat dog meat; The Germans avoid using walnut, because they think walnut is an unlucky thing, and so on. Marketers must be familiar with local customs, and carry out marketing campaigns according to different areas, different ethnic customs and habits.

(七)审美观 Aesthetic Standards

审美观通常指人们对事物的美丑、善恶的评价。不同的国家、民族、宗教、阶层和个人往往因社会文化背景不同,其审美标准也不尽一致。例如,在欧美,妇女结婚时穿白色的婚礼服,因为白色象征着纯洁和美丽。但在亚洲,白色通常是悲伤的象征。在中国,传统上,妇女结婚时穿红色的婚礼服,因为红色象征吉祥如意、幸福美满。但在西方国家红色是危险的象征。因此,不同的审美观对消费的影响是不同的,企业应针对不同的审美观所引起的不同消费需求,开展自己的营销活动。

Aesthetic standards refer to people's evaluation of beauty and ugliness, good and evil. Different nations, ethnics, religions, classes and individuals have different aesthetic standards because of different social culture backgrounds. For example, in Europe and the United States, brides wear white wedding dresses because white symbolizes purity and beauty; whereas in Asia white is usually the symbol of sadness. In China, traditionally, brides wear red wedding dresses because red symbolizes good luck and happiness; whereas in some western countries, red is the symbol of danger. Thus, different aesthetic standards have different effects on consumption behavior. Enterprises should conduct their marketing activities according to different consumption requirements caused by different aesthetic standards.

三、经济环境 Economic Environment

经济环境一般是指影响企业市场营销方式与规模的社会经济条件及其运行状况和发展趋势。它通常包括经济发展阶段与地区发展状况、消费者收入与支出状况、货币流通状况等因素。其中收入因素和消费结构对营销活动的影响较为直接。

Economic environment generally refers to the social economic condition, which influences the scale and ways of enterprise marketing, the economic operation situation and development trend. Economic environment usually includes the stages of economic development and situations of regional development, consumer income and expenses, currency circulation and some other factors, among which, income and consumption structure have more direct influence on marketing activities.

(一)经济发展阶段 Stages of Economic Development

美国学者W.W.罗斯托的经济成长阶段理论把世界各国经济发展归纳为如下五种类型:传统经济社会、经济起飞前的准备阶段、经济起飞阶段、迈向经济成熟阶段、大量消费阶段。凡属前三个阶段的国家称为发展中国家,处于后两个阶段的国家则称为发达国家。就消费品市场而言,处于经济发展水平较高阶段的国家和地区在市场营销方面则强调产品款式、性能及特色,侧重于大量广告及促销活动,其品质竞争多于价格竞争;相比之下,处于经济发展水平较低阶段的国家和地区则侧重于产品的功能及实用性,其价格因素重于产品品质。因此,对处于不同经济发展阶段的地区,企业应采取不同的市场营销策略。

According to the theory of economic growth stage proposed by American scholar W.W.

Rostow, the world economic development can be divided into the following five types: traditional economic society, preparing stage before economic take-off, stage of economic take-off, economic mature stage, and stage of heavy consumption. Countries with the first three stages are known as developing countries and countries with the last two stages are known as developed countries. In terms of consumer goods market, the countries and regions with higher economic development level emphasize on product design, performance and features. In marketing, they focus on a large number of advertising and sales promotion activities, and they pay more attention to quality competition than price competition. In contrast, the countries and regions with low economic development focus on function and practicability of products. They regard the price factor more important than product quality. Therefore, enterprises should adopt different marketing strategies for the regions of different economic development stage.

(二)地区发展状况 Condition of Regional Development

我国各地区经济发展不平衡，在东部、中部、西部三大地带之间的经济发展水平客观上存在着东高、西低的总体区域趋势。同时，每个地带的不同省市还呈现出多极化发展的趋势。这种各地区经济发展的不平衡发展对企业的投资方向、目标市场及营销战略制定等都会带来巨大的影响。随着我国西部大开发战略的实施，在今后一段时间内，国家将加大对西部地区基础设施的投资力度。建材、钢材、水利等相关行业和部门的发展也会给市场营销带来各种影响。

There is an unbalanced regional economic development in China. Among the eastern, central and western areas, the level of economic development has the following tendency, i.e. the eastern area is more developed than the western area. At the same time, different provinces and cities in the same area also presents a multi-polarization development trend. The unbalanced development of regional economic development will bring great influence on the enterprise investment direction, targeting market and developing marketing strategies, etc. With the implementation of Western Development Program, China will increase investment in infrastructure in the western areas in a period of time in the future. The development of relevant industries, such as building materials, steel, and water conservancy, will also brings all kinds of influence to marketing.

(三)消费者收入状况 Condition of Consumer Income

购买力水平是市场形成并影响其规模大小的决定因素。消费者的收入是消费者购买能力的源泉。消费者收入是指消费者个人从各种来源所得的全部收入，包括消费者个人的工资、退休金、红利、租金、赠与等收入。消费者收入水平的高低制约了消费者支出的多少和支出模式的不同，从而影响了市场规模的大小和不同产品或服务的需求状况。

The level of purchasing power is the decisive factor of market formation and market size. Consumer income is the source of purchasing power. Consumer income includes all individual's income from various sources: wages, pensions, dividends, rent, gift and so on. The level of consumer income restrains the amount of consumers' spending and spending patterns, thus influences the size of market and the market demand for different products or services.

在研究收入对消费者需求的影响时，常使用以下指标。①国民收入。指一个国家物质生产部门的劳动者在一定时期(通常为一年)内所创造的价值的总和。一个国家以一年的国民收入总额除以总人口，即得出该国的人均收入。人均国民收入大体反映了一个国家的经济发展水平和人民生活状况。②居民收入水平。它是影响购买力大小、市场规模及消费支出结构的一个重要因素。居民收入水平的分析着重于区别"个人收入""个人可支配的收入""个人可任意支配的收入"。从国民收入中减去公司(或企业)所得税、公司盈余及社会保险等，即为"个人收入"；个人收入减去应由个人直接负担的税收及其他费用，就是"个人可支配的收入"。从个人可支配的收入中减去用来购买生活必需品和固定支出(如房租、保险费、分期付款、抵押借款等)所剩下的那部分个人收入就是"个人可任意支配的收入"，这部分收入可存入银行，也可用来旅游或购买耐用消费品等。这是影响消费需求变化的最活跃因素。使用这部分收入所购买的产品与劳务的需求弹性大，因此，提供这类产品的企业间竞争较为激烈，尤其在产品与品牌方面的竞争更是如此。此外，消费者收入还应区别为货币收入和实际收入，并注意不同社会阶层、不同地区、不同职业的收入和收入增长率的差别，以深入认识各个细分市场的购买力水平。

When studying the effect of income on consumer demand, we often use the following indicators: the first is national income which refers to the total value created by the labor in material production sector within a certain period (usually a year). The national income in a year divided by the total population is the country's per capita income. Per capita national income can roughly reflect a nation's level of economic development and people's living condition. The second is the residents' income level. It is an important factor which affects purchasing power, the size of market and the consumption expenditure structure. The analysis of residents' income level focuses on the difference between "personal income" "personal disposable income" and "personal freely disposal income". The national income minus the corporate income tax, corporate surplus and the social insurance, etc., is known as "personal income"; personal income minus taxes and other fees which should be borne directly by individuals is "personal disposable income". Personal disposable income minus expenses of necessities and fixed expenses (such as rent, insurance, payment, mortgage, etc.), comes to the "personal freely disposal income". This part of income can be deposited in the bank, and can be used for travel or durable consumer goods, etc. This is the most active factor affecting consumer demand changes. There is big elasticity of demand for the products and services purchased by "personal freely disposal income". Therefore, competition among enterprises providing this kind of goods is fierce, especially in terms of product and brand competition. In addition, consumers' income can also be divided into monetary income and real income, and it should also be noticed that the income and income growth are different in different social classes, regions, and professions in order to fully understand the purchasing power level of each market segment.

(四)消费者支出模式 Consumer Spending Patterns

消费者支出模式是指消费者各种消费支出的比例关系，也就是常说的消费结构。优化的消费结构是优化的产业结构和产品结构的客观依据，也是企业开展营销活动的基本立足点。

Consumer spending patterns refer to the proportional relationship between various consumer spending, which is often called consumption structure. Optimized consumption structure is the objective basis of optimization of industrial structure and product structure, and also the standpoint for enterprises to develop marketing activities.

随着消费者收入的变化，消费者支出模式会发生相应的变化，继而使一个国家或地区的消费模式也发生变化。居民个人收入与消费之间所存在的这一函数关系在不同的国家和地区是不同的。

As consumer income changes, consumer spending patterns are changing accordingly, which in turn makes a country's or a region's consumption patterns change. There is a functional relationship between residents' personal income and consumption, and it is different in different countries and regions.

德国统计学家恩格尔提出：在一定的条件下，当家庭个人收入增加时，收入中用于食物开支部分的增长速度要小于用于教育、医疗、享受等方面的开支增长速度，即食物开支占总消费的比重越大，说明家庭收入越少，这就是恩格尔定律。食物支出占个人总支出的比例称为恩格尔系数。恩格尔系数越高，生活水平越低；恩格尔系数越小，生活水平越高。企业从恩格尔系数的大小变化中可以了解市场的消费水平及其变化的趋势。

German statistician Engel proposed that upon certain conditions, when the family income increases, the growth rate of food spending is slower than the growth of expenses used in the aspects such as education, medical treatment and entertainment. That is to say, the larger proportion of total consumption the food spending accounts for, the less the family income is. That is so called Engel's Law. The proportion of food spending to the total individual expenses is known as Engel Coefficient. The higher the coefficient is, the lower the living standards are; the smaller the Engel coefficient is, the higher the living standards are. Enterprises can know the consumption level and its change trend in the market from the change of Engel coefficient.

(五)消费者储蓄和信贷情况 Consumer Savings and Credit Condition

消费者的现实购买力受储蓄和信贷的直接影响。因为消费者的个人收入不可能全部花掉，总有一部分以各种形式储蓄起来，这是一种推迟的、潜在的购买力。当收入一定时，储蓄越多，现金消费量就越小，其潜在消费量越大；反之，储蓄越少，现实消费量就越大。所以，储蓄的增减变化会引起市场需求规模和结构的变动，这就要求企业营销人员在调查、了解储蓄率的基础上，制定不同的营销策略，为消费者提供有效的产品和劳务。同时，消费者信贷也是影响消费者购买力和支出的一个重要因素。所谓消费者信贷，就是消费者凭信用先取得商品使用权，然后按期归还贷款以购买商品，这实际上就是消费者提前支取未来的收入，提前消费。其主要形式有短期赊销、分期付款、消费贷款等。信贷消费允许人们购买超过自己现实购买力的商品，消费信贷的规模与期限在一定程度上影响着某一时限内现实购买力的大小，也影响着提供信贷的商品的销售量。例如，购买住宅、汽车及其他昂贵消费品，消费信贷可提前实现这些商品的销售，从而创造了更多的就业机会、更多的收入以及更多的需求。

Consumers' real purchasing power will be directly influenced by savings and credit. Since consumers cannot spend all their personal incomes, they usually save part of their income in various forms and this is a kind of delayed and potential purchasing power. When the amount of income is fixed, the more savings are, the smaller cash consumption is, and the greater the potential consumption is. Conversely, the less the savings are, the greater the real consumption will be. The change of savings amount may cause market demand and structure to change. Therefore, marketing personnel should know well the savings rate, and formulate different marketing strategies in order to provide effective products and services for consumers. Consumer credit is also an important factor which can affect consumers' purchasing power and spending. The so-called consumer credit means that consumers can consume goods first with credit, and then they make periodical payment to repay the loan used for buying the goods. That is, consumers spend their future income and consume goods in advance. Consumer credit has such main forms as short-term credit, installment, consumer loans, etc. Credit consumption allows people to buy more goods than their real purchasing power can afford. The scale and duration of consumer credit affect the real purchasing power within a period, and also affect the sales of credit goods. Consumer credit can realize the sales of expensive goods in advance, such as houses, cars and other expensive products. More work, income and demand are thereby created.

(六)货币流通状况 Situation of Currency Circulation

货币流通状况，主要是指货币的供应和银行利息率。货币的流通状况是指纸币发行量与商品流通量所需要的金属货币量的适应协调状况。如果纸币发行过多，将会导致通货膨胀，影响物价稳定，从而既增加了企业生产要素成本，又扰乱了市场正常秩序，造成虚假的市场机会，增加营销的风险性和威胁性。同时，利息的高低对企业营销也有一定影响，当银行利率低时，市场价格就会大幅波动，消费者就会减少储蓄，而把收入的大部分用于消费。

The situation of currency circulation mainly refers to currency supply and bank interest rates. The situation of currency circulation means the coordination between the amount of paper money and metal currency needed in commodity circulation. If paper money is issued too much, it will lead to inflation and influence price stability, thus increase the cost of production factors, disturb the normal order of market, create a false market opportunity and increase marketing risk and threat. At the same time, bank interest has some influence on enterprise marketing, too. When the interest rate is low, market price will fluctuate a lot, and consumers will save less and spend more.

四、科技环境 Science and Technology Environment

科学技术是第一生产力。科技的发展对经济的发展有巨大的影响，不仅影响企业内部的生产和经营，同时还与其他环境因素互相依赖、互相合作，给企业营销活动带来有利或不利的影响。例如，一种高新技术的应用可以为企业创造明星产品，使现有产品在功能、性能、结构上更趋于合理和完善，满足人们的更高要求，产生巨大的经济利益；也可以迫使企业的某种曾获得巨大成功的传统产品不得不退出市场。新技术的应用会引起企业市场营销策略的巨大变化,也会引起企业经营管理的变化,例如,电子计算机、传真机、办公自动化等提高了信息的接收、分析、处理和存储能力,从而有利于营销决策。它还会改变零售商业结构和消费者购物习惯,商业中自动售货、邮购、电话订货、电子商务、电视购物等引起了分销方式的变化。科技应用使生产集约化和规模化、管理高效化,所有这些导致生产成本、费用大幅度降低,为企业制定理想价格策略准备了条件。因此,企业应特别注意科学技术这一重要的环境因素对企业营销活动的影响,从而抓住机会,避免风险,求得生存和发展。

Science and technology is the first productive force. Development of science and technology has a huge impact on the development of economy, not only affecting the enterprise internal production and operation, but also having mutual dependence and cooperation with other environmental factors, which brings positive or negative influence to the enterprise marketing activities. For example, an application of high and new technology can create star products for an enterprise and make the existing products have better function, performance and structure. That could meet consumers' higher requirements and bring huge profit. Meanwhile, it can also force some of enterprises' traditional products, which were successful before, to withdraw from the market. The application of new technology will cause great changes in corporate marketing strategies; it can also cause the change of enterprise management. For example, computers, fax machines and office automation improve information receiving, analyzing, processing, and storage capacity, which is helpful to marketing decisions. The application of high and new technology will also change the structure of retailing and consumer purchasing habits. The selling forms of vending, mail order, phone order, e-commerce, TV shopping have all caused great change in distribution ways of products. Application of science and technology brings intensive and large-scale production, and efficient management. All these will reduce production cost and expense greatly, and offer the enterprise advantageous conditions for making ideal price strategies. Therefore, enterprises should pay special attention to science and technology, which is an important environmental factor influencing marketing activities, so as to seize opportunities avoid risk, survive and develop.

五、政治法律环境 Political and Legal Environment

政治法律环境是指企业市场营销的外部政治法律形势,一般分为国际政治法律环境与国内政治法律环境两部分。政治法律主要是指国家的政治变动引起经济势态的变化及政府通过法律手段和各种经济政策来干预社会的经济生活。它往往是市场营销必须遵循的准则。企业必须注意国家的每一项政策、立法和国际政治法律的约束及其对市场营销所造成的影响。此类环境包括以下内容。

Political and legal environment refers to external political and legal situation of the enterprise marketing. It is generally divided into international and domestic political and legal environment. Political law mainly refers to that the country's political change may cause the change of economic situation and that the government interferes in social economic life through legal means and various economic policies. Normally it is often the rules that marketing must obey. Enterprises must pay attention to the restriction from national policy, legislation and international political laws and their impact on marketing. Such environment includes the following content.

(1) 一国经济体制。它是一个国家组织整个经济运行的模式，是该国基本经济制度的具体表现形式，也是本国宏观政策制定和调整的依据。它由所有制形式、管理体制、经济运行方式组成。

A country's economic system is the mode of the entire economic operation organized by a country, and it is a concrete manifestation of the country's basic economic system. It is also the basis of formulation and adjustment of national macro policy. It is made up of forms of ownership, management system and economic operation mode.

(2) 政治形势。在国内主要是政治稳定性、社会治安、政府更迭、政策机构作风、政治透明度等，在国际上主要是"政治权利"与"政治冲突"。"政治权利"对于市场营销的影响多表现为由政府机构通过采取某种措施来约束外来企业或其产品，如进口限制、外汇控制、劳工限制、绿色壁垒等。"政治冲突"是指国际上的重大事件与突发性事件，这类事件在以和平与发展为主流的时代从未绝迹，对企业市场营销工作的影响或大或小，有时带来机会，有时带来威胁。

Political situation. In a country, political situation mainly means political stability, social security, change of government, policy organization style, and political transparency and so on. In international environment, it mainly refers to "political rights" and "political conflicts". The impact of political rights on marketing lies in policy measures taken by government, such as import restrictions, exchange control, restrictive labor practice, and green barriers and so on. Political conflicts refer to major international events and unexpected events. In the era of peace and development, such events have never died out. They exert big or small influence on enterprise marketing, sometimes bring opportunities and sometimes bring threat.

(3) 执政党和政府的路线、方针、政策。这些方针、政策是根据政治经济形势及其变化的需要而制定的，往往带有扶持或抑制、扩展或控制、提倡或制止等倾向性特点，直接或间接影响着企业的营销活动。

The party in power and the government's line, principles and policies. These principles and policies are drawn up according to the needs of political and economic situation and its change. They often have characteristics of support or inhibition, extension or control, advocating or restraint, directly or indirectly affecting the enterprise's marketing activities.

(4) 政治团体和公共团体。政治团体，如工会、共青团、妇联组织。公众团体，如中国消费者协会、企业家协会、个体劳动者协会、残疾人协会等。这些团体通过影响国家立法、方针、政策、社会舆论等，对企业营销活动施加影响。

Political groups and public groups. Political groups are labor unions, communist youth league, and women's federation organization and so on. Public groups include China Consumers'

Association, China Enterprise Directors Association, Individual Worker's Association, and China Disabled Persons' Federation, etc. These groups influence enterprise marketing activities by influencing the national legislation, guidelines, policies, social public opinion, and so on.

(5) 法律和法规。各个国家的社会制度不同,经济发展阶段和国情不同,体现统治阶级意志的法律制度也不同。从事国际市场营销的企业必须对有关国家的法律制度和有关的国际法规、国际惯例和准则进行学习和研究,并在实践中予以遵循。在国内,法律和法规主要是指国家或地方政府颁布的各项法规、法令和条例等,尤其是其中的经济立法。这既可保证企业自身严格依法管理和经营,也可运用法律手段保障自身的权益。

Laws and regulations. Different Countries have different social systems, economic development stages and national conditions, and legal systems which show wills of the ruling class are different, too. Companies engaged in international marketing must study and research the legal system of relevant countries and the relevant international laws and regulations, international conventions and rules, and follow them in practice. In China, it mainly refers to the laws, decrees and regulations promulgated by national or local government, especially the economic legislation. Enterprises can keep strict management and operation in accordance with the law, and also can use legal means to safeguard their own rights and interests.

六、自然环境 Natural Environment

自然环境是指影响企业生产和经营的物质因素,如企业生产前需要的物质资料、生产过程中对自然环境的影响等。自然环境的发展变化会给企业造成某些"环境威胁"或"市场机会"。

Natural environment refers to the physical factors that influence enterprise production and operation, such as material resources needed before production, influence on natural environment during the production process, etc. The development and change of natural environment will bring the enterprise some "environmental threat" or "market opportunities".

(一)自然资源的拥有及其逐渐枯竭的趋势 Possession of Natural Resources and Its' Dry-up

地球上的资源由无限资源(如阳光、空气等)、可再生的有限资源(如森林、粮食等)和不可再生的有限资源(如石油、煤、铀、锡、锌等矿产资源)所组成。目前,第一类资源面临被污染的问题;第二类资源由于生产的有限性和生产周期长,再加上因森林乱砍滥伐,导致生态失衡、水土流失、灾害频繁,影响其正常供给;第三类资源都是初级产品,且政府对其价格、产量、使用状况控制较严。因此,对市场营销来说,面临两种选择:一是科学开采、综合利用、减少浪费;二是开发新的替代资源,如太阳能,核能。从事研究与开发勘探的企业,在开发有价值的原料新来源和新材料方面有着惊人的机会。

Earth resources are composed of infinite resources (such as sunlight, air, etc.), renewable limited resources (such as forest, food, etc.) and non-renewable limited resources (such as oil, coal, uranium, tin, zinc and other mineral resources). At present, the first kind of resource is faced with the problem of pollution; The second category of resources is short of supply due to limited production, long production cycle and deforestation. There also appeared ecological imbalance, erosion of soil and water and frequent disasters; the third type of resources are primary products, and the government controls more strictly on the price, output and using condition. Therefore, marketing faces two options: one is scientific exploitation, comprehensive utilization and waste reduction. The other is to develop new alternative sources, such as solar energy and nuclear energy. For the enterprises engaged in research and development of exploration, they have amazing opportunities in the development of valuable new sources of raw materials and new materials.

(二)环境污染日益严重与重视生态平衡 Increasingly Serious Environmental Pollution and Great Importance to Ecological Balance

工业污染日益成为全球性的严重问题,要求控制污染的呼声越来越高。一方面,这使污染控制不力的企业面临压力,它们不得不采取有效措施去治理污染;另一方面,也给一些企业或行业创造了新的机会,如研究开发不污染环境的包装以及妥善处理污染物的技术等。由于生态平衡被破坏,国家立法部门、社会组织等提出了"保护大自然"的口号,使一些绿色产品被开发出来,营销学界也提出了"绿色营销"观念,从而促使企业营销活动必须按照生态平衡的要求去确定自己的营销方向及营销策略。

Industrial pollution has become a serious global problem, and clamor for the control of pollution is higher and higher. On the one hand, enterprises which lack the control of pollution will feel more pressure, and they will have to take effective measures to control pollution. On the other hand, it also creates new opportunities for some enterprises or industries, such as research and development of green packing, technology dealing with pollutant, etc. Because the ecological balance has been destroyed, state legislation departments and social organizations put forward the slogan of "protecting the nature", and some green products have been developed. Besides, the marketing academia also proposed the concept of "green marketing". All these make enterprises carry out their marketing activities in accordance with the requirements of ecological balance, and determine their own marketing orientation and marketing strategies.

(三)许多国家对自然资源管理的干预日益加强 More Management on Natural Resources by Countries

随着经济的发展和科学的进步,许多国家的政府对自然资源管理加强了干预。但是,政府机构保护环境的措施常常与增加就业的计划背道而驰,另外,企业因被强制购置昂贵的防污设备而无钱购买更先进的生产设备。有时,保护环境的问题不得不放在经济增长后面加以考虑。因此,企业的营销管理者要妥善解决这种矛盾,力争做到既能减少对环境的破坏,又能保证企业的发展。

With economic development and scientific progress, the governments in many countries have strengthened the management on natural resource. Government measures to protect the environment, however, often run counter to the plans for increasing jobs, and being forced to purchase expensive anti-pollution equipment, enterprises often lack money to buy more advanced production equipment. Sometimes, the problem of protecting the environment has to be considered after economic growth. Therefore, marketing managers of enterprises should properly solve this contradiction, try to reduce damage to the environment, and at the same time to ensure the development of the enterprise.

本 章 小 结
Summary

企业的市场营销环境,是指与企业市场营销活动有关的、影响产品的供给与需求的各种外界条件和因素的集合。市场营销环境包括微观环境和宏观环境。微观环境因素是指企业内部条件、供应商、目标顾客、竞争者、营销渠道和公众等对企业营销活动有直接影响的诸因素;宏观环境因素是指一个国家或地区的政治、法律、人口、经济、社会文化、自然、科学技术等影响企业营销活动的不可控的宏观因素。

Enterprise marketing environment means a collection of various external conditions and factors which are related to enterprise marketing activities and that influence the supply and demand of products. The marketing environment includes macro-environment and micro-environment. Micro-environment factors refer to the internal conditions of the enterprise, suppliers, target customers, competitors, marketing channels and other factors which have a direct effect on marketing activities; macro-environment refers to a country's or a region's politics, law, population, economy, social culture, nature, science and technology, and other uncontrolled macro factors which can influence enterprise marketing activities.

市场营销环境的动态性,使企业在不同时期面临着不同的市场营销环境,而不同的环境可能给企业既带来市场机会,也带来环境威胁。企业面对环境的变化会有两种基本的态度:一种态度是消极适应;另一种态度是积极适应。

Under dynamic marketing environment, the enterprise is facing different marketing environment in different periods, and different environment can bring the enterprise opportunities and may also threat the enterprise environment. Facing the changes in the environment, the enterprise may have two basic attitudes: one is negative to adapt and the other is to adapt positively.

思 考 题
Questions

1. 什么是市场营销环境?它主要包括哪些内容?

What is marketing environment and what does it basically include?

2. 消费者支出结构变化对企业营销活动有何影响?

What kind of influence will the change of consumer spending structure bring on enterprise marketing activities?

3. 政治法律环境对整个营销活动有何重要影响？

What kind of influence will the political and legal environment have on the whole marketing activities?

4. 结合实际，谈谈人口环境和社会文化环境对企业营销活动有何影响。

Combined with the reality, please talk about the influence of population environment and social culture environment on the enterprise marketing activities.

第四章 市场购买行为分析
Analyzing Market Purchase Behavior

【学习目标】
1. 消费者市场的概念及消费者购买行为模型；
2. 影响消费者购买行为的因素；
3. 消费者购买行为类型及决策过程；
4. 组织市场的概念及类型；
5. 各类组织市场的特殊购买行为。

Learning Objectives
1. Concept of consumer market and consumer purchasing behavior model;
2. Factors affecting consumer purchasing behavior;
3. Types of consumer purchasing behavior and decision-making process;
4. Concept and types of institutional markets;
5. Special purchasing behavior of various institutional markets.

按照顾客购买目的或用途的不同，市场可分为组织市场和消费者市场两大类。每类市场的购买者有不同的购买行为。

According to different purchase aims or purposes of customers, market can be divided into two major categories: institutional market and consumer market. The buyers of each market have different buying behaviors.

第一节 消费者市场及其购买行为分析
Consumer Market and Consumer Purchasing Behavior

一、消费者市场的概念及购买模式 Concept of Consumer Market and Purchasing Patterns

(一)消费者市场的概念 Concept of Consumer Market

消费者市场是指个人或家庭为了生活消费而购买产品和服务的市场。生活消费是产品和服务流通的终点，因而消费者市场也称为最终产品市场。消费者市场是市场体系的基础，是起决定作用的市场。

Consumer market refers to the market in which individuals or families purchase products and services for life consumption. Life consumption is the end of the flow of products and services, and thus consumer market is also known as the final product market. Consumer market is the foundation of market system and plays a vital role in the system.

(二)消费者购买行为模式 Patterns of Consumer Purchasing Behavior

消费者购买行为模式,是指消费者购买行为比较规范的形式,或常见的购买类型,它通常用购买行为模型来反映。

The patterns of consumer purchasing behavior mean quite formal forms of consumers' purchasing behavior, or the common types of purchase. It is often reflected by purchasing behavior model.

1. 消费者市场购买活动的内容 Contents of Purchase Activities in Consumer Market

为了搞清消费者购买行为模式,就必须首先搞清消费者购买活动的内容。为此,有些市场营销学家提出了以下七个必须研究的问题:①消费者市场由谁构成?(who)——购买者(occupants)。②消费者市场购买什么?(what)——购买对象(objects)。③消费者市场为何购买?(why)——购买目的(objectives)。④消费者市场的购买活动有谁参与?(who)——购买组织(organizations)。⑤消费者市场怎样购买?(how)——购买方式(operations)。⑥消费者市场何时购买?(when)——购买时间(occasions)。⑦消费者市场何地购买?(where)——购买地点(outlets)。

In order to understand the patterns of consumer purchase behavior, you must first find out the contents of consumer purchase activities. Therefore, some marketing experts put forward the following seven questions which are necessary to think about: ①who is the consumer market composed of? (who)—the occupants. ②what to buy in consumer market? (what) —objects. ③why to buy in consumer markets? (why)—objectives. ④who are involved in purchase activities in consumer market? (who)—organizations. ⑤how to buy in consumer market,? (how)—operations. ⑥when to buy in consumer market? (when)—occasions. ⑦where to buy in consumer market? (where)—outlets.

2. 消费者购买行为模式 Patterns of Consumer Purchase Behavior

消费者的"行为是在其动机支配下发生的,动机的形成是消费者一系列复杂心理活动过程的结果"。按照心理学上的"刺激—反应"学派的理论,人们行为的动机是一种内心活动过程,是看不见摸不着的,像一个"黑箱"。外部的刺激经过黑箱(心理活动过程)产生反应,引起行为。在这种情况下,营销人员关注的核心问题是:对于公司采取的各种营销活动,消费者会有什么样的反应?首先,让我们来研究消费者购买行为的刺激—反应模型,如图4-1所示。

Consumer behavior occurs "under the domination in of its motivation, the formation of motivation is the result of a series of consumers' complex psychological activity process". According to the theory of psychological "stimulation-response", motivation of people's behavior is a process of inner activity, imperceptible to touch, and can't be seen, just like a "black box". With the black box (psychological activity process), external stimuli causes responses and behaviors. In this case, what the marketers focus on is: for a variety of marketing activities adopted by companies, what will be the consumers' reaction? First of all, let's look at the stimulation-response model of consumer purchase behavior as shown in figure 4-1.

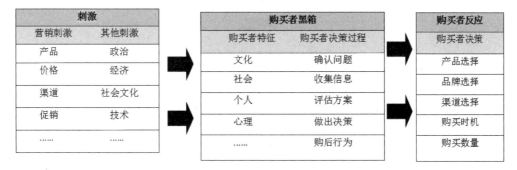

图 4-1 消费者购买行为模式

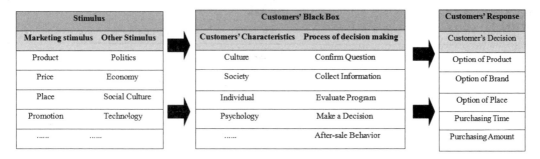

Figure 4-1　Models of Customer Purchase Behavior

运用这一模式分析消费者购买行为的关键：一是揭示形成购买者行为特征的各种主要因素以及相互之间的关系；二是揭示消费者的购买决策过程。前者影响购买者对外界刺激的反应，后者导致购买者的各种选择。

The key to analyze consumer purchase behavior with this model is as follows: one is to reveal the main factors and further the relationship between them, which form consumer behavior characteristics; another is to reveal the process of consumer purchase decision. The former influences the buyer's response to external stimuli; while the latter leads to the buyer's various options.

二、影响消费者购买行为的因素 Factors influencing Consumer Purchase Behavior

消费者行为研究的对象是消费者个人和群体的消费行为，其研究内容和体系结构由消费者行为及其影响因素所决定。刺激—反应模式反映了影响消费者行为的主要因素，将这一模式所涉及的内容适当展开，可以用图 4-2 表示。

The object of consumer behavior research is consumption behavior of individuals and groups, and research content and system structure are determined by the consumer behavior and its influencing factors. Stimulation—response model reflects the main factors influencing consumer behavior. Figure 4-2 shows the contents of this model properly.

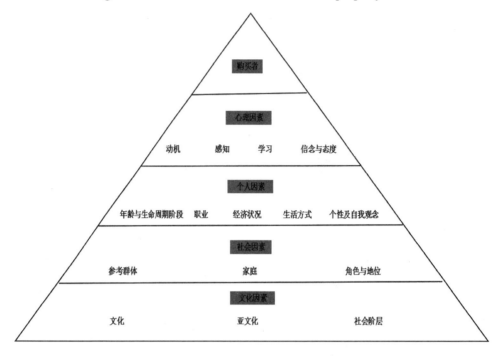

图 4-2 影响消费者购买行为的因素

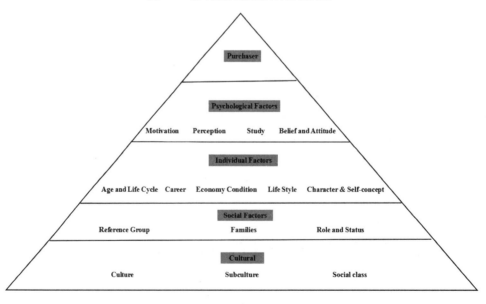

Figure 4-2 Factors Affecting Customers' Purchasing Behavior

消费者的购买行为受文化、社会、个人和心理特征的强烈影响。多数情况下，营销人员不能控制这些因素，但必须考虑这些因素。

Consumer purchase behavior is strongly influenced by cultural, social, personal and psychological characteristics. In most cases, marketers can't control these factors, but these factors must be considered.

(一)文化因素 Cultural Factors

(1) 文化。文化是指人类从生活实践中建立起来的价值观念、道德、信仰、理想和其他有意义的象征的综合体。文化是引发人类愿望和行为的最根本原因。文化的差异引起消费行为的差异，表现为婚丧、服饰、饮食起居、建筑风格、节日、礼仪等物质和文化生活等各个方面的不同特点。

Culture means that the combination of concepts of values, ethics, beliefs, ideals and other meaningful symbols that the humanity built through life practice. Culture is a fundamental cause of human's desire and behavior. Cultural difference causes the difference of the consumer behavior, which is performed by the different characteristics of marriage, funeral, clothes, diet, architecture, festivals, etiquette and other aspects of material and cultural life.

(2) 亚文化。亚文化是指某一局部的文化现象。每一个国家的文化中都包含若干不同的亚文化群，亚文化为其成员带来更明确的认同感和集体感。亚文化包括民族、宗教、种族和地域等。许多亚文化构成了重要的细分市场。亚文化主要表现为：①民族亚文化。各个民族在宗教信仰、节日、崇尚爱好、图腾禁忌和生活习惯方面有其独特之处，并对消费行为产生深刻影响。②宗教亚文化。不同宗教有不同的文化倾向和戒律，影响人们认识事物的方式、对客观生活的态度、行为准则和价值观，从而影响消费行为，每种宗教都有其主要流行地区和鲜明的特点。③种族亚文化。一个国家可能有不同的种族，各个种族都有自己独特的生活习惯和文化传统。例如，美国的黑人与白人相比，购买的衣服、个人用品、家具和香水较多，而在食品、交通运输和娱乐方面花费较少。④地理亚文化。不同的地区有不同的风俗习惯和爱好，使消费行为带有明显的地方色彩。例如，闻名中国的川菜、鲁菜、苏菜、粤菜、浙菜、闽菜、徽菜、湘菜八大菜系，皆风格各异，各成一派，就是因为地域不同而形成的。 此外，亚文化还可以分为年龄亚文化、性别亚文化、职业亚文化、社区亚文化等。

Subculture refers to a partial cultural phenomenon. Every national culture contains a number of different subcultures, which bring its members a more specific sense of identity and collective. Subcultures include nation, religion, ethnic, region, etc. Many subcultures constitute important segments of the market. Subculture is mainly shown as follows: the first is ethnic subculture. Every nation has its own way in religious beliefs, festivals, hobby, totem, taboo and living habits, and has a profound impact on consumers' behavior. The second is religious subculture. Different religions have different cultural tendencies and precepts, which can affect the way people know the things, their attitudes to the objective life, and their behavior norms and life values, and finally can influence consumer behavior. Each religion has its main epidemic areas and distinctive features. The third is ethnic subculture. A country may have different races, and each race has its own life habits and cultural tradition. Compared with the white in the United States, for example, the black buy more clothes, personal care, furniture and perfume, and spend less on food, transport and entertainment. The last is geographic subculture. Different areas have different customs, habits and hobbies, from which obvious local color can be seen from consumer behavior. For example, the well-known eight Chinese cuisines—Sichuan cuisine, Shandong cuisine, Zhejiang cuisine, Jiangsu cuisine, Cantonese cuisine, Fujian cuisine, Anhui cuisine, Hunan cuisine, have different styles because of different regions. Moreover, subculture can also be divided into age subculture, gender subculture, occupational subculture, community subculture, etc.

(3) 社会阶层。社会阶层是指社会学家根据职业、收入来源、教育水平、价值观和居住区域对人们进行的一种社会分类，是按层次排列的具有同质性和持久性的社会群体。各阶层具有特定的作用和特定的社会地位。同一社会阶层的人要比来自两个不同的社会阶层的人行为更加相似。因此，社会阶层不仅是影响消费者行为的重要因素，而且被作为细分消费者市场的重要依据。社会阶层对消费者的影响主要体现在商店的选择、消费和储蓄倾向、消费产品的品位、娱乐和休闲方式以及对价格的心态。

Social classes refer to the different social categories of people divided by the social scientists according to occupation, income, education level, values and living area; these people are social groups which are hierarchically arranged with homogeneity and persistence. Each class has a specific function and certain social status. People from the same social class are more similar in behaviors than people from two different social classes. Therefore, social class is not only an important factor that influences consumer's behavior, but also the important basis to segment the consumer market. Influences from social classes on consumers are mainly reflected in choosing stores, consumption and saving tendencies, taste of consumption products, entertainment and leisure patterns, and attitudes towards price.

(二)社会因素 Social Factors

消费者的购买行为同样受到诸如参照群体、家庭以及社会角色与地位等一系列社会因素的影响。

Consumer purchase behavior is also influenced by a series of social factors such as reference groups, family, social roles and status.

(1) 参照群体。参照群体也称作相关群体或参考群体，是指一个人在认知、情感的形成过程和行为的实施过程中用来作为参照标准的某个人或某些人的集合。换言之，参照群体是个人在特定情况下作为行为向导而使用的群体。只要某一群人在消费行为、态度或价值观等方面存在直接或间接的相互影响，就构成一个参照群体，如家庭成员、亲朋好友、邻居、同事、同学、影视明星、体育明星等。这主要表现在：一是参照群体使一个人受到新的行为和生活方式的影响；二是参照群体影响个人的态度和自我概念，因为人们通常希望能迎合群体；三是参照群体还产生某种趋于一致的压力，它会影响个人的实际产品选择和品牌选择。 参照群体的影响程度因产品和品牌而异。对于那些能被购买者的偶像所注意的产品，参照群体的影响力较大。

Reference group. Reference group is also known as relevant group. It refers to the collection of someone or some people that a person uses as a reference standard in the formation process of cognition and emotion and in the process of behavior implementation.In other words, reference group is a group which a person regards as behavior guide under certain circumstances. As long as a group of people's purchase behavior, attitudes, or values have direct or indirect influence on each other, they form a reference group, such as family members, friends, relatives, neighbors, co-workers, classmates, film stars, sports stars, etc. This is mainly reflected in: first, reference group can affect a person by the new behavior and way of life; second, reference group also influences personal attitude and self concept, because people often want to cater to the group; third, the reference group also produces a consistent pressure which will affect the individual's actual choice of products and brands. The influence of reference group varies according to products and brands. The reference group has bigger influence on those products which can be noticed by the icon of the buyer.

(2) 家庭。家庭是社会消费者购买群体中最重要的影响，而且已经被广泛地研究。它包括家庭类型与家庭成员结构。不同的家庭类型有不同的购买行为，家庭成员结构不同，消费结构不同，其购买行为也就不同。家庭成员对购买者的行为影响很大。营销人员感兴趣的，是在研究不同产品和服务的购买决策中家庭成员所发生的作用与影响。

Family. Families are the most important influence in buying groups in the society, and they have been widely studied, which includes family types and families structures. Different family types have different buying behaviors. Different member structures of the families and different consumption structures can lead to different buying behaviors. Family members have a great influence on the behavior of the buyers. What the marketers are interested in is the function and influence of family members in research of different product and service purchase decisions.

(3) 角色与地位。一个人一生中可能会从属于很多群体——家庭、俱乐部以及各类组织。每个人在群体中的位置取决于角色和地位。身份是周围的人对一个人的要求，是其在各种场合承担的角色、应起的作用。每一种身份又附有一种地位，反映了社会对一个人的评价和尊重程度。人们往往结合身份、地位做出购买选择。许多产品、品牌由此成为一种身份和地位的标志。

Role and status. A person may belong to many groups in his/her whole life—family, clubs and all kinds of organizations. Everyone's position in the group depends on his/her role and status. Identity is the request of people around to him/her; it is the role that someone should play and the function he/she should assume on various occasions. Each identity is along with a status, reflecting the social evaluation and degree of respect for him/her. People often make purchase decisions according to their status and positions. In that case, many products and brands become a symbol of identity and status.

(三)个人因素 Personal Factors

购买者的决策也受个人因素的影响，尤其是受年龄与生命周期阶段、职业、经济状况、生活方式、个性及自我观念的影响。

Buyers' decision is also influenced by personal factors, especially by age and lifecycle stage, profession, economic situations, lifestyle, personality and self-concept.

(1) 年龄与生命周期阶段。人们在一生中购买的产品与服务是不断变化的。人们在食品、服装、家具和娱乐方面的喜好与年龄有关。例如，三个月、六个月和一岁的婴儿对玩具的要求会不一样；同一消费者在不同的年龄阶段，对食物、服装和业余爱好也会有不同的嗜好。

Age and life cycle stage. Products and services people purchase in their life are constantly changing. People's preferences in the field of food, clothing, furniture, and entertainment are related to age. For example, three-month, six-month and one-year old babies have different requirement of toys; while one consumer has different appetite for food, clothes and hobbies at different ages.

家庭生命周期阶段也影响着消费。家庭生命周期是一个以家长为代表的家庭生活的全过程，从其青年阶段的独立生活开始，到年老后并入子女的家庭或死亡时为止。在不同阶段，同一消费者及家庭的购买力、兴趣和对产品的偏好都会有较大差别。

Family life cycle stage also affects consumption. Family life cycle is the whole process of family life in which parents are taken as representatives. It starts from the stage of the young with independent life to the old merging into the grown-up children's families or to the stage of death. At different stages, the same individual or family consumer can have quite different purchasing power, interests and preference to products.

(2) 职业。一个人的职业也影响其消费模式。蓝领工人会买工作服、工作鞋、午餐盒和玩保龄球游戏。公司的总裁则会买贵重的西装、进行空中旅行等。

Profession. A person's profession also affects his/her consumption patterns. Blue-collar workers will buy work clothes, work shoes, lunch boxes and play bowling game. While presidents of companies will buy expensive suits and take air travel and so on.

(3) 经济状况。个人经济状况对产品的选择有重要影响，包括可花费的收入(收入水平、稳定性和花费的时间)，储蓄和资产(包括流动资产比例)，债务，借款能力等。

Economic situation. Personal economic conditions will seriously affect the choice of the product, which includes available revenue (income level, stability, and time to expend), savings and assets (including current assets ratio), debt, ability to borrow money and so on.

(4) 生活方式。生活方式是一个人生活中表现出来的活动、兴趣和看法的整个模式。它可以由一个人的消费心态表现出来，并影响其对品牌的看法和喜好，进而影响到消费者对产品消费品种的选择与购买行为。营销者往往可以通过生活方式去理解消费者不断变化的价值观及其对消费行为的影响，如节俭者、奢华者、守旧者、革新者、高成就者、自我主义者、有社会意识者等，从而明确地针对某一群体来设计产品和广告。

Lifestyle. Lifestyle is the whole pattern of activities, interests, and opinions in personal life. It may be expressed by people's consumption psychology, and affect people's opinion to the preference and perception of the brand, thus influence the consumers' choice of product consumption and purchase behavior. Marketers can often understand customers' changing values and their influence on consumer behavior through lifestyles, for example, the life styles of thrifty people, extravagant people, conservative people, innovators, people of great achievement, egoists and people of social consciousness. Thus, marketers can design products and advertisements specifically for a group with a particular lifestyle.

(5) 个性及自我观念。每个人都有影响其购买行为的独特个性。所谓个性，是指个人独特的心理特征，这种心理特征将使个人对环境做出相对一致和持久的反应。个性通常可用自信心、控制欲、自主、顺从、交际、保守性和适应等特征来描述。

Personality and self-concept. Everyone has a unique personality which can influence his/her purchase behavior. The so-called personality refers to the unique psychological characteristics of a person, which will make the individual give a relatively consistent and lasting response to the environment. Personality is usually described with the words such as self-confidence, control freak, independence, obedience, communication, conservation and adaptability.

对于特定的产品或品牌选择，个性是一个分析消费者购买行为的很有用的变量。个性特征有若干类型，如外向与内向、细腻与粗犷、理智与冲动、乐观与悲观、领导与顺从、独立性与依赖性等。同时，不同气质的消费者的购买行为也有很大差别。他们都会将自己的气质贯彻于购买行为中。根据巴甫洛夫的高级神经活动学说，个人的气质可以划分为活泼型、兴奋型、安静型和抑制型四种。

For a specific choice of product or brand, individuality is a very useful variable for analyzing a consumer's buying behavior. There are several types of individuality, such as extroversion and introversion, exquisiteness and boldness, rationality and impulse, optimism and pessimism, leadership and submission, independence and dependence, etc. At the same time, different consumers with different qualities will also have different purchase behaviors. They all mix their qualities into their purchase behaviors. According to Pavlov's theory about higher nervous activity, personal qualities can be divided into four types: active, exciting, quiet and depressive.

所谓自我观念，其基本前提是人们的拥有物决定和反映了其地位，也就是说"我们有什么就是什么"。因此，要了解消费者的购买行为，首先要清楚他们的自我观念和他们的拥有物之间的关系。

The basic premise of self concept is that people's belongings decide and reflect their status. That is to say, "What we have is what we are." Therefore, to understand consumer purchase behavior, marketers must be clear about the relationship between their self-concept and their ownings.

(四)心理因素 Psychological Factors

个人的购买行为还受四种主要心理因素的影响，即动机、感知、学习以及信念和态度。

Personal purchase behavior is also influenced by four major psychological factors: motivation, perception, learning, beliefs and attitudes.

1. 动机 Motivation

它是推动个人进行各种活动的驱策力。动机是行为的直接原因，它促使个人采取某种行动，规定行为的方向。动机也是一种需要，它促使人们去寻求满足。消费者的购买行为，是消费者使自己的需要得以满足的行为。不同的人有不同的需要，因而人们在生理上、精神上的需要也就具有广泛性与多样性。每个人的具体情况不同，解决需要的轻重缓急的顺序自然各异，也就是存在一个梯级的"需要层次"。迫切的需要会激发起强烈的购买动机；需要一旦满足，则失去了对行为的激励作用，即不会有引发行为的动机。

Motivation. It is the driving force of all kinds of individual activities. Motivation is the direct cause of behaviors. It can prompt individuals to take a certain action and get behavior direction. Motivation is also a kind of need. It motivates people to seek satisfaction. Consumer purchase behavior aims to meet the consumer's needs. Because different people have different needs, the physical and spiritual needs have the characteristics of universality and diversity. Everyone has different specific situations, so there are different sequences when they try to meet their needs. There is a "hierarchy of needs". Urgent needs will inspire strong purchase motives. Once the needs are met, they lose the function of stimulation , which means there will not be a motivation for actions.

心理学家提出了多种人类动机理论，最著名的两种理论——西格蒙德·弗洛伊德(Sigmund Freud)理论和亚伯拉罕·马斯洛(Abraham Maslow)理论——对消费者行为分析和市场营销有着特殊的意义。

Psychologists have proposed a variety of human motivation theories, and two of the most famous theories are Sigmund Freud theory and Abraham Maslow theory, which have a special significance to the analysis of consumer behavior and marketing.

西格蒙德·弗洛伊德认为，在人们行为的过程中，真正的心理因素大多是无意识的，随着人们的成长，他们压抑了许多欲望。根据弗洛伊德的假设，人们不可能真正了解自己的动机。

Sigmund Freud argues that in the process of people's behavior, the real psychological factors are mostly unconscious. As people grow up, they depress a lot of desire. According to Freud's hypothesis, people can't really know their motivation.

为了切实掌握消费者购买动机，进而掌握其购买行为，就必须对人们的消费动机进行研究。

In order to grasp the consumer's purchase motivation, and to know well the purchasing behavior, people's consumption motivation must be researched.

亚伯拉罕·马斯洛(Abraham Maslow)提出了需要层次论，将人类的需要分为由低到高的5个层次，即生理需要、安全需要、社会需要、尊重需要和自我实现需要，如图4-3所示。

Abraham Maslow puts forward the hierarchy of needs theory, in which human needs can be divided into 5 levels from low to high: physiological needs, safety and security needs, social needs, esteem needs and self-actualization needs, as shown in Figure 4-3.

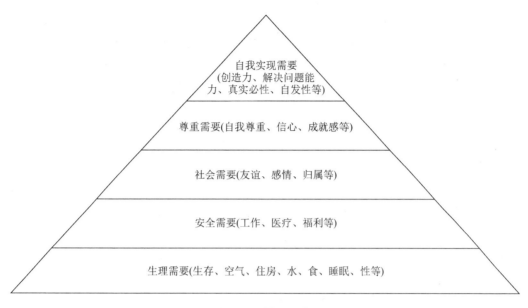

图4-3 需要层次

Figure 4-3 The Hierarchy of Needs

(1) 生理需要。指为了生存而对必不可少的基本生活条件产生需要。如由于饥、渴、冷、热，而对吃、穿、住产生需要，它能保证一个人作为生物体而存活下来。

The first is physiological needs which refer to the needs for indispensable basic living conditions in order to survive. When you feel hungry, thirsty, cold or hot, you will have needs for food, clothing and housing. These needs can guarantee a person to survive as a living organism.

(2) 安全需要。指维护人身安全与健康的需要。例如，为了人身安全和财产安全，人们对防盗设备、保安用品、人寿保险和财产保险产生需要；为了维护健康，人们对医药和保健用品产生需要等。

The second is called safety and security needs, which refer to the needs for safeguarding of personal safety and health. For example, to get personal safety and property safety, people have needs for security equipment, security products, life insurance and property insurance. In order to maintain health, people have needs for medical and health supplies, etc.

(3) 社会需要。指参与社会交往，取得社会承认和归属感的需要。在这种需要的推动下，人们会设法增进与他人的感情交流和建立各种社会联系。消费行为必然会反映这种需要，例如，为了参加社交活动和取得社会认可，人们对得体的服装和用品产生需要；为了建立友谊，人们对礼品产生需要，等。

The third is social needs, which refer to the needs for participating in social activities, and achieving social recognition and a sense of belonging. Driven by this need, people will find ways to enhance emotional communication with other people, and establish all kinds of social connections. Consumption behavior will inevitably reflect these needs. For example, in order to participate in social activities and gain social recognition, people will have needs for appropriate clothing and other things; in order to build friendship, people have needs for gifts and so on.

(4) 尊重需要。指在社交活动中受人尊敬，取得一定社会地位、荣誉和权力的需要。例如，为了在社交中表现自己的能力，人们对教育和知识产生需要；为了表明自己的身份和地位，人们对某些高级消费品产生需要；等等。

Next is esteem needs which refer to the needs for being respected in social activities and getting certain social status, glory, and power. For example, to show their ability in the social contact, people generate the needs, for education and knowledge; in order to show their identity and status, people have the needs for some high-grade consumer goods and so on.

(5) 自我实现需要。指发挥个人的最大能力，实现理想与抱负的需要。这是人类的最高需要，满足这种需要的产品主要是思想产品，如教育与知识产品等。

The last is self-actualization needs, which mean the needs for exerting a person's capacity as much as possible to realize one's ideals and ambitions. This is the highest human need, and it is always the spiritual product that can meet this need, such as products about education and knowledge.

马斯洛的需要层次论可进一步概括为两大类：第一大类是生理的、物质的需要，包括生理需要和安全需要；第二大类是心理的、精神的需要，包括社会需要、尊重需要和自我实现需要。马斯洛认为，一个人同时存在多种需要，但在某一特定时期每种需要的重要性并不相同。人们首先追求满足最重要的需要，即需要结构中的主导需要，它作为一种动力推动着人们的行为。当主导需要被满足后就会失去对人的激励作用，人们就会转而注意另一个相对重要的需要。一般而言，人类的需要由低层次向高层次发展，低层次需要满足以后才追求高层次的满足。例如，一个食不果腹、衣不蔽体的人可能会铤而走险，而不考虑安全需要。

Maslow's theory of hierarchy of needs can be further divided into two broad categories: the first category is physiology and material needs, including physiological needs and security needs; the second category is psychological and spiritual needs, including social needs, esteem needs and self-actualization needs. Maslow believes that one has many needs at the same time, but in a certain period, the importance of each need is not the same. People first pursuit the most important needs, which are the dominant needs in the need model as a kind of dynamic driving people's behavior. Once the dominate needs are satisfied, they will lose the incentive function and people will turn their attention to another important need. In general, human needs develop from the low level to the high level. People only pursuit high level needs after low level needs are satisfied. For example, a hungry, naked man might take risks to meet his needs without considering his security needs.

2. 感知 Perception

感知，是人们收集、整理并解释信息，形成有意义的客观世界图像的过程。人们通过视觉、听觉、嗅觉、触觉和味觉五种感官来获取信息，但是每个人感知、组织和解释这些感觉信息的方式各不相同。感知的性质及其在市场营销中的应用如下。

Perception is a meaningful process to form an image of the objective world by collecting, sorting out and explaining information. People get information through five senses: the senses of sight, hearing, smell, touch and taste. However, each person uses his/her own way to feel, organize, and explain these sensory information. The natures of perception and its application in marketing are as follows.

(1) 感知的整体性。也称为感知的组织性，指感知能够根据个体的知识经验将直接作用于感官的客观事物的各种属性整合为同一整体，以便全面地、整体地把握该事物。有时，刺激本身是零散的，而由此产生的感知却是整体的。

The integrity of perception is also known as the organization of perception. It means that the perception can integrate natures of objective things into a whole according to individual's knowledge and experience in order to grasp the things comprehensively and wholly. Sometimes, the stimuli are fragmented themselves, while the perception resulting from them is a whole.

(2) 感知的选择性。指感知对外来刺激有选择地反应或组织加工的过程，包括选择性注意、选择性扭曲和选择性保留。选择性注意(selective attention)，是指人们只会对少数他们感受到的刺激产生注意，多数会被有选择地忽略。人们会过滤掉大部分接触到的信息，意味着营销人员必须尽力来吸引消费者的注意。选择性曲解(selective distortion)，是指人们将信息加以扭曲，使之合乎自己意愿的倾向。人们对注意到的事物，往往喜欢按自己的经历、偏好、当时的情绪、情境等因素做出解释。这种解释可能与企业的想法、意图一致，也可能相差很大。受选择性扭曲的作用，人们在消费品购买和使用过程中往往忽视自己所喜爱的品牌的缺点和其他品牌的优点。由于选择性记忆(selective retention)的作用，人们往往会忘记接触过的大多数信息，只记住那些符合自己态度和信念的信息。企业的信息是否能留存于顾客记忆中，对其购买决策影响甚大。

Selection of perception refers to that the perception reflects selectively to external stimuli and organizes and processes the response, including the selective attention, selective distortion, and selective retention. Selective attention refers to the fact that people only pay a little attention to the stimulation they feel and most of it will be selectively ignored. People will filter most information, which means marketers must try their best to attract the attention of consumers. Selective distortion refers to that people distort the information and make it meet their intention. For the things noticed, people often explain them according to their own experiences, preference, and the mood at that time, situation and other factors. The explanation may be consistent with enterprise ideas and intentions, also it may vary considerably. Because of the effect of selective distortion, people often ignore the shortcomings of favorite brands and merits of other brands during the process of purchasing and using goods. Due to selective retention, people usually tend to forget most old information, and just remember those conforming to their attitudes and beliefs. It has great influence on consumers' purchase decisions whether the enterprise's information can be retained in customers' memory.

企业应当分析消费者的特点，使本企业的营销信息被选择成为其感知对象，形成对本企业有利的感知过程和感知结果。

The enterprise shall analyze the characteristics of consumers, and make the enterprise's marketing information chosen as their perceptive object, then consumers may form a perceptive process and result which is favorable to the enterprise.

3. 学习 Learning

学习是指由经验所引起的个人行为的改变，学习反映在驱动、刺激物、诱因、反应和强化的交互作用中。①驱动，指驱使人们产生行动的内在推动力，即内在需要。②刺激物。指可以满足内在驱使力的物品。例如，人们感到饥渴时，饮料和食物就是刺激物。③诱因。也称为提示刺激物，指刺激物所具有的能吸引消费者购买的因素，决定着动机的程度和方向。所有营销因素都可能成为诱因。④反应。指驱使力对具有一定诱因的刺激物所发生的反作用或反射行为，如是否决定购买某商品以及如何购买等。⑤强化。指驱使力对具有一定诱因的刺激物发生反应后的效果。

Learning refers to the change of individual behavior caused by experience. Learning is reflected in the interaction between motive power, irritants, incentive, reaction and intensity. First, motive power is also called internal need. It refers to the intrinsic impetus which drives people to generate actions. Second, irritants are things which can satisfy the intrinsic impetus. For example, when people feel hungry, beverage and food are irritants. Third, incentive is also known as prompt irritant. It refers to the element that can attract consumers to purchase, which determines the degree and direction of motivation. All marketing factors might be incentives. Fourth, reaction refers to the retroaction or reflection behavior of impetus caused by certain irritants, such as whether to buy a commodity, and how to buy it, etc. Last, intensity refers to the driving force that has a reaction to irritants.

4. 信念与态度 Beliefs and Attitudes

信念是指人们对事物所持的描述性的思想。人们通过实践和学习获得了自己的信念和态度，而它们反过来又影响人们的消费行为。因为信念构成了产品和品牌的形象，而人们是根据自己的信念行动的。例如，"吸烟有害健康"是以"知识"为基础的信念；"汽车越小越省油"可能是建立在"见解"之上；某种偏好很可能是出于"信任"。如果消费者存有错误的信念并因此阻碍了其购买行为，企业就应进行促销来纠正这些信念。

Belief is a descriptive thought of things held by people. People get their own beliefs and attitudes through practice and learning, which in turn affect people's consumption behavior. Beliefs constitute the image of product and brand, and people take action according to their own beliefs. Such as: "smoking is harmful to health" is the faith based on "knowledge"; "the smaller the car is, the more fuel it saves" may be based on the "view". The preference is probably due to the "trust". If the customers have wrong beliefs which hinder the purchase behavior, enterprise should do some promotions to correct these beliefs.

人们对宗教、政治、服装、音乐、食品等几乎所有事物都持有态度。态度是人对某因素(人、物、事)的全面而稳定的评价。态度导致人们喜欢或不喜欢某些事物，并对它们亲近或是疏远。态度的基本特性是持久性和广泛性。持久性，指一种态度会在相当长的时间内维持不变，转瞬即逝的评价并不构成态度；广泛性，指一种态度适用于所有同类事物，而不仅仅适用于单一事物。营销人员可以通过测试营销组合因素如产品、价格、渠道、广告、推销、服务等，以确定哪些因素才能最有力地影响消费者购买行为。

People hold attitude about almost all things: religion, politics, clothes, music, food, etc. Attitude is a person's comprehensive and stable evaluation of certain factors (people, objects, things). Attitude leads people to like or dislike something, and people may keep close to or stay away from to them. The basic characteristic of attitude is persistence and universality. Persistence refers to a kind of attitude which will remain unchanged for a long period of time, and transient evaluation does not constitute attitude; universality means a kind of attitude applying to all similar things, rather than a single thing. Marketers can determine what factors can have the most powerful influence on consumer purchase behavior through testing factors of marketing mix such as product, price, channel, advertising, promotion, service, etc.

三、消费者购买行为的类型 Types of Consumer Purchase Behavior

消费者购买行为决策随其购买决策的类型不同而变化。对于复杂、昂贵的产品的购买决策往往凝结着购买者的反复权衡，而且包含许多购买决策的参与者。阿萨尔(Assael)根据购买者在购买过程中参与者的介入程度和品牌间的差异程度把消费者购买行为分为四种类型，如图 4-4 所示。

The decisions of consumer purchase behavior vary with different types of buying decisions. Consumer purchase decisions about complicated and expensive products usually contain the buyer's repeated consideration, and also involve a lot of participants who contribute to purchase decisions. According to the participants' involvement degree and difference degree between different brands in the process of purchase, Assael distinguishes four types of consumer purchase behavior, as shown in Figure 4-4.

	高介入度	低介入度
竞争品牌之间差异性大	复杂购买行为	寻找多样化的购买行为
竞争品牌之间差异性小	减少失调的购买行为	习惯性购买行为

图 4-4 消费者购买行为的类型

	High Involvement	Low Involvement
Significant Differences Between Competitive Brands	Complex Buying Behavior	Variety-seeking Buying Behavior
Few Differences Between Competitive Brands	Dissonance-reducing Buying Behavior	Habitual Buying Behavior

Figure 4-4 Types of Consumers' Purchase Behavior

(1) 复杂购买行为。当消费者专心仔细地购买，并注意现有各品牌间的重要差别时，他们也就完成了复杂的购买行为。通常消费者在购买价格昂贵、有风险但非常有意义的、他们不常买的产品时都非常仔细。即首先产生对产品的信任，然后逐步形成，对产品的偏好，最后做出慎重的购买选择。例如，购买计算机、汽车等，就属于复杂购买行为。

The complex buying behavior. When consumers buy goods carefully, and pay attention to the major differences between existing brands, they complete the complex buying behavior. In general, consumers are very careful when they select expensive, risky and very meaningful products that they seldom buy. First of all, they have faith in the product; then they gradually form attitudes of preference for products; finally they make a mature purchase choice. Such behaviors as buying computers, cars, etc. all belong to complex purchase behavior.

(2) 减少失调的购买行为。如果消费者属于高度参与，但是并不认为各品牌之间有显著差异，则会产生减少失调感的购买行为。减少失调感的购买行为指消费者并不广泛收集产品的信息，并不精心挑选品牌，购买决策过程迅速而简单，但是在购买以后会认为自己所买的产品具有某些缺陷或其他同类产品有更多的优点，进而产生失调感，怀疑原先购买决策的正确性。在这种情况下，营销人员不仅要优化自己的营销因素，而且要通过营销沟通去树立消费者的信心，使购买者对自己选择的产品在购买之后有一种满意感。

Dissonance-reducing buying behavior. If consumers are highly involved in the buying behavior, but don't think there are significant differences between brands, in that case, dissonance-reducing buying behaviors occurs. Dissonance-reducing buying behavior means that the consumers do not collect product information widely and they do not select brands carefully either. They just make quick and simple purchasing decisions, but after buying behavior, they think what they have bought has some defects or other similar products have more advantages. In such a circumstance, dissonance mentality appears, the consumer begins to doubt the original purchase decisions. Under this circumstance, marketers should not only optimize their own marketing factors, but also build faith through marketing communication, which enables buyers to have a feeling of satisfaction after purchase.

(3) 习惯性购买行为。许多产品的购买是在消费者低度介入、品牌间无多大差别的情况下完成的，我们称之为习惯性购买行为。购买食盐就是一个很好的例证。消费者对这类产品几乎不存在介入情况。他们去商店购买某一品牌的食盐，如果他们长期保持购买同一个品牌的食盐，如加碘食盐，那只是出于习惯，而非出于对品牌的忠诚。事情很清楚，消费者对大多数价格低廉、经常购买的产品介入程度很低。营销研究人员发现，销售品牌差别很小、低度介入的产品时，在制定营销策略时要考虑运用价格和促销手段，因为购买者并不强调品牌。

The habitual buying behavior. Many buying behaviors are undertaken under the circumstances of low involvement degree of customers and low difference degree between brands, which we call habitual buying behavior. The purchase of salt is a good example. Consumers almost have no intervention of this kind of product. They go to the store to buy a certain brand of salt, and if they keep buying the same brand over a long period, such as salt with iodine, it's just out of habit, not because of brand loyalty. It is very clear that consumers have low degree of involvement for cheap products which are bought frequently. Marketing researchers find that they have to take price and promotion into consideration while making marketing strategy for selling the products with low brand difference and low involvement degree, because purchasers do not mind the brand.

(4) 寻找多样化的购买行为。寻求多样化的购买行为是以消费者低度介入但品牌差异很大为特征的。以购买小甜饼的过程为例，消费者第一次购买时挑选了某一品牌的小甜饼，但在下一次购买时，消费者也许想尝新，或想体验一下不同口味，而转向购买另外一种品牌的小甜饼，由此改变了品牌选择。但这种品牌选择的变化通常并不是因为对产品不满意，而多为寻求多样化。企业应采取多样化的营销策略去适应与鼓励消费者的多样化购买行为。

Variety-seeking buying behavior. Variety-seeking buying behavior is based on consumers' low involvement but high difference between brands. Take the process of buying cookies for example, for the first time consumers choose a brand of cookies, but in the next purchase, consumers may want to try something new, or want to try another taste, then they may buy another brand of cookies. In that case, the brand choice changes. But usually this change in brand choice is not because of dissatisfaction of products, but because of seeking more diversification. Enterprises should adopt diversified marketing strategies to adapt to and encourage the diversification of consumers' buying behavior.

四、消费者购买行为决策过程 Decision-making Process of Consumer Purchase Behavior

消费心理学在对消费者进行研究的过程中发现，广大消费者在购买过程中的心理变化一般遵循五个阶段的模式，即唤起需要、寻找信息、比较评价、购买决定和购买后感受，如图 4-5 所示。

In the study of consumers from the view of consumption psychology, researchers find that consumers' psychological changes in the purchase process generally follow the mode of five stages: arousing the need, looking for information, comparative evaluation, purchase decision and feeling after purchase, which are shown in Figure 4-5.

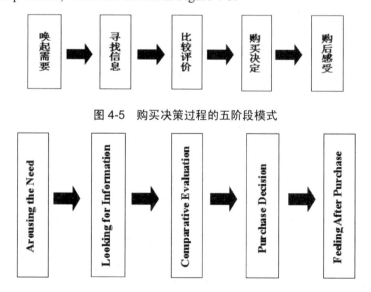

图 4-5 购买决策过程的五阶段模式

Figure 4-5　Five Stages of Decision-making Process

这个购买决策过程模式适用于分析复杂的购买行为。因为，复杂的购买行为是最完整、最有代表性的购买类型，其他几种购买类型是复杂购买行为的简化形式。这个模式强调了消费者的购买决策在实际购买行动之前就已经做出，而且在商品购买中乃至购买以后，消费者的购买心理变化仍未中止。这就要求营销人员注意购买决策过程的各个阶段而不是仅仅注意销售。

The model of purchase decision-making process is suitable for the analysis of the complex purchase behavior. The complex purchase behavior is the most complete and representative type of buying behavior, while other types of buying behavior are the simplified forms of the complex buying behavior. This model stresses that the consumers' purchase decision has been made before actual purchasing action and that the change of consumers' purchasing psychology does not stop in the process of purchase or even after the purchase. This requires that marketers should pay attention to various stages of purchase decision-making process, as well as sales itself.

1. 唤起需要 Arousing the Need

消费者购买行为过程的起点是消费者的需要。消费者的需要源于内部刺激或外部刺激，是指其具备主、客观条件(购买方与货源)的需要。因为，只有这样的需要才能形成购买需要，才对企业市场营销活动有实际意义。营销人员要了解与本企业产品有关的现实的和潜在的需要，了解消费者需要随时间推移以及外界刺激强弱而波动的规律性，并以此设计诱因、增强刺激、唤起需要，最终促成人们采取购买行动。

The need of consumers is the starting point of consumers' buying process. Consumers' needs are derived from internal or external stimuli. They are the needs with subjective and objective conditions (the buyer and supplier). Only this kind of needs can become purchasing needs and have practical significance to enterprise marketing activities. The marketing personnel should understand the real and potential needs related to the enterprise's product, understand the regularity of consumers' needs changing with time and intensity of external stimulation, and then the marketers should design incentives, increase stimulation, arouse needs, and eventually lead people to take the action of purchase.

2. 寻找信息 Looking for Information

消费者为了满足消费需要，就要寻找信息。如果消费者的驱使力很强，可供满足的产品就在近处，那么他就很可能会购买该产品。不然的话，消费者的需要就只能保留在记忆之中。消费者可能不会收集更多信息，也可能会收集更多信息，还可能会积极收集信息，这都与需求有关。

In order to meet their needs, consumers will look for information. If the consumer has a strong driving force, and the satisfying products are available to buy, it is likely for these customers to purchase the product. Otherwise, the needs of the consumer will have to be kept in memory. Consumers may not collect further information, or collect some more information, or actively collect information, which are all related to their demands.

消费者信息来源可分为四种。①个人来源。指家庭成员、朋友、邻居、同事和其他熟人所提供的信息。②商业来源。指营销企业提供的信息,如广告、推销员介绍、经销商、商品包装的说明、商品展销会等。③公共来源。指社会公众传播的信息,如消费者权益组织、政府部门、新闻媒介、消费者和大众传播的信息等。④经验来源。指消费者的亲身经历和感受,是消费者直接使用产品而得到的信息。以上这些信息来源的相对影响是随着产品的类别和购买者特征而变化的。一般来说,消费者经由商业来源获得的信息最多,其次为公共来源和个人来源,最后是经验来源。但从消费者对信息的信任程度看,经验来源和个人来源最高,其次是公共来源,最后是商业来源。因而,商业来源的信息在影响消费者的购买决定时只起告知作用,而个人来源则起确定或评价作用。

The source of consumers' information can be divided into four categories: ① Individual source. It refers to the information coming from family members, friends, neighbors, colleagues and other acquaintances. ② Commercial source. It refers to the information provided by marketing enterprises, such as advertising, introduction from sales reps, dealers, instructions of commodity packaging, trade fairs, etc. ③ Public source. It refers to the information spread by the public, such as consumer rights groups, government agencies, news media, consumers and the masses, etc. ④ Experience source. It refers to the information got through the consumer's experience and feelings produced after the use of the product. The relative influence of the above sources is changing with the product categories and buyers' characteristics. In general, consumers get most information through commercial sources, then through public sources and individual source, and the least form the experience source. From the view of the trust level in the information, however, consumers trust experience and individual sources the most, the public source the second, and commercial source the least. Thus, information from commercial source only plays the role of noticing when customers making purchase decisions, while individual source functions as determination or assessment.

企业要在对各种信息来源调查、分析的基础上,设计和安排恰当的信息渠道和传播方式,采用对目标市场影响最大、信息数量最多的促销组合。

On the basis of investigation and analysis of information, enterprises should design and arrange appropriate channels and ways of publicizing, and use promotion mix with the biggest affected on the target market and the largest amount of sales information.

3. 比较评价 Comparative Evaluation

消费者在获得全面的信息后就会根据这些信息和一定的评价方法对同类产品的不同品牌加以评价并决定选择。一般来说,消费者对商品信息进行比较评价的标准,主要集中在商品的属性、质量(包括品牌信念)、价格、效用四个方面,但有时也因人而异。不同的消费者,其消费需要的结构不同,对商品信息的比较和所得结果必然有异。在价格不变的条件下,产品有更多的属性将增加其对顾客的吸引力,但是也会增加企业的成本。营销人员应了解顾客主要对哪些属性感兴趣,以确定产品应具备的属性。

After obtaining the comprehensive information, consumers will evaluate different brands of similar products and make purchase decision according to these information and some evaluation methods. Generally speaking, consumers' standard of comparative evaluation on the commodity information is mainly concentrated in four aspects of the commodity: property, quality (including brand beliefs), price, and utility, but sometimes it also varies from person to person. Different consumers have different structures of consumption needs, so the results of comparison and evaluation are different. Under the condition of the same price, the product with more attributes will increase its appeal to customers, but also will increase the cost of enterprise. Marketers should know what attributes customers are mainly interested in so that the attributes that the product should have can be determined accordingly.

4. 购买决定 Purchase Decision

消费者在评价阶段已经对品牌进行排序并形成了购买意向，肯定态度一旦形成，就会作出购买决定。消费者购买决定的内容是多方面的，除了包括对购买商品品牌的决定之外，还包括对购买地点、购买时间、购买数量、购买方式等的决定。但是，在购买意向和购买决策之间还有以下两种因素会起作用：一是他人的态度。他人的影响力取决于他人否定的强度、他人与消费者的关系、他人的权威性等几方面。二是未预料到的影响因素。如果预期收入、预期价格、预期质量、预期服务等受到一些意外因素的影响而发生变化，购买意向就可能改变。例如，预期的奖金收入没有得到、原定的商品价格突然提高、购买时销售人员态度恶劣等都可能导致顾客购买意向改变。

In the evaluation stage consumers have already had the rank of the brands and formed purchase intention, and they would make the purchase decision after the positive attitude formed. The contents of consumers' purchase decisions are various, including not only the decision on the chosen brand, but also the decision on the location for the purchase, purchase time, purchase quantity, and the methods of purchase. However, between purchase intention and purchase decision, the following two factors can play a role: one is the attitude of others. The influence of others depends on the strength of others' negative attitude, the relationship between others and customers and the authority of others, and so on; the second is the unexpected factors. If the conditions, such as the expected revenue, price, quality, service, etc., are affected by some accidental factors and have changed, purchase intentions will change, too. For instance, the customers don't get expected bonuses, the original price suddenly increases, sales people have bad attitudes towards customers, and all these can change the customers' purchase intention.

企业要想促使消费者做出多买本企业产品的决定，就必须提供适销对路的商品和优质的服务，使其能在消费者心目中树立起良好的形象和较高的信誉，以招徕更多的顾客。

If a company wants to promote consumers to make buying decisions in its enterprise, they must provide marketable products and high quality service to set up good image and high reputation in the consumers' mind in order to attract more customers.

5. 购后感受 Feeling After Purchase

消费者购买了某一品牌的商品后，必然对商品进行观察、使用，产生相应的感受。这种感受大致有三种情况：很满意、基本满意、不满意。企业要懂得使消费者满意的重要性，用户满意是企业与消费者之间保持长久稳固关系的基础。顾客信赖产品，就会重复购买同一产品，将产品推荐给周围人群，同时会继续从这家企业购买其他产品。而不满意的消费者的反应恰好相反，他们可能会抱怨、索赔，个人抵制或不再购买，甚至劝阻他人购买，向有关部门投诉，等等。可见，买后感受对购买行为有重要的反作用，甚至是唤起需要的重要因素。

After purchasing a product of a particular brand, consumers will inevitably observe the the product and use it, then they have corresponding feelings. The feelings are roughly divided into three kinds: very satisfied, basically satisfied and not satisfied. Enterprises should understand the importance of satisfying consumers; customers' satisfaction is the basis of keeping stable and long relationship between enterprises and customers. If customers trust a product, they will buy the same product repeatedly, and recommend the product to people around. At the same time, they will continue to buy other products from the same company. However, the consumers with dissatisfaction respond contrarily. They may complain and claim for compensation, resist the product or stop buying, discourage others to buy, complain to the relevant department and so on. It's obvious that after-buying feelings have important reaction on purchasing behavior, and even become an important factor to arouse the needs.

企业应当采取有效措施减少或消除消费者的不满情绪。例如，有的耐用消费品经营企业在产品售出以后，定期与顾客联系，感谢购买，指导使用，提供维修保养，征询改进意见等，还建立良好的沟通渠道以处理消费者意见并迅速赔偿消费者所遭受的不公平损失。事实证明，售后沟通可减少退货和退订现象。

Enterprises should take effective measures to reduce or eliminate customers' dissatisfaction. For example, after selling some durable products, the enterprise which sells the durable goods will have regular contact with customers, thank them for their purchase, direct them how to use the products, provide maintenance, and ask for improvements, etc. Besides, they also establish good communication channels to deal with consumer opinions and compensate quickly for the unfair loss suffered by consumers. It has proved that after-sales communication can reduce the return of products or cancelling of orders.

第二节 组织市场及其购买行为分析
Institutional Markets and Institution Purchase Behavior

一、组织市场的概念及类型 Concept and Types of Institutional Markets

(一)组织市场的概念 Concept of Institutional Markets

组织市场是指以某种组织为购买单位的购买者因购买所需产品与服务而构成的市场。其购买目的是为了生产、销售或履行组织职能。因此，与消费者市场相比，组织市场是一个数量更大、范围更广的销售市场。就卖主而言，消费者市场是个人市场，而组织市场则是法人市场。

An institutional market refers to the market formed by some kind of institutions as the purchase unit to purchase products and services. The purchase aim is to produce, sell, or perform the institutional functions. Therefore, compared with the consumer market, institutional market has more in number and a wider range. In terms of the seller, the consumer market is a personal market, while the institutional market is a corporate market.

(二)组织市场的类型 Types of Institutional Market

组织市场包括生产者市场、中间商市场、非营利组织市场和政府市场。

Institutional market includes producer market, intermediary market, non-profit institutional market and government market.

(1) 生产者市场。指购买产品或服务用于制造其他产品或服务，然后销售或租赁给他人以获取利润的单位和个人。组成生产者市场的主要产业有工业、农业、林业、渔业、采矿业、建筑业、运输业、通信业、公共事业、银行业、金融业、保险业和服务业等。

Producer market. It refers to units and individuals who purchase products or services for manufacturing other products or services, and sell or lease them to others for profit. The main industries making up the producer market are manufacture, agriculture, forestry, fishery, mining, construction, transportation, communication, utility, banking, finance, insurance and service, etc.

(2) 中间商市场，也称为转卖者市场。指购买产品用于转售或租赁以获取利润的单位和个人，包括批发商和零售商。批发商是指为了转手而进行大宗商品买卖的经济活动组织；零售商是指为了向最终消费者(包括个人消费者和组织消费者)出售商品而进行买卖的经济组织。

Intermediary market. Intermediary market is also known as the resale market. It is composed of the organizations and individuals, including wholesalers and retailers, that purchase products for resale or lease to obtain profit. Wholesalers are organizations that engage in sales and purchase of goods in large amounts for reselling; retailers are economic organizations who sell goods to final customers (including individual consumers and organizational consumers).

(3) 非营利组织市场。非营利组织泛指所有不以营利为目的、不从事营利活动的组织。非营利组织主要分布在教育、医疗、文化、科研、体育以及各类社会团体中。非营利组织市场是指为了维持正常运作和履行职能而购买产品和服务的各类非营利组织所构成的市场。

Non-profit institution market. Non-profit institutions refers to all organizations that have no purpose for profit and are not engaged in profit-making activities. They are mainly distributed in education, health care, culture, scientific research, sports and all kinds of social groups. Non-profit institutional market is the market composed of all kinds of non-profit institutions that purchase products and services for maintaining normal operation and functions.

(4) 政府市场。指为了执行政府职能而购买或租用产品的各级政府部门。政府是特殊的非营利组织。各国政府通过税收、财政预算掌握了相当部分的国民收入，形成了潜力极大的政府采购市场。

Government market. It refers to government departments at all levels that buy or rent products in order to perform the functions of the government. The government is a special non-profit organization. The government of each country holds quite a part of national income through taxation and budget, and form the government procurement market with enormous potential.

从组织市场的构成可以看出，组织市场是一个综合性的市场，它既向生产企业提供生产资料以满足生产消费需要，又向商业企业提供消费品以满足消费者需要，还向社会机构提供各类满足社会活动和公共消费需要的产品。组织市场的这一特点决定了在组织市场中的各类购买者具有不同的消费行为，并受到不同因素的影响和制约。因此，开展对组织市场行为的研究，对于企业来说具有特别重要的意义。

It can be seen from the formation of institutional market that the institutional market is a comprehensive market. It not only provides production material to enterprises in order to meet the needs of the production and consumption, but also offers consumption products to business organizations in order to meet consumers' needs. In addition, it supplies a wide range of products to social institutions in order to meet the needs of social activities and public consumption. This characteristic of institutional market makes buyers have different consumption behavior in the institutional market, and they are influenced by different factors and restriction. Therefore, to carry out the study of institutional market behavior, for companies, is of specially vital significance.

二、组织市场购买行为 Purchase Behavior of Institutional Market

组织市场的购买行为除了区别于消费者市场的购买行为之外，不同类型的组织市场内部也存在着各自不同的差异性。

Besides the difference from the purchase behavior in consumption market, different types of institutional market also have different purchase behavior.

(一)生产者市场购买行为 Purchase Behavior of Producer Market

在组织市场中，生产者市场的购买行为有典型意义，它与消费者市场的购买行为既有相似性，又有较大的差异性，特别是在购买行为类型与购买决策过程等方面更为突出。

Purchase behavior in producer market is typical in the organization market. It has similarities with the purchase behavior of consumer market, and also has big difference from it, especially in such aspects as the type of purchase behavior and the process of making purchase decisions.

1. 购买行为类型 Types of Purchase Behavior

(1) 直接重购。指生产者用户的采购部门按照过去的订货目录和基本要求继续向原先的供应商购买产品。这是最简单的购买类型，通常由采购部门按常规原则处理，即采购部门对以往的所有供应商加以评估，选择感到满意的作为直接重购的供应商。被列入直接重购名单的供应商应尽力保证产品质量和服务质量，提高采购者的满意程度，维护重购关系。

Direct repurchase. It means that the purchase departments of producers continues buying products from the original supplier according to the past order directory and basic demand. This is the simplest type of purchase, which is usually handled by the purchasing department according to conventional process. That is to say, the purchase department evaluates all of the past cooperative suppliers, chooses the satisfying as suppliers for repurchase directly. Suppliers which are chosen should try to keep the product quality and service quality, improve the buyers' satisfaction degree, and maintain repurchase relationship.

(2) 修正重购。指生产者用户改变原先所购产品的规格、价格或其他交易条件后再行购买。这类购买较直接重购复杂，由于以前的采购单在一些项目上发生了改变，购销双方需要重新谈判，因而双方均需要较多的决策人员参加。用户会与原先的供应商协商新的供货协议，甚至更换供应商。原先选中的供应商感到有一定的压力，会全力以赴地继续保持交易。对新的供应商而言，他们会觉得这是获得交易的最好机会，因此常提出令采购者更满意的供货条件，以争取获得订单。

Revision repurchase. It refers to that the producer user changes the specifications and prices of the originally purchased product or other trading conditions before purchase. This kind of purchase is more complex than direct repurchase, because there are some changes of the projects on the previous purchase order, and purchasing party and selling party need to negotiate again. Both sides need to have some decision personnel involved in the negotiation. The user will negotiate new supply agreements with the original supplier, or even change the supplier. Previously selected suppliers may feel some pressure, and will make every effort to keep trade going on. For new suppliers, they feel this is the best chance of obtaining trading, so they often put forward more satisfying conditions for suppliers in order to get the order.

(3) 新购。指生产者用户初次购买某种产品或服务。这是最复杂的购买类型。新购产品大多是不常购买的项目，如大型生产设备、建造新的厂房或办公大楼、安装办公设备或计算机系统等。采购者要在一系列问题上做出决策，如产品的规格、购买数量、价格范围、交货条件及时间、服务条件、付款条件、可接受的供应商和可选择的供应商等。购买的成本和风险越大，购买决策的参与者就越多，需要收集的信息也越多；同时，制定决策花费的时间也就越长，购买过程就越复杂。

New purchase. It means the producer users buy a product or service for the first time. This is the most complex type of purchase. New products mostly belong to items seldom purchased, such as production equipment of large size, construction of new factories or office buildings, installation of office equipment or computer systems, etc. Buyers should make a decision on a series of issues, such as product specifications, purchase quantity, price range, delivery terms and time, service conditions, terms of payment, acceptable suppliers and alternative suppliers, etc. The higher the purchase cost and risk is, the greater the number of decision-making participants is, the more information needs to be collected; meanwhile, the time of making decisions becomes longer, and the buying process is more complicated.

2. 购买决策过程 Decision-making Process of Purchase

生产者市场购买过程一般经过八个阶段。购买者如果是新购行为，常常会经过全部阶段；如果是修正重购或直接重购，购买者可能会跳过某些阶段。这八个阶段如下所述。

The purchase process conducted by producers in the producer market generally goes through eight stages. If it is new purchase behavior, producers often experience all the stages; if it is modified repurchase or direct repurchase, the buyer might skip some stages. The eight stages are as follows.

(1) 提出需求。这是生产者用户购买决策的起点。当企业在经营中发现某个问题，有人提出可以通过增购某些产品和服务来解决时，采购过程便开始了。提出需求可以由内在刺激或外在刺激引起。从内部来看，企业可能要推出一种新产品，需要新设备或原材料来制造；机器发生故障，需要更新或更换新零件；已购进的商品不理想或不适用，需要改变供应商。从外部来说，采购人员通过广告、商品展销会或卖方推销人员介绍等途径了解到有更理想的产品，从而产生需求。

The first is putting forward the demand. This is the starting point of producer user's purchase decisions. If the enterprise finds out a problem in its operation, and someone proposes that it can be solved by purchasing certain products and services, purchasing process begins. Putting forward demand can be caused by internal or external stimuli. In terms of internal stimuli, the enterprise is likely to launch a new product which needs new equipment or raw materials for manufacturing. If the machine is out of order, it needs updating or replacing with new parts. If the product is not good or proper, it needs changing the supplier. From the outside, procurement staff has a demand for more ideal products through advertising, trade fairs, or introduction of the seller.

(2) 确定基本需求。确定所需项目的总特征和数量。标准化产品易于确定，而非标准化产品需由采购人员和使用者、技术人员乃至高层经营管理人员共同协商确定。卖方营销人员应向买方介绍产品的特性，协助买方确定需要。

The second is determining the basic requirements which is to determine the total quantity and general characteristics of the project. Standardized products are easy to determine, but non-standardized products should be determined through the negotiation of buyers, users, technical staff and even senior management personnel. The marketing personnel on behalf of the seller should introduce the product features to the buyer to assist the buyer to determine their needs.

(3) 说明详细需求。由专业技术人员进一步对所需产品的规格型号、性能、特征、数量和服务等做详细的技术说明，同时需要做价值分析，目的是降低成本，并形成书面材料，作为采购人员采购的依据。卖方也应通过价值分析向潜在顾客说明自己的产品和价格比其他品牌更理想。

The third is explaining the detailed requirements. Professional and technical personnel should give further technical instructions of specifications, models, performance, characteristics, quantity and services of required products. Meanwhile value analysis should be done to reduce costs and form a written material as the purchase basis for the procurement staff. The seller should also tell potential customers through the analysis of the value that their products and price are more ideal than other brands.

(4) 寻找供应商。采购人员根据产品技术说明书的要求寻找那些服务周到、产品质量高、声誉好的供应商。寻找的途径可通过工商名录或其他资料查找，也可借助其他企业介绍、观看商业广告、参加展览会、查找网上信息等渠道。然后，采购人员对这些工商企业的生产、供货、人员配备及信誉等方面进行调查，从中选出理想的企业作为备选供应商。

The fourth is looking for suppliers. According to the requirement of the product technical instructions, purchasing personnel look for suppliers offering good service, high-quality products and good reputation. They can find these suppliers through business directory or other sources, and can also through other enterprises' introduction, by watching commercial ads, participating in the exhibition, finding information on the Internet and so on. Then, they need to make an investigation on the manufacture, supply, staffing, and credit of these enterprises and choose the ideal one as alternative supplier.

(5) 征求供应建议书。指邀请合格的潜在供应商提交详细的书面供应建议书，以征求他们对供货的意见和建议。卖方的营销人员必须擅长调查研究、写报告和提建议。这些建议应当是营销文件而不仅仅是技术文件，以便引起对方的重视和信任。

Fifth, soliciting supply proposals. It refers to inviting qualified potential suppliers to submit detailed written supply proposals, and soliciting their opinions and suggestions of supply. The supplier's marketing personnel must be good at investigation and research, writing the report and giving advice. These suggestions should be marketing files, not only technical files, so that they can draw the attention and trust of the other party.

(6) 选择供应商。指生产者用户对供应建议书加以分析评价，从中选出最具吸引力的供应商。评价内容包括供应商的产品质量、性能、产量、技术、价格、信誉、服务、交货能力等属性，各属性的重要性依购买类型的不同而不同。此外，多数企业不愿仅依靠单一的供应商，而是取若干供货方，然后将其中较大的份额给予其中的一个厂家，这样，买方企业就不会仅依赖一个供应源。为此，各供应商都要及时了解竞争者的动向，制定相应的竞争策略。

Sixth, selecting suppliers. It means that the producer users try to analyze and evaluate the supply proposals, and then choose the most attractive supplier. Evaluation contents include the supplier's product quality, product performance, production, technology, price, reputation, service, delivery ability, etc. The importance of each item mentioned above varies according to purchase types. In addition, most companies don't want to rely on a single supplier, but find a number of suppliers, then give larger share of purchase to one of these manufacturers. iIn this way, buyer companies needn't rely on only one supply source. For this reason, all the suppliers should get to know competitors' movements in time and formulate competitive strategies accordingly.

(7) 签订合同。选定供应商后，买方即正式发出订单，订单上写明所需产品的规格、数量、交货时间、退货条款、保修条件等。双方签订合同后，合同或订单附本被送到进货部门、财务部门及企业其他有关部门。许多生产者用户愿意采取长期有效合同的形式，而不是定期采购订单。买方若能在需要产品的时候通知供应商随时按照条件供货，就可实行"无库存采购计划"，降低或免除自己的库存成本而全部由卖方承担。卖方也愿意接受这种形式，因为这样可以与买方保持长期的供货关系，增加业务量，抵御新竞争者。

The seventh stage is to sign the contract. After selecting the supplier, the buyer will formally issue orders, on which the following items should be written: the ordered product's specification, quantity, delivery time, terms and conditions of return of goods, warranty and so on. After both parties signing the contract, the contract or the copies of the order will be sent to the purchase department, the financial department and other relevant departments in the enterprise. Many producer users are willing to take the form of long-term effective contract, rather than a regular purchase order. If the buyer can ask the supplier to deliver products under the contract terms at any time when they are in need of products, "no inventory purchase plan" can be carried out to reduce or avoid inventory cost, which should be undertaken by the supplier in that case. The supplier is willing to accept this method, because they can keep a long-term business relationship with the buyer to increase business and resist new competitors.

(8) 绩效评价。产品被购进并使用后，采购部门将与使用部门保持联系，了解该产品使用情况与满意度，并考察和比较各家供应商的履约情况，以决定维持、修正或中止供货关系。

The last is performance evaluation. When the products are purchased and come into use, the purchase department will keep in touch with application department to understand the service conditions of product, satisfaction degree, and explore to compare the performance of suppliers, then determine to maintain, correct or to suspend the supply relationship.

(二)中间商市场购买行为 Purchase Behavior of Intermediary Market

中间商市场在地理分布上比生产者市场分散，但中间商购买者较为集中。故中间商购买行为与决策具有自己的独特之处。

Intermediary market scatters in a larger area than producer market geographically, but there are dense intermediary buyers. So the purchase behavior and decision of middlemen have their own uniqueness.

1. 购买行为类型 Types of Purchase Behavior

(1) 新购。指中间商对是否购进以及向谁购进以前未经营过的某一新产品做出决策。中间商会通过对该产品的进价、售价、市场需求和市场风险等因素进行分析后做出决定。其购买决策过程的主要步骤与生产者市场的购买决策过程大致相同。

New purchase. It refers to that the middlemen make a decision about whether to purchase and from whom to purchase a new product which has never been sold. The middlemen will make the decision after analyzing the purchase price, selling price of the product, market demand, and market risk. The main steps of purchase decision-making process are roughly the same as that of producer market.

(2) 直接重购。指中间商的采购部门按照过去的订货目录和交易条件继续向原先的供应商购买产品。中间商会对以往的供应商进行评估，选择感到满意的一家作为直接重购的供应商，在商品库存低于规定水平时就按照常规续购。

Direct repurchase. It refers to that the purchasing department of middlemen continues buying products from the original supplier according to their previous order directory and trading conditions. The middlemen will assess the past suppliers and choose the satisfying one as the supplier of direct repurchase. When the inventory is lower than the prescribed level, they will continue to buy the products according to the convention.

(3) 选择最佳供应商。指中间商已经确定需要购进的产品，正在寻找最合适的供应商。当中间商拟用供应商品牌销售时，或由于自身条件限制不能经营所有供应商的产品时，就需要从众多的供应商中选择最优者。

Choosing the best supplier. It means that the middlemen have identified the necessary products and are looking for the most suitable suppliers. When the middlemen want to use a supplier's brand to make a sale, or due to their own limited conditions, they can not sell all the suppliers' products, it's necessary to choose the best performer from many suppliers.

(4) 改善交易条件的采购。指中间商希望现有供应商在原交易条件上再做些让步，使自己得到更多的利益。如果同类产品的供应增多或其他供应商提出了更有诱惑力的价格和供货条件，中间商就会要求现有供应商加大折扣、增加服务、给予信贷优惠，等等。他们并不想更换供应商，但是会把这方式作为一种施加压力的手段。

Purchase based on the improvement of trade terms. It means that the middlemen expect the existing suppliers to make some concessions on the basis of the original conditions in order to gain more interests. If the supply amount of similar products increase or other suppliers come up with a much more attractive price and supply conditions, the middlemen will demand more discounts, more services, preferential credit and so on from the present suppliers. They don't want to change suppliers, but they take this method as a means of putting pressure.

2. 购买决策过程的参与者 Participants of Purchase Decision-making Process

中间商购买过程参与者的多少与商店的规模和类型有关。在小型"便利店"中，店主人亲自进行商品选择和采购工作。在大公司里，由专人或专门的组织从事采购工作，重要的项目有更高层次和更多的人员参与。虽然不同类型的中间商如百货公司、超级市场、杂货批发商等采购方式不同，同类中间商的采购方式也有差别，但是其中也有许多共性。

Participants' number of the middlemen's purchase process is associated with the size and type of the store. In the small "convenience store", the shopkeeper personally selects the items and does the purchasing work. In big companies, purchasing work is carried out by specialized staff or organization. Furthermore, more people of higher level will participate in important projects. Although middlemen of different types, such as department stores, supermarkets, grocery wholesalers, have different purchase ways, and the ways of similar middlemen's purchase are different as well, there are many commonalities between them.

以连锁超市为例，参与购买的人员和组织主要有以下几类。

Take the chain supermarket for example, staffs and organizations involved in the purchase are as follows.

(1) 商品经理。他们是连锁超级市场公司的专职采购人员，分别负责各类商品的采购任务，收集不同品牌的信息，选择适当的品牌和品种。有些商品经理被赋予较大的权力，可以自行决定接受或拒绝某种新产品或新品牌。有些商品经理权力较小，只是负责审查和甄别产品，然后向公司的采购委员会提出接受或拒绝的建议。

The product manager. They are professional procurement staffs for chain supermarket companies, in charge of purchasing all kinds of goods, collecting information of different brands, selecting the appropriate brands and categories. Some product managers are given greater power to decide to accept or reject a new product or a new brand. Some product managers' power is small, only responsible for reviewing and screening the products, and then giving proposals whether to accept or reject a product to the company's procurement committee.

(2) 采购委员会。采购委员会通常是由公司总部的各部门经理和商品经理组成，负责审查商品经理提出的新产品采购建议，做出采购与否的决策。由于商品经理控制信息和提出建议，事实上具有决定性作用。采购委员会只是起着平衡各种意见的作用，在新产品的评估和购买决策方面产生重要影响。

Procurement committee. Procurement committee is usually composed of department managers and product managers of head office, responsible for the review of managers' purchasing suggestions about new products and making purchasing decisions. Because the product manager can control information and give advice, in fact they play a decisive role. Procurement committee just balances opinions, and has vital effect in terms of new product evaluation and purchase decision.

(3) 分店经理。分店经理是连锁超市下属各分店的负责人，掌握着分店的采购权。美国连锁超级市场各个分点的货源，有三分之二是由分店经理自行决定采购的。即使某种产品被连锁公司总部的采购委员会接受，也不一定被各个分店接受，这加大了制造商的推销难度。

The branch manager. The branch manager is in charge of the branch supermarket, and owns the purchasing power of the branch. In American chain supermarkets, two thirds of products are decided and purchased by branch managers. Even if a product is accepted by the procurement committee of the chain company headquarters, it may not be accepted by each branch, which increases difficulty in the manufacturers' promotion process.

（三）非营利组织市场购买行为 Purchase Behaviors of Non-profit Institutional Markets

1. 非营利组织的类型 Types of Non-profit Organizations

按照不同的职能，非营利组织可分为如下三类。

According to different functions, non-profit institutions can be divided into the following three categories.

(1) 履行国家职能的非营利组织。指服务于国家和社会，以实现社会整体利益为目标的有关组织，包括各级政府和下属各部门、保卫国家安全的军队、保障社会公共安全的警察和消防队、管制和改造罪犯的监狱等。

Non-profit institutions, which performs national functions, refer to those serving the country and society in order to realize the goal of interests of the whole society, including all levels of government and subordinate departments, the army for the national security, police and fire brigade for social public security, prisons for control and reform of prisoners, etc.

(2) 促进群体交流的非营利组织。指促进某群体内成员之间的交流、沟通思想和情感、宣传普及某种知识和观念、推动某项事业的发展、维护群体利益的各种组织，包括各种职业团体、业余团体、宗教组织、专业学会和行业协会等。

Non-profit institutions for promoting group communication refer to the organizations for promoting communication between members within a group, exchanging thoughts and feelings, advocating and popularizing knowledge and concept, driving the development of certain business and safeguarding the interests of the community, including various professional groups, amateur groups, religious organizations, professional societies, trade associations, etc.

(3) 提供社会服务的非营利组织。指为某些公众的特定需要提供服务的非营利组织，包括学校、医院、红十字会、卫生保健组织、新闻机构、图书馆、博物馆、文艺团体、基金会、福利和慈善机构等。

Non-profit institutions providing social services refer to some non-profit organizations providing services to satisfy the public's specific needs, including schools, hospitals, Red Cross, health care organizations, news agencies, libraries, museums, art groups, foundations, welfare and charity organizations, etc.

2. 非营利组织的购买特点和方式 Purchase Characteristics and Ways of Non-profit Organization

(1) 非营利组织的购买行为主要有以下特点：①限定总额。非营利组织的采购经费总额是既定的，不能随意突破。比如，政府采购经费的来源主要是财政拨款，拨款不增加，采购经费就不可能增加。②价格低廉。非营利组织大多不具有宽裕的经费，在采购中要求商品价格低廉。政府采购用的是纳税人的钱，更要仔细计算，用较少的钱办较多的事。③保证质量。非营利组织购买商品不是为了转售，也不是使成本最小化，而是维持组织运行和履行组织职能，所购商品的质量和性能必须保证实现这一目的。比如，医院以劣质食品供应病人就会损害声誉，采购人员必须购买价格低廉且质量符合要求的食品。④受到控制。为了使有限的资金发挥更大的效用，非营利组织的采购人员受到较多的控制，只能按照规定的条件购买，缺乏自主性。⑤程序复杂。非营利组织购买过程的参与者多，程序也较为复杂。例如，政府采购要经过许多部门签字盖章，要遵守许多规章制度，准备大量的文件，填写大量的表格等。

Non-profit institutional purchase basically has the following features: the first is the limited amount. The purchasing fund of non-profit institution is limited, so it cannot be exceeded freely. For example, the source of the government procurement funds is mainly from financial allocation. If the funds do not increase, the purchasing funds can not be increased. The second is the low price. Non-profit organizations do not have plenty of money, so they mostly require low prices in procurement. Government procurement uses taxpayers' money. In that case the money should be carefully calculated to do more things with less money. The third is to ensure the quality. Non-profit organizations neither purchase goods for resale, nor minimize costs, but for maintaining the operation and the performance of the organization. So the quality and properties of products must ensure that the products can achieve this purpose. For example, if the hospital offers inferior food to patients, this behavior will damage the reputation of the hospital; so the procurement staffs should buy cheap food with the quality good enough to meet the requirements. The fourth is under control. In order to make the best use of the limited funds, non-profit organizations' procurement staffs are under more control. They can only make purchases in accordance with the regulated conditions, which is lack of autonomy. The last is complicated procedures. There are many participants during the purchase process of non-profit organization; the procedure is also complicated. For example, the government procurement need to get many signatures and stamps of many departments, follow many rules and regulations, prepare lots of documents, fill in a lot of forms, etc.

(2) 非营利组织的购买方式主要有：①公开招标选购。即非营利组织的采购部门通过传播媒体发布广告或发出信函，说明拟采购商品的名称、规格、数量和有关要求，邀请供应商在规定的期限内投标。有意争取这笔业务的企业要在规定时间内填写标书，密封后送交非营利组织的采购部门。招标单位在规定的日期开标，选择报价最低且其他方面符合要求的供应商作为中标单位。②议价合约选购。即非营利组织的采购部门同时和若干供应商就某一采购项目的价格和有关交易条件展开谈判，最后与符合要求的供应商签订合同，达成交易。这种方式适用于复杂的工程项目，因为它们涉及重大的研究开发费用和风险。③日常性采购。指非营利组织为了维持日常办公和组织运行的需要而进行采购。这类采购金额较少，一般是即期付款、即期交货，如购买办公桌椅、纸张文具、小型办公设备等，类似于生产者市场的"直接重购"或中间商市场的"最佳供应商选择"等类型。

There are many ways of non-profit organizations' purchase. The first way is through public bidding. The purchasing department of non-profit organization publishes advertisement or sends letters through media to state the name, specification, quantity and the relevant requirements of the purchasing commodity, and suppliers tender bid within the prescribed time. The business that is willing to get the deal should fill out the bid within the stipulated time, then send the sealed bidding document to the purchasing department of non-profit organization. The tenderee opens the bid within the prescribed date, chooses suppliers offering the lowest price and meeting other requirements as the winning unit. The second way is bargaining contracts. The purchasing department of non-profit organization negotiates with several suppliers at the same time in terms of the price of procurement project and the related transaction condition, and finally signs a contract with qualified supplier and makes a deal. This is suitable for complex projects, because they involve significant research and development costs and risks. The third way is daily purchase. It refers to that non-profit organizations make procurement in order to maintain daily work and the needs of the organization operation. Such purchase costs less amount of money. Generally the ways are sight payment and prompt delivery of the goods, such as buying office tables and chairs, paper, stationery, small office equipment, etc., which are similar to the "direct repurchase" in the producer market or " the best selection of supplier " in the middlemen market.

(四)政府市场及购买行为 Government Market and Its Purchase Behavior

政府市场是非营利组织市场的重要构成部分，关于非营利组织购买行为的阐述同样适用于政府市场。此外，政府市场还有其自身的特点与购买行为。

Government market is an important part of non-profit organization market. The statement about the buying behavior of non-profit organization is also applied to the government market. In addition, the government market has its own characteristics and buying behavior.

1. 政府市场的购买目的 Purchase Purpose of Government Market

政府采购的目的不像工商企业那样是为了营利，也不像消费者那样是为了满足生活需要，而是为了维护国家安全和社会公众的利益。政府采购的具体购买目的有：加强国防与军事力量；维持政府的正常运转；稳定市场，政府有调控经济、调节供求、稳定物价的职能，常常支付大量的财政补贴以合理价格购买和储存商品；对外国的商业性、政治性或人道性的援助等。

The purpose of government procurement is not for profits like business, also not for meeting the requirements of life like consumers, but for safeguarding national security and social public interests. The specific purposes of government procurement are as follows: to strengthen national defense and military strength, to maintain the normal operation of the government; to stabilize the market, the government has a function of regulating economy, adjusting supply and demand, stabilizing price, and it often pays a lot of financial subsidies to purchase and stock goods at reasonable prices; to aid foreign countries for commercial, political, or humanitarian reasons, etc.

2. 政府市场购买过程的参与者 Participants of Purchase Process in Government Market

各个国家、各级政府都设有采购组织，采购组织一般分为如下两大类。

(1) 行政部门的购买组织。如国务院各部、委、局；省、直辖市，自治区所属的各厅、局，市、县所属的各局、科等。这些机构的采购经费主要由财政部门拨款，由各级政府机构的采购办公室具体经办。

All the countries and governments at all levels have purchasing organizations which are generally divided into the following two categories.

The first is the purchasing organization of administrative department. Such as the ministries，committees, bureaus of the state council; provinces, municipalities directly under the central government; departments and bureaus in autonomous regions; bureaus and agencies subordinated to the city and county, etc. The purchasing funds of these institutions mainly from the financial department, and are handled by procurement office of government agencies at all levels.

(2) 军事部门的购买组织。军事部门采购的军需品包括军事装备(武器)和一般军需品(生活消费品)。各国军队都有国防部和国防后勤部(局)，国防部主要采购军事装备，国防后勤部(局)主要采购一般军需品。在我国，国防部负责重要军事装备的采购和分配；解放军总后勤部负责采购和分配一般军需品；此外，各大军区、各兵种也设立后勤部(局)负责采购军需品。

The second is the purchase organization of military department. The munitions of military procurement include military equipment (the weapons) and general munitions (consumer goods). The ministry of every state is equipped with the department of national defense and logistics department (bureau); the department of defense mainly purchases military equipment, while the logistics department (bureau) mainly purchases general munitions. In China, the department of defense is responsible for the procurement and distribution of important military equipments; the general logistics department of people's Liberation Army (PLA) is responsible for the procurement and distribution of general ammunition; in addition, each major military also sets up the logistics department (bureau) which is responsible for purchasing munitions.

3. 政府购买方式 Ways of Government Purchase

与其他非营利组织一样,政府购买方式有公开招标选购、议价合约选购和日常性采购三种,其中以公开招标为最主要方式。采用公开招标方式时,政府要制定文件,说明对所需产品的要求和对供应商能力与信誉的要求。议价合约的采购方式通常发生在复杂的购买项目中,往往涉及巨大的研究开发费用与风险;有时也发生在缺乏有效竞争的情况下。

Like purchasing ways of other non-profit organizations, government purchase ways conclude public bidding, negotiating contracts and daily purchase, and the public bidding is the most usual way. When adopting the public bidding method, the government should formulate file to illustrate the requirements of the required products and the requirements for suppliers' capability and credibility. The purchase way of bargaining contracts usually occurs in a complex purchase program, often involving huge research and development costs and risks and sometimes occurs in the absence of effective competition.

由于政府支出受到公众的关注,为确保采购的正确性,政府采购组织会要求供应商准备大量的说明产品质量与性能的书面文件;决策过程可能涉及繁多的规章制度、复杂的决策程序、较长的时间及采购人员的更换。政府机构也会经常地采取改革措施简化采购过程,并把采购系统、采购程序和注意事项提供给各供应商。政府采购比较重视价格。因此,有实力的供应商要经常预测政府需求,设计出适当低价的适用产品和服务,以争取中标。

Because the government spending attracts the attention of the public, in order to ensure the correctness of the procurement, government procurement organization will ask supplier to prepare a lot of written documents which can show the quality and performance of the product; the decision-making process may involve various rules and regulations, complicated decision-making procedures, a long time, and the change of purchasing personnel. Government agencies will often take reform measures to simplify the purchasing process, and provide each supplier with purchasing system, procurement procedure and matters needing attention. Government procurement focuses on price. Therefore, the capable suppliers should often predict government demands and design applicable products and services at an appropriately lower price to win the bid.

第四章 市场购买行为分析
ANALYZING MARKET PURCHASE BEHAVIOR

本 章 小 结
Summary

　　本章着重论述了消费者市场与组织市场的购买行为。首先，介绍了消费者市场及其购买模式、影响消费者购买行为的四大因素、消费者购买行为的类型和购买决策过程。其次，说明组织市场的类型分为生产者市场、中间商市场、非营利组织市场和政府市场。同时对不同市场购买行为的差异性进行了论述。

　　This chapter focuses on the purchase behavior of consumer market and organizational market. Firstly, this chapter introduces the consumer market and its purchase patterns, the four major factors affecting consumer purchase behavior, the types of consumer purchase behavior and the process of making purchase decision. Secondly, organizational market is divided into producer market, intermediary market, non-profit organization market and government market. At the same time differences of different market purchasing behaviors are discussed.

　　生产者购买行为可分为直接重购、修正重购和新购三种类型，其中，新购的购买过程最为复杂。生产者市场购买过程一般经过八个阶段，即提出需求、确定基本需求、说明详细需求、寻找供应商、征求供应建议书、选择供应商、签订合同、绩效评价。中间商的购买类型分为新购、直接重购、选择最佳供应商和改善交易条件的采购四种。中间商类别不同，购买决策的参与者也不同。非营利组织的购买特点主要有限定总额、价格低廉、质量保证、受到控制、程序复杂等五个方面。通常的采购方式是公开招标选购、议价合约选购、日常性采购等。政府市场购买组织一般分为行政部门的购买组织和军事部门的购买组织两类。

　　Producer's buying behavior can be divided into three types: direct repurchase, revision repurchase and new purchase. The process of new purchase is the most complicated. The buying process conducted by producers in the market generally goes through eight stages. They are putting forward the demand, determining the basic requirements, explaining the detailed requirements, looking for suppliers, soliciting the supply proposals, selecting suppliers, signing the contract, and the performance evaluation. Intermediary purchase is classified into new purchase, direct purchase, selecting the best suppliers and purchase based on the improvement of trade terms. Different middlemen have different participants while making purchase decision. Non-profit organization purchase basically has the following features: the first is the limited amount, the second is the low price, the third is to ensure the quality, the fourth is under control, the last is complicated procedures. The first purchase way of non-profit organizations is through public bidding. The second way is bargaining contracts. The third way is daily purchase. The purchase organizations of government market are generally divided into the purchasing organization of administrative department and the purchase organization of military department.

思 考 题
Questions

1. 什么是消费者市场？影响消费者市场的因素有哪些？

What is the consumer market? What factors can affect the consumer market?

2. 说明复杂的购买行为、减少失调感的购买行为、多样性购买行为和习惯性购买行为的产生条件以及相应的营销策略。

Describe the reason for arising the following behaviors and their corresponding marketing strategies: complex buying behavior, dissonance-reducing buying behavior, variety-seeking buying behavior, habitual buying behavior.

3. 什么是组织市场？有哪些基本类型？

What is the institutional market? What are the basic types?

4. 生产者用户一个完整的购买过程是什么？

What is a complete purchase process of producer users?

5. 中间商的购买类型对购买决策过程产生何种影响？

What influence do the intermediary purchase types have on the process of buying decision?

6. 非营利组织有哪些类型？主要购买方式有哪些？

What are the types of non-profit organizations? What are their main buying ways?

7. 政府市场的购买方式有哪些？

What are the buying ways of government market?

第五章 目标市场选择及市场定位策略
Strategies for Target Market Selection and Market Positioning

【学习目标】
1. 市场细分的含义及有效市场细分的要求；
2. 市场细分的程序、依据及方法；
3. 目标市场及目标市场选择的含义；
4. 目标市场选择的标准和策略；
5. 目标市场营销的策略及影响目标市场选择的因素；
6. 市场定位的含义、作用、步骤、方法和策略。

Learning Objectives
1. Concept of market segmentation, the requirements of effective market segmentation;
2. Procedure, basis and method of market segmentation;
3. Meaning of target market and target market selection;
4. Standard and strategy of target market selection;
5. Marketing strategy of target market and the influencing factors of target market selection;
6. Meaning, functions, steps, methods and strategies of market positioning.

成功的企业，懂得怎样把整个市场分割为有意义的顾客群体，即进行市场细分；然后在此基础上，选择企业要服务的顾客群体，即准确地选择目标市场；继而创造那些能够满足目标市场的供给物，这样就能实现对市场的准确定位。

A successful enterprise knows how to divide the whole market into meaningful customer groups, that is to make market segmentation; and then, on this basis, to select customers that the enterprise will service. This is choosing target market effectively, and then creating the supply that can meet the target market. In this way accurate market positioning can be achieved.

第一节 市 场 细 分
Market Segmentation

一、市场细分的含义 Concept of Market Segmentation

在买方市场条件下，消费者的需求和欲望日益呈现出多样化的趋势。同时，不同的企业由于受其自身的资源、技术等方面的制约，不可能满足全部顾客的所有需求，而必须根据自身的优势条件，针对不同的顾客群，选择力所能及的、适合企业经营的顾客群作为自己营销活动的主要对象。于是，市场细分应运而生。

In a buyers' market, consumers' needs and desires increasingly present a trend of diversification. At the same time, due to their own limited resources, technology, etc., enterprises cannot satisfy all the needs of all customers. Hence different companies must choose certain customer groups as their main marketing object, and according to their own advantages follow their marketing activities. Thus, market segmentation arises from this situation.

市场细分是美国市场学家温德尔·R.史密斯(Wendell R. Smith)于20世纪50年代中期提出来的。市场细分(market segmentation)是指营销者通过市场调研，依据消费者的需要和欲望、购买行为和购买习惯等方面的差异，把某一产品的市场整体划分为若干消费者群的市场分类过程。每一个消费者群就是一个细分市场，每一个细分市场都是由具有类似需求倾向的消费者构成的群体。

Market segmentation was proposed by the U.S. marketing expert Wendell R. Smith in the mid-1950s. Market segmentation refers to a process of market division during which through market research, marketers divide the whole market for one kind of product into several consumer groups according to the differences of consumers' needs and desires, purchase behaviors, buying habits and other aspects. Every consumer group is a segment market, and each segment market is a group composed of consumers with similar needs.

消费需求的多样性是市场细分的客观基础。从消费需求的状况来看，各种产品的市场可以分为两类，一类叫作同质市场，另一类叫作异质市场。凡消费者或用户在对某一产品的需要、欲望、购买动机、购买行为、购买习惯等方面具有相同或相似性，这种产品的市场就是同质市场。对于同质市场无须细分。但是，绝大多数产品的市场都是异质市场，即消费者或用户对某种产品的质料、特性、规格、档次、花色、款式、质量、价格、包装等方面的需要及欲望以及购买动机、购买行为、购买习惯是不同的。市场细分是把一个异质市场分为若干个相对说来是同质的细分市场。市场细分的目的就是把消费需求类似的消费者加以分类，以便企业了解市场中顾客需求的差异性，发现有利的营销机会。

The diversity of consumption needs is the objective basis for market segmentation. From the point of consumption needs, there are two kinds of markets for various products: one is homogeneous market, the other is heterogeneous market. Where there are some same or similar aspects in consumers' or users' needs, desires, motivation, purchase behaviors and buying habits, etc. of a product, the market for this product is called an homogeneous market. There are no specific classifications of homogeneous market. But, most markets are heterogeneous where consumers or users have different needs, desires, purchasing motivation, purchase behaviors and buying habits of one product's material, properties, specification, grade, color, style, quality, price, packaging, etc. Market segmentation divides a heterogeneous market into several relatively homogeneous segment markets. The purpose of market segmentation is to categorize consumers with similar consumption needs to help the enterprise understand the difference of customers' needs in the market and find good marketing opportunities.

二、有效市场细分的要求 Requirements of Effective Market Segmentation

从营销的角度看,虽然市场细分的方式有很多种,但是并不是所有市场细分都有意义。

From the marketing point of view, although there are many ways to segment the market, not all market segmentation is meaningful.

有效的市场细分必须满足以下几个方面的条件。

Effective market segmentation must satisfy the following conditions.

(1) 可测量性。指各个细分市场的基本情况、购买力和规模是可以测量的。如果细分变数很难衡量的话,就无法界定市场。

Measurability. This refers the basic situation, purchasing power and the size of each segment market being measured. If it is difficult to measure segmentation variables, it will be difficult to define the market.

(2) 可营利性。指企业新选定的细分市场容量足以使企业获利。

Profitability. This refers to the the capacity of segment market newly selected by the enterprise to be sufficient to allow the enterprise to achieve profits.

(3) 可进入性。指所选定的细分市场必须与企业自身状况相匹配,企业有优势占领这一市场。可进入性具体表现在信息进入、产品进入和竞争进入。市场的可进入性包含对营销活动的可行性的研究。

Accessibility. This refers to the selected segment market matching the enterprise's situation and the enterprise gaining advantages to occupy the market. Accessibility is specifically performed in information access, product access and competition access. The accessibility of the market involves studying the feasibility of marketing activities.

(4) 差异性。指细分市场在观念上能被区别并对不同的营销组合因素和方案有不同的反应。

Difference. It refers to the segment market being identified in concept and giving different reactions to different marketing mix factors and plans.

(5) 相对稳定性。指细分后的市场有相对应的时间稳定。细分后的市场能否在一定时间内保持相对稳定,直接关系到企业生产营销的稳定性。特别是大中型企业以及投资周期长、转产慢的企业,更容易出现经营困难,严重影响企业的经营效益。

Relative stability. This means there is a corresponding time for the segment market to maintain stability. Whether the segment market can remain relatively stable for a certain length of time is directly related to the stability of the enterprise production and marketing. Especially those large and medium-sized enterprises, as well as those with long investment cycle and slow production, are more likely to face operating difficulties which will seriously affect the enterprises' benefits.

三、市场细分的程序 Procedures of Market Segmentation

要使市场细分这一活动顺利进行,必须遵循一定的程序。

Certain procedures should be followed to keep activities around market segmentation running smoothly.

(1) 选定产品市场范围。企业应明确自己在某行业中的产品市场范围,同时与企业的营销目标、任务相联系,而不能脱离实际,孤立地进行市场细分。

Selecting the market scope of products. The enterprise should define the market scope of the product in a certain industry and connect it to the enterprise's marketing objective and task at the same time. The enterprise cannot be divorced from reality and segment the market in isolation.

(2) 选择符合企业实际的市场细分的依据。列举潜在顾客的需求。可从地理、人口、心理等方面列出影响产品市场需求和顾客购买行为的各项变量。

Choosing a basis for market segmentation which conforms to the enterprise and listing potential of customers' demands. All kinds of variables which can influence market demands and customers' purchasing behaviors can be listed, from aspects of geography, population and psychology.

(3) 分析潜在顾客的不同需求。企业应对不同的潜在顾客进行抽样调查,并对所列出的需求变量进行评价,了解顾客的共同需求。

Analyzing the different needs of potential customers. Companies should make a sample investigation of potential customers, evaluating the listed demand variables, and understanding the customers' common demands.

(4) 分析评价确定的各个细分市场的规模和性质,最终确定可进入的细分市场,确定市场营销策略。

Analyzing and evaluating the size and nature of every market segment and finally confirming the accessible segment market and determining marketing strategy.

四、市场细分的依据 Basis of Market Segmentation

市场细分的变量很多,而且不同类型的市场,细分变量也会有所不同。这里主要介绍消费者市场和生产者市场的细分依据。

There are a many variables of market segmentation, and markets of different types have different segmentation variables. This section introduces the segmentation basis of consumer markets and producer markets.

(一)消费者市场细分的依据 Segmentation Basis of Consumer Market

通常,企业是综合运用有关变量来细分市场,而不是单一采用某一变量。概括起来,细分消费者市场的变量主要有地理变量、人口变量、心理变量、行为变量四大类。

Usually, a combination of relevant variables is used for the enterprise to segment the market, rather than a single variable. In summary, the segmentation variables of consumer markets are geographic variables, demographic variables, psychological variables and behavioral variables.

1. 地理变量 Geographic Variable

地理变量是指消费因所处的地理位置不同和自然环境等而形成的地理上的变量。根据国家、地区、城市规模、气候、人口密度、地形地貌等方面的差异，可将整体市场分为不同的小市场。地理变量之所以可作为市场细分的依据，是因为处在不同地理环境下的消费者对于同一类产品往往有不同的需求与偏好，他们对企业采取的营销策略与措施会有不同的反应。生活在同一地区的消费者有很多相似的特点，而不同地区的消费者之间存在很多明显的差异，地区的范围大小对于人们的消费活动也构成一定的限制。

Geographic variables refer to those variables formed because of different geographical locations and natural environments where the customers live. According to the differences among countries, regions, city scales, climates, population density and topographic features, the whole market can be divided into different small markets. Geographic variables can be used as the basis for market segmentation because, in different geographic environments, consumers often have different needs and preferences regarding the same kind of products, and they have different reactions to an enterprise's marketing strategies and measures. Consumers living in the same region have many similar characteristics, while there may be many obvious differences between consumers living in different regions. Also the size of a region also poses a certain limitation on people's consumption activities.

2. 人口变量 Demographic Variable

人口变量是指人口的各种构成及其变化情况。即按人口统计变量，如性别、年龄、家庭规模、家庭生命周期、收入、职业、教育程度、宗教、种族、国籍等为基础细分市场。人口变量是市场细分常用的和最主要的依据，因为人口是构成市场营销的最根本因素，其所包含的各种因素对消费者的价值观念、生活情趣、审美观念和生活方式等都直接产生影响，而且比其他因素更容易测量。

Demographic variables refer to all conditions of the population's composition and changes. They involve segmenting the market according to variables, such as gender, age, family size, family life cycle, income, occupation, education level, religion, race, nationality, etc. Demographic variables are most commonly used in segmenting markets because population is most fundamental in constituting marketing factors, and all the factors it contains directly affect the consumers' values, life interests, aesthetic ideas and ways of life. Also it is easier to measure than other factors.

(1) 性别。由于生理上的差别，男性与女性在产品需求与偏好上有很大不同，在服饰、发型、生活必需品等方面均有差别。

Gender. Because of physical differences, men and women are quite different in demand and preference for products such as in clothing, hairstyles, basic necessities and so on.

(2) 年龄。不同年龄的消费者有不同的需求特点，例如青年人与老年人之间在对服饰的需求方面就有差异，青年人往往偏好鲜艳、时髦的服装，而老年人则更喜欢端庄素雅的服饰。

Age. Consumers of different ages have different demand features. For example, young people have different demands for clothing to elderly people; young people often prefer bright and fashionable clothing, while the elderly prefer more dignified and elegant apparel.

（3）收入。低收入和高收入消费者在产品选择、休闲时间的安排、社会交际与交往等方面都会有所不同。

Income. Low-income and high-income consumers will be different in their product selection, leisure-time arrangements, social communication and association, etc.

（4）职业与教育。消费者的职业及所受教育的不同也会导致所需产品的不同。例如，农民偏好购买载重自行车，而学生、教师则喜欢轻型、样式美观的自行车。

Career and Education. Different careers and different education levels of consumers also lead to different demands for products. For example, farmers prefer to buy heavier bicycles, while students and teachers like light and beautiful bikes.

（5）家庭生命周期。一个家庭按年龄、婚姻和子女状况，可分为单身、新婚、满巢、空巢和孤独五个阶段。在不同阶段，家庭购买力、家庭成员对商品的兴趣与偏好也会有很大的差别。

Family Life Cycle. The life of a family, according to the conditions of age, marriage and children, can be divided into five stages: single stage, married stage, full-nest stage, empty-nest stage and lonely stage. In different stages, domestic purchasing powers vary and family members have different interests and preferences in goods.

3. 心理变量 Psychological Variable

心理变量是指消费者的生活方式、个性特征和社会阶层等因素。即根据购买者所处的社会阶层、生活方式、个性特点等心理因素细分市场。

Psychological variables refer to the consumer's lifestyle, personality characteristics, social class and other factors. This is to segment the market according to the buyers' social class, lifestyle, personality, and other psychological factors.

（1）社会阶层。指在某一社会中具有相对同质性和持久性的群体。处于同一阶层的成员具有类似的价值观、兴趣爱好和行为方式，而不同阶层的成员所需的产品也各不相同。识别不同社会阶层消费者所具有的不同特点将为很多产品的市场细分提供重要依据。

Social class. This indicates a group in a society with relative homogeneity and persistence. The members of the same class have similar values, interests, and behaviors, and members of different classes require different products. Identification of consumers' characteristics in different social classes will provide important grounds for the market segmentation of numerous products.

（2）生活方式。人们追求的生活方式的不同也会影响其对产品的选择。例如，有的人追求新潮时髦，有的人追求恬静、简朴；有的人追求刺激、冒险，有的追求稳定、安逸。

Lifestyle. The pursuit of people's way of life can also affect their choice of products. For example, some people follow fashion, others like a quiet and simple life-style; some pursuit excitement and adventure, and others look for stability and comfort.

（3）个性。指一个人比较稳定的心理倾向与心理特征，它会导致一个人对其所处环境做出相对一致和持续不断的反应。一般地，个性会通过自信、自主、支配、顺从、保守、适应等性格特征表现出来。因此，个性可以按这些性格特征进行分类，从而为企业细分市

第五章 目标市场选择及市场定位策略
Strategies for Target Market Selection and Market Positioning

场提供依据。在西方国家，对诸如化妆品、香烟、啤酒、保险之类的产品，一些企业以个性特征为基础进行市场细分并取得了成功。

Personality. This refers to a person's relatively constant psychological tendencies and characteristics; they can cause a person to have relatively consistent and continuous reactions to his/her environment. Generally, personality will be characterized through self-confidence, independence, dominance, deference, conservation, adaptation and other characteristics. Hence, personality can be classified according to these characteristics and then provide a basis for the enterprise to segment the market. In western countries, for the products of cosmetics, cigarettes, beer, insurance, etc, some enterprises segment the markets on the basis of the products' personality characteristics and achieve success.

4. 行为变量 Behavioral Variable

行为变量是指消费者购买或消费某种产品的时机、追求的利益、进入市场程度、使用频率和对品牌的忠诚状况等因素。很多人认为，行为变量能更直接地反映消费者的需求差异，因而成为市场细分的最佳起点。

Behavioral variables refer to the timing for the consumers to purchase or consume a product, the pursuit of interests, the extent of entering the market, using frequency, level of brand loyalty and other factors. Many people think that behavioral variables can more clearly reflect different consumer demands, so they are the best starting point in market segmentation.

消费者在购买商品的时间上存在客观差异。一是由于消费者的购买习惯所致，例如，有的消费者喜欢在节假日或休息日集中购买，有的则在早晨上班前或傍晚下班后进行购买。二是由于商品的特性所致，如有些商品是时令商品，消费者的购买时间便有一定的规律性。

There are objective differences between consumers' purchasing timing, relating to consumers' buying habits. For example, some consumers like to make concentrated purchases during holidays or at weekends, but other consumers buy things on a daily basis before going to work in the morning or after leaving work in the late afternoon or evening. Timing of purchases may also be due to the nature of specific goods. For example, some goods are seasonal goods, influencing the regularity of the consumers' buying schedule.

按消费者进入市场的程度，通常可以将其划分为常规消费者、初次消费者和潜在消费者。

According to the extent of their entrance to the market, consumers can often be divided into regular consumers, consumers for the first time, and potential consumers.

由于不同消费者对产品的使用率有很大悬殊，可以将消费者细分为大量使用者、中量使用者和少量使用者。

Because different consumers show very great disparity of product usage, they can be divided into large-amount users, medium-amount users and small-amount users.

许多消费者在购买商品的过程中存在着"品牌偏好"。消费者对品牌的偏好程度可以用品牌忠诚度这一指标来衡量。根据品牌忠诚度可以将消费者市场划分为四个群体，即绝对品牌忠诚者、多种品牌忠诚者、变换型忠诚者和非品牌忠诚者。

In the process of buying goods many consumers demonstrate "brand preference".

Consumers' preference degree regarding brand can be measured by the index of brand loyalty. According to brand loyalty, consumer markets can be divided into four groups: absolute brand loyalists, various brand loyalists, changing brand loyalists and non-loyalists.

消费者对各种产品的了解程度往往因人而异。有的消费者可能对某一产品确有需要,但并不知道该产品的存在;还有的消费者虽已知道产品的存在,但对产品的价值、稳定性等还存在疑虑;另外一些消费者则可能正在考虑购买。针对处于不同购买阶段的消费群体,企业可进行市场细分并采用不同的营销策略。

Consumers have different understandings of various products. Some consumers may have particular needs for certain products, but don't know the existence of particular products; some consumers may already be aware of a product but doubt its value and reliability; while other consumers may be considering purchasing but have yet to take a decision. In view of consumer groups at different purchasing stages, an enterprise can carry out market segmentation and adopt different marketing strategies accordingly.

企业还可根据市场上顾客对产品的热心程度来细分市场。不同消费者对同一产品的态度可能有很大差异,如有的喜欢持肯定态度,有的持否定态度,还有的则处于既不肯定也不否定的无所谓态度。企业可针对持不同态度的消费群体进行市场细分并在广告、促销等方面采取不同策略。

Companies can also segment the market according to customers' enthusiasm for products. Different consumers may have quite different attitudes towards the same product. For example, some like to hold a positive attitude, some reject, while others show an indifferent attitude, neither yes nor no. According to different consumer groups, the enterprise can operate market segmentation and adopt different strategies regarding advertising, promotion, etc.

(二)生产者市场细分的依据 Basis of Producer Market Segmentation

很多用来细分消费者市场的标准同样也可用于细分生产者市场。例如,企业可以根据地理、追求的利益和使用率等变量对市场加以细分。不过,由于生产者与消费者在购买动机与行为上存在差别,所以,除了运用前述消费者市场细分标准外,还可用一些新的标准来细分生产者市场。

Many criteria used to segment the consumer market can also be used in producer market segmentation. For example, an enterprise can arrange market segmentation according to variables like geography, the pursuit of interests and utilization rate. However, because producers and consumers vary in buying motives and behaviors, therefore, in addition to using the former criteria of consumer market segmentation, some new standards may also be used to segment the producer market.

1. 用户规模 Customer Size

在生产者市场中,有的用户购买量很大,而另外一些用户的购买量则很小。企业应当根据用户规模的大小来细分市场,并根据用户或客户的规模不同,制定不同的营销组合方案。例如,对于大客户,宜于直接联系、直接供应,在价格、信用等方面给予更多优惠;

而对众多的小客户，则宜于让产品进入商业渠道，由批发商或零售商组织供应。

In the producer market, some users purchase more, while others purchase less. An enterprise can segment the market according to the number of customers, and formulate different marketing mix plans according to the size of different users or customers. For example, for VIPs, it's better to engage them through direct contact, direct supply, and more preferential treatment in respect of price, credit, etc; while for many other clients, it may be better to supply products through more normal commercial channels, and let wholesalers or retailers organize supply.

2. 产品的最终用途 Final Use of Product

产品不同的最终用途也是生产者市场细分的标准之一。例如，工业品用户购买产品，一般都是供再加工之用，对所购产品通常都有特定的要求。

Different final uses of products are one of the criteria to segment the producer market. For example industrial users generally buy a product for reprocessing, and they usually have specific requirements regarding the products.

3. 生产者购买状况 Producer's Buying Condition

企业也可根据生产者购买方式来细分市场。如前所述，生产者购买的主要方式包括直接重购、修正重购及新购。由于不同购买方式的采购程度、决策过程等不相同，因而可将整体市场细分为不同的小市场群。

An enterprise can also segment the market according to the producer's buying method. As mentioned above, the main methods include direct reproduction, revision repurchase and new purchase. Since procurement degrees and processes of different purchase manners vary from one to another, the whole market can be subdivided into different small market groups.

4. 行业类别 Industry Categories

不同行业的生产者对不同生产资料的需求，是为了生产不同的产品。因此，行业类别是生产资料市场细分最通用的变量。国民经济可划分为工业、农业、商业、交通运输等多个部门，每个部门还可以进一步细分。通过这种划分，企业可识别使用本企业产品的行业用户，这有利于制定生产计划与经营策略。

Producers from different industries have demand for various productive means in order to produce different products. As a result, the industry category is the most common variable for market segmentation of productive means. The national economy may be divided into industry, agriculture, commerce, transportation and other departments, and each department can be further subdivided. Through this division, an enterprise can identify the industry users requiring its products. This is beneficial for drawing up a production plan and business strategy.

企业在运用细分标准进行市场细分时必须注意：一是市场细分的标准是动态的。市场细分的各项标准不是一成不变的，而是随着社会生产力及市场状况的变化而不断变化。如年龄、收入、城镇规模、购买动机等都是可变的。二是不同的企业在进行市场细分时应采用不同的标准。因为各企业的生产技术条件、资源、财力和营销的产品不同,所采用的标准也应有所区别。

An enterprise must pay attention to the following points when applying segmentation criteria to market segmentation. Firstly, the standard of market segmentation is dynamic rather than static, changing according to change in social productivity and market conditions. For example, age, income, urban scale and buying motives, are all variable. Secondly, different enterprises should adopt different standards while carrying out market segmentation. Because each enterprise's production technology conditions, resources, financial power, and marketing products are different, standards should be adopted accordingly.

五、市场细分的方法 Methods of Market Segmentation

企业在进行市场细分时,可采用一项标准即单一变量因素细分,也可采用多个变量因素组合或系列变量因素进行市场细分。

One criterion an enterprise can utilize while operating market segmentation is called single variable segmentation. A combination of multiple variables or series of variables can also be used for market segmentation.

(1) 单一变量因素法。就是根据影响消费者需求的某一个重要因素进行市场细分。例如,服装企业按年龄细分市场,可分为童装、少年装、青年装、中年装、中老年装及老年装。

Single variable segmentation. This is according to one important element that can affect consumers' demands. For example, a garment enterprise may subdivide the market according to age categories: children, teenagers, youth, the middle-aged, the middle-aged and the old, and the elderly.

(2) 多个变量因素组合法。就是根据影响消费者需求的两种或两种以上的因素进行市场细分。例如,生产者市场主要根据企业规模的大小、用户的地理位置、产品的最终用途及潜在市场规模来细分市场。

Combination of multiple variables. This is to organize market segmentation based on two or more elements affecting consumer demand. For example, the producer market is mainly subdivided according to the size of the enterprise, the user's location, product end use and the size of potential market.

(3) 系列变量因素法。根据企业经营的特点并按照影响消费者需求的诸因素,由粗到细地进行市场细分。这种方法可使目标市场更加明确而具体,有利于企业更好地制定相应的市场营销策略。例如,自行车市场可按地理位置、性别、年龄、收入、职业、购买动机等变量因素细分市场。

Series of variables. This is to segment the market from general aspects to subtle aspects according to the characteristics of the enterprise management and according to the elements affecting consumer demand. This method can make the target market clearer and more specific, and is advantageous for the enterprise to better formulate corresponding marketing strategy. For example, the bicycle market can be segmented according to geographical location, gender, age, income, occupation, buying motivation and other variables.

第二节 选择目标市场
Selecting Target Market

一、目标市场及目标市场选择的含义 Meaning of Target Market and Target Market Selection

企业通过市场细分可以发现企业可能面临的市场机会,然后,企业必须要对各种细分市场进行评估,根据评估的结果确定进入并为之服务的细分市场,即选择目标市场。

Through market segmentation an enterprise can identify possible market opportunities. Then, the enterprise must evaluate various segment markets; according to the results of the evaluation, the enterprise confirms the segment market they will attempt to gain access to and give service to. This is "choosing target market".

著名的市场营销学者麦卡锡 McCarthy 提出,应当把消费者看作一个特定的群体,称为目标市场。通过市场细分,有利于明确目标市场,通过市场营销策略的应用,有利于满足目标市场的需要。即:目标市场就是通过市场细分后,企业准备以相应的产品和服务满足其需要的一个或几个子市场。

The famous marketing scholar McCarthy argued that consumers should be regarded as a specific group, referred to as target market. Market segmentation is beneficial to confirm target market, and the application of the marketing strategy is good for meeting the needs of the target market. That is to say, the target market is one or several submarkets where the enterprise can obtain satisfaction from supplying corresponding products and services after market segmentation.

所谓目标市场,就是企业在市场细分的基础上,结合考虑各细分市场上顾客的需求和企业自身的经营条件,而选出的一个或若干个企业能很好地为之提供产品或服务的细分市场。目标市场就是企业产品或服务的主要需要者或顾客。

The so-called target market is, on the basis of market segmentation, the one or several segment markets chosen by the enterprise in consideration of customers' demands and its own conditions in each segment market, and the enterprise can supply with good products or service. The target market are the main customers for the enterprise's products or services.

所谓目标市场选择,是指企业在划分好细分市场之后,可以进入既定市场中的一个或多个细分市场。目标市场选择是指估计每个细分市场的吸引力程度,并选择进入一个或多个细分市场。

So-called target market selection refers to the fact that the enterprise can enter one or more identified segment markets after divisions. Target market selection is to estimate the appeal degree of each segment market, and to choose to enter one or more segment markets.

二、目标市场选择的标准 Criteria of Target Market Selection

1. 有一定的规模和发展潜力 Certain Scale and Potential

细分市场的潜力是指在一定时期内,在消费者愿意支付的价格水平下,经过相应的营销努力,商品在该细分市场上可能达到的销售规模。企业进入某一市场是期望获得利润,如果市场规模狭小或者趋于萎缩状态,企业进入后难以获得发展,那么,在进入前有必要对市场进行审慎分析。

The potential of a segment market refers to the sales scale in the segment market that goods may reach following corresponding efforts in marketing, and according to the price level consumers are willing to pay in a certain period of time. The enterprise expects to obtain profits while entering a particular market. If the scale of the market is narrow, or it downsizes after entering, it will be difficult for the enterprise to develop. Thus, it is essential to carefully analyze a situation before entering.

2. 细分市场结构的吸引力 Attractive Structure of Segment Market

细分市场可能具备理想的规模和发展特征,然而从赢利的观点来看,它未必有吸引力。迈克尔·波特认为有五种因素决定整个市场或其中任何一个细分市场的长期的内在吸引力。这五种因素是:同行业竞争者、潜在的新竞争者、替代产品、购买者和供应商。它们具有如下五种威胁性。

A segment market may possess an ideal size and development characteristics. From a profit point of view, however, it may not be attractive. Michael Porter believes that there are five factors determining the long-term inherent attractiveness of the entire market or any particular segment market. The five factors are: competitors in the same industry, potential new competitors, substitute products, buyers and suppliers. There are five potential dangers as follows.

1) 细分市场内激烈竞争的威胁 Threat Caused by Severe Competition in Segment Market

如果某个细分市场已经有了众多的、强大的或者竞争意识强烈的竞争者,那么该细分市场就会失去吸引力。如果该细分市场处于稳定或者衰退状态、生产能力不断大幅度扩大、固定成本过高、撤出市场的壁垒过高、竞争者投资很大,那么情况就会更糟。这些情况常常会导致价格战、广告争夺战,使得企业要推出新产品参与竞争就必须付出高昂的代价。

If a segment market already has numerous and powerful competitors, or competitors with strong consciousness, this segment market will lose its appeal. The situation is even worse if, for example, this segment market is in a stable or recessional condition; production capacity expands greatly and continuously; fixed costs are too high; barriers are too strict while withdrawing from the market; competitor investment is very great, and so on. These conditions often lead to price wars and advertising wars, which means the enterprise pays a high price while launching new products and participating in competition.

2) 新竞争者的威胁 Threat from New Competitors

如果某个细分市场吸引了会增加新的生产能力和大量资源并争夺市场份额的新的竞争

者，那么该细分市场就会变得没有吸引力。问题的关键是新的竞争者能否轻易地进入这个细分市场。如果新的竞争者进入这个细分市场时遇到森严的壁垒，并且遭受到来自细分市场内原来的企业的强烈攻击，他们便很难推进。根据行业利润的观点，最有吸引力的细分市场应该是进入的壁垒高、退出的壁垒低。在这样的细分市场里，新的企业很难打入，但经营不善的企业可以安然撤退。

If a segment market attracts new competitors who can add new productive capacity and mobilize resources to fight for market share, then this segment market becomes less attractive. The nub of the problem is whether new competitors can easily get into this segment market. If new competitors meet substantial barriers while trying to enter this market, and suffer much aggression from the original enterprises, it is difficult for them to progress. According to the point of industry profit, the most attractive segment market should have high entry barriers but low exit barriers. In this kind of segment market, it is difficult for new enterprises to break in but easy to retreat for badly-operating enterprises.

3) 替代产品的威胁 Threat of Substitute Products

如果某个细分市场存在着替代产品或者有潜在的替代产品，那么该细分市场就会失去吸引力。替代产品会限制细分市场内价格和利润的增长。企业应密切注意替代产品的价格变化。

If there are substitute products, or potential substitute products, in a segment market, then this segment market will lose attraction. Substitute products will limit the growth of prices and profits in the segment market. The enterprise should pay close attention to price changes of substitute products.

4) 购买者讨价还价能力加强的威胁 Threat Caused by Buyers' Strengthened Bargaining capacity

如果某个细分市场中购买者的讨价还价能力很强或正在加强，该细分市场就没有吸引力。购买者会设法压低价格，对产品质量和服务提出更高的要求，并且使竞争者互相斗争，所有这些都会使销售商的利润受到损失。

If the buyers' bargaining capacity in a market segment is very strong or progressing steadily, this segment market has little appeal. Buyers will try to push down prices, put forward higher requirements as to quality and service, causing competitors to struggle against each other; all of these can cause the seller to suffer losses.

5) 供应商讨价还价能力加强的威胁 Threat Caused by Suppliers' Strengthened Bargaining Capacity

如果企业的供应商提价或者降低产品和服务的质量，或减少供应数量，那么该企业所在的细分市场就会没有吸引力。

If the suppliers to the enterprise raise prices or reduce the quality of products and services or reduce supply, the segment market where the enterprise is situated will lose its appeal.

3. 符合企业的目标和能力 In Accordance With Enterprise's Goals and Abilities

某些细分市场虽然有较大的吸引力，但不能推动企业实现发展目标，甚至分散企业的精力，使之无法完成其主要目标，这样的市场应考虑放弃。另一方面，还应考虑企业的资源条件是否适合在某一细分市场经营。只有选择那些企业有条件进入、能充分发挥其资源优势的市场作为目标市场，企业才会立于不败之地。

Although some segment markets have great attraction, they cannot promote the enterprise to realize development goals, and can even disperse the enterprise's energy, and make it unable to complete its main target. It might be better to withdraw from such a market. On the other hand, whether an enterprise's resource condition is suitable for the segment market should also be taken into consideration. Only choosing market to which those enterprises have conditional access and give full play to the resource advantages as a target market, can the enterprise be in an impregnable position.

三、目标市场的选择策略 Strategies for Target Market Selection

目标市场的选择策略，即关于企业为哪个或哪几个细分市场服务的决定。通常有五种模式可供参考。

The strategy of target market selection is the decision regarding which segment market(s) the enterprise will serve. Usually there are five models.

1. 市场集中化策略 Strategy of Centralized Market

企业选择一个细分市场，只生产一种标准化产品，供应某一单一的顾客群，集中力量为之服务，以取得企业在该细分市场上的优势。较小的企业一般这样专门填补市场的某一部分。集中营销有助于企业深刻了解该细分市场的需求特点，采用针对性的产品、价格、渠道和促销策略，以获得强有力的市场地位和良好的声誉。但此种做法同时隐含较大的经营风险。

The enterprise chooses a segment market, only produces one kind of standardized product, supplies a single customer group, and focuses on services in order to obtain advantages in this segment market. Smaller enterprises in general are dedicated to fill only a certain part of the market. Concentrated marketing helps enterprises understand more deeply the demand characteristics of a segment market, use strategy for targeting products, price, channels and promotion, in order to gain a strong market position and good reputation. But this also brings greater business risks.

2. 产品专业化策略 Strategy of Specialized Product

企业集中生产一种产品，并向所有顾客销售这种产品。由于面对不同的顾客群，产品在档次、质量或款式方面会有所不同。此种策略的优点是有利于形成和发展生产的技术上的优势，提高产品质量，降低产品成本，在该领域树立形象。但当该领域被一种全新的技术与产品所代替时，企业将面临巨大的威胁。

The enterprise is specialized in producing one kind of product and selling this to all customers. Due to confronting different customers, products will be different in grade, quality or style. The advantage of this strategy is to form and develop technical advantage of production, to improve product quality, reduce product cost and set up an image in the field. But if this field is replaced by new technology and products, the enterprise will face a huge danger.

第五章 目标市场选择及市场定位策略
Strategies for Target Market Selection and Market Positioning

3. 市场专业化策略 Strategy of Specialized Market

企业专门服务于某一特定顾客群，尽力满足他们的各种需求。例如，企业专门为老年消费者提供各种档次的服装。企业专门为这个顾客群服务，能建立良好的声誉。但一旦这个顾客群的需求潜量和特点发生突然变化，企业要承担较大的风险。

Here the enterprise serves a particular customer group and tries its best to meet their various needs. For example, the enterprise provides various grades of clothing designed for older consumers. The enterprise is dedicated to serving these customers to establish a good reputation. But if the potential demand and characteristics of the customer sudden changes, the enterprise becomes involved in great risk.

4. 选择专业化策略 Strategy of Specialized Selection

企业选择几个细分市场，每一个对企业的目标和资源利用都有一定的吸引力。但各细分市场彼此之间很少或根本没有任何联系。这种策略能分散企业经营风险，即使其中某个细分市场失去了吸引力，企业还能在其他细分市场盈利，但这种策略要求企业具有较强的资源和营销实力。

The enterprise chooses a few segment markets, each of which has certain appeal to the goals and resource utilization of the enterprise. But the segment markets have little or no contact at all with each other. This strategy can spread business risks; even if one segment market loses appeal, companies can achieve profits in other segment markets. However, this requires an enterprise with strong resources and marketing power.

5. 全面进入市场策略 Strategy of Overall Access to Market

企业力图全方位地进入各个细分市场，用各种产品满足各种顾客群体的需求。一般只有实力强大的大企业才能采用这种策略。IBM 公司在计算机市场、可口可乐公司在饮料市场的策略是很好的例子。这类公司会开发众多的产品，以满足各种消费需求。

The enterprise tries to get into each segment market, meeting the needs of various customers with a variety of products. Usually only large powerful enterprises adopt this strategy. Good examples are IBM in the computer market and Coca-Cola in the beverage market. Companies like these develop a lot of products to meet all kinds of consumer demands.

四、目标市场的营销策略 Marketing Strategies for Target Market

企业选择的目标市场不同，提供的产品或服务就不同，进占目标市场的营销策略也就不一样。一般说来，可供企业选择的目标市场营销策略主要有三种，即无差异市场营销策略、差异性市场营销策略和集中性市场营销策略。

Different target markets the enterprise chooses, different products or services the enterprise provides, mean different marketing strategies are used to occupy the target market. In general, there are mainly three available marketing strategies for target markets, which are non-difference marketing strategy, difference marketing strategy and concentration marketing strategy.

(一)无差异市场营销策略 Non-difference Marketing Strategy

无差异市场营销策略,就是企业把整个市场作为自己的目标市场,只考虑市场需求的共性,而不考虑其差异,运用一种产品、一种价格、一种推销方法,吸引尽可能多的消费者。美国可口可乐公司从 1886 年问世以来,最初采用无差别市场策略,生产一种口味、一种配方、一种包装的产品满足世界 156 个国家和地区的需要,因此它生产的是"世界性的清凉饮料"。这种营销策略除适用于市场是同质的产品外,主要适用于有广泛需求的、能够被大量生产、大量销售的产品。采用这种策略的企业一般具有大规模单一的生产线,拥有广泛的或大众化的销售渠道,并能开展强有力的促销活动,如图 5-1 所示。

Non-difference marketing strategy refers to the enterprise considering the whole market as its target market; the enterprise only considers common demands of the markets, regardless of their differences, using one product, one price, one marketing method to attract more customers. Since 1886 the Coca-Cola Company has adopted non-difference market strategy, and produced a product with one kind of taste, recipe and package, which meets the needs of 156 countries and regions all over the world. Thus it produces a "worldwide cold drink". This marketing strategy not only applies to a market composed of homogeneous products, but also is mainly suitable for products with widespread demand, mass production and big sales. The enterprise adopting this strategy generally has large single production lines, extensive or mass sales channels, and can carry out strong promotional activities, as is shown in Figure 5-1.

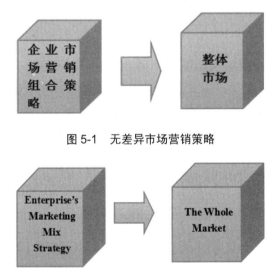

图 5-1 无差异市场营销策略

Figure 5-1 Non-difference Marketing Strategy

这种策略的优点是产品单一,容易保证质量,能大批量生产,降低生产和销售成本。但如果同类企业也采用这种策略时,必然要形成激烈竞争。所以,面对竞争强手时,无差异营销策略也有其局限性。

This strategy has the advantages of singleness of product, ease in ensuring quality, mass production, and reducing costs of production and sales. But if similar enterprises also use this strategy, it causes fierce competition. So, while the enterprises face strong competition, there are also limitations in using non-difference marketing strategy.

(二)差异性市场营销策略 Difference Marketing Strategy

差异性市场营销策略就是把整个市场细分为若干子市场,针对不同的子市场设计不同的产品,制定不同的营销策略,满足不同的消费需求。例如,美国有的服装企业按生活方式把妇女分成三种类型:时髦型、男子气型、朴素型。时髦型妇女喜欢把自己打扮得华贵艳丽,引人注目;男子气型妇女喜欢打扮得超凡脱俗,卓尔不群;朴素型妇女购买服装讲求经济实惠,价格适中。企业根据不同类妇女的不同偏好,有针对性地设计出不同风格的服装,使产品对各类消费者更具有吸引力。这一策略的运用只能限制在销售额的扩大所带来的利润超过营销总成本费用的增加时才能采用,并且只有大中型企业可以采用,实力不足的小企业不宜采用。差异性市场营销策略如图 5-2 所示。

Difference marketing strategy involves dividing the whole market into several submarkets, and designing different products according to different submarkets to formulate different marketing strategies and meet different consumer demands. For example, in the United States, some garment enterprises, divide women into three types according to way of life: modern type, manly type, and simple type. Fashionable women like to dress elegantly, gorgeously, and attractively; manly women like to dress outstandingly and free from vulgarity; women of the simple type buy clothes focusing on economic benefits and moderate price. Companies, according to different classes of women with different preferences, design different styles of clothes to make the products more attractive to all kinds of consumers. The use of this strategy is usually only undertaken when profits from the expansion of sales exceed the rise in total marketing costs, and can only be used by large and medium-sized enterprises. Smaller businesses lacking sufficient power should not use it. Difference Marketing Strategy is as shown in Figure 5-2.

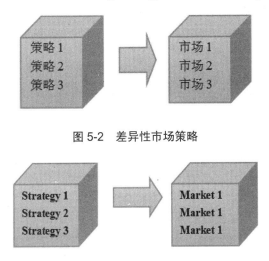

图 5-2 差异性市场策略

Figure 5-2 Difference Marketing Strategy

这种策略的优点是能满足不同消费者的不同要求,有利于扩大销售、占领市场、提高企业的声誉。其缺点是由于产品和促销方式差异化,增加了管理难度,提高了生产和销售费用。

The advantage of this strategy is that it can meet various demands of different consumers, and it is beneficial to expand sales, occupy the market and improve reputation. The disadvantages arise from differentiation of products and promotion ways, management difficulty increases, and the cost of production and sales rise.

(三)集中性市场营销策略 Concentration Marketing Strategy

集中性市场营销策略就是在细分后的市场上,选择一个或少数几个细分市场作为目标市场,集中企业的所有力量,实行专业化生产和销售,为目标市场顾客服务。在个别少数市场上发挥优势,提高市场占有率。采用这种策略的企业,不是追求在整个市场上占有较大的份额,而是在一个或几个较小的市场上取得较大的市场占有率,甚至居于支配地位。其具体做法不是把有效的人力、物力、财力分散在广大的市场上,而是集中企业的优势力量,对某个细分市场采取攻势营销策略,以取得市场上的优势地位。这是大部分中小型企业应当采用的策略。集中性商场营销策略如图 5-3 所示。

With concentration marketing strategy in a segment market, an enterprise selects one or several segments as the target market, concentrates all efforts there, and carries out specialized production and sales to serve customers in the target market. The enterprise may derive advantages in several special markets, and improve market share. The enterprise adopting this strategy does not attempt to occupy a bigger share in the whole market, but obtain larger market share and even dominance in one or a few smaller markets. This way avoids dispersing effective manpower, material resources and financial resources in a vast market, but concentrates the enterprise's strengths to carry out an offensive marketing strategy in a segment market in order to obtain the dominant position in that market. This is the strategy most small and medium enterprises adopt. Concentration Marketing Strategy is as shown in Figure 5-3.

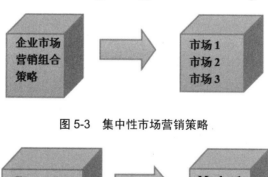

图 5-3 集中性市场营销策略

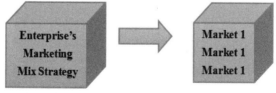

Figure 5-3　Concentration Marketing Strategy

采用集中性市场营销策略，能集中优势力量，有利于产品适销对路，降低成本，提高企业和产品的知名度。但这种策略有较大的经营风险，因为它的目标市场范围小，品种单一。如果目标市场的消费者需求和爱好发生变化，企业就可能因应变不及时而陷入困境。同时，当强有力的竞争者打入目标市场时，企业就要受到严重影响。因此，许多中小企业为了分散风险，仍应选择一定数量的细分市场作为自己的目标市场。

Concentration marketing strategy is used to focus superior forces and is advantageous in selling products in an appropriate manner, reducing costs and enhancing the reputation of the enterprise and its product. However, it leads to greater risk for the business, because the scope of its target market is small and the category of product is singular. If consumers' demands and interests in the target market change, the enterprise could find itself in trouble through slow response. At the same time, when powerful competitors enter the target market, the enterprise will be severely affected. As a result, in order to spread risks, many small and medium-sized enterprises choose a certain number of segment markets as target market.

选择适合本企业的目标市场营销策略是一个复杂多变的工作。企业内部条件和外部环境在不断发展变化，经营者要不断通过市场调查和预测，掌握和分析市场变化趋势与竞争对手的条件，扬长避短，发挥优势，把握时机，采取灵活的适应市场态势的策略，去争取较大的利益。

Choosing a strategy suitable for an enterprise in a target market is a complicated task. Because internal conditions and the external environment of the enterprise develop and change constantly, operators should constantly through market survey and prediction, control and analyze market trends and competition conditions. They need to foster strengths and circumvent weaknesses, give play to advantages, seize the moment and adopt flexible strategies to suit the market situation, and to strive for broader interests.

五、影响目标市场选择的因素 Factors Influencing Target Market Selection

上述三种策略各有利弊，企业在进行决策时要具体分析产品和市场的状况以及企业本身的特点。影响企业目标市场策略的因素主要有企业资源、产品特点、市场特点、产品生命周期和竞争对手的策略五类。

There are advantages and disadvantages of the above three strategies. An enterprise should specifically analyze products and market conditions and the characteristics of the enterprise itself while making decisions. The five major factors affecting an enterprise's target market strategy are the enterprise's resources, the nature of its products, market characteristics, product life cycle and competitor's strategy.

(一)企业的资源 Enterprise's Resources

企业的资源指的是企业在生产、技术、销售、管理和资金方面力量的总和。资源雄厚的企业，如拥有大规模的生产能力和广泛的分销渠道、高度的产品标准化、好的产品内在质量和品牌信誉等,可以考虑实行无差异市场营销策略;如果企业拥有雄厚的设计能力和优秀的管理素质,则可以考虑施行差异市场营销策略;而对实力较弱的中小型企业来说,更适合集中力量实施集中营销策略。企业初次进入市场时,往往采取集中市场营销策略;但在积累了一定的成功经验后就可以采取差异市场营销策略或无差异市场营销策略,以扩大市场份额。

An enterprise's resources refer to the sum of the enterprise's production, technology, sales, management, and capital. The enterprise could consider implementing non-difference marketing strategy if it has abundant resources such as a large-scale production capacity, a wide range of distribution channels, a high degree of product standardization, good internal quality and brand reputation, etc. If the company has strong design capabilities and outstanding management quality, it can consider adopting difference marketing strategy; but for the weaker, small or medium-sized enterprises, it is more suitable to focus on concentration marketing strategy. When an enterprise enters the market for the first time, it often focuses on concentration marketing strategy; but after accumulating some successful experience, it can adopt difference or non-difference marketing strategy to expand market share.

(二)产品的性质 Nature of Product

产品的性质是指产品是同质的还是异质的。产品的同质性表明了产品在性能、特点等方面的差异性的大小,是企业选择目标市场时不可不考虑的因素之一。一般对于同质性高的产品如食盐等,宜施行无差异市场营销;对于同质性低或异质性产品,差异市场营销或集中市场营销是恰当的选择。

Nature of product refers to whether products are homogeneous or heterogeneous. Product homogeneity shows the diversity degree of product size in the aspects of performance, characteristics and so on, which are the factors the enterprise must consider when selecting the target market. Generally for high homogeneity products like salt, an enterprise should adopt non-difference marketing strategy; but for products with low homogeneity or heterogeneity, difference marketing strategy or concentration marketing strategy may be the right choice.

(三)市场的特点 Characteristics of Market

如果市场消费者具有相同的口味、爱好,在每一个时期内购买的数量大致相同,对销售方式的要求也无大的差别,在这种情况下,可采用无差异市场营销策略;另一方面,如果市场需求的特点差别很大,企业就应选择差异性市场营销策略或集中性市场营销策略。供与求是市场中的两大基本力量,它们的变化趋势往往是决定市场发展方向的根本原因。供不应求时,企业重在扩大供给,无暇考虑需求差异,所以采用无差异市场营销策略;供过于求时,企业为刺激需求、扩大市场份额殚精竭虑,多采用差异市场营销或集中市场营销策略。

If customers have the same tastes and interests, in each period they have roughly the same buying quantity, and they also do not have big difference of requirement regarding sales manner.

In this case, non-difference marketing strategy can be used. On the other hand, if there is a great characteristic difference of market demands, the enterprise should choose difference marketing strategy or concentration marketing strategy. Supply and demand are two basic forces in the market whose changing tendencies are often the fundamental factor in determining the direction of market development. In a short supply situation, the enterprise must focus on expanding supply and is too busy to consider demand difference. Thus non-difference marketing strategy should be adopted. However, when supply exceeds demand, the enterprise should make great efforts to stimulate demand and expand market share mostly adopting difference marketing strategy or concentration marketing strategy.

(四)产品生命周期 Product Life Cycle

产品因所处的市场生命周期的阶段不同而表现出的不同特点亦不容忽视。产品处于导入期和成长初期时，消费者刚刚接触新产品，对产品的了解还停留在较初浅的层次，竞争尚不激烈，企业这时的营销重点是挖掘市场对产品的基本需求，因此往往采用无差异市场营销策略。等产品进入成长后期和成熟期时，消费者已经熟悉产品的特性，需求向深层次发展，表现出多样性和不同的个性来，导致竞争空前激烈，在这种情况下，企业应适时地转变策略为差异市场营销或集中市场营销。

Particular characteristics cannot be ignored when a product is at different life cycle stages in the market. When a product is in its introduction and early growth stages, the consumers only have contact with new products and their understanding of the product stays at a superficial level. At this moment, competition is not fierce and the enterprise's marketing strategy focuses on finding basic demand for the product in the market, and non-difference marketing strategy is often adopted. When the products are at later growth stage and maturity stage, the consumers are already familiar with the product characteristics, and demands develop at a deeper level. Thus the demand shows diversity and different personality, which can lead to unprecedented fierce competition. In this case, the enterprise should change strategy at the appropriate moment to difference marketing strategy or concentration marketing strategy.

(五)竞争者的策略 Competitor's Strategy

企业可与竞争对手选择不同的目标市场覆盖策略。例如，竞争者采用无差异市场营销策略时，企业选用差异市场营销策略或集中市场营销策略更容易发挥优势。

An enterprise can choose a different target market strategy from its competitors to cover the market. When competitors, for example, use non-difference marketing strategy, it may be easier to exert advantages by choosing difference marketing strategy or concentration marketing strategy.

企业的目标市场策略应慎重选择，应能充分发挥企业的特点和优势，生产出符合市场需要的产品。

Any enterprise must choose its target market strategy carefully. The final choice should give full play to the enterprise's characteristics and advantages in making products which can meet the needs of the market.

第三节 市场定位
Market Positioning

一、市场定位的含义 Meaning of Market Positioning

所谓市场定位就是企业根据目标市场上同类产品的竞争状况，针对顾客对该类产品某些特征或属性的重视程度，为本企业产品塑造强有力的、与众不同的鲜明个性，并将其形象生动地传递给顾客，求得顾客的认同。市场定位的实质是使本企业与其他企业严格区分开来，使顾客明显感觉和认识到这种差别，从而在顾客心目中占据与众不同的有价值的位置。

The term market positioning means that the enterprise, according to the competition situation of similar products in the target market, and in view of the importance given by customers to the degree of one product's characteristics or attributes, shapes a strong and distinctive image for this product and transfers this vivid image to customers in order to obtain approval. The essence of market positioning is to sharply distinguish an enterprise from other enterprises, and to allow customers to feel and recognize this difference. In this way, in the customers' mind it possesses a position with distinctive value.

美国著名的营销专家里斯(Ries)和特劳特(Trout)认为："定位是你对未来的潜在顾客心灵所下的工夫，也就是把产品定位在你未来顾客的心中。"即市场定位是能够让产品或企业走进顾客心灵深处的方法。所以定位是从顾客心理出发的，而不是从企业或产品出发的，不能只认识到自己的产品有特色，而是要将其传达播给顾客，这就是市场定位。

The well-known American marketing experts Ries and Trout think: "positioning is when you make efforts to make an impression in your future potential customers' hearts, also it is to position the product in the minds of your future customers." It is the manner in which the enterprise can let its products or business go into the deep minds of customers. So positioning starts from customer psychology, rather than from the enterprise itself or the product. It is not enough for the enterprise to realize that its own products are special. It must convey this information to the customer. This is the essential dimension of market positioning.

菲利普·科特勒于 20 世纪 70 年代把"positioning"引入营销中，作为"4Ps"之前最重要的另一个"P"，以引领企业营销活动的方向。他对定位的定义是："对公司的产品进行设计，从而使其能在目标顾客心目中占有一个独特的、有价值的位置的行动。"

Philip Kotler introduced the term "positioning" in marketing in the 1970s as one of the most important "P" before "4Ps" to lead the direction of the enterprise marketing activities. He defined positioning like this: "a behavior to design the enterprise's products, allowing it to occupy a unique and valuable position in the target customers' minds."

定位的应用范围很广，可以是一件商品、一项服务，甚至是一家企业、一个机构或一个人。

The application range of positioning is very wide. It can be a product, a kind of service, or even an enterprise, an institute or a person.

第五章 目标市场选择及市场定位策略
Strategies for Target Market Selection and Market Positioning

企业进行市场定位并不是要在产品上做什么重大的改变，而是要在产品的名称、品牌、价格、包装以及服务方面下工夫，为自己的产品在市场上树立一个明确的、有别于竞争产品的、符合消费者需要的形象，其目的是要在消费者的心目中占据一个有利的销售地位，这是决定一个产品成败的关键。市场定位包括品牌定位、企业定位、产品定位、价格定位、广告定位等。

The enterprise's market positioning is not about making any significant change in a product, but to pay attention to the product's name, brand, price, packaging, and service, to set up a clear and different image with regard to competing products which can conform to the consumers' needs; the aim is to occupy a favorable sales position in consumers' mind, which is the key to achieving success in selling products. Market positioning includes brand positioning, enterprise positioning, product positioning, price positioning, advertisement positioning, etc.

二、市场定位的作用 Functions of Market Positioning

市场定位有利于建立企业及产品的市场特色，是参与现代市场竞争的有力武器。在现代社会中，许多市场都存在严重的供大于求的现象，众多生产同类产品的厂家争夺有限的顾客，市场竞争异常激烈。为了使自己生产经营的产品获得稳定销路，防止被其他厂家的产品所替代，企业必须从各方面树立起一定的市场形象，以期在顾客心目中形成一定的偏好。美国摩托罗拉公司在世界电信设备市场上，成功地塑造了质量领先的形象，从而在激烈的市场竞争中居于领先地位。它在不到十年的时间内，由一家小公司上升到世界十大"名牌"公司之一。

Market positioning is conducive to building characteristics of enterprises and products in the market, and is a useful tool to participate in modern market competition. In modern society, the phenomenon of serious oversupply exists in many markets and many manufacturers producing similar products compete for limited customers, making market competition extremely fierce. In order to obtain stable sales, and preventing replacement by other manufacturers' products, an enterprise must construct a certain market image from various aspects, so as to form a certain preference in customers' minds. The American company Motorola successfully achieved a leading image of high quality in the global telecom equipment market. Thus it is the leader in a fiercely competitive market. In less than 10 years, it grew from a small company to one of the top ten "famous brand" companies in the world.

市场定位决策是企业制定市场营销组合策略的基础。企业的市场营销组合要受到企业市场定位的制约，例如，假设某企业决定生产销售优质低价的产品，那么这样的定位就决定了：产品的质量要高；价格要定得低；广告宣传的内容要突出强调企业产品质优价廉的特点，要让目标顾客相信他们能以低价买到好产品。企业的分销储运效率要高，以保证低价出售仍能获利。也就是说，企业的市场定位决定了企业必须设计和发展与之相适应的市场营销组合。

Market positioning is the foundation of an enterprise's marketing mix strategy. Indeed, the enterprise's marketing mix is restricted by its market positioning. For example, if an enterprise decides to produce and sell a high quality product at a lower price, then the location of the product is determined: the quality of the product is high; the price is low; advertising content must highlight the characteristics of the product with high quality and low price to convince target customers that they can buy good products at a low price. The enterprise must have high efficiency of distribution and storage to guarantee that it can still make profits at a low price. That is to say, the enterprise's market positioning determines that the enterprise must design and develop the corresponding marketing mix.

三、市场定位的步骤 Steps of Market Positioning

市场定位的主要任务就是在市场上，让企业及其产品与竞争者有所不同，从而吸引细分市场中的重要群体。定位的步骤包括识别可能的竞争优势、确定适当的竞争优势和选择整体定位策略。

The main task of market positioning is to distinguish the enterprise and its products from competitors to attract an important group in the segment market. The steps of positioning include identifying potential competitive advantage, determining the appropriate competitive advantage and choosing overall positioning strategy.

(一)识别可能的竞争优势 Identifying Potential Competitive Advantage

赢得并保持顾客的关键，在于比竞争对手更加了解顾客的需要和购买过程，并为他们提供更大的价值。只要企业把自己定位为向选定的目标市场提供最大价值，它就获得了竞争优势。当企业为市场提供的某种产品或服务有利于竞争对手时就要开始定位，以给消费者带来更大的价值。

The key to winning and maintaining customers is to understand more about their needs and buying process, and to offer them greater value than competitors. As long as an enterprise positions itself to provide maximum value to the selected target market, it will gain a competitive advantage. Positioning starts when the enterprise supplies the market with one kind of product or service differently to its competitors in order to give consumers more value.

为了找到差异之处，营销人员必须仔细分析顾客对企业产品或服务的全部体验。成功的企业能够在与顾客发生联系的每一处都找到使自己产品差异化的方法。企业把自己的产品或服务与竞争对手区分开来的方法，就是按照产品、服务、渠道、人员或者形象来进行差异化。

In order to distinguish differences, marketers must carefully analyze all the customers' experience regarding an enterprise's products or service. Successful enterprises can find a way to distinguish their products by contacting customers in each place. The method for enterprises to set their own products or services apart from their competitors' is to seek differentiation in accordance with the products, service, channels, people or image.

(1) 产品差异化有不同的程度。企业可以在一致性、耐久性、可靠性、维护性等方面将自己的产品进行差异化。

Products can possess different degrees of differentiation. An enterprise can distinguish its products in the aspects of consistency, durability, reliability and maintenance.

第五章 目标市场选择及市场定位策略
Strategies for Target Market Selection and Market Positioning

(2) 一些企业可以依靠快捷、方便或细致的配送来实现服务的差异化。安装和服务维修也能把一个企业和另一个企业区分开来，一些企业提供顾客培训服务或者咨询服务，包括购买者需要的数据、信息系统和广告服务，以使自己的服务差异化。

Some enterprises can rely on fast, convenient and considerate delivery to realize service differentiation. Installation, service and maintenance also can distinguish between one enterprise and another. Some enterprises provide their customers with a training service or consulting service, including data, information systems and advertising service that the buyers need.

(3) 实行渠道差异化的企业，在渠道的覆盖、专业化和绩效方面获得竞争优势。

The enterprise implementing channel differentiation can gain competitive advantages in channel coverage, specialization and performance.

(4) 企业通过人员差异化获得强大的竞争优势，也就是比竞争对手雇用并培训更优秀的员工。

With personnel differentiation, the enterprise can get strong competitive advantage; that is to hire and train more talented staff than its rivals.

(5) 企业或者品牌的形象应该传递产品独有的特点和定位，从而使企业的形象差异化。

The enterprise or its brand image should pass unique product characteristics and positioning, thus achieving image differentiation for the enterprise.

(6) 最后，企业还要考虑自身的条件。有些产品属性，虽然是顾客比较重视的，但如果企业力所不及，也不能达成市场定位的目标。

In the end, the enterprise has to consider its own conditions. Though some product properties are noticed by customers, if the enterprise can't get to that point, it can't achieve its market positioning target.

(二)确定适当的竞争优势 Determining Proper Competitive Advantage

企业所确定的产品差异化的特色，是企业有效参与市场竞争的优势，但这些优势不会自动地在市场上显示出来。要使这些独特的优势发挥作用，影响顾客的购买决策，企业需要以产品差异化特色为基础树立鲜明的市场形象，通过积极主动而又巧妙地与顾客沟通，引起顾客的注意与兴趣，求得顾客的认同。

The characteristics of product differentiation identified by the enterprise are the enterprise's advantages for effectively participating in market competition. However, these advantages will not be automatically displayed in the market. To make these unique advantages play a role and influence the customers' buying decision, it is necessary construct a distinct enterprise image based on product differentiation characteristics. Through active and skillful communication with customers, the enterprise's attraction and interest can be raised and the customer's approval can be obtained.

企业是否应该向目标市场推广一项还是一项以上的产品的特性，要视具体情况而定。那些只挑选一个特性，并且宣称自己在这个特性方面是"最好的"，购买者很容易记住。如果两家企业或者更多的企业在同样的特性上宣称自己是最好的，那企业就应该根据一个以上的差异因素进行定位，以对更多的细分市场产生吸引力。

Whether the enterprise should promote one item or more items in a target market depends on specific conditions. Buyers easily remember only one feature of a product that is promoted as the "best" with regard to this feature. If two or more enterprises claim to be the best in the same feature, the enterprise should position the product based on more than one differentiating factor, in order to appeal to more segment markets.

企业可以从产品的重要性、显著性、优越性、沟通性、专有性、经济性、营利性等角度来推广产品的差异性，然而不是每种差异性都要被强调，一种差异在增加消费者利益的同时，也有可能增加企业的成本。因此，企业必须仔细选择与竞争对手相区分的方法。

The enterprise can make its product differentiation more widespread from the aspects of product importance, significance, advantage, communication, exclusiveness, economy, profitability, etc. However, not all of these differences should be emphasized. One difference may increase consumers' interest, but at the same time, it is likely to increase the enterprise's costs. Therefore, the enterprise must choose carefully choose a method to distinguish itself from competitors.

有效的市场定位并不取决于企业怎么想，关键在于顾客怎么看。对市场定位最成功的的反映就是顾客对企业及其产品所持的态度和看法。

Effective market positioning does not depend on how the enterprise thinks; the key is what customers think. The most successful reflection of market positioning is the attitude and view held by customers to the enterprise and its products.

(三)选择整体定位策略 Choosing Overall Positioning Strategy

市场营销人员希望根据其产品或服务的关键利益，相对于竞争对手对品牌进行定位。品牌的整体定位叫作品牌价值方案，即品牌基于整体利益组合定位，从而告诉消费者这种选择可以为自己带来最大价值的产品或服务。

Marketers want to adopt brand positioning relative to competitors according to key benefits of their products or services. Overall brand positioning is also referred to as brand value program, being based on the combination of overall interests. Thus consumers may see their choice delivers the greatest value of products or service.

可能的价值方案一般有五种：高质高价、高质同价、同质低价、低质低价及高质低价。

Usually, the five available value programs are: high quality and high price, high quality and equal price, equal quality and low price, low quality and low price, high quality and low price.

(1) 高质高价定位是指提供最高档次的产品或服务，并制定更高的价格来补偿更高的成本。这不仅是提供质量上乘的产品，还给顾客带来了声望，象征着地位和高档的生活方式。

High quality and high price positioning refers to providing products or services of the highest quality, and setting higher prices to compensate for higher costs. This not only provides good quality, but also brings customers prestige, enhances status and facilitates a high-level way of life.

(2) 高质同价定位是指企业可以推出与竞争对手价格相当而质量较高的品牌，以此来吸引那些注重质量差别的消费者。

High quality and equal price positioning occurs when an enterprise launches a brand of similar price but of higher quality, compared to its competitors, in order to attract those customers who pay attention to quality difference.

(3) 同质低价可能是一种强大的价值方案，因为每个人都喜欢利好的交易。企业以较高的性价比提供同等质量的产品，可以形成旺盛的购买力，把顾客从市场领导者那里吸引过来。

Equal quality and low price positioning can be a powerful value program, because everyone loves a good deal. The enterprise provides products of the same quality with high value to enhance purchasing power and attract customers from market leaders.

(4) 低质更低价定位指用更低的价格满足消费者对产品性能或质量的较低的要求。因为很少有人对每样东西都需要并买得起"最好的"，在很多情况下，消费者也愿意接受性能不理想的产品，或者为了价格低一些而放弃花哨的东西。

Low quality and low price positioning is to use lower prices to meet consumer requirements of lower performance or quality. Because very few people need everything, or can afford "the best", in many cases, consumers are often willing to accept a product without ideal features, or forego "fancy stuff" for lower prices.

(5) 高质低价一定是成功的价值定位，许多企业宣称自己就是这么做的。但是从长远来看，企业严格坚持这种两全其美的定位是很困难的，因为质量好成本就会高。

High quality and low price usually means successful value positioning, and many enterprises claim to be doing just that. But in the long term, it is difficult for any enterprise to strictly adhere to this positioning, because good quality automatically means higher costs.

一旦企业选定了一种定位，企业必须采取有力措施向目标顾客宣传这种定位，企业的所有市场营销组合也必须支持此定位策略。

Once an enterprise selects a particular strategy for positioning, it must adopt strong measures to publicize this positioning to target customers. Also the enterprise's whole marketing mix must support this positioning strategy.

顾客对企业的认识不是一成不变的。由于竞争者的干扰或与顾客沟通不畅，会使企业形象变得模糊，同时顾客对企业的理解将会出现偏差，态度发生转变。所以建立企业市场形象后，企业还应不断向顾客提供新的论据和观点，及时矫正与市场定位不一致的行为，巩固企业形象，维持和强化顾客对企业的看法和认识。

Customer awareness of an enterprise is not set in stone. Due to competitors' interference or miscommunication with customers, this may cause enterprise image to become fuzzy; meanwhile, modification of customer understanding of the enterprise will appear and attitudes will change. After establishing an enterprise image in the market, the enterprise should also constantly offer new arguments and opinions to customers, timely correct behavior which is inconsistent with market positioning, strengthen the enterprise image, and maintain and strengthen customer views and understanding of the enterprise.

四、市场定位的方法 Methods of Market Positioning

各个企业经营的产品不同，面对的顾客不同，所处的竞争环境也不同，因而市场定位的方法也不同。总的来讲，市场定位方法有以下几种。

Because of product variety, and customer and competition environments, each enterprise uses different methods of market positioning. In general, market positioning involves the following methods.

1. 根据产品特点定位 According to Product Characteristics

构成产品内在特色的许多因素都可以作为市场定位所依据的原则，如所含成分、材料、质量、价格等。"七喜"汽水的定位是"非可乐"，强调它是不含咖啡因的饮料，与可乐类饮料不同。"泰诺"止痛药的定位是"非阿司匹林的止痛药"，显示药物成分与以往的止痛药有本质的差异。

A number of factors relating to the internal features of a product can be used as the principle of market positioning, for example, ingredients, materials, quality, price, etc. The positioning of the soft drink "7 Up" is as "not-coke", emphasizing that it is not a caffeinated beverage, and is different from cola beverages. The positioning of the painkiller "Tylenol" is as a "non-aspirin painkiller", emphasizes that the ingredients have essential differences from existing pain relievers.

2. 根据质量和价格定位 According to Quality and Price

这种定位是根据产品的质量和价格这两者的组合而创造出产品的特定目标市场定位。该定位方法突出的是在经济利益上给消费者以好处。一般有五种定位，即高质高价、高质同价、同质低价、低质低价和高质低价。

This positioning is based on a combination of product quality and price to create particular target market positioning. This method highlights economic benefits to consumers. Generally there are five types of positioning: high quality and high price, high quality and equal price, equal quality and low price, low quality and low price, and high quality and low price.

3. 根据特定的使用场合及用途定位 According to Specific Occasions and Purposes

为老产品找到一种新用途，是为该产品创造新的市场定位的好方法。例如，脑白金本是一种保健药品，但企业为了取得好的销售效果，将其定位为礼品。这种定位有利于突出本企业产品与市场上其他产品的差异，便于消费者的选购。

Finding a new use for an old product can be a successful way to create new market positioning for the product. For example, the basic nature of Naobaijin is a type of health care medicine, but the enterprise positions it as a gift in order to achieve increased sales. This positioning is beneficial for the enterprise to distinguish its product from other products in the market, and makes it convenient for consumers.

4. 根据顾客得到的利益定位 According to Customers' Interests

产品提供给顾客的利益是顾客最能切实体验到的，也可以用作定位的依据。如劳斯莱斯车豪华气派，丰田车物美价廉，沃尔沃则结实耐用。

Experience derived from using products is very practical for customers, and can also be used as the basis of positioning, such as the luxurious style of Rolls-Royce cars, high quality and low price of Toyota, and the strong and durable quality of Volvo.

5. 根据使用者类型定位　According to Type of Users

企业常常试图将其产品指向某一类特定的使用者，以便根据这些顾客的看法塑造恰当的形象。美国米勒啤酒公司曾将其原来唯一的品牌"高生"啤酒定位为"啤酒中的香槟"，吸引了许多以前不常喝啤酒的高收入妇女。公司在一项调查中发现，占30%的狂饮者大约消费了啤酒销量的80%，于是，该公司在广告中展示石油工人钻井成功后狂欢的镜头，还有年轻人在沙滩上冲刺后开怀畅饮的镜头，塑造了一个"精力充沛的形象"。该公司在广告中提出"有空就喝米勒"，从而成功地占领啤酒市场达10年之久。

An enterprise often tries aim its products at particular users in order to develop a positive image according to customer views. Miller Brewing Company in the United States repositioned the original brand "Miller High Life" as "The Champagne of Bottled Beer", attracting many high-income women who infrequently drank beer previously. In one survey, it was also found that 30% of those who drank beer accounted for about 80% of sales. Thus one beer advertisement showed two people binge drinking after a successful oil drilling episode, as well as young people on a beach sprinting, laughing and drinking. This created an image which equated beer drinking with energy. The advertisement stressed "Free to Drink Miller" and helped successfully occupation the beer market for up to 10 years.

6. 根据产品类别定位 According to Product Category

企业产品在定位时可以借助另一种已被大家所熟悉的产品，而将自己的产品定位在与这种产品相近的位置上。例如，大家对奶油都很熟悉而对麦淇淋往往不很了解，但若将麦淇淋比作人造奶油，则大家就会迅速了解并对它产生印象。

When an enterprise adopts a product positioning strategy, it can use another product which is familiar to people, and position its own product in a similar position to the better known product. For example, many people are familiar with cream but do not necessarily know margarine. But if we compare margarine to artificial cream, then customers will more quickly understand and have an impression of it.

7. 根据竞争者定位 According to the Competitor

这种定位方式是将自己的产品与竞争对手的产品进行比较后，针对竞争者产品的定位方式来决定一种既能突出自己产品的优势特性、又能削弱竞争者产品的定位方式。

This type of positioning refers to comparing an enterprise's own products with those of competitors and according to competitors' own product positioning method. The enterprise determines a kind of positioning strategy in which the product advantage can be highlighted and competitors' products can be undermined.

事实上，许多企业进行市场定位的依据往往不止一个，而是同时使用多个依据。因为要体现企业及其产品的形象，市场定位必须是多维度的、多侧面的。

In fact, many companies adopt market positioning often based on more than one criterion. Because an enterprise wants to promulgate its own image of the enterprise and its product, market positioning must be multidimensional and multifaceted.

五、市场定位策略 Strategies for Market Positioning

市场定位是一种竞争性定位，它反映了市场竞争各方的关系，是为企业有效参与市场竞争服务的。市场定位策略主要有以下几种。

Market positioning is a kind of competitive action, which reflects the relationship of various parties involved in market competition, and helps an enterprise participate effectively in market competition. The following are the main strategies in this area.

1. 避强定位策略 Strategy of Avoiding Strong Competitors

避强定位策略是指企业力图避免与实力最强的或较强的其他企业直接发生竞争，而将自己的产品定位于另一市场区域内，使自己的产品在某些特征或属性方面与最强或较强的对手有比较显著的区别。

The positioning strategy of avoiding strong competitors refers to an enterprise attempting to avoid direct competition with the most powerful or strong companies. Instead it positions its products in another market to distinguish them significantly from those strongest or relatively strong opponents in terms of certain characteristics or attributes.

避强定位策略的优点是能使企业较快地在市场上站稳脚跟，并能在消费者或用户心目中树立形象，风险小。

The advantage of this positioning strategy is that the enterprise can rapidly gain a foothold in the market and is able to establish an image in the consumers' or users' hearts, at the same time taking less risk.

此策略的缺点在于，避强往往意味着企业必须放弃追求最佳的市场位置，很可能使企业处于最差的市场位置。

The disadvantage of this strategy is that it often means the enterprise must give up chasing the best market position, and is likely to leave the enterprise in a subordinate position in the market．

2. 迎头定位策略 Head-on Positioning Strategy

迎头定位策略，这是一种与在市场上居支配地位的竞争对手"对着干"的定位方式，即企业选择与竞争对手重合的市场位置，争取同样的目标顾客，彼此在产品、价格、分销、供给等方面少有差别。

Head-on positioning strategy is to directly challenge competitors who are in the dominant position in the market. That is to say, the enterprise chooses an overlapping market position with competitors and strives for the same target customers. Usually, there is little difference with regard to product, price, distribution, supply, etc.

在世界饮料市场上，作为后起品牌的"百事可乐"进入市场时，就采用过这种方式，"你是可乐，我也是可乐"，与可口可乐展开面对面的较量。实行迎头定位，企业必须做到知己知彼，应该了解市场上是否可以容纳两个或两个以上的竞争者，自己是否拥有比竞争者更多的资源和能力，是不是可以比竞争对手做得更好。否则，迎头定位可能会成为一种非常危险的战术，对企业造成严重损害。

In the global drinks market, as the late-starter, Pepsi entered the market using the position "You are Coke, me, too!" to compete with Coca-Cola head on. With head-on positioning, the newcomer must understand the situation well, know whether the market can accommodate two or more competitors, whether it has sufficient resources and capabilities regarding competitors and whether it can do better than competitors. Otherwise, head-on positioning could be a very dangerous tactic which can severely damage the enterprise.

当然，也有些企业认为这是一种更能激发自己奋发向上的定位尝试，一旦成功就能取得巨大的市场份额。

There are, of course, some companies who believe that head-on positioning positively provides great motivation to strive for significant market share and achieve success.

3. 重新定位策略 Repositioning Strategy

重新定位策略，通常是指对那些销路少、市场反应差的产品进行二次定位。初次定位后，随着时间的推移，新的竞争者进入市场，选择与本企业相近的市场位置，致使本企业原来的市场占有率下降；或者，由于顾客需求偏好发生转移，原来喜欢本企业产品的人转而喜欢其他企业的产品，因而市场对本企业产品的需求减少。在这些情况下，企业就需要对其产品进行重新定位。例如，某些专门为青年人设计的产品在中老年人中也开始流行后，这种产品就需要重新定位。

Repositioning strategy usually refers to adopting a second positioning with those products with poor sales and negative market reaction. After initial positioning, as time passes, new competitors enter the market and choose to be close to this enterprise's market position. This causes the enterprise's original market share to drop; or, due to customer demand preferences shifting, people who originally liked this enterprise's product turn to other enterprises' products, thus reducing demand from the market. In these cases, enterprises need to reposition their products. For example, if a product specially designed for young people later becomes popular with middle-aged and old people, this kind of product may need to be repositioned.

4. 创新定位策略 Innovation Positioning Strategy

创新定位策略是指寻找新的尚未被占领但有潜在市场需求的位置，填补市场上的空缺，生产当前市场上没有的、具备某种特色的产品。例如，通过创新，日本的索尼随身听填补了迷你电子产品市场的空白，索尼公司在二战时期得到迅速发展，其后成为世界级的跨国公司。采用这种定位方式时，公司应明确创新定位所需的产品在技术上、经济上是否可行，有无足够的市场容量，能否为公司带来合理而持续的盈利。

Innovation positioning strategy refers to looking for new locations which have not been occupied previously but have potential market demand, filling gaps in the market by creating new products with unique features. For example, the Japanese Sony Walkman filled a gap in the mini-electronic products market through innovation. Sony had a rapid development during World War II, and later became a world-class multinational company. When adopting this type of positioning, the company must be clear whether the product is technically and economically feasible, whether there is enough market capacity, and whether it could bring reasonable and steady profits for the company.

本 章 小 结
Summary

成功的企业，懂得怎样把整个市场分割为有意义的顾客群体，即进行市场细分；然后在此基础上，选择企业要服务的顾客群体，即准确地选择目标市场并创造能够满足目标市场的供给物，从而进行准确的市场定位。

A successful enterprise knows how to divide the whole market into meaningful customer groups, which is market segmentation; and then on this basis, the enterprise selects the service-needing customers. This is to choose the target market accurately, and create supply that can meet the target market, thus achieving successful market positioning.

市场细分是指营销者通过市场调研，依据消费者的需要和欲望、购买行为和购买习惯等方面的差异，把某一产品的市场整体划分为若干消费者群的市场分类过程。有效的市场细分必须满足可测量性、可赢利性、可进入性、差异性和相对稳定性等条件。市场细分应遵循一定的程序。细分消费者市场的变量主要有地理变量、人口变量、心理变量、行为变量四大类。由于生产者与消费者在购买动机与行为上存在差别，所以，除了运用前述消费者市场细分标准外，还可用一些新的标准来细分生产者市场，如用户规模、产品的最终用途、生产者购买状况、行业类别。企业可采用单一变量因素、多个变量因素组合或系列变量因素进行市场细分。

Market segmentation refers to a process of market division during which through market research, marketers divide the whole market for one kind of product into several consumer groups according differences in consumer needs and desires, purchase behavior, buying habits and other aspects. Effective market segmentation must meet the following conditions: measurability, profitability, accessibility, difference and relative stability. Market segmentation should follow certain procedures. The variables of consumer market segmentation are geographic variables, demographic variables, psychological variables and behavioral variables. Because producers and consumers have different motives and behavior, therefore, in addition to using consumer market segmentation criteria, enterprises can still use some of other criteria to segment the product market, such as customer size, final use of product, producers' buying conditions and industry categories. In market segmentation, enterprises can use a single variable, a combination of multiple variables, or a series of variables.

第五章 目标市场选择及市场定位策略
Strategies for Target Market Selection and Market Positioning

所谓目标市场，就是企业在市场细分的基础上，结合考虑各细分市场上顾客需求和企业自身的经营条件，而选出的一个或若干个企业能很好地为之提供产品或服务的细分市场。目标市场选择的标准一是有一定的规模和发展潜力，二是细分市场结构具有吸引力，三是符合企业目标和能力。目标市场选择策略包括市场集中化策略、产品专业化策略、市场专业化策略、选择专业化策略、全面进入市场策略。可供企业选择的目标市场营销策略有无差异市场营销策略、差异性市场营销策略和集中性市场营销策略。

The so-called target market is, on the basis of market segmentation, one or several segment markets chosen by the enterprise in consideration of customer demands and its own conditions in each segment market which the enterprise can supply with good products or service. Criteria of target market selection involve certain scale and potential, the attractive structure of a segment market in accordance with enterprise's goals and abilities. The strategies of target market selection involve the strategy of centralized market, the strategy of specialized product, the strategy of specialized market, the strategy of specialized selection and the strategy of overall access to the market. Regarding the target market, marketing strategies available to the enterprise include non-difference marketing strategy, difference marketing strategy and concentration marketing strategy.

市场定位就是企业为其产品塑造强有力的、与众不同的鲜明个性，并将其形象生动地传递给顾客，求得顾客认同。定位的步骤包括识别可能的竞争优势、确定适当的竞争优势和选择整体定位策略。总体来说，市场定位方法有以下几种：根据产品特点定位、根据质量和价格定位、根据特定的使用场合及用途定位、根据顾客得到的利益定位、根据使用者类型定位、根据竞争者定位、根据产品类别定位。市场定位策略主要有避强定位策略、迎头定位策略、重新定位策略及创新定位策略。

The term market positioning refers to an enterprise shaping a strong and distinctive for its product and transmitting this vivid image to customers in order to obtain their approval. The steps in positioning include identifying potential competitive advantage, determining the appropriate competitive advantage and choosing an overall positioning strategy. In general, market positioning uses the following methods: according to product characteristics, according to quality and price, according to specific occasions and purposes, according to interests of customers, according to type of users, according to competitors, according to product category. Market positioning strategies include: avoiding strong competitors, head-on positioning strategy, repositioning strategy and innovation Positioning Strategy.

思 考 题
Questions

1. 什么是市场细分？市场细分的程序是什么？

What is market segmentation? What are the procedures of market segmentation?

2. 消费者市场细分的标准有哪些？生产者市场细分的标准有哪些？

What are the criteria of consumer market segmentation? And what are the criteria of producer market segmentation?

3. 什么是目标市场？目标市场选择的策略有哪些？

What is target market? What are the strategies for target market selection?

4. 目标市场营销的策略有哪些？

What are the marketing strategies for a target market?

5. 什么是市场定位？市场定位的作用是什么？

What is market positioning? What are the functions of market positioning?

6. 市场定位的策略有哪些？

What are the market positioning strategies?

第六章 产品策略
Product Strategies

> 【学习目标】
> 1. 产品整体概念及其与营销策略的关系；
> 2. 产品市场生命周期及其各个阶段的市场营销策略；
> 3. 商品品牌、商标与包装的内涵及产品品牌策略、商标策略和包装策略；
> 4. 产品组合概念和产品组合策略；
> 5. 新产品概念及新产品开发策略。
>
> Learning Objectives
>
> 1. Total product concept and its relationship with marketing strategy;
> 2. Product life-cycle and marketing strategy at every stage of product life-cycle;
> 3. Connotations and strategies of branding, trademark and packaging;
> 4. Concept and strategies of product mix;
> 5. Concept and development strategies of a new product.

所谓产品策略，是指企业制定经营战略时，首先要明确企业能提供什么样的产品和服务去满足消费者的要求，也就是要解决产品策略问题。产品策略是市场营销组合策略的基础，从一定意义上讲，企业成功与发展的关键在于产品满足消费者的需求的程度以及产品策略正确与否。

The so-called product strategy means that the first thing to make clear is what kind of products and services the enterprise can provide to satisfy consumers' demands when an enterprise creating a marketing strategy. This is to solve the problem of product strategy. The product strategy is the foundation of marketing mix strategy. To some extent, the key to achieve success and develop business is to understand how products can meet consumers' needs and whether the product strategy is correct or not.

第一节 产品概述
Overview of Products

一、产品的含义 Concept of Product

产品是指能提供给市场，用于满足人们某种欲望和需要的任何事物，包括实物、服务、场所、设计、软件、意识等。由此可见，产品不仅是指物质实体，而且指能满足人们某种需要的服务。从营销的角度来看，产品包括实物及更广泛的内容。

Product refers to anything that can be brought to the market to satisfy certain desires and needs, including material objects, services, location, design, software, consciousness, etc. Thus, not only do products refer to a physical entity, but also to services which can meet needs. From the perspective of marketing, products contain material objects and a broader range of contents.

(1) 产品的实体性，指市场上产品的具体形态，包括产品的实体及其品质、式样和包装等。它是产品的物质属性。

The substantiality of a product refers to the concrete form of the product in market, including the product's entity, quality, style, packaging, etc. These are material properties of the product.

(2) 产品的有效性，指产品提供给消费者的一种基本效用和利益，它是人们的主观价值的体现。

The effectiveness of a product is the basic utility and benefit that products can provide to consumers. It is the embodiment of people's subjective value.

(3) 产品的可靠性，指产品实现其效用的可靠程度。

The reliability of a product refers to how much the product can realize its functions.

(4) 产品的经济性，指消费者在购买和使用产品过程中所花的费用与产品的使用价值之比。消费者一般希望用尽量少的费用购买尽量多的使用价值。

The economy of a product refers to the ratio of the cost of buying the product and the use value of the product. Consumers generally want to spend as little money as possible to buy more use values.

二、产品整体概念 Total Product Concept

市场营销学中的产品概念已经远远超出了传统有形实物及生产劳动所得的范畴，这就是"产品整体概念"。

Product concept in marketing goes far beyond the category of traditionally tangible material and income from productive labor. This is what is meant by "total product concept".

根据市场营销学中的产品整体概念，产品可分为三个层次：核心产品、形式产品、附加产品，这三个层次共同组成了一个有机完整的产品共同体，其构成体系如图6-1所示。

According to the total product concept in marketing, products are divided into three classes: core product, actual product and additional product. They constitute an organic and integrated product community. The constitutional system is as shown in Figure 6-1.

第六章 产品策略
Product Strategies

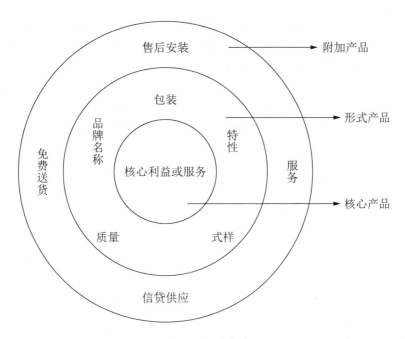

图 6-1 产品整体概念

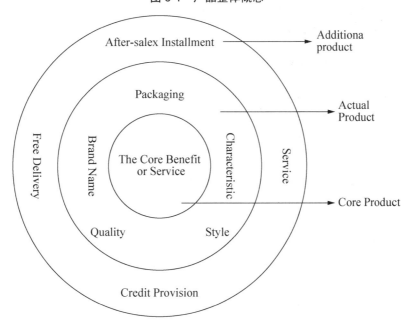

Figure 6-1　Overall Product Concept

(一)核心产品 Core Product

核心产品也称为实质产品,是指向购买者提供的能够满足其需要的基本效用或核心利益。例如,电视机产品的核心是通过图像和音响使消费者获得各种信息与娱乐的效用,而不是为了使消费者获得装有某些机械、电器零部件的一个箱子。产品实体只是产品效用或利益的载体,消费者购买产品的最终目的不是载体本身,而是通过载体达到某种功效。

Core product is also known as substance product. It can provide basic utility or core interests to meet the buyers' needs. For example, the core benefit of a TV is to allow consumers to obtain all sorts of information and entertainment through image and sound, rather than to simply permit consumers to get a box equipped with certain mechanical and electrical components. Product entity is only the carrier of utility or benefit. The final purpose for consumers to purchase products is not to obtain the carrier itself, but to access some benefits with the carrier.

(二)形式产品 Actual Product

形式产品,是指核心产品借以实现的形式。是企业向消费者提供的产品实体和服务的外观。产品的外观出现于市场时,可以为顾客提供可识别的面貌。形式产品由五个标志构成,即质量、特性、式样、品牌名称和包装。具有相同效用的产品,其存在的形态可能有较大的差别。

Actual product refers to the form in which core product can realize its core benefits. This is the appearance of the product entity and services provided by the enterprise for consumers. When the product appears in the market, customers can recognize it through its appearance. The actual product consists of five signs: quality, characteristics, style, brand name and packaging. Products with the same utility may exist in very different forms.

(三)附加产品 Additional Product

附加产品也称为延伸产品,是指顾客购买形式产品时所获得的全部附加服务和利益,包括购买合同中含有的信贷供应、免费送货、保证、安装和售后服务等条款。附加产品概念的提出满足了消费者的某种需要;另外,企业为赢得竞争优势,而着眼于向消费者提供比竞争对手更多的附加利益。

Additional product is also known as augmented product. It refers to all additional services and benefits included in the purchase agreement, including credit provision, free delivery, guarantee, installment and after-sales service, etc. The concept of additional product is developed to meet the consumers' needs. Moreover, in order to gain competitive advantage, the enterprise pays extra attention to provide consumers with more additional benefits than its competitors.

核心产品、形式产品和附加产品作为产品的三个层次,是不可分割并紧密相连的,它们构成了产品的整体概念。其中,核心产品是核心、基础和本质;核心产品必须转变为形式产品才能得以实现;企业在提供产品的同时,还要提供广泛的服务和附加利益,形成附加产品。产品整体概念的三个层次清晰地体现了以顾客为中心的现代营销观念,为企业开发适合消费者需要的有形与无形产品、挖掘新的市场机会提供了新的思路,给企业产品开发设计提供了新的方向,此外为企业的产品差异化提供了新的线索,且要求企业重视各种售后服务。

The core product, actual product and additional product, as three dimensions of products, are inseparable and interdependent, and they form the total product concept. The core product is the core, foundation and essence; the core product can only be realized by transforming into the actual product; the company provides products, and at the same time provides a wide range of services and additional benefits to form the additional product. The three dimensions of the total product concept clearly embody the modern "customer oriented" marketing notion. They provide a new direction for the enterprise to develop tangible and intangible products for consumers and to explore new market opportunities. They also offer a new direction to the enterprise's product development and design; in addition, they provide new clues for product differentiation and require enterprises to attach importance to all kinds of after-sales services.

三、产品的分类 Categories of Product

产品根据其不同特点，可分为以下几类。

According to different features, products can be classified into the following categories.

(一)根据产品的耐用性与有形性分类 Classification According to Product's Durability and Tangibility

产品根据其耐用性和有形性分类，如图 6-2 所示。

Classification according to product's durability and tangibility is as shown in Figure 6-2.

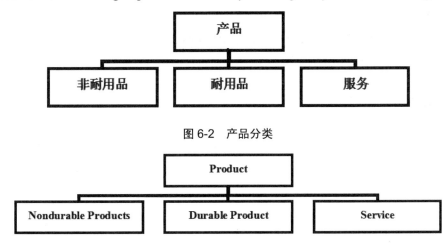

图 6-2 产品分类

Figure 6-2 Categories of Product

1. 非耐用品 Nondurable Goods

非耐用品指使用时间较短，甚至一次性消费的商品，如手纸、糖果、牙膏等。这类产品单位价值较低，消耗快；另外，消费者往往经常、反复购买，并大量使用。如果企业生产的是非耐用品，那么除了在产品质量上下功夫以外，还应在销售网点上多下功夫，才能经营成功。

Nondurable goods refer to the goods with short use time, and even one-off consumption goods, such as toilet paper, candies, toothpaste, etc. The value of these products per unit is low, and the products are consumed quickly; besides, consumers often purchase them again and again and make heavy use of these goods. If the enterprise produces nondurable goods and wants to achieve success, it must focus on both the product quality and on the sales outlet.

2. 耐用品 Durable Goods

耐用品指能使用较长时间(至少在 1 年以上)的物品,如电冰箱、汽车、电视机和机械设备等。耐用品单位价值较高,购买频率较低;需要许多的人员推销和服务,销售价格较高,利润也较大。

Durable goods refer to goods that can be used for a long time, at least over one year, such as refrigerators, cars, TVs, mechanical equipment and so on. The value of durable goods per unit is relatively high, but purchase frequency is low; they require a lot of personal selling and service with higher prices and greater profits.

3. 服务 Service

服务是指为他人做事,并使他人从中受益的一种有偿或无偿的活动。服务不以实物形式而以提供活劳动的形式满足他人某种特殊需要。

Service means to do things for others, and enable others to get benefit from paid or unpaid activities. It provides living labor but not material objects to meet others' special needs.

(二)根据销售的目标对象及产品的用途分类 Classification According to Sales Target and Use of Products

1. 消费品 Consumption Goods

消费品,是最终消费者购买的用于个人消费的产品。对消费品可从不同的角度按不同的标准划分为多种类型。例如,从营销的角度来分析,可以根据消费者的购买行为特征把消费品分成以下四种类型,如图 6-3 所示。

Consumption goods refer to products bought by consumers for personal consumption. According to different standards consumption goods can be divided into several types from different angles. For example, from the perspective of marketing, we can, according to the characteristics of consumers' buying behavior, divide consumption goods into the following four types, as shown in Figure 6-3.

(1) 便利品。便利品是指价格低廉,消费者要经常购买或需要随时购买的消费品或服务。消费者在购买此类产品时,花费的时间越少越好,不用与其他产品作任何深入的比较,希望就近、即刻买到。生活日用品,如肥皂、洗衣粉、手纸、牙膏、毛巾、饮料等类商品就是属于此类商品。对于生产经营此类商品的企业来说,应尽量增加销售此类商品的网点,把网点设在居民住宅区的附近设在就显得特别重要。

Convenience goods refer to goods or services with low price which consumers often buy or need to buy when necessary. When consumers buy such products, it is better to spend less time while purchasing and not make any deep comparison of these products, hoping to buy them nearby and immediately. Everyday goods, such as soaps, washing powder, tissue, toothpaste, towels, beverages and so on, all belong to convenience goods. The enterprises producing and selling this kind of commodity need to increase the sales outlets of this commodity as greatly as possible. It is particularly important to establish these outlets near residential areas.

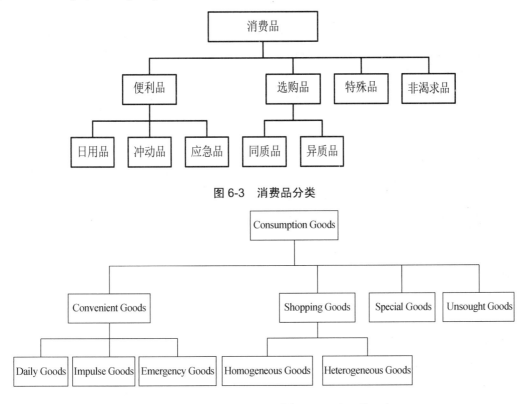

图 6-3 消费品分类

Figure 6-3 Classification of Consumption Goods

(2) 选购品。选购品是消费者购买频率比较低的消费品和服务，因其耐用程度较高，不需要经常购买。所以，消费者有必要和可能花较多的时间和精力去多家商店物色合适的商品，并注重产品的品牌、特色及价格等。服装、皮鞋、农具和家电产品是典型的选购品。为此，企业要根据消费者的购买行为，赋予自己的产品以特色，并且不断地向消费者传达有关商品的信息，帮助消费者了解有关产品的专门知识。

Shopping goods. These are goods and services that consumers don't buy frequently because they are durable. So it is necessary and possible for consumers to spend more time and energy on looking for appropriate goods in various shops and pay more attention to the brand, features and prices of products. Clothing, leather shoes, farm tools and home appliances are typical shopping goods. Therefore, according to the consumer's buying behavior, enterprises should endow their products with characteristics, and constantly convey information of the commodities to consumers to help them understand particular characteristics of the products.

(3) 特殊品。特殊品，是指具有特殊效益或特定品牌，并拥有一批购买者愿意花精力去认定其品牌而后进行购买的消费品或服务。如具有特殊品牌和造型的奢侈品、名牌服装、特殊邮票、供收藏的钱币等商品。消费者注重的是商标与信誉，而不注重价格，在购买前愿意努力去搜寻这类商品。

Special goods. These are goods or services with special benefits or specific brands that attract a group of buyers willing to spend energy to know the product's brand and then to buy it. These include luxury goods with special brand and model, designer clothes, special stamps, coins for collection and so on. Consumers focus on brand and reputation of these goods, but not on price; they are willing to make an effort to find these goods before buying them.

（4）非渴求品。指消费者不了解或即使了解也不想购买的产品。传统的非渴求品有刚上市的新产品、人寿保险、墓地、墓碑以及百科全书等。对于非渴求品，应加强广告宣传和人员推销工作，使消费者对这些产品有所了解并产生兴趣，从而吸引潜在顾客，扩大销售。

Unsought goods. These are goods that consumers don't know about or want to buy even if they do know. Traditional unsought goods include new products, life insurance, cemeteries, gravestones, encyclopedias etc. While selling unsought goods, the enterprise should supplement its advertising effort and widen personal selling to make consumers know and take an interest in the products. In this case, the enterprise can attract potential customers and expand sales.

2. 产业用品 Industrial Goods

产业用品，是购买后用来进一步加工或用于企业经营的产品或服务。依据产品在生产过程中的重要程度及其相对成本来划分，产业用品又分为原材料与零部件、资本项目、供应品和服务，如图6-4所示。

Industrial goods are products or services purchased for further processing, or for business operation. According to the importance of the product in the production process as well as their relative costs, industrial goods are divided into raw materials and components, capital items, supplies and services, as is shown in Figure 6-4.

图 6-4 产业用品分类

Figure 6-4 Category of Industrial Goods

(1) 原材料和零部件。原材料和零部件指最终要完全转化到生产者所生产的成品中去的产业用品，可分为以下两种类别：①原材料。这是农、林、渔、畜、矿产等部门提供的产品，构成了产品的物质实体，如粮食、羊毛、牛奶、石油、铜、铁矿石等。这些产品的销售一般都有国家的专门销售渠道，按照标准价来成交，并且往往要订立长期的销售合同。②零部件和半成品。零部件是被用来进行整件组装的制成品。如汽车的电瓶、轮胎、服装上的纽扣、自行车的坐垫等。这些产品在不改变其原来形态的情况下，可以直接成为最终产品的一部分。半成品，是经过加工处理的原材料，将被用来再次加工。

Raw Materials and Components. Raw materials and components are industrial articles which are later transformed completely into finished products. They can be divided into the following two categories: ①Raw materials. These are products provided by the sectors of farming, forestry, fisheries, livestock and minerals, which provide the material entity of the product, such as grain, wool, milk, oil, copper, iron ore, etc. Usually there are special national distribution channels to sell these products. The products are sold according to the standard prices, and long-term sales contracts are usually signed. ②Components and semi-finished products. Components are articles used to assemble products, such as car batteries, tyres, clothing buttons, bike seat cushions, etc. These articles can become a part of the final product directly without changing their original form. Semi-finished products are processed raw materials used for processing again.

(2) 资本项目。资本项目是指它的价值部分进入产成品中，帮助购买者生产和运营的产业用品，可以分为以下两大类：①装备。由建筑物、地权和固定设备所组成。建筑物主要指厂房、办公楼、仓库等。地权是矿山开采权、森林采伐权、土地耕种权等。固定设备指发动机、锅炉、机床、电子计算机、牵引车等主要的生产设备。②附属设备。这种设备比装备的金额要小，耐用期也相对要短，是非主要生产设备，包括各种工具、夹具、模具、办公打字机等等。购买者对此类产品的通用化、标准化的要求比较高，价格和服务是用户选择中间商时所要考虑的主要因素。促销时，人员推销要比广告重要得多。

Capital Items. Capital items are industrial articles with partial value embodied in the finished goods to help producer's production and operation. They can be divided into the following two categories: ①Equipment. Equipment is composed of buildings, land ownership and fixed equipment. Buildings mainly refer to workshops, office buildings, warehouses, etc. Land ownership includes mining concessions, forest concessions, land-use rights, and so on. Fixed equipment refers to the main production equipment such as engines, boilers, machine tools, computers, tractors, etc. ②Accessory facilities. Accessory facilities are cheaper than equipment. They are not durable and are not the main production equipment. They include all kinds of tools, fixtures, moulds, office typewriters, and so on. Buyers have high requirements for the generalization and standardization of such products, and price and service are the main factors to be considered for users while selecting middlemen. Personal promotion is more important than advertising in general promotion.

(3) 供应品。供应品并不直接参与生产过程，而是为生产过程的顺利实现提供帮助，这相当于是生产者市场中的方便品，如打字纸、铅笔、墨水、机器润滑油、扫除用具和油漆等。供应品主要是标准品,由于其消费量大,购买者分布比较分散,所以往往要通过中间商来销售。购买者对此类产品也无特别的品牌偏好,价格与服务是购买时考虑的主要因素。

Supplies. Supplies are not directly involved in the production process, but provide help to finish the production process smoothly. They are equal to the convenience goods in the producer market, such as typing paper, pencils, ink, machine oil, cleaning appliances, paint, etc. Supplies are mainly standard products. With heavy consumption and dispersed buyers' distribution, it's always the intermediaries who sell the products. The buyers also have no special brand preference, and price and service are the main factors to be considered in buying the products.

(4) 服务。服务指有助于生产过程的顺利进行并使作业简易化服务,主要包括维修服务和咨询服务,前者如清扫、刷油漆、修理办公用具等,后者主要是业务咨询、法律咨询、委托广告等。这类服务通常以签订合同的形式提供。

Services. These are beneficial to the smooth progress of the production process, and can make the operation easy. They mainly include maintenance service and consulting service; the former includes cleaning, painting, office appliance repair, etc., and the latter includes business consulting, legal consulting, advertising consignation and so on. These kinds of services are usually written in contract.

第二节　产品生命周期策略
Product Life Cycle Strategies

一、产品生命周期的概念 Concept of Product Life Cycle

产品生命周期是指一种产品从投入市场开始到退出市场为止的周期性变化的过程。每一种产品都有一个研制、生产、投放市场和被市场淘汰的过程。一种产品从试制成功到开始投放市场,直到被市场淘汰的整个阶段,称为该产品的生命周期,即该产品从上市到退出市场的时间间隔。产品的生命周期是客观存在的,主要取决于产品上市后的需求变化和新产品的更新换代速度。

Product life cycle is a process full of cyclical changes, starting from the launch of the product and ending with withdrawal from the market. Each product has a process of market research, production, launching into the market and elimination by the market. Product life cycle is the whole stage of the product from successful trial production, to its introduction into the market, then to its elimination from the market; it is the time interval from the product launch into the market to the exit from the market. Product life cycle has objective existence, which mainly depends on demanding phase of the product and renewal speed of new products.

产品的生命周期是产品的经济寿命,即在市场上销售的时间,而不是使用寿命。产品的使用寿命是指产品的自然寿命,即具体产品实体从开始使用到消耗磨损废弃为止所经历的时间。

Product life cycle is the economic life of the product. It is the sales period in the market, not the service life. Service life refers to the natural life of the product and it is the time during which the specific product begins to be used till it's consumed, worn and abandoned.

从理论上分析，完整的产品生命周期可分为导入期、成长期、成熟期和衰退期四个阶段。产品销售额和利润在市场的不同阶段有不同的表现，通常表现为类似 S 型、近似正态分布的曲线，被称为产品生命周期曲线图，如图 6-5 所示。

In theory, a complete product life cycle can be divided into four stages: introduction, growth, maturity and decline. Sales and profits of the products vary in different stages in the market. It is usually characterized by S type, and the curve with approximately normal distribution which is known as the product life cycle graph, as is shown in Figure 6-5.

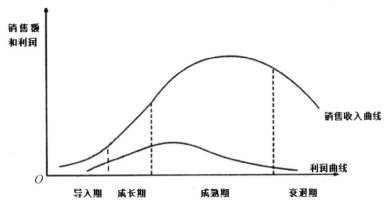

图 6-5　产品市场生命周期曲线图

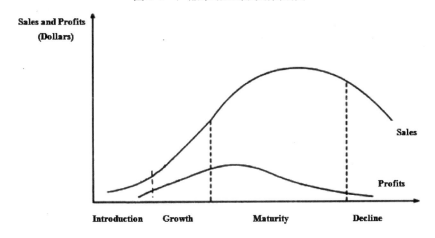

Figure 6-5　Graph of Product Life Cycle

在图 6-5 中，产品导入期，是指在市场上推出该项产品后，其产品销售呈缓慢增长状态的阶段。市场成长期，是指该产品在市场上迅速为消费者所接受，销售额迅速上升的阶段。市场成熟期，是指大多数购买者已经接受该项产品，产品市场销售额从明显上升逐步趋于缓慢下降的阶段。市场衰退期，是指销售额急剧下降的阶段。

In Figure 6-5, the introduction stage refers to the period during which sales grow slowly after the product's initial launching in the market. The growth stage means the period when the products are quickly accepted by consumers and sales increase rapidly. During maturity stage, most buyers have accepted the products and product sales increase outstandingly at first and then gradually tend to slow down, while the sales fall sharply at the decline stage.

图 6-5 中的利润曲线的变化趋向与销售额曲线大体相同，但是变化的时间却不一样。当销售额曲线还在上升时，利润额曲线已开始下降了，这是由于竞争而压低了售价所造成的。

In Figure 6-5, the changing tendency of the profit curve is approximately the same as the sales curve, but they have different time change. When the sales curve is still on the rise, the profit curve has begun to decline. The reason for this situation is that competition leads to low prices.

需要说明的是，图 6-5 显示的是产品市场生命周期的一般性特征，在现实经济生活中，并不是所有的产品生命周期都完全符合这种理论形态，还有一些其他的特殊表现形态。

What needs to be stated is that Figure 6-5 shows the general characteristics of the product life cycle, while in real economic life, not all of the product life cycles are completely in keeping with this model, and there are other special forms of expression.

二、产品生命周期各阶段的特点及营销策略 Characteristics and Marketing Strategies at Every Stage of the Product Life Cycle

研究产品生命周期规律，就是要针对产品生命周期各阶段的市场特点，采取相应的营销对策。

The purpose of research into the regularity of product life cycles is to adopt corresponding marketing strategies according to the market characteristics of a product life cycle at each stage.

(一)导入期的特点及企业营销策略 Characteristics at Introduction Stage and Enterprise Marketing Strategy

1. 导入期的特点 Characteristics at Introduction Stage

(1) 生产批量小，制造成本高。因为新产品刚开始生产时，技术不够稳定，不能批量生产，次品率较高。另外，根据市场反应测试的改进费用高，因此制造成本相对较高。

Low output and high manufacturing costs. Because the technology of the new product is not stable, it can't reach quantity production and the defective rate is high. In addition, according to market reaction tests, the improvement cost is high, and thus the manufacturing cost is relatively high.

(2) 营销费用高。新产品刚进入市场，消费者对其性能、质量、款式、价格、优点等不了解、不认识、不认同，促使企业加大推销和宣传的力度，这就必然引起营销费用的提高。

High marketing costs. When new products come into the market, consumers don't know about understand or accept their performance, quality, style, price, merits, etc. This drives the enterprise to put more effort into promotion and publicity. In this situation, all marketing expenses will increase.

(3) 销售数量少。新产品投入市场，由于消费者不了解，大部分顾客不愿放弃或改变自己以往的消费行为，只有少数创新者、早期接受者购买产品，因而销售数量少。

Small sales quantity. Because customers don't know much about the new products, most of consumers are reluctant to give up or change their previous buying behavior and only a few innovators and early adopters buy the products. So sales quantity is low.

(4) 利润较少，甚至出现经营亏损，这是企业承担市场风险最大的阶段。但这个阶段市场竞争者较少，企业若建立有效的营销系统，就可以将新产品快速推进引入阶段，进而进入市场发展阶段。

Less profit or even deficit. This is the largest marketing risk stage undertaken by the enterprise. At this stage there are few competitors. If the enterprise establishes an effective marketing system, new products can rapidly step into the introduction stage and then into the market development stage.

2. 导入期的营销策略 Marketing Strategy at Introduction Stage

根据导入期产品的特点，企业必须积极收集市场对新产品的反应，大力开展广告宣传活动，疏通销售渠道，千方百计打开销路。具体有四种策略可供选择。

According to the characteristics of the products at the introduction stage, enterprises must actively collect the consumers' reaction to new products, and carry out advertising campaigns on a big scale, clear the sales channels, and increase sales by all possible means. Here there are four specific and optional strategies.

(1) 快速掠取策略，又称"双高策略"。即以高价格和高促销推出新产品。实行高价格是为了在每一单位销售额中获取最大的利润，高促销费用是为了引起目标市场的注意，加快市场渗透。成功地实施这一策略，可以赚取较大的利润，尽快收回开发新产品的投资。实施该策略的市场条件是：市场上有较大的需求潜力；目标顾客具有求新心理，急于购买新产品，并愿意为此付出高价；企业面临潜在竞争者的威胁，需要及早树立名牌。

Fast predatory strategy, also known as "double-high strategy", involves launching new products at high price and with high promotion. With the implementation of this strategy, the enterprise can obtain the biggest profits from each sales unit. High promotion spending is to attract the attention of the target market and accelerate market penetration. Successful implementation of this strategy can earn greater profits and retrieve the development investment of a new product as soon as possible. The market conditions to carry out this strategy are as follows: there is great potential of demand in the market; the target customers are eager to buy new products and willing to pay a high price because of their psychology in seeking new products; the enterprise faces the threat of potential competitors, and needs to establish a famous brand presence as early as possible.

(2) 缓慢掠取策略，又称选择性渗透策略。即以高价格和低促销费用将新产品推入市场。高价格和低促销成本相结合可以使企业获得更多利润。实施该策略的市场条件是：市场规模相对较小，竞争威胁不大；市场上大多数用户对该产品没有过多疑虑；适当的高价能被消费者接受。

Slow predatory strategy, also known as the selective penetration strategy, aims to launch new products into the market with low promotion cost and high price. The combination of high price and low promotion cost can enable the enterprise to gain more profits. The market conditions to implement this strategy are: the market scale is relatively small and there is not much competitive threat; the majority of consumers don't have too much doubt about this product; the appropriate high price can be accepted by customers.

(3) 快速渗透策略，又称密集式渗透策略。即以低价格和高促销费用推出新产品。目的在于先发制人，以最快的速度打入市场，该策略可以给企业带来最快的市场渗透率和最高的市场占有率。实施这一策略的条件是：产品市场容量很大；潜在消费者对产品不了解，且对价格十分敏感；潜在竞争激烈；产品的单位制造成本可随生产规模和销售量的扩大迅速下降。

Fast penetration strategy, also known as intensive penetration strategy, is to launch new products at a low price with high promotion spending, aiming to make a preemptive strike and occupy the market at the fastest speed. This strategy can bring enterprises the fastest market penetration and the biggest market share. The conditions of carrying out this strategy are as follows: market capacity of the product is large; the potential customers do not understand the product and are sensitive to the price; the potential competition is serious; the product's unit manufacturing costs may drop rapidly along with the expansion of production scale and sales.

(4) 缓慢渗透策略，又称双低策略。即企业以低价格和低促销费用推出新产品。低价是为了促使市场迅速地接受新产品，低促销费用则可以实现更多的净利润。企业坚信该市场需求价格弹性较高，而促销弹性较小。实施这一策略的基本条件是：市场容量较大；潜在顾客易于或已经了解此项新产品且对价格十分敏感；有相当的潜在竞争者准备加入竞争行列。

Slow penetration strategy, also known as "double-low strategy", is that the enterprise launches new product at a low price and with low promotion cost. Low price can prompt the customers to accept the new product quickly, while low promotion cost permits greater net profit. The enterprise firmly believes that customers' price elasticity of demand is higher, but promotion elasticity is low. The basic conditions for implementing this strategy are as follows: the market capacity is big; the potential customers easily or already know the new product and are very sensitive to the price; considerable potential competitors are ready to join in the competition.

(二)成长期的特点及企业的营销策略 Characteristics and Enterprise's Marketing Strategy at Growth Stage

1. 成长期的特点 Characteristics at Growth Stage

(1) 销售量增长很快。消费者对新产品已经熟悉，其销售金额大幅度上扬。厂家和商家在经营处于这一时期的产品时,一般都可获得丰硕的经营成果。

Sales grow quickly. Consumers are familiar with the new product, so the sales rise sharply. Manufacturers and merchants often can achieve fruitful results at this stage.

(2) 产品质量日趋稳定。企业已形成规模化生产,并取得了良好的规模效益。产品已定型,技术工艺成熟。

Product quality tends to be stable. The enterprise has set up large-scale production, and achieved good economies of scale. The product has been finalized at design, and the technology is mature.

(3) 市场竞争加剧。大批竞争者加入,其产销的垄断性基本消除。

Market competition becomes more severe. A large number of competitors join in, so the marketing monopoly of the product is basically eliminated.

(4) 建立了比较理想的营销渠道。

An ideal marketing channel has been established.

(5) 市场价格趋于下降。

Market price tends to fall.

(6) 促销费用水平基本稳定或略有提高。为了适应竞争和市场扩张的需要,企业的促销费用水平基本稳定或略有提高,但对销售额的比率下降。

Promotion cost level is basically stable, or increases slightly. In order to meet the needs of competition and market expansion, the level of business promotion expense is basically stable or increases lightly, but the proportion to the sales declines.

(7) 企业利润迅速上升。这是因为促销费用分摊到更多销量上,单位生产成本迅速下降。

Profit rises rapidly because the promotion cost can be allocated to more sales, and production cost per unit falls rapidly.

2. 成长期的营销策略 Marketing Strategy at Growth Stage

这一阶段的主要任务是,防止产品粗制滥造、失信于顾客,设法使产品的销售和利润快速增长,回收投资。企业可选取的主要营销策略有以下几种。

The main task at this stage is to avoid making a product of inferior quality and losing the trust of customers. The enterprise should try to make the product sales and profit grow rapidly and recoup investment. The enterprise can choose from the following marketing strategies.

1) 规模策略 Scale Strategy

这一策略是指集中人力、物力、财力在短时间内迅速完善生产能力和生产工艺,以迅速增加或扩大生产批量,增加市场供应,形成规模效益。企业应根据用户需求和其他市场信息,不断提高产品质量,努力开发产品的新款式、新型号、新用途。

This strategy involves intensively taking advantage of human, material and financial resources to perfect production capacity and technology in a short time in order to increase or expand production, enlarge market supplies and form the scale merit. According to users' requirements and other market information, the enterprise constantly improves product quality, pays attention to developing new styles, new models and new functions.

2) 形象策略 Image Strategy

从质量、性能、式样等方面努力对产品加以改进，寻找并进入新的细分市场；使用注册商标，取得商标专用权；加强服务、加强促销，促销策略的重心从建立产品知名度转向树立产品形象，以建立品牌偏好，争取更多的顾客。

Try to improve the product from the aspects of quality, performance, style, etc, to find and enter a new market segment; use the registered trademark to get exclusive right to use the trademark; strengthen service and promotion; change the key of sales promotion from building awareness of the product to establishing product image to build brand preference and strive for more customers.

3) 降价策略 Price-cut Strategy

在扩大生产的基础上，选择时机，适当降低产品价格，以吸引对价格敏感的潜在消费者，进行有效、成功的竞争。

Achieve effective and successful competition by choosing the proper time and reducing product price to attract potential consumers who are sensitive to the price on the basis of expanding production.

4) 渠道策略 Channel Strategy

重新评价渠道选择决策，巩固原有渠道，增加新的销售渠道，开拓新的市场。

Reevaluate decisions about channel selection; consolidate old channels; increase new sales channels and exploit new markets.

(三) 成熟期的特点及企业的营销策略 Characteristics and Enterprise's Marketing Strategy at Maturity Stage

1. 成熟期的特点 Characteristics at Maturity Stage

成熟期是产品市场生命周期的一个"鼎盛"时期，其前半期的销售额逐渐上扬而达到最高峰，在稳定一个相对短暂的时期后，其销售额开始缓慢回落，这时便进入了一个转折时期，即成熟期的后半期。成熟期还可以进一步分为如下三个时期：一是成长成熟期。此时期各销售渠道基本呈饱和状态，增长率缓慢上升，还有少数后续的购买者继续进入市场。二是稳定成熟期。由于市场饱和，消费平稳，产品销售稳定，销售增长率一般只与购买者人数成比例，如无新购买者则增长率停滞或下降。三是衰退成熟期。销售水平显著下降，原有用户的兴趣已开始转向其他产品和替代品。产品过剩，竞争加剧，一些缺乏竞争能力的企业将渐渐被新的竞争者取代，同时，新加入的竞争者的数量减少。竞争者之间各有自己特定的目标顾客，市场份额变动不大，因此难以有所突破。

The maturity stage is the "peak" period of a product life cycle. The sales in the first half period rise to a peak, then stabilize in a relative short period. After that, sales begin to slow down. This is a transitional period and also the second half of the mature period. The maturity stage can also be further divided into the following three periods. The first is the growth maturity period. During this period sales channels are in a saturated state; the growth rate slowly rises and a few buyers continue to enter the market. The second is the stable maturity period. As the market is saturated, consumption is steady and product sales are stable, and the sales growth rate is generally proportional to the number of buyers. If there are no new buyers, the growth rate stagnates or falls. The third is the recession maturity stage. The sales level reduces significantly, and the original user's interest has begun to turn to other products and substitutes. Supply exceeds demand; competition increases, and some enterprises which lack competitiveness will gradually be replaced by new competitors. And the number of new competitors falls. The competitors all have their own specific target customers, and market share doesn't change much, so it's difficult to break in.

成熟期产品的特点集中体现在如下几个方面。

Product characteristics at the maturity stage are embodied in the following several aspects.

(1) 产品质量稳定,产品结构基本定型,工艺成熟。厂家在研制、生产出新产品后,将其投放市场。经过导入期、成长期的试销和成批销售,厂家根据反馈的有关产品的信息,对产品结构进行多次调整,进而使产品结构定型。同时,在较长时间的试制和批量生产过程中,厂家已积累了许多宝贵的经验,其工艺日趋完善与成熟。正因如此,成熟期的产品在性能及质量方面再度进行改进的余地已经不大。

Product quality is stable; the product structure is basically finalized and the technology is mature. After developing and producing new products, the enterprise launches them onto the market. Through trial sales and wholesale at the introduction and growth stages, manufacturers adjust the product structure many times based on feedback information. They then further finalize the product structure. At the same time, after a long process of trial production and quantity production, the enterprise has accumulated valuable experiences, and its technology has become increasingly perfect and mature. Therefore, there is less room for products to be improved in performance and quality at the maturity stage.

(2) 产品销售额在逐渐达到顶峰后开始缓慢回落。成熟期产品对广大消费者来说已属半新半旧产品,相当一部分人已购买和使用过这类商品,他们在使用这类商品时,已对产品的性能、质量有所了解,并信心十足地重复购买,从而大幅度提高了购买量,致使销售额在成熟期的前半期达到顶峰。但是在成熟期的后半期,市场上开始出现同类的新产品,一些勇敢的试用者和其他少数消费者将眼光转向外观美丽、功能更先进的新产品,从而将成熟期的相同类型的半新半旧产品的购买量减少下来。因此,成熟期又是一个由"盛"转"衰"的转折时期。

After reaching their peak, the product sales gradually begin to slow down. For consumers, the products at maturity stage have become semi-new products, because quite a number of people have bought and used these products; they know the products' performance and quality while using them and confidently repurchase them. This significantly increases purchases, and then the sales in the first half of the mature period reach their peak. But in the second half of the maturity stage, the same kind of new products start to appear in the market, a few brave testers and a few other consumers turn their sight to new products with beautiful appearance and advanced functions. This makes the purchases of the semi-new products with the same type at maturity stage decrease. Therefore, the maturity stage is a turning period from prosperity to decline.

(3) 产品价格相差不大，竞争处于"白热化"。成熟期产品生产厂家众多，其技术水平和生产成本趋于平衡，因此，产品销售价格基本相同，从导致市场竞争"白热化"。需要指出的是，在成熟期上半期，市场供应大都基本平衡，市场竞争的激烈程度较下半期相对缓和。大下半期由于市场供大于求的趋势日益明显，厂家和商家为了减少库存积压，纷纷采取各种促销手段，从而加大了市场竞争的激烈程度。

Price difference is not great and competition becomes "white-hot". There are many manufacturers at the maturity stage and the technical level and production cost are stable. Therefore, the similar sales prices, lead to "white and hot" competition. What must be pointed out is in the first half period of the maturity stage, market supply is basically in the balance, and the intensity of market competition is relatively towards detente compared with the second half of the period. During the second half of the period, because the market oversupply trend is increasingly obvious and in order to reduce inventory, the manufacturers and merchants seek all kinds of promotion methods, which strengthens the fierce market competition.

(4) 企业经营状况不尽如人意，利润开始下降。激烈的市场竞争使企业的宣传费用增加，加上库存产品的积压及资金周转速度缓慢，所付出的银行利息开始增加，企业的利润开始下降。在这种情况下，企业的经营前景不容乐观。

The operating conditions of the enterprises are not very desirable, and profits begin to fall. Fierce market competition causes the enterprises' publicity costs to increase, combined with overstocking of products and slow speed of capital turnover. This increases bank interest and decreases corporate profits. In that case, the operation prospect is not optimistic.

2. 成熟期的营销策略 Marketing Strategy at Maturity Stage

这一阶段的主要任务是集中一切力量，牢牢占领市场，尽可能延长产品成熟期，为企业带来更多的利益，积累更多的资金。企业在这一时期可以采取的营销策略有以下几种。

The main task at this stage is to focus all forces to firmly occupy the market, extend the maturity stage as far as possible, bring more benefits for the enterprise, and accumulate more money. The marketing strategies that the enterprises can apply during this period are as follows.

(1) 市场改良策略。包括寻找尚未采用本产品的新市场或市场中的新部分；增加产品的新用途，创造新的消费方式等，以增加用户使用次数和用户每次使用量。

Market improvement strategy. This includes searching for a new market which doesn't include the product or finding out new parts in the market; expanding new use of the product, creating new way of consumption, thus increasing the user frequency and amount required each time.

(2) 产品改良策略。也称为"产品再推出"，是指改进产品的品质如提高耐用性和可靠性，或改进产品的特性，如增加适应性或方便性，或改进产品的式样如提升产品的外观或服务，再将产品投放市场。

Product improvement strategy is also known as the "product re-launch". This means to put the products back on the market after improving quality aspects such as durability and reliability, or features such as increasing flexibility or convenience, or style features such as improving the appearance of the product or service.

(3) 营销组合改良。是指通过改变定价、销售渠道及促销方式来延长产品成熟期。但营销组合改进容易被竞争对手模仿，尤其是降价、附加服务等。对此，企业必须事先做好充分考虑，以防出现紧急事件。

Improvement of marketing mix. This refers to extending the maturity stage of the products by changing the pricing, sales channels and promotion methods. But these improvements can easily be imitated by competitors, especially price, additional services, and so on. So the enterprise must consider in advance any emergencies which may arise.

(4) 转移生产场地。即把处于成熟期的产品转移到某些生产成本低、市场潜力大的国家和地区。

Changing the location of production refers to transferring production at the maturity stage to countries and regions with low production cost and large market potential.

(四)衰退期的特点及企业的营销策略 Characteristics and Enterprise's Marketing Strategy at Decline Stage

1. 衰退期的特点 Characteristics at Decline Stage

产品进入衰退期，呈现以下特点。

Products present the following features at the decline stage.

(1) 消费者的兴趣转移到别处。市场上出现了功能更先进、外形更美观的同类新产品。这些新产品转移了部分消费者的注意力。于是，在这部分人的眼中，衰退期的产品已显得陈旧，不值得购买，甚至已经完全过时。

Consumer attention is transferred elsewhere. New products appear with more advanced functions and more beautiful images. These new products capture part of consumers' attention and the older products appear out-of-date, aging and unworthy to buy, even completely obsolete.

(2) 产品的销售量急剧下降。由于大部分消费者已对衰退期产品不感兴趣，并将购买力投入同类的新产品或较新产品上面，因而这一时期的旧产品的销售量开始急剧下降。

Sales fall sharply. Since most consumers are not interested in products at the decline stage, and put their purchasing power into similar new products or relatively new products, the sales of old products during this period begin to drop sharply.

(3) 利润明显下降，部分企业出现了亏损。由于产品销路受阻，企业库存出现严重积压，其仓储费增加，资金周转速度明显减慢，银行利息开始上升。由此导致企业成本大幅度上升，利润明显下降，部分企业开始出现了亏损。

Profits decline notably and some companies suffer losses. Because of poor sales, overstocking is increasingly risky, warehousing costs increase, the capital turnover speed slows down considerably and bank interest starts to rise. Consequently, costs rise dramatically, profit decline may accelerate, and some companies even begin to make losses.

(4) 价格已下降到最低水平，库存产品做大幅度削价处理，企业濒临破产的危机。严重的经营亏损最终导致企业中断生产和经营。于是，企业正式转产，开始开发、生产其他的新产品。留在市场上的企业逐渐减少产品附带服务，削减促销预算，以维持最低水平的经营。

Because price has dropped to a lower level and stock is largely sold at a low price, many enterprises may be on the verge of bankruptcy. Severe operating losses eventually lead to the suspension of enterprise production and management. So, the enterprises begin to develop and produce new products. Surviving enterprises gradually reduce additional service of the product and cut the promotion budget in order to maintain the lowest level of operation.

2. 衰退期的营销策略 Marketing Strategy at Decline Stage

这一阶段企业的主要任务是转入研制开发新产品或转入新市场，进行有计划的"撤"、有预见的"转"、有目标的"攻"。具体策略有以下两种。

The main task of the enterprise at this stage is to research and develop new products or to step into new markets, to make planned "withdrawal", predicting "transition" and targeted "attack". There are the following specific strategies.

1) 继续经营策略(也称为自然淘汰策略)Continuing operation strategy, also known as natural selection strategy

是指企业继续使用过去的营销策略，直到该产品完全退出市场为止。当企业在该市场占有绝对支配地位且产品竞争者退出市场后该市场仍有一定潜力时，通常可采用本策略，尽力把销售维持在一个较低的水平上，等待时机，退出市场。

This refers to the fact that companies continue to use the old marketing strategy until the products are completely withdrawn from the market. When an enterprise occupies an absolutely dominant position in the market and the market still has potential after competitors withdraw from the market, this strategy can often be adopted. The enterprises try to maintain sales at a low level, waiting for an appropriate opportunity to leave the market.

2) 集中策略 Concentration Strategy

它是指把企业的能力和资源集中在最有利的市场和渠道上，放弃那些没有盈利机会的市场。通过缩短战线，企业在最有利的市场上赢得尽可能多利润。本策略一般在某中心市场的顾客对本企业的特定产品的质量、品牌和服务有特殊的忠诚度时采用。

This concentrates the ability and resources of enterprises on the most advantageous market and channels and gives up unprofitable markets. By narrowing the scope of business, the enterprise achieves as much profit as possible in the most advantageous market. This strategy is generally adopted when customers in the central market have special loyalty to the quality, brand and service of particular products.

3) 放弃策略 Give-up Strategy

当某种产品已无改进和再生的希望时，企业要及时果断地停止该产品的生产和经营，转向对新产品的研究和开发。

产品生命周期各阶段的特征、目标和策略如表6-1所示。

When a product cannot be improved, enterprises should stop production and operation decisively, turning instead to research and development of new products.

Characteristics objectives and strategies at each stage of the product life cycle are as shown in Chart 6-1.

表 6-1 产品生命周期各阶段的特征、目标和策略

		导入期	成长期	成熟期	衰退期
特征	销售	低销售	销售快速上升	销售高峰	销售衰退
	成本	按每个顾客计算平均成本	按每个客户计算平均成本	按每个顾客计算平均成本	按每个顾客计算平均成本
	利润	亏损	利润上升	高利润	利润下降
	顾客	创新者	早期采用者	多数	落后者
	竞争者	极少	数量增加	稳定的数量开始下降	数量衰减
营销目标	目标	创建知名度，促进试用	最大限度地占领读市场	保卫市场份额，获得最大利润	削减支出，获取利润
营销策略	产品	提供一个基本产品	提供产品的扩展品、服务和担保	品牌和样式的多样性	逐步淘汰疲软品目
	价格	采用成本加成	市场渗透价格	较量或击败竞争者的价格	削价
	分销	建立选择性分销网	建立密集广泛的分销网	建立更密集广泛的分销网	进行选择：逐步淘汰无盈利的分销网点
	广告	在早期采用者和经销商中建立知名度	在大量市场中建立程度度和兴趣	强调品牌的差别和利益	减少到保持坚定忠诚者需求的水平
	促销	加强促销以吸引试用	充分利用有大量消费者需求的有利条件，适当减少促销	增加对品牌转换的鼓励	减少到最低水平

Chart 6-1 Characteristics, Objectives and Strategies at Each Stage of the Product Life Cycle

		Introduction	Growth	Maturity	Decline
特征	Sales	Low sales	Sales increase rapidly	Sales peak	Sales decline
	Cost	Calculate the average cost according to the number of the customer	Calculate the average cost according to the number of the customer	Calculate the average cost according to every customer	Calculate the average cost according to every customer
	Profit	Loss	Profits increase	High profits	Profits decline
	Customer	Innovators	Early adopters	Majority	Laggard
	Competitors	Minority	The number increase	The stable number begins to decline	The number declines
Marketing Objectives	Objective	Create the popularity and promote the trial	Occupy the market share to the fullest extent	Protect the market share and get most profits	Cut the expenses and get profits
Marketing Strategies	Product	Offer basic product	Offer extend product service and guarantee of the product	The variety of brand and style	Eliminating gradually the Weak products
	Price	Adopt the cost plus	Market penetration price	The price that can be compared with the competitors or beat the competitors	Cut the price
	Distribution	Create the selective distribution net	Create the intensive distribution net	Create more intensive distribution net	Make a choice Eliminating gradually the net without profits
	Advertisement	Create the popularity of the product am ong the early adopters and distributors	Create popularity and interest in a lot of markets	Focus on the difference and profits of the brand	Reduce the level which can keep the loyal customers' needs
	promotion	Enhance the promotion to attract more trial	Take full advantage of favorable conditions and promotion promotion properly	Give more encouragement to change the brand	Reduce to the lowest level

第三节 产品品牌与包装策略
Branding and Packaging Strategies

一、品牌策略 Branding Strategy

(一)品牌及品牌资产的含义 Meaning of Brand and Brand Asset

1. 品牌的含义 Meaning of Brand

品牌是用以识别某个销售者或某群销售者的产品或服务,并使之与竞争对手的产品或服务区别开来的商业名称及其标志,通常由文字、标记、符号、图案和颜色等要素或这些要素的组合构成。品牌是一个集合概念,它包括品牌名称、品牌标志和商标三部分。品牌名称是指品牌中可以用语言称呼的部分,也称"品名",如可口可乐、奥迪等。品牌标志,也称"品标",是指品牌中可以被认出、易于记忆但不能用言语称呼的部分,通常由图案、符号或特殊颜色等构成如美国米高梅电影公司的怒吼的狮子、迪士尼的米老鼠和唐老鸭等。品牌标志主要是让消费者产生视觉效果。商标,是指经过注册登记的受到法律保护的品牌或一个品牌的一部分。它作为区别不同种类商品的标记或标志,往往印在商品的包装和标签上。企业产品品牌或品牌的一部分在政府有关主管部门注册登记以后,就享有其使用专用权并受到法律保护,其他任何企业都不得使用。

Brand refers to the business name and logo used to identify a product or service of a seller or a group of sellers, and to differentiate it from competitors' products or services. Brand usually contains elements such as words, marks, symbols, patterns and color, or a combination of these elements. Brand is a collective concept which includes the brand name, brand logo and trademark. Brand name refers to the part of the brand that can be expressed in words, also known as the "name" such as Coca-cola, Audi, etc. Brand logo is the part of the brand that can be recognized and remembered easily but cannot be expressed in words. It is usually composed of patterns, symbols or special colors, etc., such as the roaring lion of the MGM movie company of the United States and Disney's Mickey Mouse and Donald Duck. Brand logo is mainly to generate visual effects for consumers. Trademark refers to the brand or part of a brand protected by law after registration. As a sign or mark of difference between different types of goods, trademarks are often printed on the packaging and the label of goods. After a brand or part of the brand is registered in relevant government departments, the enterprise can enjoy the exclusive right to use it, and be protected by law, other firms not being allowed to use it.

2. 品牌资产的含义 Meaning of Brand Asset

品牌资产,是一种超过商品或服务本身利益以外的价值。它通过为消费者和企业提供附加利益来体现其价值,并与某一特定的品牌紧密联系。某种品牌给消费者提供的超过商品或服务本身以外的附加利益越多,则该品牌对消费者的吸引就越大,品牌资产的价值也就越高。如果该品牌的名称或标志发生变更,则附着在该品牌上的财产也将部分或全部丧失。品牌给企业带来的附加利益最终源于品牌对消费者的吸引力和影响力。

Brand asset is a kind of "overvalue" exceeding the simple value of the goods or services themselves. It realizes its value through offering additional benefits to consumers and businesses, and closely links with a particular brand. The more additional benefits exceeding the goods or services a brand provides consumers with, the more attraction the brand has to consumers, and higher the value of the brand asset. If the brand's name or logo changes, the properties of the brand also disappears partially or completely. The additional benefits brought by brand to the enterprise finally come from the attraction and influence of the brand to consumers.

由品牌带来的超值利益是品牌的价值体现，是由品牌这种特殊的资产生成的，故品牌被称作特殊资产。这不仅是因为品牌是无形的，还因为它的真实价值并未在企业财务状况表中反映出来。作为企业财产的重要组成部分，品牌资产具有无形性，可以在使用中增值；另外品牌难以准确计量，具有波动性。同时，品牌资产是营销绩效的主要衡量指标。

The overvalue brought by brand is the embodiment of a brand's value, and is generated by the special asset—brand. Therefore the brand is called a special asset. This not only because brand is invisible, but also because its real value is not reflected in the enterprise's financial statements. As an important part of enterprise property, brand asset cannot be seen and can get added value in use; besides, it is difficult to measure accurately and can fluctuate. At the same time, brand asset is the main measurement of marketing achievements.

(二)品牌策略的分类 Categories of Branding Strategy

企业的品牌策略，是指企业合理地使用品牌，以达到一定的营销目的。企业在进行品牌决策时，一般可以作以下选择。

Branding strategy means the enterprise reasonably takes advantage of brand in order to achieve certain marketing purposes. While making brand decisions, an enterprise can make the following choices。

1. 无品牌策略 No Brand Strategy

一般来说，绝大部分企业或产品都使用品牌或注册商标。但在某些特殊情况下，可以不使用品牌或注册商标，只注明产地或生产厂家名称，也可使用未经注册的临时商标。无品牌策略适用于以下三种情况：一是产品技术要求简单，不同生产厂家的产品质量是同质的，故消费者没有必要凭品牌去购买，如原材料、煤炭、电力等；二是小范围的地产、地销商品，习惯上只注明产地或厂家，也可使用未注册商标，如土特产、手工艺品等；三是企业临时性加工或一次性生产的产品，如接受外商的加工业务，一般是由经营单位重新包装并使用经营者的商标。

In general, most enterprises or products have brand or a registered trademark. However, in some special circumstances, they are not used. Just the place of production or manufacturer's name are labeled, and only temporary unregistered trademarks are used. No brand strategy is suitable in the following three conditions: ①The requirements of product technique are simple. Different manufacturers' product quality is homogeneous, so the consumers don't have to buy the products according to brand. This often applies to raw materials, coal, electric power, etc. ②The local products sold in a small area only indicate production place or the manufacturer, and unregistered trademarks also can be used. Examples are native products, handicrafts, etc. ③The temporary processing of disposable products, such as in the processing business offered by foreign traders, are generally repacked by the operator, using the operator's logo.

2. 品牌归属策略 Brand Ownership Strategy

品牌归属策略是指由谁来使用产品的品牌。可供企业选择的有以下三种策略。

Brand ownership strategy refers to who will use the product brand. There are three main strategies for enterprises to choose from.

(1) 自有品牌。是指企业使用属于自己的品牌，这种品牌也称作企业品牌或生产者品牌。索尼、福特、可口可乐等均为自有品牌。企业品牌一直是品牌决策的主角，大多数企业都创立了自己的品牌。

"Own" brand. This means that the enterprise uses its own brand. This kind of brand is also called enterprise brand or producer brand. Sony, Ford, Coca Cola, etc. are all own brands; enterprise brand plays the leading role in brand creation and most enterprises have founded their own brands.

(2) 他人品牌。他人品牌又可细分为以下两种：①中间商品牌。企业将其产品售给中间商，由中间商使用自己的品牌将产品转卖出去，这种品牌叫作中间商品牌。②贴牌。贴牌是指一家厂家根据另一家厂商的要求，为其生产产品和产品配件，亦称为定牌生产或授权贴牌生产。它既可代表外委加工，也可代表转包合同加工，俗称代加工，也称 OEM(Original Equipment Manufacture)或 ODM(Original Design Manufacture)。具体来说，OEM 即原始设备制造商，又叫定牌生产和贴牌生产；ODM 即原始设计制造商；此外，还有 OBM(Original Brand Manufacture)，即原始品牌制造商，例如，A 方看中 B 方的产品，让 B 方生产，产品使用 A 方商标，对 A 方来说，这叫 OEM；A 方自带技术和设计，让 B 方加工，这叫 ODM；对 B 方来说，只负责生产加工别人的产品，然后贴上别人的商标，这叫 OBM。近年来，这种生产方式在国内家电行业比较流行，如 TCL 在苏州三星定牌生产洗衣机，长虹在宁波迪声定牌生产洗衣机等。

Others' brands. Others' brands can be subdivided into the following two categories: the first is the middleman's brand. An enterprise sells its products to middleman, and then the middleman uses their own brands to sell the products. This brand is called middleman brand. The second is OEM (Original Equipment Manufacture). OEM, also called fixed brand production or ODM (Original Design Manufacture), refers to a manufacturer producing products and product accessories according to the requirements of another manufacturer. The enterprise can process the products on behalf of the sub-contractor. Specifically, OEM is the original equipment manufacturer and OBM is original brand manufacture. For example, party A prefers party B's products, then lets party B produce with A's trademark. For party A, this is called OEM; party A provides technology and design and lets party B process, which is called ODM; party B is responsible for producing and processing other enterprises' products, and then label with the other enterprise's trademark This is called OBM. In recent years, this production arrangement is popular in the domestic appliance industry. For example, TCL produces washing machine in Sanxing, Suzhou; Changhong produces washing machine in Disheng, Ningbo, etc.

(3) 混合品牌。企业对部分产品使用自己的品牌，而对另一部分产品使用中间商品牌或者其他生产者品牌。

Mixed brand. The enterprise applies its own brand to some of the products, but applies the middleman's or other producers' brands to other products.

3. 家族品牌策略 Family Brand Strategy

企业如果已经决定了其大部分或全部产品都使用自己的品牌名称，还应决定其产品是否分别使用不同的品牌名称，或者统一使用一个或几个品牌名称。对于企业来说，家族品牌策略共有以下四种选择。

If an enterprise has decided to use its own brand name with most or all of the products, it should also decide whether to use different brand names with its products, or use a unified one or several brand names. For the enterprise, the family brand strategy has the following four options.

(1) 个别品牌是指企业决定其各种不同产品分别使用不同的品牌名称。企业使用个别品牌名称的好处是：第一，没有将公司的声誉系在某一品牌的成败上；第二，可以使公司为每一种新产品寻找最佳的名称；第三，一个新的品牌可以造成新的刺激，建立新的信念。

The individual brand means that the enterprise decides to use different brand names respectively for its various products. The benefits of using the individual brand for the enterprise are as follows: first, the company doesn't tie its reputation to one brand's success or failure; second, it can enable the company to find the best name for each new product; third, a new brand can cause new stimulus and establish new belief.

(2) 同一品牌是指企业决定其所有产品都统一使用一个品牌名称。例如，日本索尼公司的所有产品都统一使用"SONY"这个品牌名称。企业使用同一品牌名称的好处是，一方面，企业在引进一种新产品时的费用较少；另一方面，原品牌良好的声誉，会促进新产品的销售。但若某一种产品因某种原因(如质量)出现问题，就可能因此牵连到其他种类产品并影响全部产品和整个企业的信誉，即产生负面"株连效应"。

The same brand means that when the enterprise decides to use a brand name for all its products. For example, all products of Sony in Japan are unified to use the brand name "SONY". Benefits of using the same brand name are as follows. On the one hand, the cost is less when the enterprise introduces a new product; on the other hand, the good reputation of the original brand will promote the sales of new product. However, if the product has problems for some reasons, for examples, a quality problem, this can negatively influence a whole range of products and the credibility of the entire enterprise. The effect is one of "collective punishment".

(3) 类别品牌是指企业各大类产品单独使用不同的品牌名称。例如西尔斯·罗巴克公司对其所经营的妇女服装类产品统一使用"瑞溪"品牌。

The category brand refers to when products of various categories separately use different brand names. For example, the Sears Roebuck company attach the brand name "stream" to all the women's apparel products.

公司名称与单个产品的名称相结合。此品牌策略是指企业决定其各种不同的产品分别使用不同的品牌名称，而且各种产品的品牌名称前面还冠以企业名称。例如，海尔集团的洗衣机产品"海尔小神童"即采用了此种策略。企业采取这种决策的主要好处是：在各种不同的新产品的品牌名称前冠以企业名称，可以使新产品合法化，能够享受企业的信誉，并可使各种不同的新产品具有不同的特色。

The company's name is combined with one single product's name. This means that the enterprise decides to apply various different brand names to different products respectively, but all the products also carry the title of the brand name of the enterprise before their individual names; for example, the washing machine "Haier Child Prodigy" of Haier Group. The primary benefit for a company to adopt this strategy is as follows. It can make the new product legal and enjoy the credibility of the enterprise; it can also endow different characteristics to different kinds of new products.

4. 品牌扩展策略 Brand Extension Strategy

品牌扩展策略，又称特殊品牌策略，是指企业利用成功的品牌推出新产品或改良产品，包括推出新的包装规格、香味和式样等。采用这种策略，可以节省新产品的宣传广告费用，利用消费者对品牌的信任感，使新产品能够顺利迅速地进入市场；但若消费者不认可，也会影响该品牌的市场信誉，甚至会降低原有品牌的市场竞争力。

Brand extension strategy is also known as special branding strategy, which means an enterprise uses an existing successful brand to launch new products or improved products, including the launching of new packing specification, flavor and style. This strategy can save advertising costs for new products, take advantage of consumers' trust in the brand to help the new products enter the market smoothly and quickly. However, if consumers do not endorse the new product, the brand's credibility may be affected and the market competitiveness of the original brand may even be lowered.

5. 更换品牌策略 Changing Brand Strategy

更换品牌策略，就是更换原有企业的品牌，采用新的品牌。

Changing brand strategy is to replace the original enterprise's brand with new brands.

6. 品牌再定位策略 Brand Re-positioning Strategy

此策略是指在竞争者推出自己的品牌抢占市场份额、顾客偏好可能发生转移的情况下，要求企业对品牌重新定位。

Brand re-positioning strategy refers that a competitor could launch its own brand to grab market share and customer preferences may transfer to other products, which requires enterprises to re-position the brand.

7. 品牌联合策略 Co-branding Strategy

品牌联合策略是指对同一产品使用不分主次的两个或两个以上品牌。品牌联合可以使两个或更多个品牌有效地协作，结成联盟，相互借势，进而提高品牌影响力与市场接受程度。如"联想—英特尔"、"三菱重工—海尔"、"索尼—爱立信"等都是很好的例子。

This strategy refers to using two or more brands in the same product, regardless of which is primary or secondary. Co-branding strategy can make two or more brands cooperate and unite with each other effectively, and improve the brand influence and market acceptance. Good examples are "Lenovo—Intel", "Mitsubishi—Haier", "SONY—Ericsson", etc.

二、包装策略 Packaging Strategies

(一)包装的含义及其构成要素 Meaning and Components of Packaging

1. 包装的含义 Meaning of Packaging

包装是指对某一品牌商品设计并制作容器或包扎物的一系列活动。也就是说，包装有两方面含义：其一，包装是指为产品设计、制作包扎物的活动过程；其二，包装是指产品的容器和外部包扎。产品包装一般包括以下三个部分：一是首要包装，是产品紧靠着的包装容器，如酒瓶；二是次要包装，是保护首要包装的包装物，又称销售包装，如酒瓶外部的长方体纸盒；三是运输包装，是为了储存和运输的需要而形成的大包装，如集12瓶为一箱的大箱子。

Packaging concerns a series of activities around designing the brand of a product and producing containers or wrapping. That is to say, packaging has two meanings: first, packaging refers to the activities around product design and production of wrapping; second, packaging is the container of the product and the external wrapping. Product packaging generally includes the following three parts: the first is the primary packaging, referring to the packaging container in which the product is contained, such as wine bottles; the second is the secondary packaging which is the packaging protecting the primary packaging, also known as sales packaging, such as a small rectangular cardboard box around the bottles; the third is transport packaging, which is the major packaging for storing and transporting products, such as a box containing 12 bottles.

2. 包装的构成要素 Components of Packaging

一般来说，商品包装包括商标或品牌、形状、颜色、图案和材料等要素。其中，商标或品牌是包装中最主要的构成要素，应在包装整体上居于突出的位置；适宜的包装形状有利于储运和陈列，也有利于产品销售，因此，形状是包装中不可缺少的组合要素。颜色是包装中最具刺激销售作用的构成要素，突出商品特性的色调组合不仅能够加强品牌的辨识度，而且对顾客有强烈的吸引力。图案在包装中如同广告中的画面，其重要性不言而喻。包装材料的选择不仅影响包装成本，而且影响着商品的市场竞争力，开发和选用新型材料是包装设计中的一项重要工作。此外，在产品包装上还有标签，其上一般都印有包装内容和产品所包含的主要成分、品牌标志、产品质量等级、生产厂家、生产日期和有效期、使用方法等，有些标签上还印有彩色图案或实物照片。

Generally, packaging includes trademarks or brand, shape, color, pattern, material and other elements, among which trademark or brand is the most important element and should be placed at a prominent position. Suitable packaging shape is beneficial to storage, display, and product sales, so shape is an indispensable mix element in packaging. Color is the packaging element which can stimulate sales most, and the color mix highlighting the product features not only strengthens brand identity, but also has a strong appeal to customers. Also it is understood that patterns of the packaging are important, just like advertising images. The choice of packaging materials not only affects the cost of packaging, but also affects the market competitiveness of companies. Moreover, development and selection of new materials are important aspects of packaging design. In addition, there are labels on the product packaging, on which the following elements are generally printed: packaging content, ingredients, brand logo, product quality level, the manufacturer, date of manufacture, expiry date, use method and so on. There are colorful patterns or pictures of the products printed on some labels.

(二)包装策略 Packaging Strategy

可供企业选择的包装策略有以下几种。

The following packaging strategies are available for the enterprise.

1. 类似包装策略 Similar Packaging

类似包装策略是指企业在所生产的各种不同的产品的包装上采用相同的图案、色彩或其他共同的特征，有利于顾客很容易地识别出同一家企业的产品。其优点在于能节省设计和印刷费用，树立企业形象，有利于新产品推销。但也会因为个别产品质量下降而影响到其他产品的销路。

Similar packaging refers that an enterprise uses the same pattern, color or other common characteristics in a variety of different product packages in order to help purchasers easily recognize they are products from the same company. The advantages are cost savings in design and printing, establishment of a corporate image and benefits to the promotion of new products. But the sales of other products can also be affected because by quality decline of a particular product.

2. 组合包装策略 Combination Packaging

组合包装策略是指企业将几种有关联性的产品组合在同一包装物内，如家用药箱、针线包、工具箱等。该策略能够节约交易时间，便于消费者购买、携带与使用，有利于扩大产品销售，还能够在将新旧产品组合在一起时，使新产品顺利进入市场。但在实践中，还需注意市场需求的具体特点、消费者的购买能力和产品本身的关联程度大小，切忌任意配套搭配。

Combination packaging is when a company puts several related products in the same packaging container, such as household kit, sewing kit, toolboxes, etc. This strategy can save trade time, is convenient for consumers to buy, carry and use, and expands product sales. Moreover, the portfolio of the old and new products can make the new products enter the market successfully. In practice, however, it is necessary to pay attention to the specific characteristics of market demand, consumer purchasing power and the degree of association of the product itself, and avoid arbitrary combination.

3. 分量包装策略 Weight-depending Packaging

分量包装策略是指对一些称重产品，根据消费者的消费时间、地点和数量的不同，采用尺寸不同的包装。例如，对一些价格较贵的产品，可采用小包装，给消费者以优惠感。

Weight-depending packaging means that some weighed products have different-sized packages according to consumers' buying time, place, quantity and so on. For example, small packages for some expensive products can make consumers feel that they are cheap.

4. 等级包装策略 Grade Packaging

等级包装策略是指企业对自己生产经营的不同质量等级的产品分别设计和使用不同的包装。显然，这种依产品等级来配比设计包装的策略可使包装质量与产品品质等级相匹配，一般来说，对高档产品采用精致包装，对低档产品采用简略包装，这样能使消费者更容易识别和选购商品，从而有利于全面扩大销售。

Grade packaging means that products with different levels of quality are designed and packaged differently. Obviously, this packaging strategy according to product levels can help the packaging quality match the quality level of the product. Usually exquisite packaging is used for high-end products and simple packaging for low-end products. This can make it easier for consumers to identify and purchase goods, thus contributing to overall expansion of sales.

5. 再使用包装策略 Reused Packaging

此包装策略是指在原包装的商品用完后，消费者可将空的包装容器移作其他用途。例如，果汁、咖啡等的包装常常被再利用。由于这种包装策略增加了包装的用途，可以刺激消费者的购买欲望，有利于扩大产品销售，并可使带有商品商标的包装物在再使用过程中起到延伸宣传的作用。

Reused packaging means that after the goods are used, the original and empty packaging can be used by consumers for other purposes. For example, the packages of fruit juices and coffee can often be reused. This packaging strategy increases the uses of packaging, which can stimulate consumer's purchasing desire, expand product sales, and enable the packaging with the trademark to play a propaganda role in the reusing process.

6. 附赠品包装策略 Kaleidoscopic Packaging

此包装策略是指在包装物内附加赠品，以吸引消费者重复购买。赠品可以是玩具、图片，也可以是奖券。该包装策略对儿童、青少年以及低收入者比较有效。

Kaleidoscopic packaging places free gifts in the package in order to attract consumers to repurchase the product. The free gifts can be toys, pictures or lotteries. This packaging strategy is more effective for children, adolescents, and low-income people.

7. 更新包装策略 Updating Packaging

更新包装策略是指企业以改变包装的办法达到扩大销售的目的。当企业某种产品与同类产品近似而销路不好，或当一种产品的包装已采用较长时间时，企业通过改变包装设计和包装材料而使用新的包装，有利于增强消费者对产品的好感，从而扩大销售量。

Updating packaging means that enterprise changes the packaging in order to expand sales. When an enterprise cannot sell the product similar to other enterprises' products very easily, or when a product's packaging has been used for a long time, the enterprise launches new package by changing the packaging design and materials. This change can raise consumers' positive impression and expand sales.

8. 礼品式包装策略 Gift Packaging

此策略是指在包装物上冠以"禄""福""寿""喜""如意"等字样及问候语，其目的在于增添节日气氛和欢乐，满足人们交往礼仪的需要，借物寓情，以情达意。

Gift packaging refers to printing some lucky words and greetings on the package, such as "Fortune", "Blessing", "Long Life", "Happy", "Good Luck", and so on. The purpose is to add a festive atmosphere and joy, meet people's needs of good relations and exchange gifts with emotion.

9. 开窗式包装策略 Window Packaging

此策略是指在包装物上留有"窗口"，让消费者透过"窗口"来直接认识和了解产品，其目的在于直接让消费者体会、认识产品的品质。

Window packaging refers to when a "window" is left on the packaging to allow consumers to observe and appreciate the product directly. The purpose is to give consumers a chance to directly experience and recognize the quality of the product.

10. 密封式包装策略 Sealed Packaging

此策略是指将产品严实地包裹起来，接口处以胶、蜡等密封。这种策略常见于防潮、防晒、防尘等易损易变质的产品，其目的在于确保商品的质量。

Sealed packaging means to package the products tightly, and to seal the interface with glue or wax. This strategy is usually used in delicate or perishable products in a wet, sunny or dusty environment. The purpose is to maintain the quality of the goods.

11. 年龄式包装策略 Age-based Packaging

此策略是指按年龄段设计相应的包装，即包装采用适宜不同年龄的造型、图案、色彩等，其目的在于满足不同年龄段的消费者的需要。

Age-based packaging is defined as packaging according to different ages, adopting different shapes, patterns, colors and so on. The purpose is to meet the consumers' needs at particular ages.

12. 性别式包装策略 Gender-based Packaging

此策略是指按性别不同采用与之相适应的包装，如男性用品包装可以是潇洒、刚正、质朴的；女性用品包装则温馨、柔软、秀丽、新颖、典雅，其目的在于满足不同性别的消费者的需求。

Gender-based packaging means to use different packages according to different genders. The packages of male products can be natural, upright and simple; while the packages of female products are warm, soft, beautiful, innovative and elegant. The purpose is to meet the consumers' according to gender.

第四节 产品组合策略
Product Mix Strategies

一、产品组合及其相关概念 Product Mix and Related Concepts

(一)产品组合的含义 Concept of Product Mix

大多数企业生产不止一种产品，它们可能会生产若干种产品，形成一定的产品集合体。产品组合是指一个企业生产或经营的全部产品线、产品项目所构成的整体，又叫产品的各色品种的集合体。它反映了一个企业提供给市场的全部产品线和产品项目的构成，即企业的业务经营范围和产品结构。产品组合包括四个衡量变量，即宽度、长度、深度和关联度。

Most enterprises produce more than one kind of product, perhaps several, to form a particular product collection. Product mix refers to the integration of all the product lines and projects produced and operated by the enterprise. This also known as the collection of products in various colors and categories. It reflects the structure of all the product lines and product projects provided to the market by the enterprise, namely, the enterprise's business activity scope and product structure. Product portfolio includes four measurable variables: width, length, depth and correlation.

(二)与产品组合相关的概念 Concepts Relating to Product Mix

一个企业应该经营哪些产品才是最有利的，这些产品之间应该有什么配合关系，这就是产品组合问题。为了实现营销目标、充分有效地满足目标市场的需求，需要企业设计一个优化的产品组合。在研究这个问题之前，有必要先了解几个相关的概念。

Which products are the best for a business to produce, and what cooperative relationship should the products have between them are the questions product mix involves. In order to achieve the marketing goal and fully and effectively meet the needs of the target market, enterprises need to design an optimal product portfolio. Before studying this problem, it is necessary to understand several related concepts.

1. 产品线 Product Line

产品线是指能够满足同类需要，在功能、使用和销售等方面具有相似性的一组产品或产品组合中的某一产品大类。比如，以类似的方式发挥功能、售给相同的顾客群、通过同样的销售渠道出售、属于同样的价格范畴等。所以，产品线亦称产品系列。例如，海尔有彩电、冰箱、洗衣机等许多产品系列。

Product line is a set of products, or a certain category of product mix, which can satisfy the needs of similar categories and have similar features in aspects of function, use and sale, for example, functioning in a similar way, sold to the same customer groups, sold through the same sales channel, belonging to the same price category, and so on. Product line is also known as product series, for example, Haier produces TVs, refrigerators, washing machines, as well as many other product series.

2. 产品项目 Product Project

产品项目是指产品线中各种不同的品种、规格、质量的特定产品及同一品种的不同品牌。在企业产品目录中列出的每一种产品就是一个产品项目。

Product project refers to particular products in different categories, specifications, quality and different brands of the same category in the product line. In an enterprise's product catalogue, each product listed is a product project.

3. 产品组合宽度 Width of Product Mix

产品组合的宽度又称产品组合的广度，是指一个企业产品组合所包括的产品线的数量。产品线多，说明其经营的产品组合宽度较大；产品线少，说明其所经营的产品组合宽度较小。产品组合的宽度表明了一个企业经营的产品种类的多少及经营范围的大小。

The width of product mix is also called the scope of product mix. It refers to the number of product lines that an enterprise's product mix includes. A large number of product lines means that the width of product mix is great, and a small number of product lines means that it is smaller. The width of product mix shows how many categories of products an enterprise operates, and the operation scope of the enterprise.

4. 产品组合长度 Length of Product Mix

产品组合的长度是指企业产品项目的总和，即所有的产品线中产品项目相加之和。一般情况下，产品组合的长度越长，说明企业的产品品种和规格越多。由于有时候一个产品项目就是一个品牌，因此，产品组合的长度越长，企业的产品品牌也就越多。

The length of product mix refers to the sum of the enterprise's product projects in all the product lines. In general, the longer the length of the product mix, the more an enterprise's product categories and specifications there are. This is because sometimes a product project is a brand. As a result, the longer the length of the product mix, the more product brands the enterprise owns.

5. 产品组合深度 Depth of Product Mix

产品组合的深度是指企业产品组合中各产品线各自包含的产品项目的数量。每条产品线中所包含的项目愈多，产品组合愈深，表示其在某类产品中产品开发的深度就越大。

Depth of product mix refers to the number of product projects contained in each product line. The more products contained in every product line, the deeper the product mix is and the greater the depth of product development.

6. 产品组合关联度 Correlation of Product Mix

产品组合的关联度是指企业所有产品线之间相关的程度，具体是指各个产品线在最终用途、生产技术、销售方式以及其他方面的相互关联程度。产品组合的相关度与企业开展多元化经营有密切关系。例如，某家用电器厂除经营洗衣机外，还经营电冰箱、空调机、微波炉等多条产品线，因每条产品线都与电有关，这一产品组合就有较强的一致性，说明产品组合关联紧密。假如该厂还生产清凉饮料，那么，这种产品组合的关联性就显得松散了。在实行集团多角化经营的混合型公司中，其各类产品线间的相关性较小，或毫无相关性。

The correlation of product mix refers to the degree of relation between all the product lines of the enterprise. Specifically, it means the degree of relation between each product line in the aspects of end use, production technologies, marketing ways, etc. The correlation of product mix has close relations with enterprises' carrying out the diversification operation. For example, a household electrical appliance factory may produce not only washing machines, but also refrigerators, air conditioners, microwave ovens and other product lines. Because each product line is related to electricity, this product mix has strong consistency, which means the product combination is close. If the factory also makes cool drinks, the correlation of product mix is looser. In mixed-operation companies with diversification management, the correlation between different product lines is little or none.

产品组合的宽度、长度、深度和关联度不同，就构成不同的产品组合，如图6-6所示。合理的产品组合对市场营销活动具有重要意义。

Different width, length, depth and correlation constitute the basis of different product mixes, which is shown in Figure 6-6. A coherent product mix is of great significance to marketing activities.

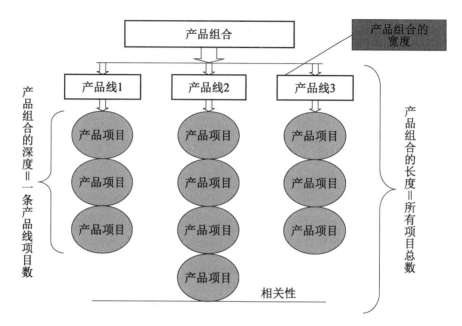

图 6-6　产品组合

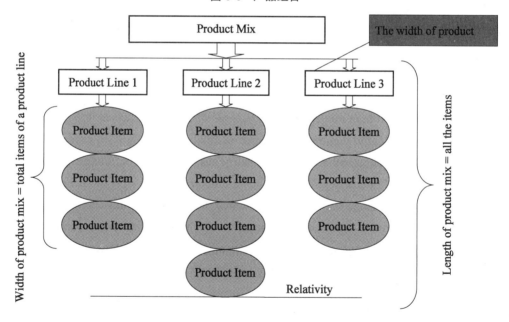

Figure6-6　Product Mix

二、产品组合策略的分类 Categories of Product Mix Strategies

产品组合策略,是指企业根据市场状况、自身资源条件和竞争态势,而对产品组合的广度、长度、深度和关联度进行不同组合的选择与运用。一个企业关于产品组合的决策并不是任意确定的,而是遵循有利于销售和增加企业总利润的原则,根据企业的资源条件和市场状况来确定。我们可以从静态与动态两个方面来分析企业的产品组合策略。

Product mix strategy is when an enterprise selects and uses different combinations of width, length, depth and correlation of product mix according to market status, resource conditions and the competition situation. An enterprise's decision-making regarding product mix is not arbitrary, but follows the principle of increasing sales and profits to create flexible selection according to enterprise resource conditions and market status. We can analyze the enterprise's product mix strategy from static and dynamic aspects.

(一)静态产品组合策略 Static Product Mix Strategy

静态产品组合策略,是指在一种特定的市场环境和企业可能承担的风险水平下,有利可图的产品组合关系一经确定,计划就不再变动。这种情况要求预测分析准确可靠,确定的产品组合来实现企业预期的利润目标。从静态的角度分析,可供选择的产品组合策略有以下几种。

Static product mix strategy means that the plan is no longer changed as soon as a profitable product mix is fixed when in a specific market environment and under risk that the enterprise may undertake. This situation requires accurate forecast analysis and the determined product mix to achieve expected profits. From the perspective of static analysis, optional product mix strategies are as follows.

1. 全线全面型策略 Comprehensive Strategy

这种策略着眼于向所有顾客提供他们所需的一切物品。其特点是尽可能地增加产品线的宽度和深度,不受产品线之间关联性的约束。例如,日本索尼公司的经营范围覆盖了从电视机、收录机、摄像机、VCD、DVD产品,到旅行社、连锁餐馆等的服务,十分宽广。全线全面型策略能较大限度地分散各种产品的经营风险,扩展企业的实力和声势,取得最大的市场覆盖面,并最大限度地满足顾客的需要。通常大工业集团或大公司采用这种策略。

Comprehensive strategy aims to provide all customers with what they need. Its characteristics are to increase the width and depth of product lines, not restricted by the correlation between product lines. For example, the business scope of Sony in Japan is very broad from TV, recorders, cameras, VCD and DVD players to services such as travel agencies, chain restaurants, etc. The comprehensive strategy can disperse operation risks of all kinds of products, expand the enterprise's strength and momentum, maximize market coverage, and meet customers' needs. Big industrial groups or companies generally use this strategy.

2. 市场专业型策略 Professional Market Strategy

这种策略即向某个专业市场(某类顾客)提供所需的各种产品。例如,以建筑业为产品市场的工程机械公司,其产品组合由推土机、翻斗车、挖沟机、超重机、水泥搅拌机、压路机、载重卡车等产品线所组成。这种产品组合策略重视各产品之间的关联程度与组合的宽度,而组合深度一般较小,它能使某一类顾客在某种消费上从一个企业获得全方位的满足，由此方便了顾客，扩大了销售。

This strategy is to provide required products to a professional market (particular customers), for example, the product mix of an engineering machinery company, whose products are related to the construction industry may consist of bulldozers, dump trucks, ditching machines, heavy machines, cement mixers, road rollers, motor trucks and other product lines. This product mix strategy attaches importance to the correlation degree and the width of the mix between products. The depth of mix is generally shallower, which can help particular kinds of customers obtain satisfaction from an enterprise. This is convenient to customers, and can expand sales.

3. 产品线专业型策略 Professional Product Line Strategy

该策略是指企业集中某一类产品的生产，并将其产品推销给各类顾客。例如，中国一汽集团公司专门生产各类小汽车，以满足不同顾客的需要。其汽车产品有普通型红旗小轿车、独具风采的旅行车、别具一格的客货两用车等。该策略产品线数目少且各项目密切相关，产品品种丰富，能分别满足不同顾客、不同用途的需要。

Professional product line strategy means that when an enterprise focuses on the production of one type of product, and sells its products to all kinds of customers. For example, First Automobile Workshop (FAW) Group Corporation in China is specialized in the production of all kinds of cars to meet the needs of different customers. Their products include ordinary Hongqi cars, wagons of unique style, distinctive vans, etc. The number of product lines is less with this strategy and all the projects are closely related to each other. Products are various and can satisfy the needs of different customers with different purposes.

4. 有限产品线专业型策略 Limited Product Line Strategy

该策略是指集中企业的力量，生产单一产品线中的几个产品项目。它一般适合生产经营条件有限的中、小型企业，这类企业以单一的市场或部分顾客作为目标市场。与产品线专业型策略相比，该策略不仅产品线数目少，且产品线内部的产品项目有限，即产品组合宽度很小，深度有限，但关联度较强。

Limited product line strategy refers to concentrating the enterprise's strength to produce several product projects in a single product line. This is suitable for medium and small enterprises with limited production and operation conditions, and the enterprises' target market is a single market or part of customers. Compared with professional product line strategy, it not only has fewer product lines, but also has limited internal product projects. This means the width of product mix is narrow and the depth is limited, but the correlation is very strong.

5. 特殊产品专业型策略 Special Product Strategy

特殊产品专业型策略是指企业根据自己所具备的特殊资源条件和技术专长，专门生产某些具有良好销路的产品项目。该策略具有组合宽度、深度小、但关联度极强的特点，所能开拓的市场是有限的。因其特殊的资源、技术产品能创造出特色产品，市场竞争威胁小。例如，某些生产特效药品、名酒、特殊用途的器械等的企业就是采用这种策略。

Special product strategy means that the enterprise is specialized in the production of certain products with good sales, according to its special resources and technical expertise. Because the strategy has characteristics of minimal mix width and depth, and strong correlation, the developed market is limited. Because special resources and technology are used to create special products, market competition is not serious, for example, some enterprises producing effective drugs, alcohol, equipment with special purposes, etc. adopt this strategy.

6. 特殊专业型策略 Special Professional Strategy

该策略是指企业凭其特殊的技术、服务，满足某些特殊顾客的需要，如提供特殊的工程设计、咨询服务、律师服务、保镖服务等。本策略组合宽度小、深度大、关联性强。

Special professional strategy means that an enterprise provides special technology and services to meet the needs of certain particular customers, such as special engineering design, consulting service, legal service, bodyguard service, etc. This strategy has narrow mix width, deep depth and strong correlation.

(二)动态产品组合策略 Dynamic Product Mix Strategy

动态产品组合策略，是指企业根据市场环境和资源条件变动的前景，适时增加应开发的新产品和淘汰应退出的衰退产品，从而随着时间的推移，仍能取得最大利润的产品组合。可见，及时调整产品组合是保证产品组合动态平衡的条件。动态平衡的产品组合亦称最佳产品组合。从动态的角度分析，可供选择的产品组合策略有以下类型。

Dynamic product mix strategy means that an enterprise should in a timely manner increase new products and phase out products which may exit from recession and obtain bigger profits with the passing of time according to changes of market environment and resource conditions. Thus, timely adjustment of product mix is the condition to ensure the equilibrium of dynamic product mix. Dynamically balanced product mix is also known as the best product mix. From the viewpoint of dynamic analysis, available product mix strategy has the following types.

1. 扩大产品组合策略 Expanding Product Mix Strategy

该策略是指扩大产品组合的宽度或深度，增加新的产品系列或项目，以扩大经营范围，生产经营更多的产品，从而满足市场的需要。它是指当企业预测现有产品线的销售额和盈利率在未来可能下降时，通过增加新的产品线或加强其中有发展潜力的产品线，去满足新的需要而采取的策略。扩大产品组合的方式包括：一是在维持产品原有的质量和价格的前提下，增加同一产品的款式和规格；二是增加不同质量和不同价格的同类产品；三是增加相互关联的产品；四是增加与现有产品使用同一材料或相同生产技术的其他产品；五是增加可获得较高利润而与现有产品完全无关的产品。

Expanding product mix strategy is to expand the width or depth of product mix, add new product series or projects to expand the scope of business, and produce and operate more products to meet market needs. This is adopted when a company predicts that the existing sales and earnings rate of a product line may decline in the future. The company will meet customers' new needs by adding new product lines or strengthening the product line with potential. Ways to expand the product mix include: first increasing the styles and sizes of the same product on the premise of maintaining the original quality and price; second, adding similar products of different quality and price; third, increasing relevant products; fourth, increasing other products using the same materials or production technology as existing products; fifth, increasing products which may obtain higher profits but are irrelevant to existing products.

2. 缩减产品组合策略 Reducing Product Mix Strategy

该策略是指减少产品组合的宽度和深度，即从企业现有产品组合中剔除某些产品大类或产品项目，集中力量生产经营一个系列的产品或少数产品项目，以提高专业化水平，力图从较少的产品中获得较多的利润。在市场繁荣时期，较长或较宽的产品组合会为企业带来更多的盈利机会；但是，在市场不景气或原材料、能源供应紧张时期，缩减产品线也能使总利润上升。

Reducing product mix strategy refers to reducing the width and depth of product mix, which means to cut some product categories or products projects from the existing product mix, and focus on producing a series of products, or a small number of product projects, in order to improve the specialization level and gain more profits from fewer products. In a booming market, longer or wider product mix will bring more profit opportunities for the enterprise; however, during the period of recession or tight raw materials and energy supplies, reduction of product line can make profits rise.

缩减产品组合有三种方式：一是保持原有产品的宽度或深度，即不增加产品大类和产品项目，只增加产品产量，以降低成本；二是缩减产品大类，即企业根据本身特长和市场的特殊需要，只生产经营某一个或少数几个产品大类；三是缩减产品项目，即在一个产品大类内取消一些利润较低的产品，尽量生产能带来较高利润的少数几个品种的产品。

There are three ways to cut product mix: one is to keep the original width or depth of the products, also not to increase product categories and product projects, but only to increase the output of products to reduce costs; another is to cut product categories, which means the enterprise only producing and operating one or a few product categories according to the speciality itself and the special needs of the market; the last is to cancel some product projects, that is to say, the company cancels some of the less profitable products of a product category, and tries to produce a few varieties of products which can bring higher profits.

3. 产品线延伸策略 Product Line Extension

产品线延伸策略，指全部或部分地改变原有产品的市场定位，即改变企业原有的产品的高档、中档或低档，有向下延伸、向上延伸和双向延伸三种方式。

Product line extension strategy refers to changing all or part of market positioning of the original product, which is to change the original high-grade, middle-grade or low-grade products. There are three ways to do this: downward extension, upward extension and two-way extension.

1) 向下延伸 Downward Extension

是指企业原来生产高档产品，后来决定增加低档产品。实行这一决策需要具备以下市场条件：利用高档名牌产品的声誉，吸引购买力水平较低的顾客慕名购买此产品线中的廉价产品；高档产品销售增长缓慢，企业的资源设备没有得到充分利用，为赢得更多的顾客，将产品线向下伸展；企业最初进入高档产品市场的目的是建立厂牌信誉，然后进入中、低档市场，以扩大市场占有率和销售增长率；补充企业的产品线空白。实行这种策略也有一定的风险，如处理不慎，会影响企业原有产品特别是名牌产品的市场形象，另外还要对销售系统重新进行设置。所有这些，将大大增加企业的营销费用开支。

This is when an enterprise originally produces high-grade products, but later decides to add low-grade products. This decision requires the following market conditions: taking advantage of the reputation of the high-end brand products to attract customers with low level of purchasing power to buy the cheap products in the product line. Because the sales of high-end products grow slowly and the resource equipment of the enterprise is underutilized, the product line extends downward in order to win more customers. The purpose of an enterprise first entering into a high grade product market is to establish brand reputation, and then go into middle and low-grade markets to expand market share and sales growth to supplement the bank of the enterprise's product line. There are certain risks in adopting this strategy. If an enterprise cannot handle the problem properly, it will affect the enterprise's market image regarding the original products, especially those famous brand products; in addition, the the sales system will have to be resetted. All of these will greatly increase the enterprise's marketing expenses.

2) 向上延伸 Upward Extension

是指企业原来生产低档产品，后来决定增加高档产品。这种策略适用于：高档产品市场具有较大的潜在成长率和较高的毛利率；企业的技术设备和营销能力已具备加入高档产品市场的条件；企业要重新进行产品线定位。采用这一策略也要承担一定的风险，如果不能改变产品在顾客心目中的地位，将会影响原有产品的市场声誉；甚至企业的销售代理商和经销商可能没有能力去经营新增的高档产品。

This is when an enterprise originally manufacturing cheap products, later decides to add high-end products. This strategy can be used when a high-end product market has great potential growth rate and higher profit margins. The enterprise's technology equipment and marketing ability meets the requirement to join a high-end product market and the enterprise wants to reposition the product line. Adopting this strategy also assumes certain risks, such as failing to change status in the eyes of customers affecting the market reputation of the original products. Indeed a company's sales agents and dealers may not be able to handle new high-end product.

3) 双向延伸 Two-way Extension

是指企业产品原定位于中档产品市场，当其占据了市场优势以后，决定向产品大类的上下两个方面延伸，一方面增加高档产品，另一方面增加低档产品，扩大市场阵地。

This refers to an enterprise first positioning the product in medium-end product market. After mastering the market advantage, the enterprise decides to extend the product categories upward and downward. On the one hand, an enterprise increases the high-end products; on the other hand, it increases the low-end products to expand the overall market.

第五节 新产品开发策略
New-Product Development Strategies

新产品开发是企业未来生命的源泉。在现代社会，消费者的需求不断变化，技术也在迅速发展和传播，产品生命周期则相应缩短，企业积极寻找、开发新产品，以适应市场需求，提升自我。

New-product development is the source of life for an enterprise in the future. In modern society, consumer demand changes constantly, and technology also develops and spreads rapidly. So product life cycle is shortened accordingly. In this case, the enterprises actively seek and develop new products to adapt to market demand and to improve their position.

一、新产品的概念及类型 Concept and Types of New Products

市场营销学对新产品概念的解释同从科学和技术发展的角度对新产品的定义不完全相同，前者包含的内容更为广泛。从技术角度来讲，只有采用了新工艺、新技术、新材料，从而使产品的功能、结构、技术特征等发生显著变化，才称其为新产品；而从市场营销的角度看，只要在功能或形态上得到改进或与原有产品产生差异，并为顾客带来新的利益，即视为新产品。根据后者，新产品包括以下几种类型。

The concept of a new product from the point of view of marketing is not exactly the same as the concept from the view of science and technology development. The former contains more content. Technically, only using new technology and material to make significant changes to product function, structure and technical characteristics can not denote a new product. But from the marketing point of view, as long as the products are improved in function or form different from the original products, and could more benefits to customers, they are new products. According to the latter, there are the following several types of new product.

(一)完全创新产品 Innovative Products

是指应用科学技术的新发明而研制成功的，具有新结构、新技术、新材料等特征的，市场上从未有过的新产品。一项科技从发明到将科研成果转化为产品，需要花费很长的时间和巨大的人力、物力、财力，因此，绝大多数企业很难提供这样的全新产品。一种全新的产品要经国家科学技术部门的鉴定批准，方可申请专利，受到法律保护。

This refers to new products which are the consequence of scientific and technological development, have new structure, new technology, new material and other characteristics, and have not appeared in the market previously. It takes long time and huge human, material and financial resources to transform technological development into new products applying scientific research achievements. Therefore, most enterprises have difficulty in providing such new products. Only after a new product is approved and identified by State Science and Technology Department, can an enterprise apply for a patent and get legal protection.

(二)换代新产品 Replacement Products

这是对原有产品全部或部分采用新技术、新材料、新结构,而制造出来的使原有的产品的性能有飞跃性提高的新产品。这种换代产品比原有的产品增添了新的功能,给顾客带来了新的利益。例如,彩色电视机是黑白电视机的换代产品,如今已发展到与计算机、录音机、自动电话、传真等兼容,可直接接受卫星电视信号,并带有立体声、遥控等设备。

This is a route for adopting new technology, new materials and new structures, completely or partially, while producing the original products with higher performance than the original product. New functions are added to the successor which can bring new benefits to customers. For example, color TVs were a replacement of black and white televisions. Now TVs have the mixed functions of computers, tape recorders, automobile phones, fax, machines etc, and can directly receive satellite TV, and contain stereo and remote control devices, etc.

(三)改进新产品 Improvement of New Products

这种新产品不是由科学技术的进步而导致对产品的重大改革,只是对现有产品的品质、性能、款式等进行一定的改进。其类型有如下几种:一是采用新设计、新材料改变原有产品的品质、降低成本,但产品用途不变;二是采用新式样、新包装、新商标改变原有产品的外观而不改变其用途;三是把原有产品与其他产品或原材料加以组合,使其增加新功能;四是采用新设计、新结构、新零件增加其新用途,如不同型号的汽车及不同款式、不同质量的服装等。

This is not great innovation of original products caused by the development of science and technology, but certain changes of existing products such as quality, performance, design, etc. There are the following types: first, to use new design and material to change the product quality, reducing costs, but the purpose remains the same; second, to adopt new style, new packaging, new trademark to change the appearance of the original product without changing its functions; third, to add new features by combining the original products with other products and raw materials; fourth, to adopt new design, new structure and new components to increase new functions, for example, different models of cars and garments with different patterns and quality.

(四)仿制新产品 Imitation of New Products

这是指企业模仿市场上正在销售的产品的性能、工艺而生产的产品,是企业的新产品。开发仿制新产品,对于许多产品研发能力比较薄弱的中小企业来说很实用,但要注意在仿制的时候,应符合专利法等法律的规定。

This means new products that an enterprise produces imitating the performance and technology of products which are already sold in the market. The development and imitation of new products is practical for small and medium-sized enterprises whose ability of product development is weak. However, while imitating, it is necessary to comply with the provisions of patent law and other laws.

新产品开发的实质,是推出具有不同内涵与外延的新产品。对大多数企业来说,多改进现有产品比创造全新产品更好。

The essence of the new product development is to introduce new products with different connotations and extension. For most enterprises, it's better to improve existing products, rather than to create new products.

二、新产品开发的策略 Strategies of New-product Development

(一)领先型开发策略 Leadership Development Strategy

企业努力追求产品技术水平和最终用途的新颖性,保持技术上的持续优势和市场竞争中的领先地位。当然这需要企业有很强的研究、开发能力和雄厚的资源。

Companies strive for technical levels and novelty of end use to sustain technological advantage and leading positions in market competition. Of course, this requires that an enterprise has strong research and development ability and abundant resources.

(二)追随型开发策略 Following Development Strategy

采取这种策略,企业并不抢先研发新产品,而是当市场上出现较好的新产品时,对产品进行仿制并加以改进,迅速占领市场。这种战略要求企业具有较强的跟踪竞争对手情况与动态的技术信息机构与人员,具有很强的消化、吸收与创新能力。这种策略在专利制度环境下不容易实施。

This is when an enterprise has a strategy, not for developing new products, but imitating and improving products to quickly occupy the market when there are good new products already in the market. This strategy requires companies with strong ability to track rivals, dynamic technical information institutions and personnel, strong digestion, absorption and innovation ability. This is not easy to implement in the context of a patent system.

(三)替代型开发策略 Alternative Development Strategy

采取这种策略,企业有偿运用其他单位的研究与开发成果,替代自己研究与开发新产品。研究与开发力量不强、资源有限的企业宜采用这种策略。

Adopting this strategy, an enterprise uses paid research and development skills of other units instead of researching and developing its own technology. Enterprises with weak research and development ability and limited resources might find this strategy appropriate.

(四)混合型开发策略 Mixed Development Strategy

以提高产品市场占有率和企业经济效益为准则,依据企业实际情况,综合运用上述几种产品开发策略。

This refers to a situation in which an enterprise uses a mixture of the above several product development strategies in order to improve product market share and the enterprise's economic benefits, according to the enterprise's actual situation.

本 章 小 结
Summary

产品，是指能够在市场上得到的，用于满足人们欲望和需要的任何东西，包括实物、服务、场所、设计、软件、意识等多种形式。系统(整体)产品概念是核心产品、形式产品、附加产品三个层次有机结合的系统。依据耐用性，产品可分为非耐用品、耐用品和服务；依据销售的目标对象（购买者的身份）及其对产品的用途，产品可大致分成两大类：消费品和产业用品。

Products refer to anything that can be provided to the market to satisfy certain desires and needs, including material objects, services, locations, designs, software, consciousness, etc. Total product concept is the organic combination of three levels: core product, actual products and additional products. On the basis of durability, products are divided into nondurable goods, durable goods and services; according to sales target (the buyers' identity) and use, products can be divided into two categories: consumption products and industrial products.

产品市场生命周期是指一种产品从投入市场开始到退出市场为止的周期性变化的过程。它包括投入期、成长期、成熟期、衰退期四个阶段。不同阶段有其不同特点，应采取不同的营销策略。品牌策略和包装策略是企业产品策略的重要内容。产品组合是指一个企业生产或经营的全部产品线和产品项目的集合体，它包括四个变数，即产品组合的宽度、长度、深度和关联度。

Product life cycle is a process full of cyclical changes starting from the launching of the product and ending with withdrawal from the market. It includes introduction stage, growth stage, maturity stage and decline stage. There are different characteristics at different stages, and different marketing strategies should be adopted accordingly. Branding strategy and packaging strategy are important aspects of an enterprise's product strategy. Product mix refers to the integration of all the product lines and projects produced and operated by an enterprise. It includes four measured variables: width, length, depth and correlation.

产品组合策略是指企业根据市场状况、自身资源条件和竞争态势对产品组合的广度、长度、深度和关联度进行不同组合的选择与运用。

Product mix strategy involves different combinations of selection and use shown between width, length, depth and correlation of a product portfolio according to market conditions, resource conditions and the competitive situation.

新产品是指企业向市场提供的较原先的产品有根本不同的产品。新产品开发策略有领先型开发策略、追随型开发策略、替代型开发策略和混合型开发策略四种类型。

New products refer to products developed and launched by an enterprise being totally different from past products. There are four strategies of new product development: the leading development strategy, the following development strategy, the alternative development strategy and the mixed development strategy.

思 考 题
Questions

1. 产品整体概念的含义是什么？产品的类别有哪些？

What is the meaning of total product concept? What are the categories of product?

2. 什么是产品生命周期？产品生命周期各阶段的特点及其营销策略的类型是什么？

What is product life cycle? What are the characteristics of product life cycle at every stage of types of marketing strategy?

3. 品牌与包装策略有哪些类型？

What are the types of branding and packing strategies?

4. 什么是产品组合？产品组合的宽度、长度、深度和关联度对营销活动的意义是什么？产品组合策略类型有哪些？

What is product mix? What are the meanings of width, length, depth and correlation of the product mix to marketing activities? What are the types of product mix strategies?

5. 新产品开发的策略有哪些？

What are the strategies of new product development?

第七章 价格策略
Pricing Strategies

【学习目标】
1. 了解定价的基本程序和定价方法；
2. 分析企业定价的基本策略；
3. 企业调价的方式和技巧。

Learning Objectives
1. Pricing procedures and pricing methods;
2. Firms' basic pricing strategies;
3. Enterprises' methods and techniques for adjusting prices.

在市场营销活动中，价格永远都是市场中最活跃的因素，而定价是标在商品上的市场零售价格。定价直接影响消费者的购买行为动机，也是企业获取利润的最活跃的因素。价格策略能否为消费者或用户接受，决定了企业市场占有率和企业盈利水平。

In marketing, price is always the most active factor and is marked on the goods for sale. Pricing directly affects the consumer's purchase behavior and motivation and also actively affects enterprises' profit. It decides enterprises' market share and benefit level whether the pricing strategies can be accepted by consumers or not.

第一节 定价的程序与方法
Pricing Procedures and Methods

一、定价程序 Pricing Procedures

企业定价的主要程序包括：明确定价目标、测定市场需求、估算成本费用、分析竞争状况、选择定价方法和确定最后价格。

The main procedures of pricing are setting pricing objectives, determining market demand, estimating cost, analyzing competition situation, choosing pricing approaches and determining the final price.

(一)明确定价目标 Setting Pricing Objectives

定价目标是企业选择定价方法和制定价格策略的依据。企业在不同营销环境中进行经营，应该有不同的营销目标，因此，企业在选择定价目标时，应权衡各种定价目标的因素和利弊，慎重地加以选择和确定。企业定价目标主要包含以下五个方面。

Pricing objectives are the foundation for selecting pricing methods and strategies. Enterprises should have different marketing objectives in different marketing environment. Enterprises, therefore, should consider the advantages and disadvantages in pricing objectives and decide on the right ones. Enterprises' pricing objectives mainly include the following five aspects.

1. 以追求利润最大化为定价目标 To Pursue Maximum Profit

追求利润最大化，是指企业在一定时期内可能获得的最高利润总额。利润最大化往往与较高的价格相联系，但与最高价格没有必然的联系。企业利润来自全部收入扣除全部成本以后的余额，而不是单位产品价格中包含的预期赢利水平。最大的利润往往更多地取决于合理价格推动产生的需要量和销售规模。企业利润最大化分为短期和长期两种。在有较好的市场环境时，企业更愿意追求短期最大利润。

The pursuit of maximum profit means the possible highest amount of profit the enterprise can achieve in a certain period. Profit maximization is often associated with higher prices, but not necessarily with the highest price. The profit is the balance from the total income with all the cost deducted, rather than the expected benefit level contained in the unit price. The maximum profit often depends on the demand and sales scale which are driven by reasonable price. The enterprise's maximum profit can be ranged into short-term and long-term types, and the latter is more often pursued while there is a better marketing environment.

2. 以市场占有率最大化为定价目标 To Maximize Market Share

市场占有率是企业经营状况和产品竞争力状况的综合反映，它是指本企业产品销售量在同一产品市场销售总量中所占的比率。它有两种表示方法：一是产品数量的市场占有率，二是产品销售的市场占有率。二者之间的区别是前者不涉及产品价格，后者则反映了与价格间的关系。企业在赢得高市场占有率之后，能产生规模经济效益并获得较高的长期利润；同时低价位还可以有效地排斥竞争对手，因此企业应制定尽可能低的价格来追求市场占有率的领先地位。

Market share reflects comprehensively the enterprise's operating conditions and product competitiveness. It refers to the ratio of the enterprise's sales in the total sales of the same product. It can be expressed in two ways, market occupation of product quantity and market occupation of product sales. The difference is that the former does not involve product prices while the latter reflects the relationship with the price. Enterprises can achieve scale economy and higher long-term profits after winning a big market share. Meanwhile, low prices effectively exclude competitors, so enterprises should set the lowest possible price to lead in market share.

3. 以提高市场竞争能力为定价目标 To Improve Market Competition Ability

价格竞争是市场竞争的重要方面，因此处在激烈竞争中的企业经常从价格竞争的角度来确定定价目标。以提高市场竞争能力为定价目标有三种情况：一是进攻性定价，其目标是打击竞争对手；二是防御性定价，这一般是为了应付竞争被动地保持与竞争者相近的价格；三是预防性定价，这是在产品上市之初，企业为了维护自己产品的市场优势地位，常常采用低价的方法以抵制更多的企业加入竞争，有时也采用特别高价的方法出售商品，排斥其他竞争者进入同一市场。

Price competition is an important aspect in market competition. The enterprise in fierce competition, therefore, often sets its pricing objective from the view of price competition. There are three types of pricing which aim to enhance market competition ability: aggressive pricing with the goal to fight against rivals; defensive pricing, which is typically used to cope with competition and passively keep close to competitor's price; preventive pricing often used to resist other enterprises joining the competition with low prices to maintain advantageous market position when the enterprise has just launched the product. Sometimes, very high prices are also used to dispel other competitors.

4. 以维持生存为定价目标 To Survive as the Pricing Objective

当企业生产力过剩或面临激烈竞争，或者消费者的需求发生变化时，需要把维持生存作为主要目标。企业为了能继续生产，使存货尽快周转，就必须降低价格，以弥补可变成本和固定成本。

An enterprise will try to survive when there is excess production capacity, fierce competition or change of consumer demand. The enterprise must lower its price to make up for some variable and fixed costs in order to sustain production and inventory turnover.

5. 以实现预期的投资收益率为定价目标 To Achieve the Expected Rate of Return on Investment

投资收益率反映着企业的投资效益。确立这种定价目标的过程是以企业投资额和预期产量为出发点，根据投资额规定一定的投资收益率，然后计算出各单位产品的利润额，把它加到产品成本上，就是该产品的出售价格。由于各单位产品的利润是固定的，企业生产的产品数量越大，则利润额越大。

Rate of return on investment reflects the enterprise's investment efficiency. The pricing process is from the starting point of the enterprise's investment amount and expected output, a certain rate of return on investment is set according to the investment amount, and profit margin of unit output is calculated then added to the product cost, which will be the price for sale. Due to the fixed profit from unit output, the more the enterprise produces, the greater the profits can be.

(二)测定市场需求 Determining Market Demand

企业商品的价格会影响需求，需求的变化影响企业的产品销售以至企业营销目标的实现。因此，测定市场需求状况是制定价格的重要工作。一般情况下，价格与需求成反比方向变化。价格上升，需求减少；价格下降，需求增加，这是供求规律的客观反映。测定需求弹性，就要计算价格弹性系数，即价格变动而引起的需求的相应变动率，它反映了需求变动对价格变动的敏感程度。需求的价格弹性可用公式表示：

$$E_d = -\frac{需求量变动的百分比}{价格变动的百分比}$$

Product price will influence demand and change of demand will affect the enterprise's sales and even its realization of marketing objectives. So determination of market demand is important to pricing. In general, the price changes inversely with the demand. When the price goes up, the demand will decrease and vice versa, which is an objective reflection of the law of supply and demand. Price elasticity coefficient will be calculated to determine demand elasticity. Price elasticity coefficient is the rate of change in demand caused by price change, which reflects how sensitive the demand change is to the price change. Price elasticity of demand formula is:

$$E_d = \frac{\Delta Q/Q}{\Delta P/P} = -\frac{\Delta Q}{\Delta P} \cdot \frac{P}{Q}$$

以 E_d 来表示需求弹性，Q 代表需求量，ΔQ 代表需求量的变动量，P 代表价格，ΔP 代表价格的变动量。

E_d stands for price elasticity of demand, Q for demand quantity, ΔQ for the change in demand quantity, P for price and ΔP for the price change.

计算结果有三种情况。

There are three results of the calculation.

(1) 当 $E_d>1$，即价格变动率小于需求量变动率时，此产品富于需求弹性，或称为弹性大。这类商品价格的上升(或下降)会引起需求量较大幅度的减少(或增加)。对其定价时，应降低价格、薄利多销，以达到增加盈利的目的；提价则务求谨慎，以防需求量发生锐减，影响企业收入。

When $E_d>1$, i.e., the price change rate is less than the demand change rate, the product is of elasticity, or has great elasticity. The increase (or decrease) of this product price will cause significant decrease (or increase) in demand. On pricing this kind of product, the price should be lowered in order to sell more to gain more profit. It should be careful to increase the price in case there is a sharp collapse in demand which will influence enterprise income.

(2) 当 $E_d=1$ 时，即价格变动率同需求量的变动率一致，此产品具有一般需求弹性。这类商品价格的上升(或下降)会引起需求量等比例的减少(或增加)，因此，价格变化对销售收入影响不大。

When $E_d=1$, i.e., the price change rate is the same as the demand change rate, the product is of usual elasticity. The increase (or decrease) of the price will cause decrease (or increase) of the demand accordingly. The price change, therefore, does not have much influence on sales.

(3) 当 $E_d<1$ 时，即价格的变动率大于需求量的变动率时，此产品缺乏需求弹性或者非弹性需求。这类商品价格的上升(或下降)仅会引起需求量较小程度的减少(增加)。对其定价时，较高水平的价格往往会增加盈利，低价对需求量刺激效果不强，薄利并不能多销，反而会降低收入水平。

When $E_d<1$, i.e., the price change rate is greater than the demand change rate, the product lacks demand elasticity or is of non-elasticity. The increase (or decrease) of price will cause a minor decrease (or increase) of demand. On pricing this kind of product, high price will lead to profit increase. Low price does not stimulate sales very much, so small profit cannot bring more sales, but will reduce income.

(三)估算成本费用 Estimating Cost

企业在制定商品价格时，要进行成本估算。企业商品价格的最高限度取决于市场需求及有关限制因素，而最低价格不能低于商品的经营成本费用，这是企业价格的下限。

When enterprises set commodity price, the cost must be estimated. The ceiling of the price depends on market demand and other related factors, and the bottom of the price can not be lower than management cost, which is the lowest limit.

企业的成本包括两种：一种是固定成本，另一种是变动成本，或称可变成本、直接成本。固定成本与变动成本之和即为某产品的总成本。

Enterprise cost includes two kinds, fixed cost and variable cost (or direct cost). The sum of fixed cost and variable cost is the total cost of a product.

在成本估算中，离不开对"产量—成本—利润"关系的分析，而其中一个要分析的重要概念是分析"边际成本"。所谓边际成本是指企业每增加(减少)一个单位生产量所引起的总成本变动的数值。因为边际成本影响到企业的边际收益，所以企业必须对其予以极大的关注。

The relation between production, cost and profit must be analyzed in order to estimate the cost. One important analysis is "marginal cost". Marginal cost is the change in the total cost that arises when the quantity produced changes by one unit. Because the marginal cost affects the marginal revenue, enterprises must pay a lot of attention to it.

(四)分析竞争状况 Analyzing Competition Situation

在制定价格的时候，企业还必须考虑竞争者的成本和定价，以及竞争者对企业定价策略的可能反应。想购买索尼数码照相机的消费者会将其价格与价值、尼康、柯达、佳能、奥林巴斯以及其他类似的照相机相比较。另外，企业的定价策略可能会影响竞争的性质。如果索尼公司实行高价格、高利润的方针，它可能会吸引竞争。一个低价格、低利润的方针将会阻挡竞争者，甚至将它们挤出市场。

When setting the price, an enterprise must consider the cost and pricing of its competitors, and their possible reactions to its pricing strategy. Consumers who want to purchase Sony digital cameras will compare prices and values of similar products like Kodak, Canon, Nikon and Olympus. What's more, pricing strategy will affect the nature of the competition. If Sony company adopts the policy of high price and high profit, it will attract competition. A policy of low price and low profit would push out competitors and even put them out of the market.

(五)选择定价方法 Choosing Pricing Approaches

详见第二节"定价的基本策略"。

For details, see Pricing Strategies in section 2.

(六)制定最终价格 Determining the Final Price

最后确定价格时，必须考虑遵循这样四项原则：①商品价格的制定与企业预期的定价目标要一致，这有利于企业总的战略目标的实现；②商品价格的制定符合法律规定和政策的有关规定；③商品价格的制定符合消费者整体及长远利益；④商品价格的制定要与企业市场营销组合中的非价格因素协调一致、互相配合，以达成企业营销目标。

Four principles should be observed in deciding on the final price: ①The price making should be consistent with the expected pricing objective, which would be favorable to the realization of an general strategic goals of an enterprise. ②The price making complies with relevant laws, policies and regulations. ③The price making is in line with the overall and long-term interests of consumers. ④The price setting should work well with the non-price factors of the enterprise marketing mix in order to achieve marketing objectives well.

二、定价方法 Pricing Approaches

定价方法是企业为实现其定价目标所采取的具体做法。按照定价依据的不同，定价方法通常可以分为如下三大类：成本导向定价法，需求导向定价法和竞争导向定价法。每一类中又包含多种不同的具体定价法。在制定价格策略时，必须慎重选择定价方法。

Pricing approaches are used to achieve pricing objectives. According to different criteria, pricing approaches can be classified into three categories, cost-oriented pricing, demand-oriented pricing and competition-oriented pricing. Each category has many specific pricing methods. Pricing approaches must be selected with care when setting pricing strategies.

(一)成本导向定价法 Cost-oriented Pricing

成本导向定价法，是以企业生产商品的全部成本和企业预期利润为基础的定价方法。它的主要优点是简便易行，定出的价格风险较小，缺点是难以确定各行各业的加成比例，灵活性不大，市场竞争不得力。它主要包括以下几种具体方法：

Cost-oriented pricing is based on the absorption cost of production and expected profit. This pricing is easy and less risky, but it is difficult to determine the markup rate in all industries. It lacks flexibility and competitiveness. It mainly includes the following specific methods.

1. 加成定价法 Cost-plus Pricing

加成定价法包括完全成本加成定价法和进价加成定价法。

The cost-plus pricing includes absorption-cost-based pricing and purchase-price-based pricing.

(1) 完全成本加成定价法多为蔬菜、水果商店采用，其计算过程是：首先确定单位变动成本；再加上平均分摊的固定成本组成单位完全成本；然后加上一定的加成率(毛利率)；最后形成销售价格。

Absorption cost-based pricing is often adopted by greengrocers. Its calculation process is like this: first, the Unit Variable Cost, after being identified, and Fixed Cost, which is equally shared, form Unit Absorption Cost. Certain Markup Ratio (rate of gross profit) is then added to the Unit Absorption Cost, and the selling price is therefore formed.

其计算公式为：产品售价=单位完全成本×(1+成本加成率)

The formula is: Selling Price=Unit Absorption Cost×(1+Markup Ratio)

其中，成本加成率=(售价-进价)÷进货成本×100%

Markup Ratio=(Selling Price-Purchase Price)/Purchasing Cost×100%

(2) 进价加成定价法多被零售业(百货商店、杂货店等)所应用。

Purchase price-based pricing is often used by retailers like department stores and grocers.

其计算公式为：产品售价=进货价格÷(1-加成率)

The formula is: Selling Price=Purchase Price/(1−Markup Ratio)

其中，加成率=(售价-进价)÷售价×100%

Markup Ratio=(Selling Price−Purchase Price)/Selling Price×100%

在以上两种定价方法中，加成率的确定是定价的关键。一般来说，加成率的大小与商品的需求弹性和企业的预期盈利有关。在实践中，同行业往往形成一个为大多数企业所接受的加成率。

Setting markup ratio is the key for the above two pricing methods. In General, markup ratio is related to product demand elasticity and desired profit. In practice, a markup ratio is usually formed within an industry which is accepted by most enterprises in the industry.

2. 目标收益定价法 Target Profit Pricing

目标收益定价法，又称投资收益率定价法。它是根据企业的投资总额、预期销量和投资回收期等因素来确定价格的方法。例如，建设一空调厂的总投资额为1000万元，投资回收期为10年，预期销售2000台，总固定成本600万元，每台空调的变动成本为500元。其采用目标收益定价法确定价格的基本步骤如下。

Target profit pricing is a pricing method by rate of return on investment. It is based on a company's total investment, expected sales, payback period and other factors. For example, 10 million Yuan is needed for the construction of an air conditioner plant, payback period is 10 years, expected sales are 2,000 sets, total fixed cost is 6 million Yuan and unit variable cost is 500 Yuan. If the method of target profit pricing is taken, the pricing steps are as follows.

1) 确定目标收益率 Setting Target Rate of Return

$$目标收益率=1/投资回收期×100\%=1/10×100\%=10\%$$

$$\text{Target Profit Rate}=1/\text{Payback Period}×100\%=1/10×100\%=10\%$$

2) 确定单位产品目标利润额 Setting Target Profit of Unit Production

$$单位产品目标利润额=总投资额×目标收益率÷预期销量$$
$$=10\,000\,000×10\%÷2000$$
$$=500(元)$$

Target Profit of Unit Product=Total Investment×Target Rate of Return÷Expected Sales

$$=10\,000\,000 \times 10\% \div 2000$$
$$=¥500 \text{ RMB}$$

3) 计算单位产品价格 Calculating Unit Price

单位产品价格=企业固定成本÷预期销量+单位变动成本+单位产品目标利润额
$$=6\,000\,000 \div 2000 + 500 + 500$$
$$=4000(元)$$

Unit Price=Fixed Cost÷Expected Sales+Unit Variable Cost + Target Profit of Unit Production =6 000 000÷2000+500+500=¥4 000RMB

该方法多适用于那些需求比较稳定的大型制造业的产品、供不应求且价格弹性小的商品、市场占有率高并具有垄断性的商品，以及大型的公用事业、劳务工程和服务项目等服务产品价格的制定。

Target Profit Pricing is suitable for those products of large manufacturing industries which have steady demand, those of small elasticity in short supply, those products which command high market share and monopoly, and service industries in large public utilities, labor and service projects.

3. 盈亏平衡定价法 Break-even Pricing

盈亏平衡定价法又称保本定价法或收支平衡定价法，是指在销量既定的条件下，企业产品的价格必须达到一定的水平，才能做到盈亏平衡、收支相抵。而既定的销量就称为盈亏平衡点，故将其称为盈亏平衡定价法。科学地预测销量和已知固定成本、变动成本，是盈亏平衡定价的前提；盈亏平衡分析原理是其理论基础；盈亏平衡分析的核心点是确定盈亏平衡点，即企业收支相抵、利润为零时的状态。

Break-even pricing means, with fixed sales, the price must remain at a certain level in order to achieve break even. The fixed sales is called Break-even Point, and that is why this pricing method is called Break-even Pricing. The premise of this pricing is to forecast sales scientifically and to know fixed cost and variable cost. Its theoretical basis is the principle of break-even analysis, the core point of which is to determine the break-even point, i.e. the state of break-even and zero profit.

其计算公式为：单位产品价格=(固定成本/损益平衡销售量+变动成本)/(1−税率)

The formula: Unit Price=(Fixed Cost/Break-even Sales+Variable Cost)/(1−tax rate)

例：某旅游饭店共有客房 300 间，全部客房年度固定成本总额为 300 万美元，每间客房每天变动成本为 10 美元，预计客房年平均出租率为 80%，营业税率为 5%，求该饭店客房保本时的价格。

Example: a hotel has 300 rooms. Its total fixed cost per year is 3 million dollars and variable cost of each room is 10 dollars. It is expected that the rent rate is 80% and business tax rate is 5%. What is the break-even price?

解：根据所给数据和公式，计算如下：

$$单位产品价格 = \frac{\dfrac{3\,000\,000}{300 \times 365 \times 80\%} + 10}{1-5\%} = \frac{34.25+10}{0.95} = 46.58(美元/间 \cdot 天)$$

According to the given data and the formulas, the calculation process is as follows:

$$\text{unit price} = \frac{\frac{3\,000\,000}{300 \times 365 \times 80\%} + 10}{1 - 5\%} = \frac{34.25 + 10}{0.95} = \$46.58\text{USD (Per day Per room)}$$

根据盈亏平衡定价法确定的旅游价格,是旅游企业的保本价格。低于此价格旅游企业会亏损,高于此价格旅游企业则有盈利,实际售价高出保本价格越多,旅游企业盈利越大。

The price determined by Break-even Pricing Method is the tourism enterprise's break-even price. The enterprise will lose money if its price is lower than the break even price, and will make a profit if higher. The higher the actual price is than the break-even price, the more profit the enterprise can make.

(二)需求导向定价法 Demand-oriented Pricing

需求导向定价法,是指企业在定价时不仅考虑到成本,而且注意到消费者对产品价值的理解和市场需求强度。市场需求较多时,可以将价格定得低些。这种定价法主要包括以下几种具体方法。

Demand-oriented pricing means that the enterprise considers not only the cost but also buyers' perceptions of product value and demand intensity. When there is more demand, the price can be set low. It includes several specific pricing methods.

1. 认知价值定价法 Perceived Value Pricing

这是根据购买者对产品的认知价值来制定价格的一种方法。认知价值定价与现代市场定位观念相一致。采用这种定价方法,企业必须根据自己产品的投资额、销售量、单位产品成本和盈利来研究该种产品在消费者心目中的地位,做出恰当的判断,进而有针对性地运用市场销售组合中的非价格因素去影响消费者,使消费者形成一定的价格观念,制定消费者需求的希望价格。认知价值定价的关键在于准确地计算产品所提供的全部市场认知价值。企业如果过高地估计认知价值,便会定出偏高的价格;如果过低地估计认知价值,则会定出偏低的价格。因此,为准确地把握市场认知价值,必须进行市场营销研究。

This method bases the price on the buyers' perceptions of product value. It is consistent with modern market concept. With this method, an enterprise must study the status of its product in consumers' minds according to its own investment, sales, unit cost and profit. The enterprise then makes a proper judgment and tries to influence consumers with non-price factors in the marketing mix so that consumers will form certain price perceptions and desired price by consumers is therefore set. The key point of this pricing method is to calculate all the perceived value accurately. If the enterprise overestimates the perceived value, a price on the high side would be set. If the enterprise underestimate the perceived value, a price on the low side would be set. So marketing research must be done in order to grasp the market perceived value.

2. 需求差别定价法 Demand Differential Pricing

该种定价方法是以不同时间、地点、商品及不同消费者的消费需求强度差别为定价的基本依据,进而针对每种差异,在其基础价格上相应地加价或减价。例如,对于不同季节消费的商品，可以制定不同的季节差价；对于不同的销售区域和服务区域，可以采用不同的地区差价；对于外观不同的同种商品，可以确定不同的销售价格；对因职业、阶层、年龄等原因而形成不同需求的顾客，零售店在定价时要给予相应的优惠或提高价格。

It is a pricing method according to different time, place, commodity and intensity demand. On the basic price, markup or markdown is made according to each difference. Seasonal goods, for example, can be given different seasonal prices. For different marketing and service regions, different regional prices can be adopted. For goods with different appearances, different prices can be set. For customers with different demand due to different occupations, classes, ages and so on, retail price should be reduced or raised accordingly.

总之，实行差别定价需要以下条件：市场能够根据需求强度的不同进行细分；细分后的市场在一定时期内相对独立，互不干扰；高价市场中不能有低价竞争者；价格差异适度，不会引起消费者的反感。

Overall, the conditions of demand differential pricing are as follows. Market can be subdivided according to different demand intensity; the subdivided markets are relatively independent and will not interfere with each other; there are no competitors of low price at high level market; price difference is moderate and will not cause resentment among consumers.

3. 比较定价法 Comparison Pricing

这是在比较不同价格所能获得的最终利益大小的基础上来制定价格的一种方法。采用这种方法，必须努力把握商品的需求弹性。需求弹性相对大的商品可以将价格定得低一些，薄利多销，而需求弹性相对小的商品可将价格定得稍高一些，以增加收入。

By this method, the ultimate profits that can be made at different prices are compared. The demand elasticity of goods must be grasped if this pricing method is adopted. The price of goods with larger elasticity can be set lower for small profits but quick return. For goods of small elasticity, the price can be set a little higher to increase income.

4. 习惯定价法 Customary Pricing

这是基于消费者长期使用某种产品的习惯而定价的方法。某些商品由于长期保持稳定价格，就会在消费者心中形成一种习惯，例如，食盐的价格就相对稳定。

Customary pricing is based on consumers' habits of using some goods for a long time. Some goods' prices remain stable for a long time and therefore a custom is formed in the minds of consumers, for example, the price of salt is relatively stable.

(三)竞争导向定价法 Competition-oriented Pricing

竞争导向定价法，就是指企业在定价时，以竞争对手同类产品的价格为主要依据，根据企业产品的市场竞争能力，选择有利于市场竞争的定价方法。其特征是产品价格与成本及需求不发生直接关系，即使是成本和需求发生变化，只要竞争对手的价格和其他竞争环境没有大的变动，价格也不变化，反之亦然。这种定价方法通常有以下几种具体的做法。

By competition-oriented pricing, the firm bases its price largely on competitors' prices, and chooses the competitive way according to its products' competitiveness. The feature lies in that there is no direct connection between price, cost and demand. Even if cost and demand have changed, the price will not change as long as competitors' prices and other competitive conditions have not changed much, and vice versa. There are the following common forms.

1. 随行就市定价法 Going-rate Pricing

随行就市定价法，又称流行水准定价法。它是指在市场竞争激烈的情况下，企业为保存实力而采取按同行竞争者的产品价格定价的方法。这种定价法对完全竞争市场和寡头垄断市场尤其适合。随行就市定价法主要适用于需求弹性比较小或供求基本平衡的商品，如大米、面粉、食油以及某些日常用品。这种定价法的主要优点：一是平均价格水平在人们的观念中常被认为是"合理价格"，易为消费者接受；二是可以避免挑起价格战，与同行和平共处，减少市场风险；三是可以补偿平均变动成本，获得适度利润，易为消费者所接受。采用这种方法既可以追随市场领先者定价，也可以采用市场的一般价格水平定价，具体要视企业产品的特征及产品的市场差异性而定。

In going-rate pricing, the firm sets its price based on the prices that competitors charge for similar products to maintain strength in fierce market competition. This pricing is especially suitable for perfectly competitive market and oligopoly market, and for the commodities of small demand elasticity and of balancing supply and demand, such as rice, flour, cooking oil and some daily necessities. The main advantages are as follows: the average price level in people's ideas is considered to be "reasonable"and easy to accept; this pricing helps to prevent harmful price wars and firms can live in peace to reduce market risks; the average variable cost can be compensated for and modest profit can be achieved which is easily accepted by consumers. With this pricing method, an enterprise can follow the leader in pricing or adopt average price at market, which depends on the characteristics of the product and market differences of the product.

2. 跟踪竞争定价法 Tracking Competition Pricing

跟踪竞争定价法又称高于或低于竞争者产品价格的定价方法。生产特种商品和高质量商品的企业依靠其商品优势和声誉以及自己所能为消费者提供的特定服务，制定高于或低于竞争者商品的价格。采用这一定价方法的企业，一般都实力雄厚，拥有高质量的服务设施，能够提供特定的服务，或者享有某种特殊商品的专利保护权。

Tracking competition pricing is also known as pricing above or below the price of competitors. Relying on its products' advantages and good reputation as well as the special service, it can provides for consumers, the enterprise, who produces special goods and goods of high quality, sets a price higher or lower than its competitors'. Enterprises that adopt this pricing method are generally strong, with service facilities of high quality, able to provide special services or enjoy patent right dealing in special goods.

3. 密封投标定价法 Seal-bid Pricing

密封投标定价法，又称为投标竞争定价法。它是指在招标竞标的情况下，企业在对其竞争对手了解的基础上定价。报价时，企业既要考虑怎样实现目标利润，也要结合竞争状况考虑中标概率。最佳报价应是使预期利润达到最高水平的价格。显然，最佳报价即为目标利润与中标概率两者之间的最佳组合。

Seal-bid pricing is also called competitive bidding pricing. In the case of bidding, the firm sets its price after knowing its competitors'. When quoting, the firm has to consider how to achieve the profit target, and in the meantime, to consider the competition situation and the winning probability. The best quotation is the price at which the expected profits can reach the highest level. Obviously, the best price is the combination of profit target and winning probability.

密封投标定价法主要用于投标交易方式，如建筑施工、工程设计、设备制造、政府采购、科研课题等需要投标以取得承包合同的项目。使用这种方法定价的步骤如下：一，企业估算此次竞标的标的物的成本，依据成本利润率计算出企业可能盈利的各个价格水平，确定几个备选的投标价格方案，并计算各方案收益。二，估计各个竞标对手的情况和可能的报价，估计出各方案的中标概率。三，根据每个方案可能的收益和中标概率，计算每个方案的期望利润，其计算公式为利润期望值＝可能收益×中标概率(%)。四，根据企业的投标目的来选择投标方案。运用这种方法，首先，企业要尽可能多地收集投标项目和竞标对手的信息；然后，通过对中标概率的历史数据的统计分析，估算竞标对手高于某一价格的概率并计算出本公司赢得标的概率。

Seal-bid pricing is mainly used for the transactions by bidding, for the projects that require bids to obtain the contract, such as construction, engineering design, equipment manufacturing, government procurement and research projects. The pricing steps are as follows. First, the enterprise estimates the cost of the subject matter, calculates each profitable price according to rate of cost-profit, then decides on a few alternative programs for bid price and then evaluates the revenues of each program. Second, the enterprise estimates competitors' situation, possible quotations, and winning probability of each program. Third, according to the revenues and winning probability of each program, the enterprise calculates the expected profit of each program. The formula is: the expected value of profit=possible revenues × probability of winning(%). Fourth, the enterprise chooses the bidding program according to its aim. To use this method, the enterprise first of all needs to collect the tender project information as much as possible. Then by statistically analyzing the historical data of winning probability, the enterprise estimates the probability that the competitor may bid higher than a certain price, and works out the probability that the firm itself could win.

4. 变动成本定价法 Variable Cost Pricing

变动成本定价法，又称边际贡献定价法。这是指企业以变动成本为依据，考虑市场环境，对付竞争对手的一种方法。一般在市场产品严重过剩、竞争十分激烈的条件下才采用这一定价方法。采用这一定价方法的理念，只要售价能够保证收回全部变动成本后还有剩余，就可以对固定成本作一定的补偿。这比停产后固定成本全部不能补偿合算，并能够在特殊情况下稳定职工队伍，保持企业实力。

Variable cost pricing is also called Marginal Contribution Pricing. The firm considers market environment and variable cost to deal with competitors. Generally, this pricing method is adopted when there is significant product excess on the market and intense competition. The idea of this method is that the fixed cost can be compensated for as long as the selling price can guarantee a surplus after recover of the total variable cost. It is better than the situation that the fixed cost can not be compensated at all after shutdown. It also helps to keep workforce stable and maintain firm strength.

第二节　定价的基本策略
Pricing Strategies

定价策略是指企业为达到总体经营目标，根据产品的特点、市场供求状况和竞争状况、产品成本变动情况及消费者购买行为的动向等，采取的各种定价技巧和措施。企业确定价格或对价格进行调整时，可采取以下策略。

The firm adopts various pricing techniques and measures, which are called pricing strategies, according to product features, supply-demand situation, competition condition, cost change and trends in consumer purchasing behaviors. When the firm decides on price or trims price, the following strategies can be adopted.

一、产品组合定价策略 Portfolio Pricing Strategies

产品组合，是指一个企业所生产经营的全部产品线和产品项目的组合。对于生产经营多种产品的企业来说，定价需着眼于整个产品组合的利润实现最大化，而不是单个产品。

Portfolio refers to the combination of all the product lines and projects of a firm. For a firm that operates a variety of products, the portfolio profit should be focused on and maximized rather than a single product when pricing.

(一)产品线定价策略 Product-line Pricing Strategy

当企业生产的系列产品存在需求和成本的内在关联性时，为了充分发挥这种内在关联性的积极效应，需要采用产品线定价策略，即对同一产品线中不同产品之间的价格步幅做出决策。采用这种定价策略的一般步骤为：首先，确定某种产品的最低价格，吸引消费者购买产品线中的其他产品。其次，确定产品线中某种产品的最高价格，它在产品线中充当品牌质量象征和收回投资的角色。最后，产品线中的其他产品也分别依据其在产品线中的角色不同而制定不同的价格。如果产品线中前后两个相互关联产品的价格差额较小，顾客就会更多地购买性能比较先进的产品。此时，若这两个产品的成本差异小于价格差额，企业的利润就会增加。

When there is inherent relevance between demand and cost of series products, the strategy of product-line pricing is used to get fully the positive effect of the inherent relevance, i.e., a decision should be made on price stride between different products of the same product line. General steps for this pricing strategy are as follows, first, setting the lowest price for a product to attract consumers to buy the other products of the product line; second, setting the highest price for the product of the line which plays the role of investment recovery and symbol of brand quality; third, prices of other products of the same line are set on the basis of their roles. If the difference between the prices of two related products in the same line are relatively small, customers will purchase more advanced products. At this time, if the cost difference is smaller than price difference, corporate profits will increase.

(二)互补产品定价策略 Pricing Strategy for Complementary Products

互补产品,又称连带产品,是指两种或两种以上功能互相依赖、需要配合使用的商品。一般说来,价值高而购买频率低的主件价格应定得低些,而与之配合使用的价值低而购买频率高的易耗品价格应适当定高些。例如,剃须刀架的价格可以定低一些,而刀片的价格可以适当高一些。

Complementary products, also known as captive products, refer to two or more products which depend on each other in use. Generally, the main piece with high value but low purchase frequency should be priced lower, while the consumable pieces, which are with low value but high purchase frequency, can be priced higher. For example, shaver frames can be priced low but blades can be priced relatively higher.

(三)任选品定价策略 Pricing Strategy for Optional Products

任选品,是指在提供主要产品的同时,还附带一些可供选择的产品或特征。任选品是指那些与主要产品密切相关的可任意选择的产品。例如有些饭馆将饭菜的价格定得较低,而酒水的价格定得较高,靠低价饭菜吸引顾客,以高价酒水赚取厚利。在这里,饭菜是主要产品,烟酒和饮料就是任选品。

Optional products mean a number of optional products or features offered when the main product is provided. They are optional products which have close relation with the main products. For example, some restaurants set low prices for the dishes but high prices for drinks. Cheap dishes are to attract customers and expensive drinks are to earn huge profit. Here, the dishes are the main product and drinks and tobacco are optional products.

(四)副产品定价策略 Pricing Strategy for Byproducts

在酿酒、榨油、生产石油化工产品的过程中,经常会产生副产品,如酿酒厂的酒糟、榨油厂的豆饼、石化厂的沥青。处理这些副产品,需要花费一定的费用。如果副产品价值很低,处理费用昂贵,就会影响到主产品的定价。制造商制定的价格必须能够弥补副产品的处理费用。如果副产品对某一顾客群有价值,就应该按其价值定价。副产品如果能带来收入,将有助于企业整体利益的提升。

In the process of making wine, oil and petrochemical products, byproducts are often produced, such as lees in the distillery, soya-bean cake in the oil mill, and asphalt in the petrochemical plant. It will cost some money to deal with these byproducts. If the byproducts have low value but high processing cost, the pricing of the main product will be affected. The price set by the producer must be able to compensate for the processing cost. If the byproducts are useful to a certain clientele, they should be priced according to the value. If byproducts can generate revenue, it will help to improve the firm's overall interests.

(五)产品群定价策略 Product Bundle Pricing

为了促销，有时企业不是销售单一产品，而是将有连带关系的产品组合在一起，进行捆绑降价销售。例如，图书经销商将整套书籍一起销售，价格就要比单独购买低得多。采用这种策略，价格的优惠程度必须有足够的吸引力。

The firm sometimes sells more than one single product for promotion instead, it bundles related products and sells the bundle at a lower price. For example, book dealers sell books by sets at much lower price than a single purchase. The price discount must be attractive enough for this pricing strategy.

(六)分部定价策略 Division Pricing Strategy

服务性企业经常收取一笔固定费用，再加上可变的使用费。例如，游乐园一般先收取门票费，如果有额外游玩的项目，游客就要再交费。

Service firms often charge a fixed fee plus a variable cost. For example, amusement parks usually charge entry fees and then charge more if there are extra amusement items.

二、新产品定价策略 New Product Pricing Strategies

新产品与其他产品相比，具有竞争程度低、技术领先的优点，但同时也有不被消费者认同和产品成本高的缺点。因此，在为新产品定价时，企业既要考虑尽快收回投资、获得利润，又要使消费者很快接受新产品。常见的定价基本策略有以下三种。

Compared with other products, new products have the advantages of low competition and leading technology, but they also have the disadvantages of no recognition and high cost. When pricing new products, the firm has to consider a quick return on investment and profit as well as easy acceptance by the consumer. There are three common pricing strategies.

(一)撇脂定价策略 Market-skimming Pricing

这是一种高价策略，是指在产品生命周期的最初阶段，利用一部分消费者的求新心理，定一个高价，像撇取牛奶中的脂肪层那样先取得一部分高额利润。该策略的优点是：高价格、高利润，能迅速补偿研究与开发费用，便于企业筹集资金，并掌握调价主动权。其缺点是：定价较高会限制需求，销路不易扩大；高价会诱发竞争，企业压力较大；新产品的高价高利时期通常较短。

This is a high pricing policy. At the beginning of a product life cycle, a high price is set for some consumers who have the mental characteristic of seeking what is new. A high profit is obtained first which is like skimming the fat layer of milk. The advantages are: high price and good profit can make up the cost of research and development very quickly and it is easy for the firm to raise fund and have the initiative to regulate the price. The disadvantages are: high price will limit demand and it is not easy to expand the market; high price will also invite competition and high pressure; the period of high price and profit is usually short.

撇脂定价策略一般适用于生命周期较短，但高价仍有需求的产品，或者有专利权的产品。它适用于制造新产品的技术已公开或者易于仿制，竞争者容易进入该市场的产品；也适用于企业新开发的产品在市场上已有同类产品或替代产品，但是企业拥有较大的生产能力并且该产品的规模效益显著的产品；还适用于市场需求价格比较敏感的产品。

Market skimming pricing is usually suitable for those products of short life cycle, high price and demand or proprietary products. Skimming pricing is suitable for the following cases, the new manufacturing technology has been open to the public; the products are easy to copy; it is easy for competitors to enter the market; there have been similar or substitute products at the market, but the firm has a large production capacity and product's scale economy is significant; the products are sensitive to the demand price at the market.

(二)渗透定价策略 Market-penetration Pricing

这是一种低价策略，是指企业在产品上市初期，利用消费者求廉的消费心理，有意将价格定得很低，使新产品以物美价廉的形象吸引顾客，占领市场，以谋取远期的稳定利润。采取渗透定价策略不仅有利于迅速打开产品销路，抢先占领市场，提高企业和品牌的声誉。价低利薄也有利于阻止竞争对手进入市场，可以使企业保持一定的市场优势。但是，由于这种定价策略使价格变动余地小，故企业难以应付在短期内突发的竞争或需求的较大变化。

This is a low-price strategy. At the early stage of the product launch, the price is set low intentionally for consumers have the mental characteristic of seeking what is cheap. Then the new product will attract customers and occupy the market with an image of good quality and low price so that a long-term steady profit can be obtained. Market-penetration pricing helps open and occupy the market quickly and enhance the reputation of the firm and its brand. Low price and thin profit also helps to prevent competitors from entering the market, so the firm can maintain certain market advantage. This pricing, however, has little room for price change, so it is difficult for the firm to deal with a sudden change in demand or competition.

(三)温和定价策略 Moderate Pricing Strategy

这是介于撇脂定价和渗透定价之间的一种定价策略，温和定价策略既能使企业获取适当的平均利润，又能兼顾消费者的利益。但是，该定价策略的缺点是比较保守，不适于需求复杂多变或竞争激烈的市场环境。

This pricing is between skimming pricing and penetration pricing. It enables the firm to obtain adequate average profit and balance consumers' interests. However, it has disadvantages too. This pricing strategy is conservative and not suitable for complicated or fierce market environment.

三、心理定价策略 Psychological Pricing Strategies

心理定价是一种基于消费者的心理要求而采用的定价策略，是指企业运用心理学的原理，依据不同类型的消费者在购买商品时的不同心理要求来制定价格，以引导消费者购买。常用的心理定价策略有以下几种方式。

Psychological pricing is based on the psychological demands of consumers, following psychological principles to set prices according to psychological demands of different consumers so that consumers can be led to purchase. Psychological pricing strategies have the following forms.

(一)整数定价策略 Integer Pricing Strategy

整数定价策略是指在定价时，把商品的价格归整，不带尾数，使消费者产生质量好的感觉。整数定价策略适用于需求的价格弹性小、价格高低不会对需求产生较大影响的商品，如流行品、时尚品、奢侈品、礼品、星级宾馆、高级文化娱乐城以及消费者不太了解的产品。

Integer pricing means that the price of goods is an integer without decimal part so that consumers would feel that the quality is good. This pricing is suitable for the goods of small elasticity of demand and the demand of which will not be affected very much by whether the price is high or low, such as pop goods, fashion goods, luxury goods, gifts, star-rated hotels and casinos as well as the goods that consumers do not know very well.

(二)尾数定价策略 Mantissa Pricing Strategy

尾数定价策略是指在定价时，利用消费者求廉的心理，常常以奇数作尾数，尽可能在价格上不进位。例如，把一种香皂的价格定为2.97元，而不定3元。这样可以在直观上给消费者一种便宜的感觉，从而激起消费者的购买欲望，并且使消费者对企业产品及其定价产生信任感，促进产品销售量的增加。

Mantissa pricing means that the price ends with odd numbers and the decimal part tries not to carry on because consumers have the mental characteristic of seeking what is cheap. For example, a soap is priced at 2.97 yuan, rather than 3 yuan, which gives consumers the impression of cheapness and arouses purchasing desire. Consumers would believe in the products and its price, so the sales can be increased.

(三)声望定价策略 Prestige Pricing Strategy

声望定价策略是指在定价时，根据产品在消费者心中的声望、信任度和社会地位来确定价格的一种定价策略。声望定价可以满足某些消费者的特殊欲望，如地位、身份、财富、名望和自我形象等，还可以通过高价格显示名贵优质。因此，这一策略适用于一些传统的名优产品、具有历史地位的民族特色产品，以及一些知名度高、有较大的市场影响、深受市场欢迎的品牌产品。例如，台湾地区的宝丽来太阳镜、我国的景泰蓝瓷器，都是成功运用声望定价策略的典范。

Prestige pricing means that the price is set according to the product's prestige, credibility and social position from the aspect of consumers. It can satisfy some consumers' special desires, such as positions, status, wealth, fame and self-image. The high prices also indicate the preciousness and rare quality. Therefore, the prestige pricing strategy applies to some traditional products, with historical status of national characteristics, or some well-known brand with high visibility, recognition and popularity. Taiwan Polaroid sunglasses, and Chinese Cloisonne are both successful examples of prestige pricing strategy.

(四)习惯定价策略 Customary Pricing Strategy

经常购买的日用品,在市场上长期地形成了一种为消费者习惯且熟识并愿意接受的价格,即"习惯价格",如大米、调味品等。对此类商品,企业定价时需注意按惯例定价,否则,会影响产品的销售。

The commodity, with a relatively long market history of being sold, has a longstanding price based on the perceived expectations of customers, named "customary price", such as rice, spices etc. The customary price needs to be respected when pricing for the commodity, otherwise the sales could be greatly affected.

(五)招徕定价策略 Loss Leader Pricing Strategy

招徕定价策略是常被零售商使用,用以吸引顾客。它包括将某几种商品的价格定得非常低或者降低利润,以引进品牌或以激发消费者的购买兴趣。这一定价策略常为综合性百货商店、超级市场、甚至高档商品的专卖店所采用。

Loss leader pricing is a common pricing strategy used by retailers to attract customers. It involves setting lower price points and reducing typical profit margins to introduce brands or stimulate interest in the business. This strategy is always implemented by the department store, supermarket and even exclusive store.

(六)分级定价策略 Tiered Pricing Strategy

分级定价策略是指在定价时,把同类产品分为几个等级,不同等级的产品价格有所不同。等级的划分应适当,级差不能太大或太小,否则起不到应有的分级效果。这种定价策略能使消费者产生货真价实、按质论价的感觉。

Tiered pricing strategy is a promotional tool pricing items differently based on the levels of a certain product. The differential of division should be appropriate, which cannot be too significant or too slight. The tiered pricing would not be effective without correct classification. Also, the pricing strategy can make consumers feel that they are willing to pay relatively high price for better quality.

四、地理定价策略 Geographical Pricing Strategies

地理定价策略是一种根据商品销售地理位置的不同而规定差别价格的策略。其主要价格形式有以下几种。

Geographical pricing is a selling strategy that involves consideration of the various prices of goods with different geographic area. Some main pricing forms are described as the following.

(一)产地交货价格 FOB Origin Price

产地交货价格也称为离岸价格(FOB)或船上交货价格,是指卖方按出厂价格交货或将货物送到买方指定的某种运输工具上交货的价格。这种价格条件下,交货前的有关费用由卖方承担,交货后的产品所有权归买方所有,运输过程中的一切费用和保险费均由买方承担。产地交货价格对卖方来说较为便利,其费用最省、风险最小,但对扩大销售有一定不利的影响。

Origin delivery price is also named FOB price, which means that the cost of movement of goods on board of Airlines or on board of ship will be borne by the seller. The ownership of goods after delivery belongs to the buyer; all the expenses and insurance premium shall be borne by the buyer. It is considered as a convenient, economical and less risky method to the seller. However, it will have certain negative influences on the sales extension.

(二)目的地交货价格 CIF Price

目的地交货价格又称到岸价格(CIF)或成本加保险费和运费价格。卖方把产品运到买方指定的目的地,到达目的地之前的一切运费和保险费等费用均由卖方承担。使用这种策略,卖方承担的费用和风险较大,但有利于扩大产品销售。

CIF is short for Cost, Insurance and Freight (to the named destination port). The seller is responsible for paying for the costs associated with transport of the goods to the named port of destination. Additionally, the seller is responsible for paying for marine insurance in the buyer's name for the shipment. It will be costly and risky to the seller under this condition; however, it is beneficial for sales development.

(三)统一运送价格 Unified Price

统一运送价格就是卖方不分路途远近,将产品送到买方所在地,统一收取相同的价格和相同的运费。这样,可减轻较远地区顾客的价格负担,使买方认为运送产品是一项免费的附加服务,从而乐意购买,有利于扩大市场占有率。同时,能使企业维持一个全国性的广告价格,易于管理。

Unified price means that the cost of delivery shall be collected at the same rate without considering the actual distance to the destination. Therefore, the buyer, especially with long distance, considering the delivery service as a free bonus, will be pleased to do the business. It is a method to develop the future market, meanwhile, it helps maintain the national charging standard, which is easier to manage for companies.

(四)分区运送价格 Regional Shipping Price

分区运送价格,是根据距离的远近将市场分成若干个区域,并在每个区域内实行统一价格。实行这种办法，处于同一价格区域内的顾客能得到来自卖方的价格优惠；而处于两个价格区域交界地的顾客之间就得承受不同的价格负担。它适用于交货费用在价格中所占比重大的产品。

Regional shipping price refers to the unified delivery price within certain regions set by different distance. Under this condition, the customers in the same area will get the favorable prices from the seller. The delivery cost varies based on distance. It applies to the large amount of delivery cost.

(五)运费补贴定价 Primage Pricing

运费补贴定价是指为弥补产地交货价格策略的不足，减轻买方的运杂费、保险费等负担，而由卖方补贴其部分或全部运费。该策略有利于处于较远地区的顾客，使企业保持市场占有率并不断开拓新市场。

Primage is a kind of subsidies, aiming to make up the shortages of FOB strategy and to ease the burden of paying freight and insurance etc, which shall be borne by the seller. This strategy is beneficial to the customers with relatively long distance, and helps maintain the current market share while exploiting new market.

(六)基点定价 Basing Point Pricing

基点定价是指企业选定某地作为定价的基点，然后加上按顾客所在地与该地之间的距离而收取的运费覆盖面广。基点定价方式适用于产品运费成本所占比重较大、企业产品市场范围大、产品的价格弹性小的产品定价。

The basing point pricing system sets a predetermined location, known as the basing point, and then adds a transportation charge depending on how far away the buyer is from that location. This strategy applies to the large amount of freight cost and the product with large market coverage and weak price elasticity.

五、折扣定价策略 Discount Pricing Strategies

折扣定价策略是指对基本价格做出一定的让步，直接或间接降低价格，以争取顾客、扩大销量的一种定价策略。折扣定价有以下类型。

Discount and allowance pricing refers to the direct or indirect reductions to a basic price of goods or services, which aims to attract customers or develop sales. The discount pricing includes the following types.

(一)现金折扣 Cash Discount

现金折扣，是对在规定的时间内提前付款或用现金付款者所给予的一种价格折扣，其目的是鼓励顾客尽早付款，加速资金周转，降低销售费用，减少财务风险。例如，购买商品房时，如果一次付清全部现金，则享受98折优惠。

A cash discount is a deduction allowed by the seller of goods or by the provider of services in order to motivate the customer to pay within limited time. The aim of cash discount is to accelerate the capital turnover and reduce the cost of sales and financial risk. Take buying commercial residential apartment as an example, the buyer can have a 2% off once he or she has a lump sum payment in cash.

(二)数量折扣 Quantity Discount

数量折扣，又叫总额折扣，是指购买大量商品的实体买家的价格优惠，也可以看作是对买家因购买量大而使单位商品价格降低的一种激励。数量折扣包括以下两种形式：一是累计折扣，即按顾客在一定时期内购买商品所达到的一定数量或金额给予不同的折扣。此种方法可以鼓励顾客经常购买本产品。二是非累计折扣，即按规定一次购买某种产品达到一定数量或购买多种商品达到一定金额时，给予一次性折扣，其目的在于鼓励消费者大量购买，从而节约营销费用。

A quantity discount, also called a volume discount, is a reduction in price given to an entity that buys a large quantity of items and goods. It can also be seen as an incentive offered to buyers that results in a decreased cost per unit of goods or materials when purchased in greater numbers. There are two types of quantity discount: the first one is called accumulation discount, which means that the discount comes from the quantity accumulated to a certain amount in a given period of time; the buyers can be motivated to frequent consumption in this way. The second one is noncumulative discount, which refers to that the discount would be given when the quantity of a one-off purchase once reaches a certain amount. It aims to motivate buyers to consider bulk-buying, and save the marketing cost meanwhile.

(三)功能折扣 Functional Discount

功能折扣，又称贸易折扣，是指制造商根据中间商的不同类型和分销渠道所提供的不同服务给予不同的额外折扣，以促使它们执行某种市场营销功能(如推销、储存、服务)。功能折扣鼓励中间商大批量订货，扩大销售，争取顾客，并与生产企业建立长期、稳定、良好的合作关系。

Functional discount, also called trade discount, refers to the price reduction offered by the seller of goods to those trade channel members that perform certain functions, such as selling, storing and service. The functional discount can encourage the reseller ordering in larger volumes, expanding the sales and attracting more customers, and building the long-term stable relationship with manufacturers.

(四)季节折扣 Seasonal Discount

季节折扣，是企业给那些购买过季商品或服务的顾客的一种减价，使企业的生产和销售在一年四季保持相对稳定。例如，旅馆、航空公司等在营业额下降时给旅客以季节折扣，以避免因季节需求变化所带来的市场风险。

Seasonal discount refers to a discount put on goods out of season which may get people to purchase now when they are discounted. It can help to keep the balance relatively between manufacture and sales all the year around. For instance, hotel and airline company will offer seasonal discount to avoid marketing risks brought by the sales volume problems of seasonal changes.

(五) 折让 Trade Allowances

折让是指生产企业为了回馈顾客在产品促销方面的参与，在价格方面提供的一定比例的优惠；或者是企业收进顾客交回的本企业的旧商品，在新商品价格上给予老顾客的一种折让优惠。例如，一台冰箱4000元，顾客以旧冰箱折价500元，购买新冰箱只需3500元。

Sellers use trade allowances to reward buyers a certain proportional reduction on price for their participation in promoting the seller's products or collecting the used products from buyers to cover a certain amount of money when they buy new products. For instance, the buyer gives the used fridge priced 500 RMB to exchange a new fridge priced 4000, in this situation, the buyer needs to pay the rest 3500 RMB to take the new one.

六、差别定价策略 Segmentation Pricing Strategies

差别定价策略是指在对产品定价时根据消费者类型、订单数量、发货时间和付款方式等因素，采取不同的价格的策略。具体方式有以下几种。

Segmentation ricing means that a product has different prices based on the type of customer, rdered quantity, delivery time, payment terms, etc. The followings are the specific types of differential pricing.

(一) 顾客差别定价 Customer Segmentation Pricing

这种定价是指企业按不同的价格把同一产品或服务卖给不同顾客。如公交车对老人和学生的收费与普通乘客是不同的。

Customer segmentation pricing is the practice of dividing a customer base into groups of individuals that are similar in specific ways relevant to marketing, therefore, a certain product can be bought by groups with different prices. For instance, the bus ticket can be sold at different rate to children and the seniors from common passengers.

(二) 产品形式差别定价 Product Form Differential Pricing

这种定价是指企业对某种产品的不同规格型号和种类制定不同的价格，但不是根据它们的不同成本按比例制定的，如听装啤酒与瓶装啤酒的价格差别。

This pricing method refers to that the different prices come from the specifications and models or the varieties of a certain product, not according to the different costs, like the different prices between canned beer and bottled beer.

(三) 产品地点差别定价 Location Differential Pricing

这种定价是指企业对处在不同位置的产品或服务分别制定不同的价格，即使这种产品或服务的成本费用没有任何差异。例如，飞机上的舱位不同，票价不同。

This method means that the price difference is based on different location, even though the costs have no differences. For instance, ticket prices of airplane are different according to location of seats.

(四)时间差别定价 Time Differential Pricing

这种定价是指企业对于不同季节、不同时期甚至不同钟点的产品或服务分别制定不同的价格。例如，电话在不同时段收取不同标准的话费。

This pricing method means that various prices are set according to different season, time period or even different hour for a certain product or service. For example, telephone services charge different price based on specific calling time.

七、价格调整策略 Price Adjustment strategies

价格调整策略是指企业为了发展而对市场竞争做出价格调整的反应。价格调整主要有两种情况：一是市场供求环境发生了变化，这种调整称为主动调整；二是由于竞争者的反应，企业不得不对价格进行调整，这种调整称为被动调整。

This strategies refers to the price adjustment reacting to market competition for company's development. There are two main situations: the first one is adjustment according to the changes of market supply-demand system, known as the initiative adjustment; and the second one is forced price adjustment because of the competitors' action, also known as passive adjustment.

(一)产品价格的主动调整策略 Initiative Adjustment Strategy

企业对价格采取主动调整，通常有两种具体情况：一是提价策略，二是降价策略。

Generally, there are two specific circumstances for initiative adjustment strategy: price increase and price decrease.

1. 提价策略 Price-increasing Strategy

1) 企业提价的主要原因 Main Reasons of Price Increase

(1) 成本上涨因素。大多数企业因成本费用增加而产生提价意向时，企业可以适当提高产品价格。

The factor of cost inflation. The price could be approximately raised due to cost inflation trend.

(2) 当市场上商品供不应求时，企业在不影响消费需求的前提下可以采取提价措施。

When the demand of a certain product exceeds the supply, the price could be raised without affecting consumption requirement.

(3) 通货膨胀。由于通货膨胀，货币贬值，使得产品的市场价格低于其实际价值，迫使企业不得不通过涨价来减少因货币贬值造成的损失。

Inflation. The currency is devaluated because of inflation, so the market price of a certain product stays lower than its real price. The price has to be increased to cover the loss of currency devaluation.

(4) 改进产品。当企业改进生产技术，增加产品功能，加强售后服务时，可以在广告宣传的辅助下，适当提高产品价格。

Product improvement. When the manufacturing techniques, product functions or services after sale have been improved, the price could be raised properly with the assistance of advertising.

(5) 市场上品牌信誉卓著的产品，如果原定价格水平较低，可考虑适度调高价格。

Products with distinguished reputation but lower original prices could be considered to increase the prices moderately.

2) 提价的方式与技巧 Methods and Skills of Price Increase

(1) 推迟报价，即产品的最后价格，在产品制成或交货时才确定。

Offer postponing. It refers to that the final prices will be set when the producing or at the point of delivery is completed.

(2) 在合同上规定调整条款，即在合同中规定，企业在一定时期内可按某种价格指数来调整价格。

State the terms of price adjustment on the contract. It means price can be adjusted in a period of time according to some certain price coefficient.

(3) 降低价格折扣，即削减正常的现金和数量折扣。

Lower the price discount, which means to reduce the regular cash and quantity discount.

(4) 取消低利产品。

Cancel the production of low-profit products.

(5) 减少产品特色和服务。

Reduce the specialties and services of a certain product.

2. 降价策略 Price-decreasing Strategy

1) 企业降价的原因 Main Reasons of Price Decrease

(1) 生产成本下降后，为了扩大产品的市场占有率，企业可以降低产品价格。

When the cost of production decreases, the price can be cut for expanding the market share.

(2) 市场上同类商品供过于求，企业可以考虑降价销售。

When the market shows that the supply exceeds the demand within similar products, the prices can be considered to be cut.

(3) 当竞争激烈时，如果竞争对手采取降价措施，企业也应进行相应的调整，以保持较高的竞争能力。

When the competitors have lowered their prices when facing the fierce competition, the prices should be reduced to maintain the competitive advantages.

(4) 产品市场占有率出现下降趋势后，降价竞销是企业对抗竞争的一个有效办法。

When the market share shows the tendency of decrease, price decreasing could be an effective method for sales competition.

(5) 商品陈旧落后时，企业应该降价销售，以收回占用资金；残损变质的商品更需要采取降价措施，从而最大限度地减少现有损失。

When the products are old-fashioned or falling behind, prices should be deceased for withdrawing tied-up capital; for damaged or degenerative products, prices have to be deceased to prevent the loss to the utmost.

2) 企业降价的方式与技巧 Methods and Skills of Price Decrease

(1) 增加额外支出费用。在价格不变的情况下，企业增加运费支出，免费送货上门，或免费安装、调试、维修以及为顾客上保险等。

Adding additional expenditure. When the prices remain the same, the extra expenditures such as free delivery, installment, adjustment and insurance can be added.

(2) 改进产品的性能，提高产品的质量；增加产品的功能，在价格不变的情况下，实际上等于降低了产品的价格。

Improving product function and quality. Improvement of function actually means reduction of price when the price remain the same superficially.

(3) 增大各种折扣比例。

Increase the proportion of discount.

(4) 馈赠礼品给顾客。

Giving presents to consumers.

(二)产品价格的被动调整策略 Passive Adjustment Strategy

被动调整是指在竞争对手率先调价之后，企业在价格方面所做的反应。一般情况下，对调高价格的反应比较容易，方法主要有：跟随提价和价格不变。对调低价格的反应有以下三种：①置之不理；②价格不变；③跟随降价。

The passive pricing adjustment strategy refers to the reaction when facing the pricing changes of competitors. Generally, the methods towards price increasing include following the increase and remaining the same. When facing the price decreasing, the methods include ignoring, remaining the same and following the decrease.

企业在调整价格时还要注意到顾客与竞争者对价格变动的反应。这就要求分析顾客的心理变化，研究顾客是如何理解本次调价的，还要分析竞争者的财务状况、近年来的生产、销售、顾客的忠诚度和企业目标状况等，以便从中找出正确的答案，采取有效的措施。

Reaction of customers and competitors should be observed when enterprises adjust price. Therefore, the customers' psychological changes, or how the consumers understand the changes of price, the financial situation of competitors, including the recent production, sales, customer loyalty and targets are all necessary to be analyzed, so as to get the answers and implement the strategy correctly and productively.

本 章 小 结
Summary

在市场营销活动中，价格永远都是市场中最敏感的因素。一般企业定价的主要程序有六个步骤：明确定价目标、测定市场需求、估算成本费用、分析竞争状况、选择定价方法和确定最后价格。定价方法是企业为实现其定价目标所采取的具体做法。按照定价依据的不同，定价的方法通常可以分为如下三大类：成本导向定价法；需求导向定价法；竞争导向定价法。其中每一类又包含了多种不同的具体定价法。在制定价格策略时，必须慎重选择定价方法。企业必须要在采用某种方法的基础上，根据目标市场状况和定价环境的变化，采用适当的策略，保持价格与环境的适应性。差别定价、组合定价、折扣定价和新产品定价等就是一些适应性定价策略。除此之外，在必要的时候还要对价格进行适当的调整。

Prices constantly are the most sensitive factor in all marketing activities. Normally, there are six steps in the pricing procedure: clarifying the pricing target, predicting the market demand, estimating the cost expenditure, analyzing competition situation, choosing pricing approaches, and determining the final price. Pricing methods refer to specific ways to achieve pricing target. According to the different basis of pricing strategy, the methods can be generally classified into three groups, cost-oriented pricing, demand-oriented pricing and competition-oriented pricing, which all include detailed methods. The pricing methods must be cautiously chosen when making pricing strategy. The prices must be set based on a certain method then implement the suitable strategy referring to the situation of target market and pricing environment. To maintain the adaption between prices and environment, methods like differentiation pricing, portfolio pricing, discount pricing and new product pricing have been developed to adapt the pricing strategy. Beyond that, the prices also can be adjusted moderately when necessary.

思 考 题
Questions

1. 简述企业定价的程序。
Briefly describe the procedure of pricing
2. 定价的主要方法有哪些？
What are the main methods of pricing?
3. 举例说明定价的基本策略。
Introduce basic strategies of pricing with relevant examples.

第八章 分销渠道策略
Distribution Channel Strategies

【学习目标】
1. 分销渠道的职能与类型；
2. 分销渠道策略的选择；
3. 批发商与零售商的分销策略；
4. 分销渠道管理。

Learning Objectives
1. Functions and types of distribution channels;
2. Selecting distribution strategies;
3. Wholesaling and retailing distribution strategies;
4. Distribution channel management.

分销渠道，是产品从制造商向消费者流转的通道。如何选择正确的分销渠道，使产品在适当的时间、地点，以适当的价格供应给适当的顾客，满足市场的需求，已成为企业面临的最复杂和最富挑战性的问题。因此，分销渠道策略是市场营销组合中的一个重要策略。

Distribution channels are the path for products to flow from manufacturers to consumers. The firm's most complex and challenging problem is how to choose the right channel and supply products to customers at the right time, place and price. Therefore, distribution channel strategy is very important in the marketing mix.

第一节 分销渠道的职能及类型
Functions and Types of Distribution Channels

一、分销渠道的概念 Definition of Distribution Channels

美国市场营销学会(AMA)为分销渠道所下的定义是："企业内部和外部代理商和经销商(批发和零售)的组织机构，通过这些组织，商品(产品或劳务)才得以上市销售。"菲利普·科特勒则将分销渠道定义为："某种货物或劳务从生产者向消费者移动时，取得这种货物或劳务的所有权的企业和个人。"也有一些学者认为分销渠道是"促使产品(服务)能顺利地经由市场交换过程，转移给消费者(用户)消费使用的一整套相互依存的组织"。

American Marketing Association (AMA) gives the definition of distribution channel-organizations composed of internal and external agents and distributors (wholesalers and retailers), through which goods (products and services) can go to the market for sale. Philip Kotler defines distribution channels as "firms and individuals that have acquired the ownership of the goods or services when moving from producers to consumers." Some scholars think that channels are "a set of interdependent organizations that help make a product or service go through market exchange smoothly and available for use or consumption by the consumer or business user".

分销渠道是指某种货物和劳务从生产者向消费者移动时取得这种货物和劳务的所有权或帮助转移其所有权的所有企业和个人,主要包括商业中间商、代理中间商以及处于渠道起点和终点的生产者与消费者。

Distribution channels refer to the firms and individuals that acquire or help transfer the ownership of the goods or services when moving from producers to consumers. Distribution channels consist of business brokers, agents, as well as producers and consumers at the starting and ending points.

二、分销渠道的职能 Functions of Distribution Channels

分销渠道对产品(或服务)从生产者转移到消费者所必须完成的工作加以组织。分销渠道的主要职能有如下一些种类。

Distribution channels organize the work that must be done when the product or service is transferred from the producer to the consumer. The main functions are as follows.

(1) 研究。取得制订计划和进行交换时所必需的各种信息。

Research: gathering all the information needed for planning and aiding exchange.

(2) 促销。对所售产品进行说服性的沟通。

Promotion: developing and spreading persuasive communications about an offer.

(3) 接洽。寻找可能的购买者并与其进行沟通。

Contact: finding and communicating with prospective buyers.

(4) 订货。渠道成员与制造商进行有购买意图的沟通行为。

Order: channel members communicate with producers with purchase intent.

(5) 配合。按照购买者的需要供应货物,包括制造、评分、装配、包装等活动。

Matching: shaping and fitting the offer to the buyer's needs, including activities such as manufacturing, grading, assembling, and packaging.

(6) 谈判。为敲定最终价格及有关条件而进行斡旋。

Negotiation: reaching an agreement on price and other terms of the offer.

(7) 实体分销。将商品进行运输和储存。

Physical distribution: transporting and storing goods.

(8) 融资。对渠道工作的成本费用进行必要的资金取得与支用。

Financing: acquiring and using funds to cover the costs of the channel work.

(9) 风险承担。承担与之相关的各种风险。

Risk-taking: assuming the risks of carrying out the channel work.

(10) 付款。买方向销售者支付账款。

Payment: the buyer pays the seller.

(11) 所有权转移。所有权从一个组织或个人向其他组织或个人转移。

Transfer of property: property transferring from an organization or individual to other organizations or individuals.

(12) 服务。渠道提供附加服务支持，如安装、维修等。

Services: the channel provides support services, like installation and maintenance, etc.

三、分销渠道的类型 Types of Distribution Channels

(一)层级结构渠道 Channels of Level Structure

同一种产品的分销渠道，根据在生产者和消费者之间是否使用中间商或使用的中间商的类型和环节的多少可将分销渠道分为零级渠道、一级渠道、二级渠道、三级渠道。基本的分销渠道结构类型如图 8-1 所示。

The channels of the same product can be divided into Direct Channel, Channel Level One, Channel Level Two and Channel Level Three depending on the numbers and types of intermediaries. Figure 8-1 shows basic types of channel structures.

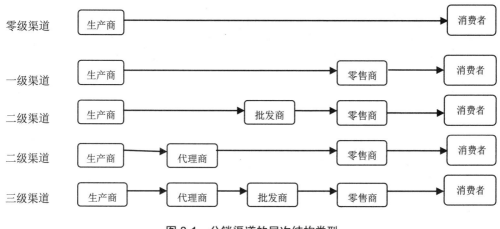

图 8-1 分销渠道的层次结构类型

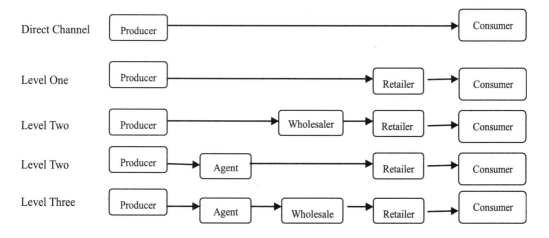

Figure 8-1 Types of Channel Structures

(1) 零级渠道。它是指产品从制造商流向最终消费者的过程中不经过任何中间商转手的直接营销渠道。直接营销渠道多用于分销产业用品。当然，一些消费品也可通过直接营销渠道销售。直接营销的主要方式有上门推销、邮购、电子通信营销、电视直销和制造商自设商店等。

Direct Channel. The product is sold directly from the manufacturer to consumers without any intermediary trader. Direct marketing channel is often used for distribution of industrial goods. Some consumer goods, of course, can also be sold through direct marketing channels. The main ways of direct marketing are door-to-door sales, mail order, email marketing, TV direct sales and stores set by manufacturer itself.

(2) 一级渠道。它是指一个渠道系统中只包括一级中间机构。在消费品市场，这个中间机构通常是零售商；而在工业品市场，它通常是销售代理商或佣金商。

Level One Channel. The channel contains only one intermediary. In the consumer goods market, the intermediary is often the retailer; while in the industrial goods market, it is usually a sales agent or commission agent.

(3) 二级渠道。它是指一个渠道系统中包括两级中间机构。在消费品市场上，它们通常是批发商和零售商；在工业品市场上，它们可能是代理商或工业品批发商与零售商。

Level Two Channel. It contains two intermediary levels. In consumer goods markets, they are usually wholesalers and retailers; in the industrial goods market, they may be agents and industrial goods wholesalers.

(4) 三级渠道。这一渠道系统中包括三级中间机构，即在代理商和零售商之间通常还有中间商或专业批发商以服务于一些小型零售商。

Level Three Channel. It contains three intermediary levels, i.e. there are middlemen or professional wholesalers who serve small retailers between agents and retailers.

(二)直接与间接渠道 Direct and Indirect Channels

按照有无中间环节，分销渠道可以分为直接分销渠道与间接分销渠道。

There are direct and indirect distribution channels depending on whether there are intermediary levels.

(1) 直接分销渠道。它是生产商将产品直接销售给消费者的分销渠道类型。在产业用户市场上，制造商通常采用直接营销渠道，例如，生产零配件的企业直接将产品出售给总装厂。在消费者市场上，直接销售也有发展，如部分由生产企业直接组织的门到门销售、邮购及电话订购等。服务业的渠道一般属于直接渠道，尤其是生活服务。

Direct distribution channels. The producer sells products directly to consumers. In the industrial goods market, the producer usually uses direct channels, for example, the producer of spare parts sells its products directly to the assembly plant. Direct sales have also developed in the consumer goods market, for example, some producers organize door to door selling, mail and telephone order, etc. The channels for service industry are usually direct, especially living services.

(2) 间接分销渠道。它是至少含有一层中介机构的分销渠道类型，且是消费者市场上占主导地位的分销渠道类型。根据其所含中间环节的多少，可分成上述的一级渠道、二级渠道、三级渠道等。

Indirect distribution channels. These channels contain at least one intermediary organization and are the main type of distribution channels in consumer goods market. According to the number of intermediary links, there are Level One Channel, Level Two Channel, Level Three Channel, and so on, as mentioned above.

(三)长渠道与短渠道 Long and Short Channels

按照经过的环节多少，分销渠道可以分为长渠道和短渠道。商品在从生产者流向最终消费者的过程中，经过的环节越多，分销渠道就越长；反之则越短。显然，直接营销渠道最短。采用长渠道可发挥各层次中间商的辐射、宣传作用，扩大产品市场。但其环节多、费用高，影响最终零售价格，会增加消费者负担，且不利于信息的及时反馈。一般对低价的日用百货商品使用长渠道较多。采用短渠道，产品专营性强，受市场影响小，但对中间商的约束较高，易于控制。一般对高价商品如电器、汽车、高技术产品使用短渠道较多。

According to the number of intermediary levels, there are long channels and short channels. The more levels the products go through in the process travelling from the producer to consumers, the longer the channel is. Otherwise, the channel is shorter. Obviously, direct channels are the shortest. Long channels can take advantage of the radiation and publicity functions of intermediary levels so market can be expanded. But so many levels and high cost influence the final retail price, increase customers' burden, and go against timely information feedback. Long channels are often used for low-priced articles of daily use. For short channels, there are more product franchises and less marketing influence, but the control of the middle traders is stronger. Short channels are often used for high-priced products such as appliances, automobiles, and high- tech products.

(四)宽渠道与窄渠道 Wide and Narrow Channels

按照渠道的每个环节中使用同种类型中间商数目的多少，分销渠道可以分为宽渠道和窄渠道。当企业使用的同类中间商较多时，产品在市场上的分销面广，就形成了宽渠道；当企业使用的同类中间商较少时，就形成了窄渠道。市场需求面广、重复性消费、均衡性消费的日用百货宜选择宽渠道；市场挑选性强的选购品，如自行车、手表、照相机、眼镜、化妆品、彩电、服装和机电配件等，可使用有选择性的分销渠道；某些特殊消费品，如小汽车、大型机电产品和技术性要求极高的产品，可使用独家经销、包销的专营分销渠道。

Channels can be divided into wide and narrow ones according to the number of the same type of intermediaries at each level. When the firm has more intermediaries of the same type, its products have more distribution areas in the market and wide channels are therefore formed. When the firm uses fewer intermediaries of the same type, narrow channels are therefore formed. For daily necessities which have large market demand, repeated and balanced consumption, wide channels are suitable. For products with strong market selection, such as bicycles, watches, cameras, glasses, cosmetics, color TV, clothing and electrical and mechanical parts, selective distribution channels can be chosen. For some special consumption goods, like cars, large mechanical and electrical products, and products with high-tech requirements, franchise or exclusive distribution channels can be adopted.

(五)单渠道和多渠道 Single and Multi Channels

企业全部产品都由自己所设的直属门市部销售或全部交由批发商经销时,称为单渠道;而企业为扩大市场采用多种分销渠道混合使用时,称为多渠道。例如,企业可能对消费品市场采用长渠道,而对生产资料市场则采用短渠道分销;在本地区采用独家经销,在外地采用多家分销;在有些地区采用直接渠道,在另一些地区采用间接渠道等。

Single channel means all products are sold by producers' sales departments or by wholesalers. When the producer uses various distribution channels to expand the market, it is called multi channel. For example, the producer may adopt long channels to sell consumer goods, short channels to sell industrial goods, exclusive distribution in the local, multi distribution channels in other areas, direct channels in some areas and indirect channels in some other areas.

第二节 选择分销渠道策略
Selecting Strategies for Distribution Channels

分销渠道策略,是指企业为了使产品进入目标市场所进行的路径选择,它涉及企业在什么地点、什么时间、由什么组织或公司向消费者提供商品和劳务。企业应选择经济、合理的分销渠道,把商品送到目标市场。

The strategy for distribution channels means how to choose the ways that the firm launches its products into the market. It is concerned with the place, time and organizations (or companies) when the firm supplies its products or services to consumers. The firm should select economical and reasonable distribution channels to deliver the goods to the target market.

一、影响分销渠道策略设计的因素 Factors Influencing the Design of Channel Strategies

分销渠道策略的设计是指为实现分销目标而对各种被选渠道结构进行评估和选择,从而开发新型的分销渠道或改进现有分销渠道的过程。渠道设计问题的中心环节是确定到达目标市场的最佳途径。为了正确设计分销渠道策略,必须系统地分析其影响因素。影响分销渠道策略设计的主要因素如下。

The design of distribution channels is the process of evaluating and selecting channel structures to achieve distribution objectives so that new channels can be developed or the existing channels can be improved. The central part of channel design is to determine the best way to reach the target market. The influencing factors must be systematically analyzed in order to design the right channel strategies. Influencing factors are mainly as follows.

(一)企业因素 Firm Factor

企业因素主要是指企业内部影响分销渠道策略选择的各种因素。主要有以下几种。

Firm factors refer to the factors inside the firm that influence the selecting of channel strategies. They are as follows.

(1) 总体规模和资金实力。企业规模大，资金雄厚，具备管理分销渠道的经验以及很好的管理经验，在渠道选择上的主动权就大，甚至可以建立自己的销售机构，渠道就短一些，反之，就要更多地依靠中间商。

Firm's overall scale and financial strength. If the firm has a large scale, great financial strength, the ability to manage distribution channels, and good management experience, it has initiative to choose distribution channels, and can even establishes its own sales organizations to have shorter channels. Otherwise, the firm will depend on intermediaries more often.

(2) 产品组合。如果制造商的产品组合宽度和深度大，即产品的种类多、规格全，则制造商可能直接销售给零售商。反之，如果制造商的产品组合宽度和深度小，即产品种类少、规格少，则制造商只能通过批发商到零售商再转售给消费者。而且，产品的关联性对分销渠道也有很大影响，其关联性越大，越可能通过同一渠道销售，分销渠道的效率越高；而产品关联性小的企业，在其产品分销过程中，往往需要选择多种渠道推销其不同种类的产品，这会降低分销渠道的效率。

Product mix. if the producer's product mix has a great width and depth, i.e., more categories and specifications, the producer may be sold directly to retailers. Otherwise, if the product mix has less width and depth, i.e., fewer categories or specifications, the producer will have to sell products to consumers via wholesalers and retailers. Moreover, the relevance of products also has significant impact on distribution channels. Products with more relevance are more likely to be distributed through the same channel and make the channel more efficient; products of low relevance are often distributed through various channels, which will reduce efficiency of the channels.

(3) 渠道费用的投入。渠道费用主要包括渠道的开发和维护所投入的资金。总的说来，高额投资有利于扩大销售网络、增加销售额，更能提高企业的知名度；而低费用经销则有利于产品低价促销，但势必会由此缩小产品的销售网络，从而丧失一部分市场。

Input of channel costs. channel costs include the money used in the development and maintenance of channels. In general, high investment is good for expanding sales network, increasing sales and producers' popularity; low-cost distribution is good for sales promotion at low price, but the sales network will be reduced and part of market will be lost.

(4) 渠道经验。如果企业有足够的营销人员及渠道经验，曾经通过特定的中间商销售产品，则会形成渠道偏好。

Channel experience. If the firm has sufficient marketing staff and channel experience, the firm will have a channel preference once it has sold its products through particular intermediaries.

(5) 企业的服务能力。如果企业有能力为最终顾客提供各项服务，如安装、调试、维修及操作服务等，则可取消一些中间环节，采用短渠道。如果服务能力有限，则应充分发挥中间商的作用。

Service ability. If the firm has the ability to offer final customer services such as installation, commissioning, maintenance and operation service, then some intermediate steps can be canceled and a short channel can be taken. If the firm has limited service ability, it should take good advantage of the intermediaries.

(6) 产品。产品的体积、重量与销售渠道的长度呈反方向变动关系，如机床设备等体积大的产品要采用短渠道。产品的技术特性涉及专有技术的使用和保护，通常也关系到特殊服务的提供和质量保证。对于高新技术含量高、结构复杂、需要特殊服务的产品，如专用汽车，应采用短且窄的渠道；对于通用性强、服务技术含量低的产品可采用较长、较宽的分销渠道。价格高的商品多采用直接渠道或一级渠道，而价格相对较低的产品大多采用二层或以上的、较宽的渠道来分销。耐损性好的产品即使经历多次运输，也不会损坏，因此可以采用较长的渠道；对于那些易破、易坏、易腐的产品，应当采用较短但是较宽的渠道。

Products. The size and weight of products go reverse direction with the length of distribution channels. For example, large machine tools and equipments usually use short channels. Technical characteristics of products involve the use and protection of proprietary technology, and are often related to provision of special services and quality guarantee. As for the product of high-tech and complex structure which needs special service such as special purpose vehicles, a short and narrow channel should be taken. For products of common use and low service-tech, a longer and wider channel can be taken. Direct channel or M-R-C channel (Manufacturer-Retailer-Consumer) is suitable for high price products, while M-W-R-C or wider channels are often used for products of relatively low price. For durable products which can go through repeated transport, long channels are proper. And short but wider channels are suitable for fragile, weak and perishable products.

(二)环境因素 Environment Factor

环境因素对分销渠道设计的影响既多又复杂，如经济发展状况、社会文化变革、竞争结构、技术以及政府管理等。例如，当经济萧条时，生产者都希望采用能使最后顾客廉价购买的方式，将产品送到市场。这也就意味着使用较短的渠道，并免除那些会提高产品最终售价但又不必要的服务。

Environment factors have various and complex effect on the design of distribution channels. The factors include economic condition, social and cultural changes, competition structure, technology, government management and so on. For example, during recessionary period, the producer hopes to launch the products by the way that they can reach the final customers at the lowest price. It means that short channels should be used and unnecessary services, which would increase the price, should be dispensed.

(三)消费者因素 Consumer Factor

首先，消费者可分为产业客户和一般消费者。通常，产业客户数量少、购买次数少，但每次购买数量大，制造商可以将产品直接销售给产业客户；而对于一般消费者，中间商则在分销渠道中起着重要作用。其次，消费者对不同产品的购买习惯也会影响分销渠道的设计。当消费品中便利品的消费者较多且购买次数频繁时，生产者可利用由批发商与零售商组成的细密的分销渠道，到达市场的各个角落，方便消费者购买；当消费品中专业性较强的产品或贵重耐用品的消费者较多且购买次数较少时，生产者可利用独家代理等方式进行分销。

First of all, there are industrial consumers and common consumers. In general, there are not many industrial consumers but they buy fewer times with large quantities. Producers are able to sell products directly to industrial consumers. For average consumers, intermediaries play an important role in the distribution channels. Secondly, consumers' purchasing habits will also affect the design of distribution channels. When there are more customers of convenience products, and they buy very often, the producer can use serried distribution channels, which are composed of wholesalers and retailers, to reach each corner of local market and to make it convenient for consumers to buy. When there are more consumers of highly specialized or expensive durable goods and they buy fewer times, the producer can use exclusive agency to distribute products.

(四)竞争者因素 Competitor Factor

竞争者因素主要是指竞争者的渠道状况。竞争者的分销渠道对企业自身的分销渠道设计会产生重要影响，企业可以选择积极竞争或完全不同的竞争策略。在实力较为对等时，企业可以选择与竞争对手相同或类似的分销渠道；在实力对比悬殊且不占优势时，也可以回避竞争对手，选择截然不同的分销渠道。

Competitor factor refers to the channel conditions of competitors. Competitors' channels will have significant impact on the design of the producer's distribution channels. The producer can choose either positive competition or completely different strategy. If the producer has similar strength, it can choose similar channels or the same channels as competitors. If there is a sharp contrast in strength and the producer does not have advantage, it can choose distinct distribution channels.

(五)中间商因素 Intermediary Factor

设计渠道时，必须考虑承担不同任务的中间商的有利条件和不利条件，在成本、可获得性及提供的服务三方面对中间商进行评估。中间商在执行运输、广告、储存及接纳顾客等方面以及信用条件、退货特权、人员训练和送货频率方面，都有不同特点和要求。

Advantages and disadvantages of intermediaries of different tasks should be considered when designing channels. Intermediaries should be evaluated on three aspects-cost, availability and services provided. Intermediaries have different characteristics and requirements in the implementation of transport, advertising, storage, attending to customers, as well as in credit conditions, return privilege, personnel training and delivery frequency.

(六)市场潜力因素 Market Potential

市场潜力包括销售潜力以及潜在的风险。通过对收集的公开数据和原始数据的评估,企业可大致预测市场潜力与潜在风险,并比较企业自身的生产能力和风险承受力,以做出正确的战略决策。

Market potential includes sales potential and potential risks. Through the evaluation of public data and original data, the producer can predict roughly market potential and potential risks, and compare their productivity and risk tolerance so as to make right decisions.

二、分销渠道选择的策略 Strategy for Selecting Distribution Channels

(一)分销渠道选择的程序 Procedures of Selecting Distribution Channels

(1) 确定渠道目标与限制条件。有效的渠道设计应以确保企业的产品到达市场为目标。渠道目标的确定会受顾客、产品、中间商、竞争者、企业策略和环境等因素的影响。

Defining channel objectives and limits. Effective channel designs should ensure that products reach the market. The factors of customers, products, intermediaries, competitors, corporate strategy and environment will influence the decision on channel objectives.

(2) 明确各种渠道交替方案。渠道的交替方案主要涉及四大基本要素,即中间商的基本类型、渠道成员的特定任务、分销渠道的宽度、生产者与中间商的交易条件及相互权责。

Defining alternatives of channels. Alternative plan of channels involves four key elements-basic type of intermediary; specific tasks of channel members; channel width; trading terms and mutual responsibilities between the producer and the intermediary.

(3) 评价各种可能的渠道交替方案。每一渠道交替方案都是企业将产品送达消费者的可能路线。生产者所要解决的问题,就是从那些看似合理但又相互排斥的交替方案中挑选最能满足企业长期发展目标的方案。因此,企业必须对各种可能的渠道交替方案逐一进行评估。评估标准包括方案的经济性、适应性和控制性三个方面。使用经济性标准对分销渠道进行评价时,一方面,要评价不同渠道所能完成的销售额;另一方面,是评价不同渠道分销成本的变化。企业应根据产品销售特性对分销成本进行对比分析,从不同的分销渠道方案中找出分销成本最低的分销渠道。适应性标准是指随着环境条件的变化,所选的分销渠道能否适应这种变化,或企业能否灵活地对其分销渠道进行调整。对分销渠道控制能力的评价,一是看企业与中间商利害关系处理的难易程度,二是看同一层次中间商之间关系协调的难易程度。

Evaluating possible alternative plans. Each channel alternative plan is a possible route for the producer to deliver products to consumers. From the plausible but repelling alternatives, the producer needs to choose the plan that can best meet its long-term goal. The producer, therefore, should evaluate every possible alternative. The evaluating criteria include three aspects-economic efficiency, adaptability and controllability. When distribution channels are evaluated on economic efficiency, sales accomplished through different channels should be assessed, and on the other hand, cost changes in different channels should be assessed too. The firm should compare and analyze distribution cost according to sales characteristics, and find out the channel with the lowest distribution cost from different channel plans. Adaptability checks whether the chosen distribution channel can adapt to environment changes or whether the producer can adjust its distribution channels. Controllability checks the degree of difficulty in relationship between the producer and its intermediary, and that between intermediaries at the same level.

(二)分销渠道选择的策略 Strategies for Selecting Distribution Channels

1. 分销渠道长度的选择策略 Strategies for Selecting the Length of Channel

通常情况下，在确定渠道长度时，首先，要决定是采用直接渠道还是间接渠道，或者以哪一种渠道模式为主；其次，如果采用间接渠道，则还要确定中间商的类型与层次。从企业加快实现产品价值和提高经济效益的目的来看，一般来讲，减少中间环节可以节省流通时间和流通费用。但是，不是所有不经过中间环节的直接分销都能带来最好的经济效益。因为通过批发商的集散作用和零售商的扩散作用往往会加快整个社会再生产的过程，大大减轻企业的销售业务和经营负担，加快资金周转，增加企业盈利。

Usually the first thing is to decide whether to use direct channels or indirect ones or to decide what channel can be the main mode when choosing the length of channels. Secondly, the types and levels of intermediary should be determined if indirect channels will be adopted. The producer has the goal to achieve product value and enhance economic efficiency, so fewer intermediaries will reduce circulation time and costs. However, not all direct distribution which without intermediaries can bring better economic benefits, for through wholesalers' distribution function and retailers' diffusion effect, the process of social reproduction will often speed up. Therefore, sales and operating costs will be greatly reduced, cash flow will be accelerated and profit will then increase.

2. 分销渠道宽度的选择策略 Strategies for Selecting the Width of Channel

所谓分销渠道的宽度，是指分销渠道同一环节或层次选用中间商数目的多少，多者为宽，少者为窄。根据同一层次中间商数目的多少，可以有三种形式的渠道宽度策略，即独家分销渠道策略、密集型分销渠道策略、选择性分销渠道策略。

The so-called "width" of the distribution channel means the numbers of intermediaries at the same level or layer. It is "wide" if there are many intermediaries and "narrow" if there are few. There are three forms of strategy for selecting channel width according to the numbers of intermediaries. They are exclusive distribution, intensive distribution and selective distribution strategies.

(1) 独家分销渠道策略。它是指生产企业根据产品特点在一个地区、一定时期内仅选择一家中间商独家经营自己的产品。采用这一渠道的生产企业必须与被选中的独家经销商签订独家经销的协议，即要求其在经销本企业产品的同时，不得经销其他厂家的同类产品。生产企业还需要经常性地对产品的供应、运输和管理技术等方面给此经销商以特殊的便利条件或支持。采用独家分销渠道可使企业十分容易地控制渠道行为。但由于采用这种渠道后，厂商与独家经销商之间的互相依赖性大大增强了，可能会使制造商受控于独家经销商，或由于经销商经营的失误，使企业失去一条分销渠道，甚至失去一个目标市场。这种策略一般适用于需要售后服务的产品，如高档消费品、多数生产资料、拥有专利技术及品牌优势的特异性商品。

Exclusive distribution. The producer chooses only one intermediary in an area during a certain period according to its product characteristics. The producer who uses exclusive distribution must sign an agreement with the chosen exclusive dealer who may not sell similar products from other producers at the same time. The producer also needs to give special facilities or regular support in product supply, transport and management techniques. It is easy for the producer to control channel behaviors if exclusive distribution is adopted. However, mutual dependence between the producer and the exclusive distributor will also increase. The producer may be controlled by the distributor. It may also happen that the producer loses a channel or the target market due to the distributor's failure. Exclusive distribution generally applies to the products that require after-sales service such as luxury goods, most production materials and special goods with advantages of patent technology and brands.

(2) 密集型分销渠道策略。密集型分销渠道也称普遍型或广泛型分销渠道，它是制造商在同一渠道层次选用尽量多的中间商经销自己的产品，使产品在目标市场上迅速普及，以达到最广泛地占领目标市场的分销渠道。采用密集型分销渠道的企业必须充分预计到每个中间商可能同时经销几个厂家的多种品牌产品的情况，这使得中间商不可能为每一产品的促销都提供相应的费用，这就要求企业在资金上给予一定的支持，从而会相应地增加企业的渠道费用支出。从经济角度看，密集型分销所产生的费用较大；同时，由于中间商数目众多，企业无法控制各渠道成员的具体行为，这些都是采用密集型分销渠道给企业带来的不利之处。目前市场上的日用品和大部分食品、工业品中的标准化和通用化商品、需要经常补充和替换或用于维修的商品、替代性强的商品等，多采用这种分销渠道。

Intensive distribution. Intensive distribution channels, known as common or extensive channels, mean that the producer uses intermediaries as many as possible at the same level to sell and popularize its products. Therefore, the target market can be occupied rapidly. The producer to use intensive channels must expect that each intermediary may sell products of different brands at the same time. The intermediary, therefore, can not provide money for every product promotion so the producer needs to give financial support to the intermediary and channel cost will rise accordingly. From an economic point of view, intensive distribution costs a lot and the producer can not control channel members' behavior. Those are the disadvantages of intensive distribution channels. This distribution is suitable for daily commodities, most food, standard and general commodities in industries, products used for refilling, replacing or repairing, and products of strong substitutability.

(3) 选择性分销渠道策略。它是指生产企业在某一地区仅通过几个精心挑选的、最合适的中间商推销产品的策略。与密集型分销相比，它可以更集中地使用企业的资源，相对节省费用并能较好地控制渠道行为；同时，企业可以获得与采用密集型或独家经销两种渠道相比更多的利益。当然，分销渠道也不是尽善尽美的。这种策略可应用于适用范围广的产品。一般说来，这一策略对所有的产品都适用，但对一些特殊的贵重的商品更适用一些。

Selective distribution. It means that the producer selects only a few of most appropriate intermediaries to distribute its products. Compared with intensive distribution, selective distribution can use resource more intensively, reduce more costs and control the channels better. The producer can achieve more benefit than those who use intensive distribution or exclusive distribution. The selective distribution channels are not perfect of course. This strategy applies to a large range of products. Generally speaking, it applies to all products especially some special and precious products.

3. 对中间商的选择策略

所谓中间商，是指在商品流通领域中担任各种商业职能的商业企业和个体商人的总称。按其在分销渠道中的地位和作用可分为批发商和零售商两大类。企业必须根据各类中间商在分销渠道中不同的地位和职能加以选择，以适应企业和市场的实际，从而降低费用、提高销售率。这一策略在选择处在销售终端的零售商时尤为重要。

The so-called intermediaries are the business firms and individuals who perform various commercial functions in circulation. They can be divided into two categories: wholesalers and retailers according to their status and functions in distribution channels. The producer has to choose intermediaries according to their status and functions in distribution channels so as to meet the actual needs of the firm and market. Therefore costs can be reduced and sales can be improved. It is even more important to choose the right retailers who are at the end of the sales terminals.

终端销售点是企业实现经营目的的前沿，企业能否实现既定的经济效益同它对终端销售点的选择和经营直接相关。正因如此，终端销售点的选择被企业定位为"进入市场组织商品销售的第一步"，也是最重要的一步。企业在选择合适的终端销售点时，需要考虑以下几个方面。

The sales terminal is the forefront for firms to realize their business purposes. Whether the firm can realize its fixed economic benefits depends on its selection and operation of sales terminals. So the choice of sales terminal is defined as the first step to enter the market and also the most important step. The firm needs to consider the following aspects when choosing appropriate sales terminals.

第一，根据销售方式选择。销售方式，主要是指企业销售产品所采取的形式，它包括店铺销售和无店铺销售两种形式。企业可选择其中一种销售方式，也可以两种销售方式同时使用作为其终端销售点。

Sales pattern. It means the ways taken by the firm to sell products, including the forms of stores and non-stores. The firm can choose either form or both forms as its sales terminal.

第二，根据消费者的收入和购买力水平等选择。不同收入水平的消费者对商品购买的方式和地点不同。在竞争者数量不变的情况下，收入水平较高的区域，其消费者购买能力较高，对消费场所的规模、声誉、售后服务以及店面装潢等方面的要求也较高，因此，企业进入该地区设立终端销售点的必要性和可能性就大；反之，收入水平较低的区域，消费者购买能力也较低，企业进入时要谨慎。

The level of consumer income and purchase power. Consumers with different income purchase at different places by different ways. In the case that the number of competitors remains the same, the consumers have higher purchase power in high income areas. The business scale, reputation, after-sales service and the store decoration also have to satisfy more requirements. So it is more necessary and possible for firms to set up sales terminals in such an area. In contrast, firms need to be careful when entering low income areas where consumers have low purchase power.

第三，根据商品经营费用和投资风险选择。在进入收入水平较高的区域时，区域内的大型商场往往会收取较高的"产品进场费""上架费""条码费"等，这样会大大降低资金的盈利率。因此，企业在进入这些区域之前必须考虑自身整体实力，如果核算后的收益较差或者投资风险较高，则需要为产品另辟蹊径。

 Management fees and investment risks. In higher income areas, shopping malls tend to charge "slotting fees", "shelving fees", "barcode fees", etc., which will reduce profitability significantly. Therefore, the firm has to consider its own overall strength before entering such areas. If earnings are poor or investment risk is too high after evaluation, the firm can take other ways to sell its products.

第四，根据目标顾客出现的位置选择。一般而言，在人流密集的场所，目标顾客也较多。这些场所包括：商业街、交通干线、工作场所周边、居民区、学校、游乐场和休闲场所等。

Target consumers' places. Generally there are more target customers where there are large crowds. These places include: commercial streets, traffic arteries, workplace surroundings, neighborhood, schools, playgrounds, recreation places, and so on.

第五，根据顾客购买心理选择。不同顾客的购买兴趣、关注因素、购物期望等心理特征是不同的。顾客的购买心理直接影响其购买行为。因此，要研究企业产品主要顾客的购买心理，否则难以达到销售预期。

Consumers' psychology. Customers have different psychological characters in purchase interests, attention, shopping expects, etc. The customers' purchase psychology affects directly their buying bahaviors. So the psychology of the firm's main customers should be studied ,otherwise sales expectations can not be reached.

第六，根据竞争者策略选择。企业在选择终端销售点时还需考虑竞争对手的数量及其分销策略、企业自身战略目标以及产品所处生命周期阶段等诸多因素。

Competitors' strategies. When choosing sales terminals, the firm needs to consider the number and distribution strategies of competitors, the firm's own strategic objectives as well as the product life cycle stages, etc.

第八章　分销渠道策略
Distribution Channel Strategies

第三节　批发商与零售商的分销策略
Wholesaling and Retailing Distribution Strategies

中间商指处于生产者和消费者之间，参与商品交换，促进买卖行为的发生和实现，具有法人资格的经济组织或个人。中间商包括批发商和零售商。本节将考察不同种类的批发商和零售商的特点以及分销策略。

Intermediaries are the economic organizations or individuals with legal personality, who participate in goods exchange and promote transactions between producers and consumers. Intermediaries include wholesalers and retailers. In this section, characters of different types of wholesalers and retailers as well as distribution strategies will be studied.

一、批发商的分销策略　Wholesaling Distribution Strategies

(一)批发商的含义及特点　Meanings and Characteristics of Wholesaler

批发商是指在产品流通过程中，不直接服务于最终消费者，只通过转售等方式实现产品在空间上、时间上的转移的中间环节的统称。

Wholesalers are the general name of middlemen, who, in the distribution process, do not serve ultimate consumers and only transfer goods in time and space by reselling.

批发商的特点有：①处于流通领域的中间环节；②服务对象是零售商业；③从事的是大宗买卖活动；④不同规模的批发商的地区分布不同。

Wholesalers' characteristics are as follows: ①in the intermediary position in circulation; ②serving retail businesses; ③engaged in big trading activities; ④different sizes of wholesalers with different regional distribution.

(二)批发商的类型　Types of Wholesalers

批发商主要有以下三种类型：经销批发商、代理商批发商、生产者的分销机构和办事处。

Wholesalers have three main types: distribution wholesaler, agent wholesaler, producer's sales branch and office.

(1) 经销批发商。是指自己进货，取得产品所有权后再批发出售的商业企业，也就是人们通常所说的独立批发商或商人批发商。经销批发商是批发商的最主要的类型。如按职能和提供的服务来分类，经销批发商可分为完全服务批发商和有限服务批发商两大类。

Distribution wholesalers are those who purchase goods and then wholesale them after obtaining the ownership. They are so-called merchant wholesalers or wholesale merchants. Distribution wholesaler is the main type of wholesalers. There are full-service and limited-service wholesalers according to functions and services provided.

(2) 代理批发商。是指从事购买或销售或二者兼备的洽商工作，而不取得产品所有权的商业单位。与经销批发商不同的是，它对其经营的产品没有所有权，所提供的服务比有限服务批发商还少,其主要职能在于促成产品的交易,借此赚取佣金作为报酬。代理批发商主要分为产品经纪人、制造商代表、销售代理商、采购代理商等。

Agent wholesalers are those engaged in purchase or sale or in negotiation of the both without obtaining the ownership of goods. Different from distribution wholesalers, agent wholesalers have no ownership of the goods in their operation. They provide less service than limited-service wholesalers and their main role is to facilitate transactions for commission as a reward. Agent wholesalers can be product brokers, manufacturers' agents, selling agents, purchasing agents, and so on.

(3) 生产者的分销机构和办事处。是指买方或卖方自行经营批发业务,而不通过独立的批发商进行。这种批发业务,可分为以下类型:销售分店、销售办事处和采购办事处。

Producers' sales branches and offices wholesale products to buyers without wholesale merchants in the middle. Types of this wholesale can be POS (Point of Sales), sales offices and procurement offices.

(三)批发商的分销策略 Wholesaler Distribution Strategies

1. 目标市场决策 Target Market Decision

批发商必须界定其目标市场,并且对自己进行有效的定位。它们可以根据客户的规模、客户类型、对服务的需要或者其他因素来选择目标顾客群。在目标顾客群内,批发商可以识别出更有利可图的客户,提供强有力的产品和服务,并且与客户信建立更好的关系。

Wholesalers must define their target market and position themselves effectively. They can base the selecting of target customers on customer sizes, types, service needed or other factors. They can identify more profitable customers in target customer group and provide powerful products and services to build better relationship with customers.

2. 营销组合决策 Marketing Mix Strategies

批发商必须就产品组合和服务、价格、促销、分销进行决策。批发商的"产品"是其提供的一组产品和服务的组合。批发商的定价通常将商品的成本加上一个标准的百分比。批发商也需要借鉴零售商所使用的一些非人员促销技巧。它们需要制定整体战略,并且更好地运用供应商的促销材料和计划。批发商必须精心选择地点、设施和网址。典型的批发商会选址在低租金、低税收的地区,并且在建筑物、设备和系统上投入不多。

Wholesalers must make decisions on product assortments, services, price, promotion and distribution. The wholesaler's "product" is the assortment of products and services that it offers. For price, wholesalers usually mark up the cost of goods by a standard percentage. Wholesalers also need to draw some non-staff promotion techniques used by retailers. They need to develop overall strategies, and make better use of promotional materials and plans from suppliers. Wholesalers must choose their location, facilities and Web locations carefully. Wholesalers typically locate in low-rent, low-tax areas and tend to invest little money in their buildings, equipment, and systems.

二、零售商的分销策略 Retailing Distribution Strategies

(一)零售商的含义 Meanings of Retailer

零售商是指将产品或服务直接销售给最终消费者的组织或个人。任何从事这种销售活动的机构，不论是制造商、批发商还是零售商，也不论这些产品和服务是经由个人、邮寄、电话或自动售货机销售的，还是在商店、街上或消费者家中销售的，都属于此范畴。

Retailers are organizations or individuals who sell products or services directly to final consumers. Any institutions engaged in such sales activities, regardless of manufacturers, wholesalers or retailers, fall into this category, no matter how the products and services are sold-by individuals, mails, phone or vending machines, or where they are sold-at shops, on the street or at consumers' places.

(二)零售商的类型 Types of Retailers

零售商可以根据几个不同的特征进行分类，主要包括以下几类。

Retailers can be classified in terms of several characteristics, including the following.

1. 依据服务的数量分类 According to the Offered Amount of Services

(1) 自助服务零售商。它服务于那些愿意自己进行"寻找—比较—选择"的过程从而省钱的顾客。

Self-service retailers. They serve customers who are willing to perform their own "locating-comparing-selecting" process to save money.

(2) 有限服务零售商。它提供更多的销售支持，因为它们更多地销售那些顾客需要了解相关信息的商品。它们由此提高的运营成本导致了更高的价格。

Limited-service retailers. They provide more sales assistance because they carry more shopping goods about which customers need information. Their increased operating costs result in higher prices.

(3) 全面服务零售商。它一般是专卖店和一流的百货店，销售人员在购物过程的每个阶段都为顾客提供帮助和支持。全面服务的商店通常更多地经营那些顾客喜欢接受"服侍"的特种商品。

Full-service retailers. In full-service retailers, such as specialty stores and first-class department stores, sales people assist customers in every phase of the shopping process. Full-service stores usually carry more specialty goods for which customers like to be "waited on".

2. 按产品线的宽度和深度分类 According to Length and Breadth of Product Line

(1) 专卖店。它经营狭窄的产品线，而这些产品线内产品的花色品种很多，如运动用品店。

Specialty stores. They carry a narrow product line with a deep assortment, such as sporting goods stores.

(2) 百货店。经营种类繁多的产品线，一般包括服装、家具和家居用品。

Department stores. They carry many product lines—typically clothing, home furnishings and household goods.

(3) 超级市场。通常规模很大、成本低、薄利多销，采用自助服务的方式来满足顾客对食品、洗涤品、家居日常用品的需要。

Supermarkets. They are relatively large, low-cost, low-margin, high-volume, and self-service operation designed to serve consumer's needs for food, washing articles and household articles, etc.

(4) 便利店。规模相对较小，位于居民区附近，一周营业七天，每天营业时间很长，经营品种不多、周转速度快的便利品。

Convenience Stores. They are relatively small stores located near residential areas, opening long hours seven days a week, and carrying a limited line of high-turnover convenience products.

(5) 超级商店。比一般的超市大得多，提供种类繁多的日用食品、非食品商品和服务。其中包括超级购物中心——超级市场和折扣店的复合体。

Superstores. They are much larger than usual supermarkets supplying various daily food, nonfood items and services, including supercenters—combined supermarket and discount stores.

3. 按索要的相对价格分类 According to Relative Prices

(1) 折扣店。通过销售较大的批量、接受较低的毛利，以较低的价格销售标准商品。

Discount stores sell standard merchandise at lower prices by accepting lower margins and selling higher volume.

(2) 低价零售商。当主要的折扣商店提高档次的时候，新一轮低价零售商则进入，填补低价格和大批量的空缺。低价零售商有三种类型：独立低价零售商、厂家门市部和仓储俱乐部。

Off-price retailer: As the major discount stores have traded up, a new wave of off-price retailers move in to fill the ultralow-price and high volume gap. The three main types of off-price retailers are independents, factory outlets and warehouse clubs.

(三)零售商的市场营销决策 Retailer Marketing Decisions

零售商处于商品流通的最终端，直接将商品销售给最终消费者。他们是联系生产企业、批发商与消费者的桥梁。

Retailers are at the end of commodity circulation and sell products directly to final consumers. They are the bridge connecting manufacturers, wholesalers and consumers.

1. 目标市场决策 Target Market Decision

目标市场的决策包括商店应面向高档、中档还是低档购物者，对目标顾客的商品供应是多类化、专类化还是特色化等。

Target Market Decision involves what customer markets shops should target at, whether up-market, mid-grade market or mass market. It also involves what products to supply, whether various, special or distinctive ones.

2. 产品组合和服务决策 Product Assortment and Service Decision

零售商必须就三个主要产品变量做出决策：产品组合、服务组合、店面气氛。

Retailers must decide on three major product variables: product assortment, services mix, and store atmosphere.

零售商的产品组合应与目标市场的购物期望相匹配，这是决定零售商在激烈竞争中能否取胜的关键因素。零售商必须决定产品组合的宽度、深度以及产品的质量，才能选择适合商品销售的渠道。

The retailer's product assortment should match target shoppers' expectations, which is the key element whether the retailer can win in fierce competition. Retailers must decide on the breadth and depth of product assortments and product quality in order to choose the right channels for the sales of goods.

零售商必须确定向顾客提供的服务组合，因为服务组合是竞争中商店之间实现差异化的主要手段，其中包括售前服务(是否接受电话订购、邮购等)、售后服务(是否接受调换、退货等)、附加服务(是否支票付现、可否免费停车等)。

The retailer must define the services mix because it is the main means to differentiate the retailers in competition. The mix includes pre-sales service (whether telephone order or mail order is accepted, etc.), after-sales service (whether replacement or return is accepted, etc.), additional services (whether payment by check or is available free parking, etc.).

商店气氛也是进行竞争的重要因素，商店必须具备井然有序、适合并吸引目标顾客的气氛。

The store's atmosphere is another element in competition. Stores must provide attractive environments that are orderly and fit for customers.

3. 价格决策 Price Decision

商品价格是一个关键的定位因素，零售商都希望产品能以较高的价格实现较大的销售量，但这不符合经济规律。因此，零售商只能在高价位、低销量和低价位、高销量这两个组合中任选其一。零售商必须根据目标市场、产品服务搭配组合和竞争情况来确定商品的最终价格。

The product's price is a key element in positioning. All retailers want to sell at high prices and large sales but it is not in line with economic laws. Retailers have to choose either high markups on lower volume or low markups on higher volume. Retailers must decide on the final price in terms of target market, product and services mix, and competition condition.

4. 促销决策 Promotion Decision

零售商使用常规的促销工具，即广告、人员推销、销售促进、公共关系和直销等来与消费者取得联系。零售商必须选择适当的促销手段来达到吸引顾客的目的。

Retailers use regular promotion tools-advertising, personal selling, sale promotion, public relations, and direct marketing- to reach consumers. They must select the right promotion means to attract customers.

5. 地点决策 Place Decision

零售商经常指出，零售成功的三个关键因素就是：地点、地点、地点！一个零售商的店址对其吸引顾客的能力而言相当重要。建筑的成本或者租用设施的费用对零售商的利润有显著影响。

Retailers often point out that the essential three elements to success are location, location and location! The retailer's shop site is very important to the ability of attracting customers. Construction costs or the cost of renting facilities can influence retailers' profit significantly.

第四节 分销渠道管理策略
Channel Management Strategies

渠道管理是指生产者为实现其分销的目标对现有渠道进行管理，目的是加强渠道成员间的合作，调解渠道成员间的矛盾，从而提高整体的分销效率。

Channel management means that the producer manages its existing distribution channels in order to achieve distribution goals. The goals are to strengthen cooperation between channel members and mediate conflicts so as to improve the overall distribution efficiency.

一、渠道管理的内容 Contents of Channel Management

(1) 对经销商的供货管理，保证供货及时，在此基础上帮助经销商建立并理顺销售子网，减轻销售库存压力，加快商品的流通速度。

The producer manages the supply for distributors, and ensures timely delivery. On such a basis, it helps distributors set up and arrange subnet of sales, relieve inventory pressure and accelerate the pace of goods flow.

(2) 加强对经销商广告、促销的支持，减少商品流通阻力；提高商品的销售力，促进销售；提高资金利用率，使之成为经销商的重要利润源。

The producer enhances support for distributors' advertising and promotion, reduces circulation resistance of the products; increases product sales force, promotes sales; improves utilization of funds to make it an important source of profit for distributors.

(3) 对经销商负责，在保证供应的基础上，对经销商提供产品服务支持。

The producer is responsible for distributors. On the basis of sufficient supply, it provides service support for distributors.

(4) 加强对经销商的订货处理管理，减少因订货处理环节中出现的失误而引起发货不畅。

The producer manages order processing, and reduces impeded delivery due to the mistakes in the order process.

(5) 加强对经销商订货的结算管理，规避结算风险。

The producer manages the settlement of distributors' orders and avoids settlement risks.

(6) 其他管理工作。包括对经销商进行培训，增强经销商对企业理念、价值观的认同以及对产品知识的认识；还要负责协调生产者与经销商之间、经销商与经销商之间的关系。

Other management work includes training of distributors for them to increase recognition of corporate philosophy, values and product knowledge. The producer also needs to coordinate relations between producers and distributors.

二、渠道管理的策略 Channel Management Strategies

(一)选择渠道成员的策略 Selecting Channel Members

生产者在确定中间商时，首先要明确所选的中间商需要满足什么条件。这些条件一般包括从业时间、发展情况、信誉、财务能力、经营的产品组合、覆盖的市场面、仓储条件和发展潜力等。一般来说，中间商不可能面面俱到，各方面都做得很好，因而企业必须对所要求的条件按照重要性进行排序，然后按照预选中间商的条件与排序标准相对照，从中优选最好的中间商作为分销渠道成员。在生产者评估中间商的条件时，要注重评估中间商的经营时间的长短及其成长记录、清偿能力、合作态度、声望等条件。

When selecting intermediaries, the producer should determine what criteria the chosen intermediary should meet. They are the channel member's years in business, growth situation, reputation, financial capacity, product lines carried, market coverage, storage condition and growth potential. Intermediaries generally can not do everything very well, so the producer must sort the required criteria in terms of importance. Then comparing the criteria with the ranking, the producer chooses the best intermediary as the channel member. When the producer evaluates intermediary conditions, it should evaluate the intermediary's years in business, growth record, solvency, cooperativeness and reputation, etc.

(二)激励渠道成员的策略 Motivating Channel Members

为了采取有效的激励策略，必须做好以下几方面的工作。

The following must be done in order to adopt better motivating strategies.

1. 了解中间商的心理状态与行为特征 Understanding Mentality and Behavior Characteristics of Intermediaries

为了激励渠道成员使其具有良好表现，生产者首先必须从了解各个中间商的心理状态与行为特征入手。许多中间商常受到如下批评：①不重视某些特定品牌的销售；②缺乏产品知识；③不认真使用供应商的广告资料；④忽略了某些顾客；⑤不能准确地保存销售记录，甚至有时遗漏品牌名称。

The producer must understand intermediaries' mentality and behavior characteristics first in order to encourage channel members to perform well. Many intermediaries are often criticized for the following reasons: ① failing to cherish the sale of certain brands; ② lacking product knowledge; ③ not able to use advertising materials given by the producer carefully; ④ ignoring some customers; ⑤ not able to keep sales records accurately and even missing some brands.

2. 奖励渠道成员 Rewarding Channel Members

对配合的渠道成员给予奖赏以鼓励其行为，如许诺较高的毛利率、给予促销支持等。

The producer should encourage and reward the cooperative members such as promises of higher gross margins, promotion support and so on.

3. 惩罚渠道成员 Punishing Channel Members

对不配合的渠道成员实施惩罚，如减少利润、收回奖赏许诺、减慢运货速度等。

The producer should impose penalty on uncooperative channel members, such as reducing profit, recover the reward promise, slowing down shipping speed, etc.

4. 提供相关知识 Providing Relative Knowledge

掌握扶助渠道成员成功经营的知识，如提供促销规划、培训、商品陈列技术等。

The producer should master the knowledge of assisting channel members, such as providing marketing plan, training and exhibition techniques.

5. 施加影响 Influencing Channel Members

利用被赋予的权力对渠道成员施加影响。

The producer should influence channel members with the given power.

（三）妥善处理生产者与经销商关系的策略 Handling the Relationship Between Producers and Distributors

生产者在处理与经销商的关系时，常依不同情况而采取三种激励策略，即促进合作、合伙，进行分销规划。

When the producer deals with relationship with its distributors, three motivating strategies are often taken: to promote cooperation and partnership, and to make distribution planning.

1. 促进合作策略 To Promote Cooperation

大部分生产者认为，解决问题的办法是设法得到中间商的配合。他们常常采取软硬兼施的方法：一方面，使用积极的激励手段，如较高的利润、交易中的特殊照顾、奖金等额外酬劳、合作广告资助、展览津贴、销售竞赛等；另一方面，偶尔使用消极的制裁，如威胁减少中间商的利润、推迟交货、甚至终止关系等。在应用该种策略时，不要简单地套用"刺激—反应"模式，而要谨慎地使激励与制裁相适应，否则会产生较大的负面影响。

Most producers believe that the solution is to get the intermediaries' cooperation. They often take a carrot approach: on the one hand, they take incentive means, such as higher profits, special favor in transaction, bonuses and other additional reward, financial aid in cooperative advertising，exhibition subsidy and sales contests; on the other hand, negative sanctions are occasionally taken, such as threatening to reduce intermediaries' profits, deferring delivery, or even terminating relationship. When applying this strategy, producers should not simply use the "stimulus-response" model, but adapt incentives carefully to sanctions; otherwise there would be great adverse effect.

2. 促进合伙策略 To Promote Partnership

生产者要着眼于与经销商或代理商建立长期的伙伴关系。首先，生产者要仔细研究并明确在销售区域、产品供应、市场开发、财务要求、技术指导、售后服务和市场信息等方面，生产者和经销商彼此之间的相互要求。其次，根据实际可能，双方共同商定在这些方面的有关政策，并按照其信守这些政策的程度给予奖励。

Producers need to focus on long-term partnership with distributors or agents. First, producers have to study carefully and define requirements of both parties in the following aspects: sales area, product supply, market development, financial requirements, technical advice, after-sales service and market information. Then both parties, if possible, decide on related policies in those fields and should be rewarded according to the extent to which they have complied with these policies.

3. 实行分销规划 To Make Distribution Planning

所谓分销规划，是指建立一个有计划的、实行专业化管理的垂直市场营销系统，把生产者的需要与经销商的需要结合起来。生产者可在市场营销部门下专设一个分销关系规划处，负责确认经销商的需要，制订交易计划及其他各种方案，帮助经销商以最佳方式经营。该部门和经销商合作确定交易目标、存货水平、产品陈列计划、销售训练要求、广告与销售促进计划等，引导经销商认识到他们是垂直营销系统的重要组成部分，从而积极做好相应的工作，以从中得到更高的回报。

The so-called distribution planning is to establish a vertical marketing system which is well planned and professionally managed to combine the needs of the producer and distributors. The producer can establish a distribution planning office under its marketing department. The office is responsible for identifying the needs of distributors, making trade plans or other programs, and helping distributors operate in the best way. It can cooperate with distributors to determine trade objectives, inventory levels, product display, training requirements, as well as advertising and promotion programs, so as to make distributors realize that they are an important part of the vertical marketing system. Distributors will then work well to gain higher returns.

(四)分销渠道的评估策略 Evaluating Distribution Channels

企业应该通过一系列对分销渠道运行过程的评估来做出及时的调整。对分销渠道运行状态的评估可以分为分销渠道运行成效评估和赢利能力评估两个方面。

The firm should make adjustments according to the evaluation of channel's running condition. The evaluation can be divided into two sides: annual evaluation of channels' economic returns and evaluation of profitability.

1. 对渠道运行成效的评估 Evaluation of Channels' Running

对渠道运行成效的评估主要依靠五种绩效工具，即销售分析、市场占有率分析、市场营销费用与销售额的对比分析、财务分析和顾客态度追踪等。其中，销售分析主要用于衡量和评估企业所制定的销售目标与实际销售额之间的关系；市场占有率分析，是用来考察企业本身的经营状况；市场营销费用与销售额的对比分析，是用来检查与销售有关的市场营销费用；财务分析，是用来识别影响企业资本净值收益率的各种因素；顾客态度追踪，是企业对顾客偏好和满意度的分析。通过以上分析，当发现实际绩效与年度计划发生较大偏差时，企业可以采取相应措施，及时做出调整。

The main evaluating tools used for evaluation of channels' running are sales analysis, market share analysis, the ratio analysis of marketing cost to sales amount, financial analysis, customer attitude tracking, etc. The sales analysis is used to measure and evaluate the relation between target sales and actual sales; market share analysis is used to examine firm's operation condition; the ratio analysis of marketing cost to sales is for the checking of marketing cost related to sales; financial analysis is used for identifying factors that influence profit margin on net assets; customer attitude tracking is used to analyze customer preferences and satisfaction. By the above analysis, when there is a large deviation from actual performance to annual plan, the firm is able to adopt appropriate measures and make timely adjustments.

2. 对分销渠道盈利能力的评估 Evaluation of Distribution Channel Profitability

对分销渠道盈利能力的评估可以用来测定不同分销渠道的经济效益，此种评估可以帮助企业对各种产品或市场分销渠道应该扩展、减少还是取消做出客观的判断。在总投资一定的情况下，提高企业分销渠道盈利能力的主要方法是大量降低分销渠道的成本，包括直接渠道费用、促销费用、仓储费用、运输费用等；同时，资产管理效率的提高也会使渠道的盈利能力得到提升。

Assessment of distribution channel profitability can be used to measure the economic benefits of different distribution channels. This assessment can help companies objectively judge whether its various products or market distribution channels should be extended, reduced or canceled. In case of a fixed total investment, the major method of improving enterprise's distribution channel profitability is greatly reducing the cost of distribution channels, including costs of direct channel, marketing costs, warehousing costs, transportation costs, etc; At the same time, the improvement in efficiency of asset management will also promote the profitability of channel.

本 章 小 结
Summary

分销渠道，是指某种货物和劳务从生产者向消费者转移时取得这种货物和劳务的所有权或帮助转移其所有权的所有企业和个人。企业仅有好的产品并不是占领市场唯一的决定性因素，它还必须建立、开发和设计有效的分销渠道，使产品能够顺畅地流转到消费者手中。因此，在竞争日益激烈的今天，选择正确的分销策略已成为决定企业成败的又一重要因素。中间商指处于生产者和消费者之间，参与商品交换，促进买卖行为发生和实现、具有法人资格的经济组织或个人。中间商包括批发商和零售商。批发商和零售商的分销策略在营销成功中作用重大。渠道管理是指生产者为实现其分销的目标对现有渠道进行管理，目的是加强渠道成员间的合作，调解渠道成员间的矛盾，从而提高整体的分销效率。渠道管理策略包括选择渠道成员策略、激励渠道成员策略、妥善处理生产者与经销商关系的策略、分销渠道的评估策略。

Distribution channels refer to the firms and individuals that acquire or help transfer the ownership of the goods or services when moving from producers to consumers. It is not the only decisive factor for enterprises to occupy the market because of their good products, they must also establish, develop, and design effective distribution channels, so that products can be smoothly flow into the hands of consumers. Therefore, with today's increasingly fierce competition, to choose the right distribution strategy has become another important factor deciding the success or failure of a company. Intermediaries refer to economic organizations or individuals with legal personality who participate in commodity exchanges and promote the sale to take place between producers and consumers. Intermediaries include wholesalers and retailers. Wholesaler and retailer's distribution strategy plays an important role in marketing success. Channel management that the producer manages existing channels of distribution in order to achieve its goal and with the aim of strengthening cooperation between channel members, mediates conflict between channel members, so as to improve the overall efficiency of distribution. The channel management strategies include selecting the channel members strategy, encouraging channel members policy, the strategy of properly handling the relationship between producers and distributors, and the assessment strategies of distribution channels.

思 考 题
Questions

1. 分销渠道的含义是什么？它包括哪些类型？

What is the meaning of distribution channels? What types of channels does it have?

2. 影响分销渠道策略选择的因素有哪些？选择分销渠道策略应考虑哪几点？

What are the factors that influence the choice of distribution channel strategy? What should be considered when selecting distribution channel strategies?

3. 批发商和零售商的含义是什么？零售商分销策略的选择包括哪些内容？

What is the meaning of wholesalers and retailers? What is the content of retailer distribution decisions?

4. 企业为何需要对分销渠道进行管理，其管理包括哪些策略？

Why do enterprises need to manage distribution channels, and what strategies does its management include?

第九章 促销策略
Promotion Strategies

【学习目标】
1. 促销及促销的作用，促销组合的概念以及影响促销组合制定的因素；
2. 人员推销的特点，人员推销的形式、对象、策略和人员推销的过程以及人员推销的管理过程；
3. 广告的类型及制定广告策略的程序；
4. 公共关系的概念及基本特征、公共关系策略及活动方式和原则；
5. 营业推广的概念、营业推广策略的类型和活动方式及实施程序。

Learning Objectives
1. Promotion and its function, the concept of promotion mix, and the factors that influence the making of promotion mix;
2. The characteristics of personal selling, the form, target and strategies of personal selling, and the management process of personal selling;
3. The types of advertisements and the strategy-making process of advertisements;
4. The concept and essential features of public relations; strategies, activity patterns and principles of public relations;
5. The concept of sales promotion; types, activity patterns and implementation procedures of sales promotion strategies.

促销策略是四大营销策略之一。正确制定并合理运用促销策略是企业在生产市场营销中获得优势、获取较大经济效益的必要保证。企业需要采取适当的方式进行促销，促销不是单独的一项工具，而是若干工具的一个组合，主要包括人员推销、广告、营业推广和公共关系。

Promotion strategy is one of the four key marketing strategies. Correctly making and properly applying promotion strategies is the essential guarantee to get the advantages of production and marketing, and obtain bigger economic benefits. Enterpriser should choose right ways to carry out the promotion, for promotion is not a single tool, but a combination of tools, including mainly personal selling, ad, sales extension and public relations.

第一节 促销与促销组合策略
Promotion and Promotion Mix Strategies

一、促销的含义 Meaning of Promotion

促销是促进产品销售的简称。从营销的角度看，促销是企业通过人员和非人员的方式，沟通企业与消费者之间的信息，激发、刺激消费者的购买欲望，使其产生购买行为的全部活动的总称。从这个概念出发，促销有以下几层含义。

Promotion is short for promoting product sales. In view of marketing of enterprises, promotion means the general activities that, in personal and non-personal ways, the enterprises communicate information to consumers, stimulate and trigger customers' desire to purchase, and make them purchase the products. From this concept, promotion has the following meanings.

(1) 促销活动的实质是沟通信息。在市场经济条件下，社会化的商品生产和商品流通决定了生产者、经营者与消费者之间客观上存在着信息的分离。对于企业生产和经营的商品性能、特点，顾客不一定知晓，工商企业有必要将有关商品和服务的存在及其性能特征等信息，通过声音、文字、图像或实物传播给顾客，以增进顾客对其商品及服务的了解，引起顾客的注意和兴趣，帮助顾客认识商品或服务所能带给他们的利益，从而激发他们的购买欲望，为顾客最终做出购买决定提供依据。

The essence of promotion activities is to communicate information. In market economy conditions, the socialized commodity production and circulation result in the existence of the separation of information among producers, operators and consumers, and consumers probably do not know the performance and characteristics of the commodity produced and operated by the company. It is necessary for the industrial and commercial enterprises to transmit related commodities, services, performance and characteristics to the consumers in the forms of sound, letters, images, and objects. In doing so, the enterprises can help consumers learn more about the services, arouse the consumers' attention and interest, help them recognize what benefits the commodity or service can bring them, trigger their desire to buy and provide a sound foundation for consumers to buy.

(2) 信息传递方式体现为双方互动的特点。在现代营销理念下，促销作为一种沟通活动，其帮助和说服消费者所采取的信息传递方式可分为两类：一类是单向传递，指单方面将商品或服务信息传递给消费者的方式，也就是以"卖方→买方"方式传递商品或服务信息。另一类是双向传递，就是双方沟通信息的方式，亦即以"卖方↔买方"方式传递商品或服务信息。这种方式的信息传递有两个好处，一方面向消费者宣传介绍商品和服务，激发其购买欲望；另一方面，企业同时直接获得消费者的反馈信息，从而不断提高商品和服务的适销对路程度，更好地满足消费者的需要。

The means of information transmitting represents the features of interaction. In modern marketing idea, promotion is a kind of communicating activity to help and persuade consumers to adopt two ways of information transmission: one is unidirectional transmission, which means unilaterally transmit goods and service information to the consumers, in other words, to transmit the goods and service information to the consumer in the form of "seller→buyer". The other is bi-directional transmission, which means the form of two sides communicating information, namely, to transmit goods and service information in the form of "seller↔buyer". This form of information transmitting has two benefits: on the one hand, the sellers advertise and introduce goods and service to the consumers to trigger their desire to buy; on the other hand, the sellers get the consumers' feedback at the same time to improve marketable degree of goods and service to better meet the demands of consumers.

(3) 促销的目的是引发、刺激消费者产生购买欲望。在消费者可支配收入既定的条件下，消费者是否产生购买行为主要取决于消费者的购买欲望，而消费者的购买欲望又与外界的刺激、诱导密不可分。促销正是针对这一特点，通过各种传播方式把产品或劳务等有关信息传递给消费者，以激发其购买欲望，使其产生购买行为。

The promotional purpose is to trigger and stimulate consumers' desire to buy. Under the given condition that consumers have some disposable income, whether consumers have purchase behavior depends on their desire to buy, and their desire is inseparable from external stimuli and induction. Because of this, promotion is a way to transmit goods, service and the related information to consumers by all kinds of transmission to trigger consumers' desire to buy and produce purchase behavior.

(4) 促销的方式有人员促销和非人员促销两类。人员促销，亦称直接促销或人员推销，是企业派出推销人员向消费者推销商品或劳务的一种促销活动，它主要适合于消费者数量少但比较集中的情况。非人员促销，又称间接促销或非人员推销，是企业通过一定的媒体传递产品或劳务等有关信息，以促使消费者产生购买欲望、发生购买行为的一系列促销活动，包括广告、公关和促售等。它适合于消费者数量多但比较分散的情况。通常，企业在促销活动中将人员促销和非人员促销两种方式结合起来运用。

The two forms of promotion are personal and non-personal. Personal promotion, also known as direct marketing or personal selling, is a promotion activity that the business appoints the sales persons to promote commodity or service. This fits the situation in which there are small-numbered but more concentrated consumers. Non-personal promotion, also called indirect promotion or non-personal selling, is a series of promotion activities that the business transmits the information about the commodity or service by way of some media to trigger consumers' desire to buy and produce purchase behavior. It includes advertisements, public relations and promotion, appropriate for a situation in which there are large but scattered numbers. As usual, a business often combines the personal selling with the non-personal selling in promotion activities.

二、促销的作用 Effects of Promotion

现代企业越来越重视促销活动，这是因为促销有以下几方面的作用。

Modern enterprises attach more and more importance to promotion activities. This is because promotion has the following effects.

1. 有助于加强买卖双方的有效沟通 Reinforcing Communication Effectively between Sellers and Buyers

在促销过程中，一方面，卖方(企业或中间商)向买方(中间商或消费者)介绍有关企业现状、产品特点、价格及服务方式和内容等信息，以此来诱导消费者对产品或劳务产生需求欲望并采取购买行为；另一方面，买方向卖方反馈对产品价格、质量和服务内容、方式是否满意等有关信息，促使生产者和经营者更好地满足消费者的需求。

During the process of promotion, one the one hand, the seller (the business or the intermediate) recommends some related information about the present situation of the company, characteristics of products, prices, and the way and content of service to induce the consumer to have the desire to buy their products and services so as to produce the purchase activity. On the other hand, the buyer provides the seller with the feedbacks about whether they are satisfied with the price and quality of a product and the content and way of their service so as to stimulate the producer and the proprietor to better satisfy customers.

2. 有助于刺激并诱导需求，开拓市场 Triggering and Inducing Demands and Exploiting the Market

有效的促销活动不仅能够诱导和激发需求，而且能在一定条件下创造需求。当企业营销的某种商品处于低需求时，促销可以招徕更多的消费者，扩大需求；当需求处于潜伏状态时，促销可以起催化作用，实现需求；当需求波动时，促销可以起到导向作用，平衡需求；当需求衰退、销售量下降时，促销可以使需求得到一定程度的恢复。

The effective promotion activity can not only induce and stimulate customers' need, but also create demand. When some commodity on sale is in light demands, promotion will appeal to more customers; when the commodity on sale is in a latent state, promotion will be a catalyst to realize the demand; when the demand is fluctuating, promotion will be a guide to balance the demands; when the demand is in a recession and sales drop off, promotion will restore the demands to some extent.

3. 有助于突出产品特色，树立企业形象 Highlighting Product Features and Establishing the Company's Image

在激烈的市场竞争中，企业的生存与发展越来越需要强化自身的经济特色。与众不同、独树一帜，是多数企业成功的秘诀。企业通过促销，突出宣传本企业经营的商品不同于竞争对手商品的特点以及它给消费者带来的特殊利益，有助于加深消费者对本企业商品的了解。

In the severe market competition, survival and development of enterprise increasingly needs to strengthen its own economic characteristics. Being distinctive and unique is the secret of success to an enterprise. By way of promotion, the enterprise advertises that their goods are different from their opponent's and they can bring special benefits to the consumers, so the consumers can know better about the company's commodity.

4. 有助于形成顾客偏爱，稳定和扩大销售 Cultivating Customers' Preference to Stabilize and Expand Sales

企业通过促销活动，能使消费者对本企业产品产生偏爱并成为企业的忠诚顾客，进而稳住已占领的市场，达到稳定销售的目的。偏爱本企业产品的顾客越多，企业的销售额也就越高，市场份额也就越大。

By way of of promotion, the enterprise can make the consumers have preference for their commodity and become its loyal customers , so as to stabilize the market that they have already captured and have steady sales. The more customers who have preference for their commodity there are, the higher sales of the enterprise will be, and the larger market they will share.

三、促销组合策略 Strategies of Promotion Mix

(一)促销组合的概念 Concept of Promotion Mix

为了把有关企业和产品的信息传递给消费者，有效地发挥促销作用，企业不得不采取一定的促销手段。促销手段可以分为两大类：一类是人员推销；另一类是非人员推销，又可分为广告、营业推广和公共关系。所谓促销组合，就是指企业为了达到促销目标，对人员推销、广告、营业推广和公共关系四大促销手段的选择、搭配及综合运用，以形成一个统一的促销整体。

In order to transmit the related information about the enterprise and the commodity to consumers and make promotion effective, the enterprise has to take some promotion measures. The measures can be divided into two types: one is personal promotion, the other is non-personal promotion which can be classified into advertising, sales promotion and public relations. The so-called promotion mix is the measure that the enterprise selects, matches and comprehensively employs personal promotion, advertising, sales promotion and public relations to form a whole sales plan.

(二)促销组合策略的含义与类型 Meaning and Types of Promotion Mix Strategies

1. 促销组合策略的含义 Meaning of Promotion Mix Strategy

促销组合策略是指企业通过对人员推销、广告、公共关系和营业推广这四个基本手段的不同组合方式，包括每个手段内部要素的不同组合方式的不同选择，以更有效地向消费者或用户传递产品信息、引起他们的注意和兴趣、激发他们的购买欲望和购买行为，从而扩大销售。因此，不同的促销组合方式可以形成不同的促销策略类型。

Promotion mix strategy is the marketing management with different combinations of the four basic means: personal promotion, advertisements, public relations and sales promotion, including different choices and different combinations of the internal elements in each means. The enterprise is then able to transmit the information of commodity effectively to the user and the consumer to attract their attention and arouse their interest to trigger their desire to buy and purchase behavior, so as to expand sales. Consequently, different combinations of promotion mix can cultivate different types of promotion strategy.

2. 促销组合策略的类型 Types of Promotion Mix Strategy

促销组合策略一般可分为促销整体组合策略与单项促销组合策略。整体促销组合策略，是指促销的四个基本构成要素的不同组合方式，即人员推销、广告、营业推广、公共关系的整体组合与差别组合所形成的策略类型。这里所说的差别组合，是指如人员推销与广告、公共关系的组合，或人员推销与营业推广的组合等不同的组合方式。单项促销组合策略，是指促销组合基本要素各自内部要素的不同组合方式所形成的人员推销、广告、营业推广、公共关系组合策略。

There are overall promotion mix strategy and single promotion mix strategy. The overall promotion mix strategy refers to different combinations of the four basic elements, that is, the type of overall mix strategy or the differential mix strategies which is a combination of personal promotion, advertisements, sales promotion and public relations. The differential mix here means different combinations of personal promotion, ads and public relations, or the combination of personal promotion and sales promotion, etc. Single promotion mix strategy refers to different combinations of the inner parts of basic sales promotion elements, i.e., personal promotion, ads, sales promotion and public relations.

我们目前常用的促销策略类型，多按促销组合要素划分为人员推销策略、广告策略、营业推广策略、公共关系策略，即单项组合策略。整体组合策略按生产者与消费者之间不同的互动关系，可划分为推式策略和拉式策略两大类，如图9-1所示。

What we commonly apply at present is single mix strategy, which can be classified as personal promotion strategy, ads promotion strategy, sales promotion strategy, and public relation strategy according to sales promotion mix elements. The overall promotion mix strategy can be classified into push marketing strategy and pull marketing strategy according to different interactions between the producer and the consumer. The main form of this strategy is as shown in Figure 9-1.

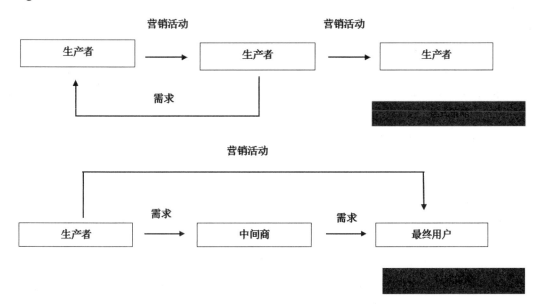

图 9-1　促销组合策略的主要形式

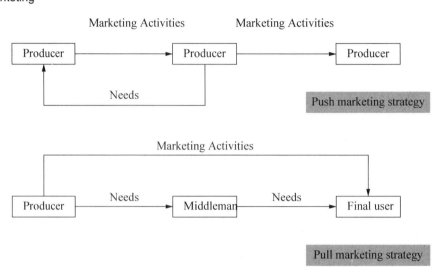

Figure 9-1　The Main Form of Promotion Mix Strategy

推式策略，是指企业运用人员推销的方式，把产品推向市场，即从生产企业推向中间商，再由中间商推给消费者，故也称人员推销策略。推式策略一般适合于单位价值较高、性能复杂、需要做示范的产品，即根据用户需求特点设计的、流通环节较少、流通渠道较短、市场比较集中的产品。拉式策略，也称非人员推销策略，是指企业运用非人员推销方式把顾客拉过来，通过宣传，使消费者对商品或服务发生兴趣，使其对本企业的产品产生需求，以扩大销售。它适用于单位价值较低、流通环节较多、流通渠道较长、市场范围较广、市场需求较大的产品。企业在促进产品销售的过程中，究竟是实行"推"式策略，还是实行"拉"式策略，要根据具体情况而定。一般说来，应当二者兼顾，各有侧重。这两种策略各具特点，在促销中各有作用、相辅相成。

The push marketing strategy refers to that the enterprise adopts the way of personal promotion to launch the product, that is, from the manufacturing enterprise to the intermediate, and then from the intermediate to consumers, which is also named personal promotion strategy. The push marketing strategy is fit for a product with high unit value, complex performance and the need of demonstration, that is, the product which is designed according the user's demand, has fewer circulation links, shorter circulation channels and more concentrated market. The pull marketing strategy refers to the non-personal promotion strategy, that is, the enterprise adopts the non-personal way to attract customers. Through the way of advertisements, the consumer will be interested in the commodity and service. Therefore, they will have needs for its products. So the enterprise can expand the sales. This strategy is fit for a product with lower unit value, more circulation links, longer circulation channels, broader market segments, and bigger market demand. During the process of promotion, whether the enterprise will apply the push marketing strategy or the pull marketing strategy depends on the real situation. Generally speaking, the enterprise should give consideration to both and have their own focuses. Both strategies have their own characteristics, have their own functions, and complement each other during promotion.

(三)影响促销组合策略制定的因素 Elements That Influence Establishing the Promotion Mix Strategy

鉴于四种促销方式各有特点,适用于不同对象,企业在进行促销活动时就要根据营销目标和商品特点等,有针对性地进行单项与不同组合的选择。一般来说,在确定促销组合策略时,应考虑以下因素。

Considering that the four ways of promotion have their own characteristics and each is fit for different targets, the enterprise should choose single promotion strategy or different promotion mix strategies according to the characteristics of its products. Generally speaking, when choosing the promotion mix strategy, the enterprise should consider the following factors:

1. 促销目标 Target of Promotion

企业促销目标不同,需采取的促销组合也不同。如果促销目标是树立企业形象,提高产品知名度,其促销重点就应放在广告上,同时辅之以公关宣传;如果促销目标是让顾客充分了解某种产品的性能和使用方法,则印刷广告、人员推销或现场展示是较好的办法;如果促销目标是在近期内迅速增加销量,则营业推广并辅之以人员推销和适量的广告最易立竿见影;而公共关系手段则着重用于企业的长期促销目标。

Different promotion targets will need to apply different promotion mixes. If the promotion target is establishing the company's image and improving the reputation of their product, the importance of the promotion should be attached to advertisements and complemented with generating publicity. If the promotion target is to make the consumer fully aware of the property and application method of some products, the good ways should be printing ads, personal promotion and live demonstration. If the promotion target is to rapidly increase the sales in a short period, sales promotion should be supplemented with personal promotion and appropriate ads should produce immediate effects, while the strategy of public relation will emphasize the long-term promotion target of the enterprise.

2. 产品因素 Product Factors

关于产品因素,我们主要从两个方面来分析,包括产品的性质和产品的市场生命周期。

For product factors we will mainly analyze from two aspects which include the properties and the market life cycle of the product.

(1) 产品的性质。不同的产品有不同的用途,为满足不同消费者的需求,需要采取不同的促销组合。

The properties of a Product. Different products have different purposes and in order to meet different consumers' demands, the enterprise will take different promotion mixes.

对营销消费资料的企业来说,最重要的促销手段是广告,其次是营业推广、人员推销,最后是公共关系。而对营销生产资料的企业来说,最重要的促销手段是人员推销,其次是营业推广、广告,最后是公共关系。各种促销手段对消费品和工业品有不同的重要性,这是由不同产品的特点所决定的。因为多数消费品价格较低,使用简单,消费者市场人多面广,每次购买数量少,因此,广告是消费品的最重要的促销手段,可以通过广告以较低的相对成本达到广而告之的目的。相反,多数工业品的价格较高,技术性强,用户数量较少且分布较为集中,每次购买数量较大,因而适宜人员推销。

For the enterprise marketing consumption goods, the most important promotion way is ads, followed by sales promotion and personal promotion, and finally the public relations. Whereas for the enterprise that sells industrial goods, the most important promotion way is personal promotion, followed by sales promotion and ads, and finally the public relations. All promotion ways are important to both consumer goods and industrial products. This is determined by characteristics of different products. Because consumer goods are cheap and simple to use, and the consumer market has the feature of wide range of people and low quantity per purchase, ads are the most important way of promotion. Through ads, the enterprise can publicize widely with relatively low cost. On the contrary, the personal promotion is fit for most industrial products because they are expensive with high technology, and it's market has the feature of fewer users, more concentrated distribution and high quantity per purchase.

(2) 产品的市场生命周期。在产品市场生命周期的不同阶段,由于促销目标不同,应相应地选择、编配不同的促销组合策略。如表 9-1 概括介绍了在产品市场生命周期的不同阶段应采取的促销组合策略及其目标重点。

Market life cycle of a product. Because the promotion target is different in different phases of the market life cycle, it is necessary to select and orchestrate different promotion mix strategies. Chart 9-1 provides a general introduction of promotion mix strategy and the important points of its target in different phases of market life cycle of the product.

表 9-1 产品市场生命周期不同阶段促销组合及其重要目标

产品生命周期	重点促销目标	促销组合
投入期	使消费者了解产品	各种介绍性广告、人员推销、导入 CIS 策略
成长期	提高产品的知名度	改变广告形式(如形象广告)
成熟期	增加产品的信誉度	改变广告形式(如形象广告)
衰退期	维持信任和偏好	营业推广为主,提醒性广告
整个周期阶段	消除顾客的不满意感	利用公共关系

Chart 9-1 Promotion Mix Strategy and the Important Points of Its Target

Market life cycle of products	Key goals of promotion	Promotion mix
input stage	to make consumers know the product	all kinds of industry ads, personal selling and leading-in CIS strategy
growth stage	to enhance the reputation of the product	to change the form of ads. (e.g., image advertising)
mature stage	to increase the credibility of the product	to change the form of ads. (e.g., image advertising)
decline stage	to maintain trust and preference	marketing promotion oriented, reminding advertising
the phase of the whole cycle	to eliminate the customer's dissatisfaction	to make use of the public relations)

3. 市场条件 Market Conditions

(1) 从市场地理范围大小看，若促销对象是小规模的本地市场，应以人员推销为主，而对广泛的全国甚至世界市场进行促销，则多采用广告形式。

Considering the size of geographic extent, if the promotion target is a small local market, personal promotion should be focused on, but for the national and international market, ads are the main promotion way.

(2) 从市场类型看，消费者市场因消费者数量多而显得分散，应重点采取广告等非人员推销形式；而对用户较少、批量购买、成交额较大的生产者市场，则主要采取人员推销形式。

Considering the type of the market, because the market is scattered due to the large number of consumers, the non-personal promotion ads should be focused on. For the market which contains fewer users who buy goods in bulk and have large turnover, personal promotion should be taken.

(3) 在有竞争者的市场条件下，制定促销组合和促销策略还应考虑竞争者的促销形式和策略，要有针对性地不断变换自己的促销组合及促销策略。

In the competitive market, before making promotion mix and promotion strategies, the competitor's ways of promotion and strategies should be considered. It is necessary to specifically change promotion mix and promotion strategies of one's own.

4. 促销预算 Promotion Budget

企业确定的促销预算额，应该是企业有能力负担的，并且能够适应竞争需要，能在满足促销目标的前提下，做到效果好而费用省。促销费用的多少，直接影响到促销方式的选择。一般说来，广告宣传的费用较高，人员推销次之，营业推广花费较小，公共关系的费用最少。

The promotion budget determined by the business should be the one that the business can afford, and it can meet the needs for competition with good effect and less cost on the premise that it can satisfy promotional goals. The amount of cost will directly affect the choice of promotion ways. Generally speaking, the cost of advertisements is the highest, personal promotion comes second, next comes the cost of sales promotion, and the cost of public relations is the least.

5. 消费者的购买时间 Buying Time of Consumers

对最早和早期购买者要进行针对性宣传，并通过广告以最快速度将商品信息告知购买者，以扩大影响；对晚期和最晚购买者，要采取各种优惠措施，以吸引顾客，扩大商品销售。

To extend influence, it is necessary to have targeted advertising to the earliest and early buyers and to tell them information of the products as soon as possible. For the latest and late buyers, all kinds of preferential measures should be taken to attract customers and extend sales.

(四)开展促销组合策略的步骤 Carrying Out the Steps of Promotion Mix Strategies

1. 明确目标受众 To Define Target Audience

目标受众可能是个人、小组、特定公众或一般公众。通过企业目标市场的研究与市场调研，界定其产品的销售对象是现实购买者还是潜在购买者，是消费者个人、家庭还是社会团体。明确了产品的销售对象，也就明确了促销的目标受众。

The target audience refers to certain individuals, groups, some specific people or the general public. Whether the target customers will become real buyers or potential buyers, the individual, family or the social group should be defined through the research and investigation of a target market. Defining the target customers is defining the target audience.

2. 确定促销目标 To Define Promotion Goal

在不同时期和不同的市场环境下，企业开展的的促销活动都有着特定的促销目标。对于短期促销目标，宜采取广告促销和营业推广相结合的方式。对于长期促销目标，公关促销具有决定性意义。须注意企业促销目标的选择必须服从企业营销的总体目标。

In different periods and different market environments, the promotional activities carried out by the business all have specific promotion goals. For short-term promotion goals, the business should take the strategy of combining the advertising promotion and sales promotion. For long-term promotion goals, the public relations promotion is of decisive significance. What should be noticed is the choice of promotion goals must comply with the overall sales promotion goal.

3. 设计促销信息 To Design Promotion Information

企业须重点研究信息内容的设计，要清楚企业促销对目标对象所要表达的诉求是什么，并以此刺激其反应。诉求一般分为理性诉求、感性诉求和道德诉求三种方式。理性诉求与受众的自身利益密切相关，显示产品所能带来的预期收益。感性诉求旨在激起积极的情绪，以刺激购买。沟通人员可以使用诸如爱、自豪、愉快和幽默等正面的感性诉求。道德诉求针对的是受众对什么是"正确"和"适当"的理解。它们通常会用来激励人们支持社会事业，例如清洁环境、改善种族关系、提倡男女平等以及帮助弱势群体。

The enterprise must focus on the design of information contents, and should be clear about it's appeals to target customers. The enterprise then stimulates customers according to the appeals. The appeals can be divided into rational appeals, emotional appeals and moral appeals. Rational appeals are closely related to the target audience's self-interest. They demonstrate the expected benefits that a product will bring. Emotional appeals aim to trigger consumers' active emotion to stimulate purchases. Communications staff will make use of positive emotional appeals such as love, pride, happiness and humor. Moral appeals aim at the understanding of what is "right" and what is "appropriate". They are used to encourage people to support social undertakings such as cleaning the environment, improving ethnic relations, equality of men and women, and helping vulnerable groups.

促销人员还必须确定如何处理三个信息结构：第一，是应该下结论还是留给受众判断。第二，是应当将强有力的证据放在开始还是最后。第三，是否只提出单方面的论据(仅提出产品的优点)，还是提出两方面的论据(在向顾客宣传产品优点的同时，也承认其不足之处)。

Sales promotion staff have to make sure how to deal with three information structures. First, whether they should draw a conclusion or leave it for audiences to judge? Second, whether they should put sound evidence at the beginning or in the end? Third, whether they should put forward unilateral arguments (only mentioning the good characteristics of products) or put forward two-side arguments (admitting shortcomings when advertising the good characteristics of the products).

4. 选择沟通渠道 To Select Communication Channels

传递促销信息的沟通渠道主要有人员沟通渠道与非人员沟通渠道。人员沟通渠道向目标购买者当面推荐，能得到反馈，可利用良好的"口碑"来扩大企业及产品的知名度与美誉度。非人员沟通渠道主要指大众媒体沟通。大众传播沟通与人员沟通有机结合才能发挥更好的效果。

The communication channels for transmitting promotional information can be divided into personal communication channels and non-personal communication channels. The personal communication channel is to recommend products to the buyers face-to-face and get the feedbacks, so as to make use of positive reactions to popularize products. The non-personal communication channel mainly refers to mass media communication. The dynamic integration of mass media communication and personal communication can gain better results.

5. 确定促销的具体组合 To Define Specific Promotion Mix

根据不同的情况，将人员推销、广告、营业推广和公共关系四种促销方式进行适当搭配，使其发挥整体的促销效果。应考虑的因素有产品的属性、价格、寿命周期、目标市场特点以及"推式"或"拉式"策略。

According to different situations, an overall promotion results can be obtained through the proper combination of personal promotion, advertisements, sales promotion and public relations. The factors to be considered are the properties, prices, life cycles of products, the characteristics of the target market and the Push or Pull strategy.

6. 确定促销预算 To Determine Promotion Budget

企业在确定促销组合方式时，应考虑自身的经济实力和受财务影响的程度。如果企业促销费用宽裕，应同时使用几种促销方式；否则，就要考虑选择耗资较少的促销方式。

The enterprise should determine the way of promotion mix according to its economic strength and the degree of financial influence during the promotion period. If there are more funds for promotion, several ways of promotion should be used simultaneously. Otherwise, the ways of low cost should be considered.

7. 收集反馈信息 To Collect Feedbacks

信息传递出去后，促销人员必须调查它对目标受众的影响。这包括询问目标受众是否记得该信息，看过多少次，还记得哪些要点，对信息的观感如何，以及对产品和企业的态度等。对信息反馈的结果可能意味着改变促销计划，甚至改变产品本身。

After transmitting the information, the promotional staff have to investigate the influence on the audience. The investigation includes asking the audience whether they remember the information or not, how many times they have viewed the information, what key points they remember, how they feel about the information, and their attitude toward the product and its enterprise. The result of the feedbacks may mean changing the plan of promotion, even changing the product itself.

第二节 人员推销策略
Personal Selling Strategies

人员推销是促销组合中人与人之间直接接触的推销方式。它是企业的推销人员直接向顾客进行介绍、说服工作，促使顾客了解、偏爱本企业的产品，进而采取购买行为的一种手段。

Personal selling strategy is a promotional way of people's direct contact with each other in the promotion mix. It is a means that sales promotion staff introduce products and persuade the customers directly so that they can have a better understanding and preference for products, thus taking purchase actions.

一、人员推销的含义及特点 Meaning and Characteristics of Personal Selling

(一)人员推销的含义 Meaning of Personal Selling

人员推销是企业运用推销人员直接向顾客推销商品和劳务的一种促销活动。在多数场合下，人员推销是一种最有效的促销手段，特别是在促使消费者对企业和产品产生偏好、采取购买行为等方面能发挥特殊的作用。通过推销人员与推销对象之间的接触、洽谈，推销人员使推销对象购买推销品并达成交易。人员推销能够实现既销售商品、又满足顾客需求的双重目标。

Personal selling is a kind of promotional activity that the enterprise chooses salesmen to directly sell goods and services. In most occasions, personal selling is the most effective way of promotion, and especially it can play a special role in making consumers have a preference and take the purchase action. By the contact and negotiation between them, the salesmen make the target customer to buy their products and conclude the transaction. Personal selling can realize the dual goals of selling the goods and meeting the customers' needs.

(二)人员推销的特点 Characteristics of Personal Selling

人员推销与非人员推销相比，具有以下优势和特点。

Compared to non-personal selling, personal selling has the following advantages and characteristics.

(1) 面对面洽谈业务，信息传递双向性。推销人员直接和顾客洽谈业务，可进行双向信息沟通，使买卖双方能够清楚地了解各自的需要和特征，并根据各种情况做出及时的调整。

Personal selling means bidirectional transfer of information through face-to-face business negotiations. Salesmen conduct direct business negotiations with the customer and they will have a bidirectional communication of information, and then the buyers and the sellers can clearly learn of their own needs and characteristics, thus timely adjusting according to various situations.

(2) 推销具有选择性和灵活性。推销员在每次推销之前，可以选择有较大购买潜力的顾客，有针对性地进行推销；并可事先对未来顾客作一番调查研究，确定具体推销方案，提高推销的成功率。另外，他们还可以及时发现、答复和解决顾客提出的问题，消除顾客的疑虑和不满意感。

Promotion is selective and flexible. Before each promotion, salesmen should select customers with more purchasing potential and make the targeted promotion. A study and investigation about the customers before promotion is necessary so they can define a detailed plan for promotion and improve the success rate. Moreover, the salesman can also timely discover, reply and solve the questions raised by customers and clear up doubts and dissatisfaction.

(3) 推销过程的完整性。人员推销过程是从市场调查开始，经过选择目标顾客，当面洽谈，说服顾客购买，提供服务，促成交易，到顾客对产品及企业做出反馈的完整过程。

The completeness of promotion process. Personal selling is a process that starts from market investigation, selecting targeted customers, face-to-face negotiation, persuading customers to buy, providing the service and making deals to the feedback of the customers to the enterprise.

(4) 培养和建立友好关系与协作长期性。推销人员与顾客直接见面、长期接触，可以促使买卖双方建立友谊，密切企业与顾客之间的关系，有助于建立长期的买卖协作关系，从而稳定地销售产品。

Long-term of cultivation and establishment of friendly relationship and cooperation. If a salesman directly meets a customer and has a long-term contact with the customer, this will lead to the establishment of friendship between the enterprise and the customer. It is also helpful to establish a long-term cooperation relation between buyers and sellers, ensuring steady sales.

二、人员推销的任务 Assignments of Personal Selling

1. 寻找顾客 To Find Customers

推销人员不仅要与现有的顾客保持联系,更重要的是要不断地寻找、发现潜在的顾客,开拓市场,这是人员推销的首要任务。

Salesmen should not only keep in contact with their customers, but also look for and find out potential customers and expand the market. It is the essential task of personal selling.

2. 沟通信息 To Communicate Messages

市场营销是买卖双方之间的信息循环。顾客通过推销员可了解公司的经营状况、经营目标、产品性能、用途、特点、使用、维修、价格等诸方面信息,这能刺激消费者完成从需求到购买的行为。同时,推销员还肩负着搜集和反馈市场信息的任务,应及时了解顾客需求的特点和变化趋势,了解竞争对手的经营情况,了解顾客的购后感觉、意见和看法等,从而为公司制定有关政策、策略提供依据。

Marketing is the message circulation between the seller and the buyer. Customers can get some messages about the company's status and target of operation, property, purpose, characteristics, usage, maintenance and price of the products. It can stimulate customers to accomplish the action from needs to purchase. At the same time salesmen also undertake the task of collecting and feeding back the market information, timely learn of customers' needs, the characteristics and changing trends of their needs, the status of their rivals' operation, and their impression, views and opinions after buying their goods, thus providing a basis for the company to decide on related policies and strategies.

3. 推销商品 To Promote Goods

推销人员不仅要说服顾客购买产品,沟通与老顾客的关系,而且要善于培养和挖掘新顾客,并根据顾客的不同需求,实施不同的推销策略,满足顾客的需要,实现商品价值的转移。推销员在向顾客推销产品时,必须明确他推销的不是产品本身,而是隐藏在产品背后的对顾客的一种建议,即告诉顾客,通过购买产品能得到某些方面的满足。同时,要掌握顾客心理,善于应用推销技巧。

Salesmen should not only persuade customers to buy goods and keep a good relationship with the regular customers, but also carry out different promotional strategies according to customers' different needs and realize the value transition. When salesmen popularize their goods to customers, they must identify what they are promoting is not goods itself, but the suggestion behind the goods which is to tell the customers they can get some satisfactions from buying. At the same time, it is necessary to master customers' minds and be good at applying the skills of promotion.

4. 提供服务 To Provide the Service

良好的服务是推销成功的保证。推销员在推销过程中,应积极向顾客提供多种服务,如业务咨询、技术咨询、信息咨询等。推销中的良好服务能够增强顾客对企业及其产品的好感和信赖。

Good service is a guarantee of promotion success. During the process of promoting, the salesmen should actively provide many kinds of services to customers, such as business consultation, technology consultation and informational consultation and so on. The good service during promotion can improve customers' impressions and trust.

5. 协调平衡 To Coordinate the Balance

推销人员为供需双方穿针引线，调剂余缺，协商分配紧缺产品，积极为积压产品寻找销路，解决此地积压、彼地脱销的不平衡状态。

Salesmen serve the function of go-between for the two sides of supply and demand. They regulate the surplus and deficiency and negotiate to distribute the products in short supply products. They actively find the market to deal with the unbalanced state of overstock here and out-of-stock there.

三、人员推销策略的含义及内容 Meaning and Contents of Personal Selling Strategies

人员推销策略是指企业根据外部环境变化和内部资源条件建立和管理销售队伍的系统工程的策略。为了增加利润，企业应将较多的资源分配在人员推销上，并制定对营销人员的奖惩办法，最大限度地调动营销人员的积极性和潜能。

Personal selling strategy refers to the systematic engineering strategy of establishing and managing the promotional staff. In order to increase profits, the enterprise should attribute more resources among personal selling, and making regulations of rewards and punishment to motivate salesmen's initiative and potential to a maximum.

其内容主要包括：一是确定人员推销在企业市场营销组合中的地位，选择适宜的人员推销的形式；二是制定人员推销的基本策略；三是确定人员推销的工作流程策略；四是确定人员推销的管理策略。

The content mainly includes: defining the status of personal selling in marketing mix and choosing the appropriate form of personal selling; making basic strategy of personal selling; conforming working procedures strategy of personal selling; determining managing strategy of personal selling.

四、人员推销的形式策略 Form Strategy of Personal Selling

(一)人员推销的形式 Forms of Personal Selling

一般来说，人员推销有以下三种基本形式。

Generally speaking, there are three basic forms of personal selling.

(1) 上门推销。上门推销是最常见的人员推销形式，它是由推销人员携带产品的样品、说明书和订单等走访顾客，推销产品。

Door-to-door selling. It is the most common form of personal selling, which refers to salesmen visiting customers with samples, instructions and order forms.

(2) 柜台推销。又称门市推销或售点推销，是指企业在适当地点设置固定的门市，由营业员接待进入门市的顾客，推销产品。门市的营业员是广义的推销人员。柜台推销适合于零星小商品、贵重商品和容易损坏的商品推销。

The counter sales. It is also termed as retail sales or store sales. It is conducted in a store in an appropriate place where the shop assistant welcomes customers and sells products. The shop assistant is the salesman in a general sense. The counter sales is suited for selling petty commodities, valuable merchandise and the vulnerable goods.

(3) 会议推销。它是指利用各种会议向与会人员宣传和介绍产品，开展推销活动。例如，在订货会、交易会、展览会、物资交流会等会议上推销产品均属会议推销。

The meeting sales. It is the process of advertising and introducing the products to the attendees in various meetings and carrying out the promotion activities. For example, selling products in purchasing meetings, trade fairs, exhibitions and commodity fairs are all meeting sales.

(二)人员推销的对象 Objects of Personal Selling

人员推销对象是推销活动中接受推销的主体，是推销人员说服的对象。推销对象有消费者、生产用户和中间商三类。

The object of promotion is the one who accepts the promotion in the activities of personal selling, a person to be persuaded. The objects of personal selling can be divided into consumers, production users and the intermediates.

(1) 向消费者推销。推销人员向消费者推销产品时，必须对消费者有所了解。为此，要掌握消费者的年龄、性别、民族、职业、宗教信仰等基本情况，进而了解消费者的购买欲望、购买能力、购买特点和习惯等，并且要注意消费者的心理反应。对不同的消费者应施以不同的推销技巧。

Promotion to consumers. When a salesman is selling products to the consumer, he must know something about the consumer. So, it is necessary to master the fundamental information about their age, sex, nationality, profession, religious belief and so on. Then they should know customers' desire to buy, their purchasing capabilities, their purchasing characteristics and their habits, at the same time paying attention to the customers' psycho-reaction. They should employ different promoting skills according to different customers.

(2) 向生产用户推销。将产品推向生产用户的必备条件是熟悉生产用户的有关情况，包括生产用户的生产规模、人员构成、经营管理水平、产品设计与制作过程以及资金情况等。在此前提下，推销人员还要善于准确而恰当地说明自家产品的优点；能对生产用户使用该产品后所得到的效益做简要分析，以满足其需要；同时，推销人员还应帮助生产用户解决疑难问题，以取得用户的信任。

Promoting to production users. The essential condition of promoting products to users is to know something about the related situation of production users, including the scale of production, the staff composition, the level of operation and management, the design and production process of products and funds. Under this premise, the salesmen should be good at illustrating the advantages of their products correctly and properly. They are able to briefly analyze the profits after using their products and meet their needs, and at the same time, the salesmen should help the production users solve problems to gain their trust.

（3）向中间商推销。推销人员在向中间商推销产品时，首先要了解中间商的类型、业务特点、经营规模、经济实力以及他们在整个分销渠道中的地位；其次，要向中间商提供有关信息，为中间商提供帮助，建立友谊，扩大销售。

Promoting to the intermediates. When salesmen are promoting products, they should at fist know the type, service features, scale of operation, economic strength of intermediates and the status during the whole channel of distribution. What's more, they should provide the related information and help to the intermediates, establish friendship, and expand sales.

五、人员推销的基本策略 Basic Strategies of Personal Selling

在人员推销活动中，一般采用以下三种基本策略。

In the activities of personal selling, the following basic strategies are generally adopted.

1. "刺激—反应"策略 Strategy of "Stimulus-Response"

这种策略是在不了解顾客的情况下，推销人员运用刺激性手段引导顾客产生购买行为的策略。推销人员事先设计好能引起顾客兴趣、能刺激顾客购买欲望的推销语言，通过渗透性交谈进行刺激，在交谈中观察顾客的反应；然后根据其反应采取相应的对策，并选用得体的语言再对顾客进行刺激，进一步观察顾客的反应，以了解顾客的真实需要，诱发其购买动机，引导其产生购买行为。这种策略最适合推销日用工业品。

Under the circumstances of not knowing the customers, this kind of strategy is that salesmen make use of stimulus to induce the customers to produce the purchasing behavior. Salesmen should design the language of promotion which can arouse customers' interests and trigger their purchasing desires. They can conduct the stimulation through permeable conversations and observe the response of customers; and then they choose the corresponding strategy and the appropriate language to stimulate the customers by observing their further response so as to know their real needs and trigger their purchasing motivation to produce the purchasing behavior. This strategy is best suited for selling manufactured goods for daily use.

2. "配方—成交"策略 Strategy of "Recipe-Deal"

此策略是指推销人员在基本了解顾客情况的前提下，有针对性地对顾客进行宣传、介绍，以引起顾客的兴趣和好感，从而达到成交的目的。因推销人员常常在事前已根据顾客的有关情况设计好推销语言，这与医生对患者诊断后开处方类似，故称为"配方—成交"策略。

This strategy is that on the premise of knowing the situations of customers, salesmen advertise and introduce their products specifically to arouse the customers' interests and good feelings to make a deal. Salesmen often organize the language previously according to customers' situation, which is something like a doctor writing out a prescription, so it is called "recipe-deal" strategy.

3. "诱发—满足"策略 Strategy of "Induction-Satisfaction"

此策略是指推销人员运用能激起顾客某种需求的说服方法，诱导顾客产生购买行为。这种策略是一种创造性推销策略，它要求推销人员能因势利导、诱发、唤起顾客的需求，并能不失时机地宣传介绍和推荐所推销的产品，以满足顾客对产品的需求。

This strategy is that salesmen take the method of persuasion to trigger customers' needs and induce them to produce purchasing behavior. This strategy is a creative promotion strategy that the salesmen are required to improve the occasion, induce and trigger customers' needs and take the opportunity to advertise and recommend the promoted products to meet their needs.

六、人员推销的工作流程策略 Working Procedure Strategy of Personal Selling

1. 寻找并识别目标顾客 To Find and Identify Targeted Customers.

推销人员首先要善于寻找产品购买者，包括有支付能力的现实购买者及潜在购买者。推销人员可以通过多种途径寻找目标顾客：一是本企业已有的推销对象的姓名和地址；二是请求介绍，可请老顾客、供应商、中间商、行业协会、亲戚朋友等帮助介绍和推荐；三是参加某些团体以及各种社交活动；四是通过报刊、工商名录、电话、信函等资料查寻信息；五是陌生访问。

Salesmen should first be good at finding shoppers of their products, including real purchasers and potential purchasers. The salesmen are able to find targeted customers through many ways. First, to use the names and addresses of targeted customers that the enterprise has already had. Second, to ask for introduction. The enterprise can request the regular customers, suppliers, intermediates, industry association and friends and relatives to help to introduce and recommend. Third, through taking part in some organizations and social activities. Fourth, to inquire some information through materials such as newspapers, directories of industries and businesses, telephone numbers, letters and so on. Fifth, to visit as a stranger.

2. 拜访准备 Preparation for Visiting

(1) 调研顾客信息。对于已确定的目标顾客，推销人员应当首先收集他们的有关资料，包括需求状况，顾客的经济来源和经济实力，拥有购买决策权的对象，购买方式以及顾客的性格、脾气、嗜好等，以便制定推销方案。

To investigate and survey the information of customers. For identified targeted customers, salesmen should collect related information first, including the circumstances of needs, sources and capability of finance, the objects with buying decisions, the means of purchasing, and customer's personality, disposition, hobbies and so on, thus making the policies of promotion.

(2) 准备洽谈资料。按照顾客的需求准备洽谈资料，重点是产品资料，如销售手册、样品、名片、笔记用品、协议书、客户资料卡和拜访计划书等。

To prepare materials for negotiation. The materials for negotiation should be prepared according to customers' needs. The most important ones are those of products, such as promotion manuals, samples, business cards, paper sheets, agreements, cards of customer's data, plan for visiting and so on.

(3) 自我准备。除了物质准备还包括精神准备，如良好的仪容仪表、自信、乐观、热情等。

Self-preparation. It includes not only material preparation but also mental preparation such as good appearance, self-confidence, optimism and enthusiasm.

3. 试探式接触，拜访客户 Heuristic Contact, Visiting Customers

推销人员应以合适的方式接近客户，接近客户的方式包括约见和贸然去见两种。约见，是指与客户事先预约然后见面，约见的方式包括电话约、信函约、通过第三方约等几种方式。贸然去见，是指事先不与客户约见而直接贸然与客户见面，即不约而见。

Salesmen should approach customers in appropriate ways, including making an appointment and meeting by chance. The former is making an appointment beforehand, and then both sides meet. The ways of making an appointment includes telephone appointment, letter appointment and third party appointment. Meeting by chance refers to going to meet customers without careful consideration, namely to meet without appointment.

4. 介绍和示范 Introduction and Demonstration

在对目标顾客已有充分了解的基础上，推销人员可以直接向目标顾客进行产品介绍，甚至主动地作一些产品的使用示范。首先要向顾客说明本企业产品的特点，然后说明该特点所带来的优点，最后向顾客说明能为顾客带来的实际利益，以增强目标顾客对产品的信心。

On the basis of being fully aware of targeted customers, salesmen can introduce the products directly to targeted customers, even actively demonstrate some products. They should first illustrate the characteristics of their products, and then explain the advantages resulting from the characteristics. Finally, they should introduce potential real profits the products can bring to customers, so that the customers' confidence can be increased.

5. 处理异议 Objection Handling

顾客往往会提出一些异议，如价格、发货时间、产品的某些特征等方面的不同意见。为了解决这些异议，推销人员要采取积极的态度，运用各种推销艺术，如向顾客解释某些误会、向顾客提供某些保证等，以消除顾客的后顾之忧。

Customers often put forward some objections, such as different advice about prices, delivery time, some characteristics of the products and so on. In order to handle these objections, salesmen have to take a positive attitude and make use of various kinds of salesmanship, for instance, explaining some misunderstanding and providing some guarantee to customers to eliminate customers' worries.

6. 协商谈判 Negotiation

顾客异议处理之后，双方合作的主要障碍基本消除，然后就应进入协商谈判环节，双方就合作数量、价格、结算、售后支持等方面进行磋商。

After handling the objections, the major barrier in the bilateral cooperation will be basically eliminated. Then they should come to the stage of negotiation. Both parties will carry on the consultation on quantity, price, closing accounts, after-sales support and so on.

7. 达成交易 Making a Deal

成交是推销的目标，当各种异议被排除之后，要密切注意顾客发出的成交信号，即通过顾客的言语动作、表情等流露出的购买意向，要抓住这一成交的良好机会及时达成交易。

Making a deal is the goal of promotion. After various objections have been eliminated, close attention should be paid to the signals of deal the customers send, which means the intention of buying expressed by customers' speeches, behaviors and expressions. The opportunities to transact should be seized to make a deal.

8. 后续工作 Follow-up Activities

交易达成并不意味着推销工作的结束，而应将其看作新的推销工作的开始。因此，各种后续工作必须及时跟上，如备货、送货、配套服务及售后服务等。推销人员还应再次访问顾客，以了解顾客的满意程度，处理事先没有考虑到的问题，并表示对顾客的关切，以促使顾客再次购买本企业的产品。这不仅有利于企业同目标顾客建立长期稳定的购销关系，而且可以吸引新的顾客。

Closing a deal does not mean the closure of promotional activities. It should rather be considered to be the beginning of the promotion. Therefore, various succeeding activities should follow up, such as preparing goods, delivering goods, supporting services and after-sales services. Salesmen should visit customers once more to know the satisfaction degree of customers, to deal with problems that were not taken into account and express the concern to the customers to make them buy their products again. This procedure is not only helpful to establishing a long-term and stable purchase-and-sale relationship between the enterprise and customers and to attract new customers.

七、人员推销的管理策略 Management Strategies of Personal Selling

人员推销的管理策略是一个系统工程，是分析、计划、执行和管理销售人员的活动，包括筹划销售队伍策略及结构以及招聘选拔、培训、激励、监督和评估销售人员，使之为实现企业目标而努力。

Management strategy of personal selling is a systematic engineering. It is to analyze, plan, carry out, and control salesmen's activities, including planning the strategies and structures of sales force and recruiting, cultivating, encouraging, supervising, and assessing salesmen, and make them work hard to realize the goals of the enterprise.

(一)销售队伍结构的设计策略 Strategy of Designing the Structure of Sales Staff

人员推销队伍组织结构的不同直接影响其效率,可供企业选择的组织结构有四种。

The different structure of sales staff will directly influence its efficiency. There are four kinds of structures for enterprises to select.

1. 地区式结构 Regional Structure

每个销售代表被指派负责一个地区。这种结构使得销售人员的责任明确。地区责任可以促使销售代表与当地商界和个人加强联系。由于每个销售代表只在一个很小的地理区域内活动,其费差旅费开支相对较少。

Each sales representative will be assigned to a region. This structure will lead to the clear responsibility of the representatives. The regional responsibility can make the representative strengthen the contacts with local business and people. As each representative only acts and operates in a small geographic region. Their traveling expense is relatively low.

2. 产品式结构 Product Structure

这是指按照产品类别来设置销售人员队伍。特别是当产品技术复杂、产品间毫无关联或产品类别很多时,按产品专门化组成销售队伍就显得特别适用。

The team of sales staff should be established according to the type of the products. It is applicable to set up a team of sales staff according to the product specialization, especially when the technique of the product is complicated and there is no relevance among products and there are so many types of products.

3. 顾客式结构 Customer Structure

这是指按行业或顾客类别来组织销售队伍。企业对不同行业甚至不同的顾客安排不同的销售人员。这种顾客专门化结构最明显的好处在于每个销售人员对顾客的特定需要非常熟悉。

The team of sales staff should be organized according to industries and types of customers. The enterprise will assign different salesmen to different industries and customers. The most obvious advantages of customer specialization structure lie in each salesman who should be very familiar with customers' special needs.

4. 复合式结构 Composite structure

当在一个相对广阔的区域内向不同类型的顾客推销多种产品或者在一个区域内要对多种不同顾客和产品精耕细作时,为了特殊的目的,需要将上述方式结合起来使用。例如,为了突出某一产品的地位或将此产品当作战略性产品,为了不使其他销售人员被其他产品分心，应按"产品结构"单独组建一支销售队伍，而对其他产品则应按"地区结构"为组建。

For a special purpose, we should employ a mixture of the above structures to sell many kinds of products to different types of customers in a relatively wide region or to illustrate the products in detail to different customers in one region. To highlight the status of a product or make it a strategic product and not to distract other salesmen with other products, a team of sales staff should be set up alone according to the "product structure", while for other products, we should establish a team according to the "regional structure".

(二)推销人员的选拔策略 The Selection Strategy of Salesman

一个企业推销能力的强弱不仅取决于推销人员的数量，还取决于推销人员的质量。优秀的推销人员能为企业带来很大的经济效益，吸引许多新顾客。

The promotional ability of an enterprise not only depends on the number of salesmen, but also on the qualities of salesmen. The excellent salesmen will bring great economic benefits and attract many customers.

1. 选拔标准 The Selecting Criteria

一个优秀的推销人员应具备以下几个方面的品质。

An excellent salesman should have the following attributes:

(1) 要有正确的经营思想和良好的道德修养。优秀的推销人员应具有强烈的事业心和责任感，具有集体利益高于个人利益的思想境界，具有公道、正派的思想作风和合作共事的精神，能以消费者为中心、以满足顾客需要为己任，不弄虚作假、损公肥私。

It is necessary to have the idea about business operation and moral cultivation. They should have the strong sense of dedication and high sense of responsibility, the mental stature of putting the group interest ahead of individual interest, the ideological style of integrity and decency and team spirit. They should center on customers and deem it their duty to meet customers' needs without any cheating and injuring the good for own benefits.

(2) 具有吃苦耐劳的实干精神和强烈的进取心。优秀的推销人员总是精力充沛，具有很强的进取精神，工作勤奋，能把握他人的感情，富有自信力，能随时应付各种困难和挑战。

Salesmen should have the pragmatism of enduring hardship and strong enterprise. They should always be energetic, have strong enterprising spirit, work diligently, understand others, be very confident and handle any kinds of hardships and challenges.

(3) 具有丰富的业务知识和一定的推销技能。一般来讲，一个优秀的推销人员应该懂得政治法律知识，懂得经济学、财务、市场营销学和推销业务知识，懂得社会学、心理学等多种知识。应有旺盛的求知欲，善于学习并掌握多方面的知识。合格的推销人员应具有业务推销能力、处理人际关系的能力、为顾客服务的能力以及较强的应变能力。

They should be knowledgeable on their profession and skillful in certain promotion salesmanship. Generally speaking, an excellent salesman should know the knowledge of laws, economics, finance, marketing, and sociology and psychology. They should have a strong thirst for knowledge, be good at learning and mastering the knowledge in many fields. A qualified salesman should have the ability to promote, deal with personal relationships, serve the customers, and respond properly to emergent affairs.

(4) 具有健康的体魄。这是承受销售工作压力和强度的前提条件。

It is necessary to have a sound body, which is a prerequisite of enduring working under pressure and intensity.

(5) 具有端正的仪表和良好的语言表达能力。在人员推销活动中,推销人员要注意推销礼仪,讲究文明礼貌,仪表端庄,热情待人,举止适度,谦恭有礼,谈吐文雅,口齿伶俐;在说明主题的前提下,语言要诙谐、幽默,给顾客留下良好的印象,为推销获得成功创造条件。

Salesmen should have good appearance and the language competence. During the promotional activities, they should pay attention to the rituals of promotion, and have good manners, dignified appearance, warm-hearted treating, moderate behaving, courtesy, elegant and articulate conversation. Under the premise of illustrating the theme, the language should be witty and humorous and make a good impression on customers, which is to create a condition for successful promotion.

2. 推销人员的甄选策略 The Strategy of Selecting Salesman

甄选推销人员,不仅要对未从事过推销工作的人员进行甄选,使其中品德端正、作风正派、工作责任心强的胜任推销工作的人员加入推销人员的行列,还要对在岗的推销人员进行甄选,淘汰那些不适合推销工作的推销人员。

To select salesman, the enterprise will not only select those who never specialize in promotion and train them so that they have good behavior, moral integrity, strong responsibility and who will be qualified for the promotion to join in the promotional team, but also select those who have been salesmen for a while to knock out unqualified ones.

推销人员的来源有二:一是来自企业内部。就是把本企业内德才兼备、热爱并适合推销工作的人选拔到推销部门工作。二是从企业外部招聘。即企业从大专院校的应届毕业生、其他企业或单位中物色合格人选。无论哪种来源,都应经过严格的考核,择优录用。

There are two sources of salesman: one is within the enterprise. That is to select the staff who have the talent and virtue and who love and are qualified for the promotional job to work in the marketing department. The other is recruiting outside of the enterprise. That is to say, to look for candidates from the current year's graduates, the qualified candidates from other enterprises or companies. Whichever source should undergo strict examination, and the best examinee will be admitted.

甄选推销人员有多种方法,为准确地选出优秀的推销人才,应根据推销人员素质的要求,采用报名、笔试和面试相结合的方法。

There are many ways of selecting salesmen. In order to accurately select excellent salesmen, the method of combined application, written examination and interview should be adopted according to the qualified qualities of the salesmen.

(三)推销人员的培训策略 The Strategy of Cultivating Salesmen

推销人员需经过培训、学习和掌握有关知识与技能后才能上岗。同时,还要对在岗推销人员每隔一段时间进行培训,使其了解企业的新产品、新的经营计划和新的市场营销策略,进一步提高素质,以适应市场形势发展的需要。

Salesmen should start to work after being trained to make them learn and master the related knowledge and skills. At the same time, the training should be carried out every once in a while to make them know new products, new business plan and new marketing strategy of the enterprise, so their qualities will be improved to suit the development of the market.

1. 培训内容 The Content of Cultivation

推销人员培训的主要内容如下。

The main contents of cultivation are as the follows.

(1) 企业知识,包括企业的历史、战略目标、组织机构、财务状况、主要商品的销售情况和政策、市场竞争对企业的影响等。

The knowledge of enterprise, which includes the history, strategic goals, organizational structure, condition of the finance, the promotional situation and policy of the main products and the influence of the market competition to the enterprise.

(2) 产品知识,包括本企业营销商品的范围、结构,所售商品的性能、用途、使用和保管方法等。

The knowledge of the product, which includes the promotional scope and structure of the products and the property, application, use and the preservation of the product to be sold.

(3) 市场知识,包括本企业目标顾客的分布、需求特点、购买力水平、购买动机、购买行为、消费习惯以及市场情况、本企业的市场地位、竞争者商品的市场地位和营销策略。

The knowledge of market, which includes the distribution of targeted customers, the characteristics of their needs, the level of purchasing power, the motivation of purchasing, the behavior of purchasing, the habit of consumption, the circumstances of market, the market position of the enterprise and the market position of rivals' products and the strategy of promotion.

(4) 推销技巧,包括推销原则和推销策略、推销人员的工作程序和责任、良好的个性、处理公众关系和人际关系的能力等。

The skills of promotion, which includes the principle and the strategy of promotion, the working procedure, responsibility, personality, and the ability to deal with public relations and interpersonal relations of salesman.

(5) 业务程序和职责,包括掌握如何制订计划、如何合理分配时间、洽谈、订立合同、结算方法、开销范围、编写报告等。推销人员应尽可能节约费用、避免损失、增加销售。

The business procedure and responsibility, which includes drafting a plan and allocating time reasonably, negotiating, drafting a contract and the method of closing accounts, defining the scope of expenditure and writing a report. They should try their best to save cost, prevent loss,

第九章 促销策略
Promotion Strategies

and increase the sales.

2. 培训方法 The Method of Cultivation

培训推销人员的方法很多,常被采用的方法有三种:一是讲授培训。这是一种课堂教学培训方法。一般是通过举办短期培训班或进修等形式,由专家、教授和有丰富推销经验的优秀推销员来讲授基础理论和专业知识,介绍推销方法和技巧。二是模拟培训。它是受训人员亲自参与的有一定实战感的培训方法,具体做法有实例研究法、角色扮演法和业务模拟法等。例如,由受训人员扮演推销人员向由专家或有经验的优秀推销员扮演的顾客进行推销,或由受训人员分析推销实例等。三是实践培训。实际上,这是一种岗位练兵。让甄选的推销人员直接上岗,与有经验的推销人员建立师徒关系,通过传、帮、带,使受训者较快地熟悉业务,成为合格的推销人员。

There are many ways of cultivation. The most commonly adopted are the following three: one is teaching to cultivate. This is a method of class-teaching, which is always in the form of organizing a short-term class to study further. Professionals, professors or excellent salesmen who have rich experience will teach the class the basic theory, the professional knowledge, the skills and the methods of promotion. The second one is imitating to cultivate, which is a situational training method in which trainees join and behave as if they were in real situations. The concrete way includes the case study method, role playing method and business simulation. For example, the trainee can play the role of salesman and conduct promotion to the professional or the excellent salesman. The trainee can also analyze the instance of promotion. The third one is practical training. Actually, this is a method of duty training. The candidate will be allowed to take up his post and establish the relationship of master and apprentice with the experienced salesman, and they will be familiar with the business quickly and become qualified salesmen by way of transmitting experience, aiding with ideology and leading the work style.

(四)推销人员的激励策略 The Motivation Strategy of the Salesman

激励在管理学中被解释为一种精神力量或状态。它能够增强、激发和推动员工的工作热情,并指导和引导行为指向目标。企业应该掌握影响推销人员工作的因素,并采取相应的鼓励措施。

In management, motivation can be explained as a spiritual strength or played as a role of state strengthening, motivating and promoting. It directs and guides the target of its behavior. The enterprise should master elements of influencing salesmen and take the corresponding encouraging measures.

为了调动推销人员的积极性,企业必须体现"按劳分配"的原则,为推销人员制定合理的劳动报酬制度。企业必须确定推销人员报酬的组成部分,如固定收入、可变收入、费用津贴和附加利益。固定收入能使推销人员有稳定的收入;可变收入包括佣金按推销额的一定比例提取的报酬、奖金等,它们用来刺激推销人员积极推销产品;费用津贴能鼓励推销人员进行必要的推销工作;附加利益包括免费休假、伤病保障、退休和人寿保险等,它能使推销人员具有安全感和对工作的满意感。总的来说，推销人员的劳动报酬有薪金制、佣金制、薪金和佣金结合制三种基本类型。

In order to arouse salesmen's motivation, the enterprise has to embody the principle of "distribution according to one's performance" and establish a reasonable system of remuneration. The enterprise has to define the components of salesmen's salary, such as regular income, variable income, allowances and the additional benefits. The regular income ensures that salesmen can have stable income; the variable income includes the commission (minus the reward according to a certain rate of the sale) and the bonus which stimulate salesmen to actively promote the products; the expense allowance can encourage the salesmen to carry out the necessary promotional work; the additional benefit includes paid vacation, sick and wounded insurance, pension and life insurance that can give salesmen a sense of security and satisfaction. All in all, there are three basic systems of remuneration for the salesmen: the salary system, the commission system and the combining system of salary and commission.

企业还应为推销人员创造一种受人尊敬的气氛。企业领导要经常关心推销人员的工作和生活，尽可能解决推销人员的困难，并使推销人员有晋升的机会。企业可以定期召开推销人员的会议，鼓励他们相互交流经验，融通感情。企业还可以举办推销竞赛，并根据推销人员的工作成绩给予荣誉和物质奖励，采取礼物、奖金、旅游、利润分成、佣金制度等措施，把政治思想工作和物质激励结合起来。

Some respectable atmosphere should be created for the salesmen. The leaders of the enterprise should often show concern for salesmen's work and life, try their best to deal with salesmen's difficulties and provide the opportunity of promotion. The enterprise can hold a periodical meeting of salesmen encouraging them to exchange experiences and feelings with each other. The enterprise can also hold promotion competitions and grant prizes and materials according to their results. They can take the measures of presidents, bonus, travelling and profit sharing and combine the political and ideological work with material incentives.

(五)监督与评估销售人员策略 The Strategy of Supervising and Evaluating Salesmen

各企业对销售人员监督的密切程度是不一样的。有些企业帮助销售人员识别目标顾客并制定拜访标准，有些企业则明确规定销售人员必须花一定时间用于寻找新客户，还明确时间安排上的其他先后顺序。许多企业采用销售自动操作系统，即采用计算机帮助销售人员更有效地输入订单、改进顾客服务以及为销售人员提供更多决策支持。管理人员可以通过组织气氛、销售配额以及正面刺激来激励销售人员的士气和提高业绩。

Each enterprise has different degrees of closely supervision to salesmen. Some enterprises help salesmen to identify targeted customers and decide on visiting criteria, while other enterprises formulate that salesmen must take the certain time to find the new customers and time schedules. Many enterprises apply the automatic operating system of promotion, which is to apply the computer to help salesmen to input orders more effectively, and to improve their service to customers and to provide more decision support for salesmen. The administrator can encourage salesmen's spirit and improve their performance through an atmosphere of organization, sales quota and positive stimulation.

销售经理可以通过使用各种销售报告以及其他信息来评估每一个销售人员。评估针对两个方面：销售人员规划工作的能力和完成计划的能力。正式的评估要求管理层制定明确的业绩评估标准并及时沟通。评估也为销售人员提供了建设性的反馈，从而促进他们更努力地工作。

The sales manager can evaluate every salesman by using many kinds of sales report and other information. The evaluation aims at two aspects: salesmen's competence of planning the work and accomplishing the plan. The formal evaluation demands the management to make the definite criteria of performance assessment and communicate timely. The evaluation also provides the constructive feedbacks for salesmen so they can work harder.

第三节 广 告 策 略
Advertising Strategies

一、广告的含义及类型 The Meaning and Types of Advertisement

(一)广告的含义 The Meaning of Advertisement

作为一种传递信息的活动，广告是企业在促销中应用最广的促销方式。广告是由明确的发起者以促进销售为目的，付出一定的费用，通过特定的媒体传播商品或劳务等有关经济信息的大众传播活动。从广告的概念可以看出，广告是以广大消费者为广告对象的大众传播活动；广告以传播商品或劳务等有关经济信息为其内容；广告是通过特定的媒体来实现的，并且广告发起者要对使用的媒体支付一定的费用；广告的目的是为了促进商品销售，进而获得较好的经济效益。

Advertisement, as an activity of transmitting the information, is the most widely used form of promotion for an enterprise. Advertisement is mass media activities for the purpose of promotion and initiated by the defined initiator who pays some fees to transfer goods and related economic information by certain media. In view of the concept of advertisement, it is a mass media activity which takes the mass consumers as the objects advertised; it takes the transmission of goods, service and the related economic information as the content. Advertisement was realized by a certain media, and the initiator should pay certain fees for relevant media. The aim of advertisement is to promote the sales of goods to gain better economic benefits.

(二)广告的类型 The Types of Advertisement

广告按照不同的分类标准，有以下几种类型。

Advertising can be divided into the following types according to different categories.

1. 广告的内容 Content of Advertisement

按照广告的内容划分,可分为商品广告和企业广告。

According to the content, the advertisement can be divided into product advertising and the corporate advertising.

(1) 商品广告。它是以产品或服务本身为内容的广告,目的在于直接推销商品或服务。

Product advertising. It is based on product or service itself as its content and with the aim of directly promoting goods or service.

(2) 企业广告,又称商誉广告。它着重宣传、介绍企业的品牌、商标、厂址、厂史、生产能力、服务项目等情况,目的是提高企业的声望、名誉和形象,从而间接促进产品销售。

Corporate advertising, namely business reputation advertising. It stresses propaganda and introduction of the brand, trademark, factory address, history, production ability, service, items and so on, with the aim of improving the enterprise's prestige, reputation, and image to indirectly promote products selling.

2. 广告的目的 Aim of Advertisement

根据广告的目的划分,可分为商业广告和非商业广告。

According to the aim of advertisement, it can be divided into commercial advertising and non-commercial advertising.

(1) 商业广告。它是指以经营产品或服务为目的的广告。

Commercial advertising. It is the advertisement based on selling products or service as its goals.

(2) 非商业广告。主要包括政治广告、公益广告和个人广告。政治广告是指为政治活动服务的广告;公益广告也称公共广告,它是指维护社会公德、宣传公益事业的广告;个人广告是指为个人利益或目的运用媒体发布的广告,如启事、声明、寻人、征婚等。

Non-commercial advertising. It mainly includes political advertising, public service advertising and personal advertisement. Political advertising refers to the advertisements serving political activities; public service advertisement, namely the public ads, refer to ads protecting the public morals and adverting public welfare undertakings; personal ads refer to the ads broadcasted by media and with the aim of personal benefits, such as announcement, statement, search notices, marriages and so on.

3. 广告的促销目标 Promoting targets of Advertisement

按照广告在商品促销不同阶段的促销目标划分,可分为开拓性广告、劝告性广告和提醒性广告。

According to the division of promoting targets in different stages of promoting, it can be divided into pioneering advertising, persuasive advertising and reminding advertising

(1) 开拓性广告，亦称报道性广告。它是以激发顾客对产品的初始需求为目标，主要介绍刚刚进入导入期的产品的用途、性能、质量、价格等有关情况，以促使新产品进入目标市场。

Pioneering advertising, namely informative advertising. It mainly introduces the conditions of application, property, quality and price with the goal of triggering the customers' initial needs for their products to make new products enter the market.

(2) 劝告性广告，又叫竞争性广告。它是以激发顾客对产品产生兴趣、增进"选择性需求"为目标，是对进入成长期和成熟前期的产品所做的各种传播活动。

Persuasive advertising, namely the competitive advertising. It aims to trigger customers' interest and promote "the selective needs". It involves all kinds of spreading activities for popularizing adolescent and pre-mature products.

(3) 提醒性广告，也叫备忘性广告或加强性广告。是指对已进入成熟后期或衰退期的产品所进行的广告宣传，目的在于提醒顾客，使其产生"惯性"需求。

Reminding advertisement, namely the memo ads or the reinforcing ads. It refers to advertise for post-mature or recessive products and aims to remind the customers to form the "sluggish" needs.

4．广告的传播区域 Districts the Advertisement transmits

按照广告传播的区域划分，可分为世界性广告、全国性广告和地区性广告。

According to the districts the advertisement transmits, ads can be divided into worldwide advertising, national advertising and regional advertising.

(1) 世界性广告。通常是在主销市场或所欲打入的国际市场所做的广告，它通过国际咨询及使馆商务部门的参谋等途径来选择适当的媒介，广告内容要求符合所在国际市场的营销环境。

Worldwide advertising. It refers to the ads in main sales markets or desire to enter the international market. It is a properly chosen media by way of international consultation and the advice from the commercial department of the embassy. It is demanded that the content of the ads should conform with the sales environment of the international market.

(2) 全国性广告。是指采用信息传播能覆盖全国媒体的广告，以激发分散于全国各地的消费者对该广告的产品产生需求。在全国发行和发放的报纸、杂志、广播、电视等媒体上所做的广告，均属全国性广告。这种广告要求广告产品是适合全国通用的产品，并且因其费用较高，也只适合生产规模较大、服务范围较广的大企业，而对实力较弱的小企业可应用性较差。

National advertising. It refers to the ads adopting media that can transmit the information all over the country to trigger the nationally scattered consumers' needs for the advertised products. The ads that issued and issuing in the newspaper, magazine, radio, TV media are all belongs to national ads. This kind of ads demands advertised products are all suitable for national popularity, and for their high expenses, it is suitable for enterprise with larger scale production and wider range of service. But it is less applicable for small weaker enterprises.

(3) 地区性广告。是指采用信息传播只能覆盖一定区域的媒体的广告，以刺激某些特定地区消费者对产品的需求。在省县报纸、杂志、广播、电视上所做的广告均属此类，路牌、霓虹灯上的广告也属地区性广告。此类广告传播范围小，多适于生产规模小、产品通用性差的企业和产品进行广告宣传。

Regional ads. It refers to the ads adopting the media which can transmit the information only in some certain area to stimulate some certain regional customers' needs. The ads that issued in province (county) newspapers, magazine, radio, TV, etc. fall into this kind, including the billboard advertising and the ads in neon lamps. This kind of ads transmits on a small scale and is suitable for an enterprise with small scale production and poor popularity and its products to carry out advertising.

5. 广告的表现形式 Forms of Advertisement

按照广告的表现形式划分，可分为印象型广告、说明型广告和情感诉说型广告。

According to the performance form of advertising, advertisement can be divided into impression ads, illustration ads and emotion provoking ads.

(1) 印象型广告。广告时间一般很短，只宣传一个简单而最为重要的广告主题。

Impression ads. The time of advertising is very short, only for advertising a simple and the most important advertising theme.

(2) 说明型广告。要对产品进行较为详尽的说明。

Illustration ads. It should illustrate a product in detail.

(3) 情感型广告。以特定的情感诉求方式影响消费者的态度。

Emotion provoking ads. It will influence consumers' attitude by a particular way of emotion telling.

此外，还有一些广告分类。例如，按广告的形式划分，可分为文字广告和图画广告；按广告的媒体不同，可分为报纸广告、杂志广告、广播广告、电视广告以及其他媒体广告等。

In addition, there are other classifications of ads. For example, according to the form of ads, it can be divided into letter ads and picture ads. According to the media applied, it can be divided into newspaper ads, magazine ads, radio ads, TV ads, other media ads and so on.

二、广告策略的概念及其程序 The Concept and Other Procedures of Ads

(一)广告策略的概念 The Concept of Ads. Strategy

广告策略是指广告策划者在广告信息传播过程中，为实现广告战略目标所采取的对策和应用的方法、手段。

The ads strategy refers to the strategy, approach, and means adopted by the ads planners during the process of transmitting ads information to realize the strategic targets of ads.

(二)制定广告策略的程序 The Procedures of Defining Ads Strategies

营销者要开发一个广告计划时，要针对以下几个方面进行决策：广告要达到的目的、传递的信息、媒体的选择、传送的时机、广告预算和衡量效果。

When a marketer develops an ads plan, he or she should carry out the following decisions: the aims the ads want to achieve, the information it transmits, the media it will choose, the time it is broadcast, the budgets and the appraised effects.

1. 确定广告目标 To Identify Targets of Ads

广告目标是在一定期限内, 针对特定目标对象设定的一项具体的沟通任务。通过宣传, 在消费者中提高广告商品的知名度, 促使消费者在购买同类商品时, 能提名购买, 达到扩大市场占有率的目的, 从而使营销者赚得更多利润。

The target of ads is a specific task of communication that is designed for a particular target in a certain period. By popularizing, consumers will better know of the reputation of advertised goods and they can nominate, which can achieve the goal of expanding the market share and give the market more profits.

广告目标可以分为告知、劝说和提醒三类。

The target of ads can be divided into three types: Information advertising, persuasive advertising and reminding ads.

(1) 告知性广告目标。此类广告的目的在于介绍新产品和开拓新市场。它通过对产品的性能、特点和用途的宣传介绍, 提高消费者对产品的认识程度, 其中着重要求提高消费者对新产品的认知度、理解度和厂牌商标的记忆度。

The goal of information advertising. This kind of advertising aims at introducing new products and developing new markets. By introducing the property, characteristics and the applications of products, customers' awareness will be improved, especially the consumers' awareness, intelligibility and memory of new products should be improved.

(2) 劝说性广告目标。此类广告的目的在于巩固已有市场, 并在此基础上深入开发潜在市场和刺激购买需求。它在竞争日趋激烈时愈来愈重要。它主要通过比较性广告的形式, 直接或间接地与一个或几个其他品牌作比较, 使消费者加深对已有商品的认识, 养成消费习惯, 产生兴趣和购买欲望。

The targets of persuasive advertising. This kind of ads aims at consolidating the existing market position and deeply exploring potential markets and stimulating the buying demands on this base. It will become more and more important with increasing fierce competitions. Mainly through comparative ads, it will compare directly or indirectly with one or other brands to make consumers better understand existing goods and cultivate a habit of consuming, and show interests and purchasing desire.

(3) 提醒性广告目标。此类型广告的目的在于使消费者一直记住该产品, 它在产品成熟期阶段很重要。如可口可乐广告的目的是提醒人们不要忘记可口可乐, 而不是告知或劝说他们。

The targets of reminding ads. This kind of ads aims at making consumers always remember the product. It is essential at the mature stage of products. For example, the target of Coca-Cola is to remind people not to forget Coca-Cola, not to tell or persuade them.

2. 形成广告创意策略 To Form the Creative Strategy of Ads

有效地进行创意的第一步是决定向顾客说什么的问题。广告信息的传播周期短，强调一种即时的效果，这就要求信息内容要抓住顾客的注意力。顾客只有觉得自己会受益时才会有反应。理想的情况是，广告创意策略能够紧随企业更广泛的定位策略。

The first step of effectively carrying out the originality is the question of deciding what to say to customers. The transmitting period of advertisement is short, and it stresses a kind of immediate effect, which requires that the content of the information can attract customers' attention. Only when the customers get the benefit will they have the response. The ideal situation is that the creative strategy of ads needs to follow the enterprise's more extensively oriented strategy.

好的创意应具有以下几个特点。
(1) 具有一个醒目的标题来强调产品所提供的主要好处；
(2) 用简洁的表现方式吸引顾客的注意力；
(3) 提供顾客需要的信息——商品的类型、品牌、价格、型号、款式等；

Good originality should possess the following characteristics:
(1) To have an obvious title to stress the goods the product can provide;
(2) To have a brief way of expression to attract customers' attention;
(3) To provide the information the customers need——such as the type, brand, price, model, style and so on.

广告信息必须真实可靠，且具有独特性和艺术性。这是非常有必要的。创意人员必须找出最好的式样、格调、用语及格式来执行创意。例如，可以采用生活片断、幻境、场景情调或人物形象、专业技术、人物象征、科学证据和推荐等方式加以表现。

It is necessary that ads information should be true, reliable, unique and artistic. The creative people have to find the best pattern, style, wording, and format to carry out the originality. For example they can adopt the form of life episodes, dreamland, emotional appeal or image, the professional techniques, character symbol, scientific evidence, recommendation and so on.

3. 广告媒体选择策略 The Strategy of Selecting the Ads Media

1) 广告媒体的种类及特点 The Sort and Characteristic of Ads Media

广告媒体，也称广告媒介，是广告主与广告接受者之间的连接物质。它是广告宣传必不可少的物质条件。广告媒体是随着科学技术的发展而发展的。

Ads media, also known as ads intermediary, is the connected substances between ads and ads receiver. That is an essential material requisite for advertising. Ads media develops with the development of science and technology.

广告媒体的种类很多，不同类型的媒体有不同的特性。目前比较常用的广告媒体有以下几种。

There are many kinds of ads media. Different kinds of media have different properties. At present, the commonly used ads media has the following types.

(1) 电子媒体 Electronic Media

它是通过广播、电台、电视、电影、幻灯、电子显示大屏幕、互联网等媒体传递广告。

It transmits ads by way of radio stations, TV, movies, slide shows, electric display screens, the Internet and so on.

广播媒体的优越性有：传播迅速、及时；制作简单，费用较低；具有较高的灵活性；听众广泛，不论男女老幼、是否识字，均能受其影响。使用广播做广告的局限性在于：时间短促，转瞬即逝，不便记忆；有声无形，印象不深；不便存查。

The advantages of radio are: fast and timely transmitting; simple and low-cost expense producing; high flexibility; extensive audience, whether they are men and women, young and old, literate or illiterate, they will be influenced and without any exception. The limitations of radio ads are: the time is brief and not easy to remember; it is audio but intangible, which can not make a deep impression; it is not convenient to preserve for reference.

电视广告媒体的优点有：因电视有形、有色，听视结合，使广告形象、生动、逼真、感染力强；由于电视已成为人们文化生活的重要组成部分，收视率较高，使电视广告的宣传范围广，影响面大；宣传手法灵活多样，艺术性强。电视广告媒体的缺点是：时间性强，不易存查；制作复杂，费用较高；因播放节目和广告多，易分散受众的注意力。

The advantages of TV media are: because TV is visible and colorful and it combines listening with watching, TV ads will be vivid, lively and lifelike and have the strong appeal; for TV has become an essential part of people's cultural life with high viewing rate, the scale of TV advertising is wide, the scope of influence is widespread; the advertising is flexible and diverse with strong artistic quality. The shortcomings of TV ads are: it is transient and not convenient to preserve for reference; it is complicatedly made with high expenses; it is easy to distract the audience's attention due to the many programs and advertisements.

互联网有其得天独厚的优势，表现在：互联网传播范围广，网络广告可跨越时空，有广泛的传播力；内容详尽，交互查询，互动性和针对性强，无时间约束；广告效果易统计；广告费用较低。与此相反，网络广告不足之处表现在：有的网络广告缺乏诱惑力；互联网的虚拟性致使网上浏览者对广告心存抵触。

The Internet has its own unique advantages, and they are performed in such aspects: the scope of transmitting is wide, the Internet ads can come across time and space with strong transmissibility; its content is elaborate and can interactively inquire with strong interactivity and purpose without any time constraint; the effects of ads is easy to calculate, and its expenses are lower. On the contrary, the shortcomings of the Internet ads are shown in such aspects: some of the Internet ads lack temptation; the virtuality of the Internet ads leads to its browsers having contradictions in their minds.

(2) 印刷媒体 Printing Media

它是通过报纸、杂志、电话簿、画册、火车时刻表等媒体传递广告。其中最为典型的是报纸和杂志这两种广告媒体。它们各有自己的优缺点。

It transmits ads by way of newspapers, magazines, phone books, picture albums, and train timetables, of which, the newspaper and magazine are the most typical ones. They have the advantages and disadvantages of their own.

报纸这种广告媒体的优越性在于影响广泛。这是因为报纸是传播新闻的重要工具之一，与人民群众有密切联系，而且发行量大。报纸传播迅速，可及时地传递有关经济信息。它简便灵活，制作方便，费用较低。它还便于剪贴存查且可信度高。借助报纸的威信，能提高广告的可信度。报纸媒体的不足是：因报纸登载内容庞杂，易分散对广告的注意力；印刷不精美，吸引力低；广告时效短，重复性差，只能维持当期的效果。

Newspaper. The advantages of newspaper advertising can be seen in its extensive influence. This is because newspaper is one of the key tools to transmit news, and it is closely related with the masses and has the large circulation. It can transmit economic related information very fast and on time. This kind of media is simple, flexible, easy to produce and with lower expense. It is convenient to clip for pasting and preserve for reference. It has high credibility. The credibility of ads can be improved by virtue of the authority of newspaper. The shortcomings of newspaper media are: because the published content is numerous and disordered, it will distract readers from ads; there is no fineness of printing and less attraction; the timeliness is short and the repeatability is poor which can only maintain the effect of that issue.

杂志以登载各种专门知识为主，是各类专门产品的良好广告媒体。它作为广告媒体，其优点表现为：广告宣传对象明确，针对性强，有的放矢；广告附于杂志而有较长的保存期，读者可以反复查看；因杂志发行面广，可以扩大广告的宣传区域；由于杂志读者一般有较高的文化水平和生活水平，比较容易接受新事物，故利于刊登开拓性广告；印刷精美，能较好地反映产品的外观形象，易引起读者注意。其缺点表现在：发行周期长，灵活性较差，传播不及时；读者较少，传播不广泛。

Magazine. It focuses on publishing various kinds of professional knowledge, and it is a good ads media for various kinds of particular products. As a kind of ads media, it has the following advantages: the definite advertising objects, being position-relevant and targeted; ads attached to magazines can be preserved for a longer period, for readers can read it over and over again; the large publishing scope of ads allows the advertising scale to be enlarged; magazine readers have a better education and living standard and would like to accept new things, which is helpful to publish pioneering ads; its elegant printing can better reflect the appearance and image of a product so to attract readers' attention easily. The shortcomings are reflected in the following aspects: the long issue circulation, poor flexibility, untimely transmitting; fewer readers and narrowly transmitting.

(3) 户外广告媒体 Outdoor Advertising Media

在街头、建筑物、车站、码头、体育场馆、展览馆和旅游点等公共场所，按规定允许设置或张贴广告的路牌、霓虹灯、招贴等，称为户外广告媒体。户外广告媒体的优点是醒目、易引人注意、复现率高、能够对目标顾客反复宣传；其缺点是宣传范围小、广告形式相对比较简单。

It refers to ads making use of streets signs, neon lights and posters according to regulations permitted to post on streets, buildings, stations, wharfs, stadiums, exhibition halls, tourist spots and other public places, which is also called outdoor advertising media. The advantages of outdoor advertising media are striking, easy to catch attention, with a high repetition rate and ability to reach targeted customers repeatedly. The disadvantages are that their scope is limited and their forms are simple compared with other forms of advertisement.

(4) 交通广告媒体 Transportation Advertising Media

利用车、船、飞机等运输工具作为媒体,在其体内设置或张贴的广告,称为交通广告。由于各种工具常年定期、定点往返运行,客流量大,具有影响广、动态性好、成本低、媒介作用多的特点。它也有针对性不强、范围有限等缺点。

It refers to ads making use of autos, ships, airplanes and other vehicles as its media, in which the ads are set or posted. Because all kinds of vehicles run back and forth regularly along fixed routes and have a large passenger flow, these ads have the advantages of wide impact, high pertinency, good dynamics, low costs and many roles of media. Its disadvantages are that they lack pertinency and the scale is limited.

(5) 售点广告媒体 POS Advertising Media

它是指售货点和购物场所的广告媒体,例如,可以在商店、商品橱窗内设置广告。售点广告媒体有利于提醒消费者,促成购买行动;有利于营造气氛,吸引消费者;实效性强,认知度高。但此媒体形式也有对设计要求比较高、维护费很高的不足。

It refers to the ads media in the spots of sales and shopping places, such as the ads set in stores or shop windows. POS ads are helpful to customers, reminding them to make a deal. They are also beneficial for producing an atmosphere to attract consumers' attention. They are strongly effective and broad cognitive. But it also has its disadvantages of higher demand of design and higher cost of maintainance.

(6) 邮寄广告媒体 Mailshot Media

它是指通过邮政直接投递企业介绍、产品说明书等函件。邮寄广告媒体的优点是:对象明确,有较强的选择性和针对性;提供信息全面,有较强的说服力;具有私人通信性质,容易联络感情。其缺点表现在:宣传面较小并有可能忽视了某些潜在的消费者;不易引起注意;广告形象较差,有可能成为"三等邮件"。

It refers to the ads through directly delivering the introduction of the enterprise and the instruction of products. The advantages of mailshot media are: providing comprehensive information, strongly persuasive; possessing the characteristics of personal letters, and with it, it is easy for people to communicate. The shortcomings are: the transmitting scope is small, so it is likely to omit some potential consumers; it is not easy to attract people's attention; the advertising image is poor and may become the "third-class mail".

此外还有一些广告媒体,如电梯、橱窗、霓虹灯、商品包装等。

In addition, there are other ads media, such as elevators, cabinets, neon lights, product packaging and so on.

2) 广告媒体选择依据的因素 The Elements of Selecting Ads Media

不同的广告媒体有不同的特性,这决定了企业从事广告活动必须对广告媒体进行正确的选择决策。正确地选择广告媒体，一般要考虑以下影响因素。

Different ads media have different features, which determines that the enterprise should select ads media properly before working on advertising activities. To correctly select ads media, the following influencing elements should be considered.

(1) 产品因素。可以按照企业产品的不同特性，来选择相应的广告媒体，如需展示的、有色泽或式样要求的产品，应选择电视、电影或印刷品做媒体，以增加美感和吸引力；对只需要通过听觉就能了解的产品，应选择广播做媒体等。

Elements of products. To select corresponding ads media according to different features of a product. For example, if it is necessary to show colorful and patterned products, the TV, movie or printing should be chosen as the media to increase its beauty and attraction; for products can simply known by auditory sense, the radio should be chosen as the media.

(2) 消费者接触媒体的习惯。一般认为，能使广告信息传到目标市场的媒体是最有效的媒体。例如，对儿童用品进行广告宣传，宜选电视作为媒体；对妇女用品进行广告宣传，宜选用妇女喜欢阅读的妇女杂志或电视，其效果较好。

The habits of consumers contacting the media. It is generally believed that the media which can transmit ads information to a targeted market is the most effective media. For example, when advertising children products, we'd better choose TV as the media; when advertising women products, we'd better select women's magazines or TV programs which are popular with them.

(3) 媒体传播范围。不同媒体的传播范围有大有小，能接近的人有多有少。市场的地理范围关系到媒体的选择，因此，行销全国的产品，应选择全国性的报刊和中央电视台、中央人民广播电台做广告；局部地区销售的产品，企业可根据所销产品的目标市场，选择地方性的报刊、电视台、广播电台或广告牌及样品台等媒体做广告宣传。

Transmitting scope of media. The transmitting scope of different media may be large or small, and the number of people who can approach the product varies. The regional scope of a market is related to the choice of the media, so the marketing products all over the country should select national newspapers, CCTV, and CNR to advertise; while for the regional selling products, the enterprise should choose regional newspapers, TV stations, billboards and samples stations to advertise according to a targeted market.

(4) 媒体的影响力。媒体的影响力应到达目标市场的每一角落，但越出目标市场则造成浪费。季节性强的产品应考虑媒体的时效性，到期不能刊登或发行的媒体就不宜选择。

The impact of media. The impact of media should reach every corner of the market, but it will result in wasting once stepping over a targeted market. For seasonal products, we should consider their effectiveness. It is not suitable to choose media that can not publish or issue on time.

(5) 媒体的费用。各广告媒体的收费标准不同。广告活动应考虑费用与效果的关系，既要使广告达到理想的效果，又要考虑企业的负担能力。应尽量争取以较低的成本达到最大的宣传效果。

Cost of media. Various media have different charging standards. For advertising activities, it is necessary to consider the relationship between cost and effects. Not only should the ideal effects be achieved, but the affordability of the enterprise should be considered. It is expected to achieve the maximum advertising effects with lower costs.

3) 广告媒体选择策略的类型 The Types of Selecting Strategy of Advertising Media

(1) 无差别策略，也称无选择策略。是指选择所有媒体同时展开立体式广告攻势，即不计时间段、不计成本的地毯式广告。

Indiscrimination strategy, which is also called nonselective strategy. It refers to choosing all kinds of media to carry out advertising, namely, blanket-advertising without considering periods of time and costs.

(2) 差别策略。是指有针对性地选择个别媒体进行广告宣传。

Discrimination strategy. It refers to selecting respective media to advertise specifically.

(3) 动态策略。是指根据广告媒体的传播效果和企业目标市场需达到的需求状态灵活地选择广告媒体。

Dynamic strategy. It refers to flexibly selecting advertising media according to transmitting effects of ads media and state of needs which the enterprise's targeted market will achieve.

4. 决定广告时间策略 The Strategy of Selecting the Ads Time

广告时间策略，就是对广告发布的时间和频度做出统一的、合理的安排。广告时间策略的制定，要视广告产品的生命周期阶段、广告的竞争状况、企业的营销策略、市场竞争等多种因素的变化而灵活运用。一般而言，即效性广告要求发布时间集中、时限性强、频度大。迟效性广告则要求广告时间发布均衡、时限从容、频度波动小。广告的时间策略是否运用得当，对广告的效果有很大影响。广告的时间策略在时限运用上主要有集中时间策略、均衡时间策略、季节时间策略、节假日时间策略等四种；在频度上有固定频度和变动频度两种基本形式。

The strategy of selecting ads time is to make a uniform and reasonable arrangement to select ads time and frequency. The decision of selecting ads time should be applied flexibly according to the life cycle phase of advised products, the competitive status of ads, the promoting strategy of the enterprise, market competition and such kind of elements. Generally speaking, the immediate effective ads demands for concentrating a release time, time-bounded, and high frequency. While late effective ads ask for a balanced release time, calm time-bounded and low frequency. Whether the strategy of ads time can be properly applied or not is closely related to the effects of ads. The strategy of ads time applied within time limits mainly includes four types: the strategy of concentrating time, the strategy of balancing time, the strategy of seasonal time, and the strategy of festival and holiday time; as for frequency, it includes two basic forms as the fixed frequency and the varied frequency.

1) 集中时间策略 The Strategy of Concentrating Time

此策略主要是集中力量，在短时期内对目标市场进行突然、大量的广告攻势。其目的在于集中优势，在短时间内迅速造成广告声势，扩大广告的影响，迅速提高商品的声誉。这种策略主要运用于新产品投入市场前后、新零售店开张前后、流行性商品上市前后、广告竞争激烈时以及商品销量急剧下降时。运用这种策略时，一般都采取媒体组合方式，掀起广告高潮。

It mainly refers to the concentrating the strength to strike on intrusive ads to a targeted market in a short period. Its aim focuses on concentrating the advantages to result in an impetus of ads and rapidly expand the influence of ads in a short period. This kind of strategy is mainly applied before or after the new products being put into the market, before or after the opening of a new retailer, before or after the popular goods coming into the market, when the ads competition is intense and the promotion of goods is decreasing sharply. When applying the strategy, generally we adopt the strategy of media mix to reach a climax of ads.

2) 均衡时间策略 The Strategy of Balancing Time

这是一种有计划地反复对目标市场进行广告的策略，目的是为了持续加深消费者对商品或零售店的印象，保持消费者的记忆，发掘潜在市场，扩大商品知名度。运用该策略时应注意广告表现要有变化，要不断给消费者以新鲜的感觉，广告的频率也要有适当的变化，不要长期重复同一广告内容。

This is an ads strategy to advertise to a targeted market repeatedly and prepensely, whose aim is to continue deepening the consumers' impression of certain goods and retailers, to keep consumers' memory of it, to explore a potential market and to expand goods' reputation. When employing this strategy, it is worth noticing there should be some changes to give a fresh feeling to consumers and there should also be some frequency changes without repeating the same content for a long time.

3) 季节时间策略 Strategy of Seasonal Time

此策略主要用于季节性很强的商品广告，一般在销售季节到来之前就要展开广告活动，为销售旺季的到来做好信息准备和心理准备。销售旺季时，广告活动达到高峰；旺季过后，广告要收缩；销售季节到尾声时，广告便可以停止。运用这类广告策略，要掌握好季节性商品的变化规律，过早地开展广告活动，会增加广告费；过迟则会延误时机，直接影响商品的销售。

It is mainly applied to seasonal ads of goods. Generally speaking, ads activities should be carried out before the sales season to make a good informational and psychological preparation for the advent of the peak season. During the peak season, ads activities should achieve the peak; after the peak season, ads should be reduced. When the sales season is coming to an end, ads can be stopped. While using this kind of ads strategy, we need a good command of the changing rules of seasonal goods. Prematurely carrying out ads activities will increase the cost of ads, while carrying out these activities too late will lose the opportunity and directly affect commodity sales.

4) 节假日时间策略 Strategy of Festival and Holiday Time

这是零售店和服务行业常用的广告时间策略，在节假日之前便开展广告活动。这类广告策略要求有特色，把品种、价格、服务时间以及特殊之处等信息突出地、快捷地告知消费者。

It is a commonly-used strategy of ads time for retailers and service industry. The ads activities should be carried out before festivals or holidays. This strategy should be distinctive. The information about variety, price, servicing time and specialties of the products should be strikingly and rapidly told to the consumers.

广告宣传频率是指在一定时间内，在广告实际到达范围内，每个人受到广告影响的平均次数。举例来说，如果一个广告连续发布 5 天，如果平均每人看见三次广告，那么，此广告宣传频率为 3 次。

Ads frequency refers to the average times during a certain period when each person is influenced by the ads in the real scope that ads reach. Let's take an example，if an ad is issued continuously for five days, and if each person reads the ad three times on average, then the advertising frequency should be three times.

5. 制定广告预算策略 Strategy of Working out the Ads Budget

制定广告预算策略，即为企业的各种产品制定广告预算。其依据可以是广告的销售反应，以便估算不同的广告预算战略的获利结果。也可以根据历史数据资料及新的情报，求出销售反应函数的估计参数作为确定新的广告预算的依据。此外，对竞争者的广告支出情况也应加以考虑。当两个竞争者同时运用各自认为恰当的方法在不同领域分配其广告预算时，其中一方可利用对方的失策来获得最大优势。

The strategy of working out the ads budget refers to the ads budgets worked out for the enterprise's various products. Its foundation should be the sales responses of ads to calculate the profits result of different strategies of ads budgets. The foundation of the new ads budget can also be identified by working out estimated parameters of the sales response function according to historical data and some new information. Besides, the ads expenses of rivals' should also be considered. Two rivals can get the maximum advantages by making use of rivals' mistakes and by employing an appropriate method to distribute its ads budget in different fields.

1) 量力而行法 The Method of Acting According to One's Ability

一些小企业由于资金有限，只能拨出很少一部分资金作为广告费。这些企业应在确定了自己的预期销售额、业务经营费用和预期利润以后，再考虑在广告上所能花的费用。

Some small businesses have limited funds, so the funds left can be used as advertising expenses. After identifying their expected sales, costs of business operation and the expected profits, the businesses will take the advertising expenses into account.

2) 销售额比例法 The Method of Sales Ratio

销售额比例法将促销预算设定为预期销售额中的一个确定的比例。这个比例可能是企业历史上曾达到的比例或者是为同类企业所使用的平均比例。

The method of sales ratio refers to setting the promotion budget as the identified ratio in expected sales. This ratio may be the one that the enterprise has achieved or the average ratio used by the similar enterprises.

3) 目标任务法 The Method of Aim and Task

目标任务法决定着为实现交流目标而采用的特定任务所需要的预算。使用这种方法时，企业首先要确定一系列交流目标。然后企业要决定必要的任务及其成本。执行这些任务所带来的所有成本的总和即为促销预算。

The method of aim and task determines the budget needed by adopting special task with the aim of realizing communication. When using this method, the enterprise first and foremost should identify a series of aims of communication. Then the enterprise should determine the necessary task and cost. The sum total of all the costs spent by carrying out the task is the expected sales.

6. 广告评估 The Assessment of Advertising

广告评估是衡量一个广告的沟通效果，即效果测试，它被用来研究该广告是否得到了有效传播。

To measure the communicative effects of ads is to test the effect, which is used to study whether ads are transmitted effectively and well.

第一，沟通效果的测定。沟通效果的测定主要有广告的事前测试和广告的事后测试。事前测试的主要方法有直接评分法、组合测试法、实验室测试法。事后测试主要用来评价在媒体刊播出广告信息之后实际产生的沟通效果，常用的方法有回忆测试和识别测试。

Firstly, test of communicative effects, which includes: the test before the ads and the tests after the ads. The methods of testing before ads mainly include: directly giving the score, combined testing and lab testing. Testing before the ads is mainly used to assess the real effects after media broadcasting ads information. The commonly used methods are memory test and recognition test.

第二，销售效果的测定。一种是将广告费用和销售额作比较，另一种是做实验。

Secondly, test of sales effects. One is making a comparison between ads costs and sales, and the other is to make experiments.

第四节 公共关系策略
Public Relation Strategies

一、公共关系的概念及特征 Concept and Essential Characteristics of Public Relations

(一)公共关系的概念 Concept of Public Relations

"公共关系"又称公众关系，它译自英文public relations，简称"公关"或PR。按照美国公共关系协会(AAPR)的理解，"公共关系有助于组织企业和公众相适应"，包括设计用来推广或保护一个企业形象及其品牌产品的各种计划。也就是说，公共关系是指企业在从事市场营销活动中正确处理企业与社会公众的关系，以便树立品牌及企业的良好形象，从而促进产品销售的一种活动。

"Public relations" can also be termed as mass relations, and it is translated from English, and is called PR for short. According to the Association of American Public Relations, it can be understood that "public relations is helpful for organizing the enterprise to fit in the public", which includes the design of recommending and protecting the company's image and various plans of its brand products. That is to say, public relations refers to relations between the company and the public with which the company is dealing when marketing sales activities are carried out to build a brand and set a good image to promote product sales.

公共关系的作用，在于工商企业通过种种公关活动使社会各界公众了解本企业，以取得他们的信赖和好感，从而为企业创造一种良好的舆论环境和社会环境。公共关系的核心是交流信息，促进相互了解，宣传企业的经营方针、经营宗旨、经营项目、产品特点和服务内容等，从而提高企业的知名度和社会声誉，为企业争取一个良好的外部环境，以实现推动企业不断向前发展的目的。

The function of public relations lies in how industrial and commercial enterprises make all social circles know the enterprise by various activities to gain their trust and favorable impressions to create a social environment of good public opinion. The core of public relations is to exchange information to improve mutual understanding, to advertise management principles, aims of management, project management, product characteristics and the content of service to promote the popularity and social reputation of the enterprise and strive for a good external environment to realize the aim of an enterprise's sustainable developing.

(二)公共关系的基本特征 The Essential Characteristics of Public Relations

公共关系的基本特征表现在以下几个方面。

The essential characteristics of public relations are shown in the following aspects.

(1) 公共关系是一定社会组织与其相关的社会公众之间的相互关系。具体地说，就是表现为公关活动的主体一定的组织，如企业、机关、团体等以各种信息沟通工具和大众传播渠道为媒介进行联系、沟通、交往、作用于公关活动的客体内部公众和外部公众。

Public relations refer to the relations between some certain organizations and their related public. Specifically, it can be shown as the subject of PR activities (some organizations, such as enterprises, offices, groups and so on) take all kinds of communication tools and mass communication channels as the media to contact, exchange, associate and act on the objects of PR activities (external public and internal public).

(2) 公共关系是一种信息沟通活动，主客双方以真诚合作、平等互利、共同发展为基本原则，并且相互协调、兼顾企业利益和公众利益；能沟通企业上下、内外的信息，建立相互间的理解、信任与支持，协调和改善企业的社会关系环境。

Public relation is an activity of exchanging information, in which both the subjects and the objects perform sincere cooperation, equality and mutual benefit, mutual development as the basic principle, and coordinate and take into account the enterprise's benefits and the public's benefits. Both of them are able to exchange the information of all the staff inside and outside the enterprise and establish an environment of mutual understanding, trust and support, and coordinate and improve the social environment of the enterprise.

(3) 公共关系的目标是在社会公众中创造良好的企业形象和社会声誉。企业以公共关系为促销手段，让社会公众熟悉企业的经营宗旨，了解企业的产品种类、规格以及服务方式和内容等有关情况，从而使企业在社会上享有较高的声誉和较好的形象，以求得社会公众的理解和支持。

The aim of public relations is to create a good business image and social reputation among the public. The enterprise always takes the means of promotion to make the social public familiar with operating principles, know the sorts and standards of products, and the way and content of service. As a result, the society will enjoy a higher reputation and a good image to win the public's understanding and support.

(4) 公共关系是一种长期活动。公共关系着手于平时努力，着眼于长远打算，需要连续地、有计划地努力，要追求长期稳定的战略性关系。

Public relations is a long-term activity. It starts with the usual endeavor, with a view to thinking in the long run, and it needs a successive and planned strive and seek out long-term and stable strategic relations.

(5) 公共关系可以消除公众思想上的疑虑，可信度高。公共关系的直接表现形式不是推销产品，而仅仅是某种形式的广告宣传，因此公众在思想上一般不存在受骗上当的戒心，从而可以使其思想上的疑虑得以消除。

Public relations can clear up the public's doubts on their minds with higher level of credibility. Their direct form of performance is not selling the products, but just some forms of advertising. Thus, the public will not have the alertness of being cheated and will remove their misgivings.

二、公共关系策略 Public Relations Strategy

(一)公共关系策略的概念 The Concept of Public Relations Strategy

所谓公共关系策略就是企业通过一系列活动的运作来树立并维护企业的公共形象，传递企业文化，建立企业与社会间的沟通桥梁，有目的、有计划地影响公众心理，从而使企业处于一个良好的社会环境当中的具体的措施和办法。

The so-called public relations strategy is detailed measures and methods with which the enterprise uses to establish and maintain its public image, transmit the enterprise's culture, build the bridge to communicate between the enterprise and the society, and influence the public's minds purposefully and designedly to place the enterprise in a good social environment.

(二)公共关系策略类型 The Type of Public Relations Strategy

(1) 宣传性公关策略。此种策略是运用报纸、杂志、广播、电视等各种传播媒介，采用撰写新闻稿、演讲稿、报告等形式，向公众宣传企业的经营思想、产品质量、服务项目、为社会做出的贡献等内容，以形成有利于企业形象的社会舆论导向，从而扩大企业影响，加深顾客印象，激励推销人员及其他职工的工作热情。

The advertising PR strategy. We should make use of newspapers, magazines, TV and various media, and adopt the form of writing news release, speech drafts, reports and so on to popularise to the public the operating ideal, quality of products, service items of the enterprise, to make contributions to the society, to cultivate a public opinion guide which is favorable to the enterprise image, to expand its influence and strengthen customers' impression, and to encourage sales force and other staff's enthusiasm to work.

(2) 交际性公关策略。是通过语言、文字的沟通，为企业广结良缘，巩固传播效果。可采用宴会、座谈会、招待会、谈判、专访、慰问、电话、信函等形式向公众进行市场教育，推荐产品，介绍知识，以获得公众的了解和支持。

Communicative PR strategy. It refers to making friends and strengthening communicating effects through oral and written language. It will adopt the form of banquets, symposiums, conferences, negotiations, interviews, comforts, phone calls and letters. It is necessary to give marketing education, recommend products and introduce knowledge to the public to gain their understanding and support.

(3) 服务性公关策略。企业可以通过各种方式为公众提供服务，如消费指导、消费培训、免费修理等。事实上，只有把服务提到公关这一层面上来，企业员工头脑中牢记公关这一点，才能真正做好服务工作。

The service PR strategy. The enterprise may provide service for the public in various ways, such as directions and training of consumption, repairing for free and so on. Actually, only when promoting service to the level of public relations can they serve well and transfer the public relations to all the staff's behavior.

(4) 社会性公关策略。是指企业通过赞助文化、教育、体育、卫生等事业，支持社区福利事业，参与国家、社区重大社会活动等形式来塑造企业的社会形象，提高企业的社会知名度和美誉度，树立企业形象，以有利于企业市场营销目标的实现。

Social PR strategy. It refers to shaping the enterprise's image and gaining more popularity and reputation by sponsoring cultural, educational, physical education and sanitation undertaking, supporting community welfare, and taking part in national and important community activities, which will be favorable for the enterprise to realize its marketing goals.

(5) 征询性公关策略。是指通过开办各种咨询业务、制定调查问卷、进行民意测验、设立热线电话、聘请兼职信息人员、举办信息交流会等各种形式，逐步形成效果良好的信息网络。

The consultative PR service. It refers to establishing a good information net gradually by carrying out various consultancies, making questionnaire, carrying out public opinion poll, setting telephone hotlines, employing part-time informational staff, holding information exchange meetings, and so on.

(三)公共关系策略的原则 The Principles of PR Strategies

1. 事实在先原则 The Principle of "Facts First"

这是程序方面的一个原则。也就是说，企业在进行具体公共关系活动时，不管是为了提升企业的形象，还是解决企业形象不好的问题；不管是协调平衡企业与公众之间出现的矛盾和利益冲突，还是解决已出现的公共关系危机，在这之前都要先调查了解掌握事实，然后再有的放矢地去进行公共关系活动。

This is a principle on the aspects of program. That is to say, when an enterprise is carrying out PR activities, whether it is to promote the image of the enterprise or to deal with the bad image of the enterprise, and whether to balance and coordinate the contraction and benefit conflict or to deal with existing crises of public relations, it should carry out the public relations activities with a target before surveying and having a command of facts.

2. 公众在先原则 The Principle of "the Public First"

企业要生存下去．要持续稳定发展，就要依赖公众的谅解与合作，而不是公众请求企业生存下去。既然如此，企业在公共关系活动中就应把公众利益放在企业本身利益的前面，即先满足公众的利益再满足本企业的利益；否则，企业所希望的公众对企业的谅解与合作就不可能实现。因此，企业在考虑和平衡双方利益时应首先考虑和满足公众的利益，然后才是企业本身的利益。

In order to survive and keep a continuous and stable development, the enterprise should relay on the public's understanding and cooperation, not because the public appeal to the enterprise to do. Under such circumstances, during the PR activities, the enterprise should place the public's interests behind, namely, to satisfy the public's benefits and then to satisfy itself. Otherwise, the public's understanding and cooperation that the enterprise expects will not be realized. Thus, the enterprise should balance and satisfy the public's interests before considering and satisfy the mutual benefits.

3. 平等互利原则 The Principle of "Equality and Mutual Benefit"

尽管企业是法人并具有一定的规模和经济实力，而公众或是自然人或是法人，在各方面的实力都较小，但在法律上两者是平等的。按照法律的规定，公众的利益是受法律保护的，公众的人格也是受到法律保护的。只有当双方的利益达到基本平衡时，双方才能产生和谐的关系。这就是说，企业在制定公共关系策略时要坚持对企业对公众双方都有利的原则。

Although the enterprise is the legal person and possess a certain scale and economic power, the power of the public, the natural person or the legal person is of little importance, they are equal in front of the law. The public's benefit is protected by laws, and human dignity of the public is also protected by laws. Only when the mutual benefit achieving the balance will a harmonious relationship be produced. That is to say, when the enterprise is making a PR strategy, whey should stick to the principle of being beneficial to both the enterprise and the public.

4. 情感相随原则 The Principle of "Emotion"

一个社会组织，不管是一个企业、一家剧团，还是一家研究所，若内部成员之间情感冷漠，那么这个组织的整体运转就不会太好。相反，若内部成员之间情感融洽、亲密无间，那么这个组织的整体运转就会比较好。这其中的原因是心理学研究出来的一种客观结论，即情感是一个社会组织运转的润滑剂，又是社会上人际关系的黏合剂。

A social organization, whether it is an enterprise, a troupe or a research institution, if its members are indifferent towards the feelings of each other, the whole operation of the organization will not be on a sound track. On the contrary, if there is harmonious emotion and intimacy among staff, there will be a sound operation in this organization. Its reason is an objective conclusion of a psychology research, which is to say, emotion is not only an lubricant for the operation of an organization, but also an adhesive of interpersonal relationship in a society.

5. 柔性原则 The Principle of Flexibility

当企业在公共关系活动中协调企业与公众的关系时，不能采取命令的方式强制公众服从，而只能采取信息交流的方式来互相交换信息，最终达到理解、谅解和平衡。

When the enterprise coordinates the relations between itself and the public in activities, they cannot take the imperative way to force the public to obey, but to take the way of informational communication to exchange information and finally to reach understanding, forgiving and balancing.

6. 补偿原则 The Principle of "Compensation"

企业的产品和营销活动长期大量地影响了公众的利益，其中有些影响是难免的甚至是合法的，例如，自来水含有一定比率的对人体有害的消毒剂是合法的。公众并不认为这理所当然，他们要求的是自己的利益丝毫不受损害，即公众自己的利益没有任何理由可以遭到企业的损害。在此情况下，企业除了不断改进自己的产品和营销活动外，对难以避免或已经造成的损害，就应给予经济和精神补偿，只有这样企业才能得到公众的谅解与合作，否则企业的形象将受到严重损害。

The products and promotional activities have long been influencing the public's benefits, some of the influence is inevitable and even legal. For example, it is true that tap water contains a certain ratio of sanitizer which is harmful to human body, but it is legal. The public do not think it a matter of course, they demand that their own benefit not be damaged at all, that is to say, there is no reason for the benefit of the public to be damaged by the enterprise. Under such circumstances, the enterprise should improve its products and promotional activities, they should also grant the financial and spiritual compensation to the public's inevitable damage. Only by doing so can the enterprise gain the public's forgiveness and cooperation. Otherwise, the enterprise's image will be damaged seriously.

7. 长期性原则 The Principle of "Long-term"

此原则是指企业的公共关系活动，更具体地说就是企业开展树立企业形象的活动和企业与公众关系的协调平衡活动，必须要长期坚持下去，不能是间断的，更不能是短期的。大多数企业像通用汽车公司、IBM 公司、雀巢公司、丰田汽车公司、松下电器公司、菲利浦电子公司、西门子公司等的企业形象都是经过半个多世纪的不懈努力才逐渐树立起来的。

It is the public relations activities, to put it specifically, the activities carried out by the enterprise to establish its business image and to coordinate and balance with the PR relations have to be held for a long term, and it should not be occasional or short. In most enterprises, such as General Motors, IBM, Nestle, Toyota, Panasonic, Siemens Company, Philips Electronic Company, etc., their images are all set up across more than half a century and with prolonged efforts.

8. 综合性原则 The Comprehensive Principle

企业进行公共关系活动的方式多种多样，每一种都有优点和缺点，都有其适用情况，企业在进行公共关系活动时不能仅仅采用某一种或某几种方式，而是要综合利用每一种方式的优点，使其互相配合，发挥最大组合效果。

There are various activities for the enterprise to carry out, each having its own advantages and disadvantages and its applicable situations. When the enterprise is carrying out PR activities, they can not merely adopt one way from several, but comprehensively make use of and coordinate the advantages of each and bring the combination into its full play.

第五节　营业推广策略
Sales promotion Strategies

一、营业推广的概念 The Concept of Sales Promotion

营业推广（sales promotion）是指企业运用各种短期诱因鼓励消费者和中间商购买、经销或代理企业产品或服务的促销活动。它是为刺激消费者迅速购买商品而采取的营业性促销措施，以及为配合一定的营销任务而采取的特种推销方式。

Sales promotion refers to the promotional activities in which the enterprise adopts all kinds of short-term temptation to encourage consumers and brokers to purchase and sell (or act as an agent of) products or services of the enterprise. It is an operating measure of promotion to encourage consumers to purchase their goods, and an adopted way of promotion coordinated with a certain task of sales promotion.

二、营业推广策略的含义 The Meaning of Sales Promotion Strategies

营业推广策略是指企业在某一特定时期内，采用特殊的方法和手段对购买者实行强烈的刺激，以达到促进企业销售量迅速增长的一种促销策略。

It refers to a kind of promotion strategy which can promote the enterprise's sales volume to increase fast in a certain period by adopting particular means and methods to give buyers strong stimulation.

三、营业推广策略的类型及活动方式 The Types of Sales Promotion Strategies and the Ways of Activities

营业推广策略包括对消费者进行营业推广、对中间商进行营业推广和对推销人员进行营业推广三种策略类型,每种策略类型又有多种形式。企业在营销活动中应根据市场情况、政策、法令、企业性质、商品特点、销售情况等选择适当的营业推广形式。对这些形式的不同组合或选择就形成了不同的营业推广策略。

Sales promotion strategies include three types: the sales promotion to the consumers, the sales promotion to brokers and the sales promotion to the sales force, with each types of strategy having its own form. The enterprise should choose the appropriate form of sales promotion according to the circumstances of the market, policies, status, the quality of the enterprise, the characteristics of goods, sales situations and so on. The different mix or choice of these forms formulates different sales promotion strategies.

1. 针对消费者的营业推广策略 The Sales Promotion Strategies to Consumers

此类策略可以鼓励老顾客继续使用、促进新顾客尝试使用企业产品,动员顾客购买新产品或更新设备等。其策略一般有如下几种。

It can encourage regular customers to continue using and promote new customers to use, mobilize customers to buy new products or renew equipment and so on, with the following strategies:

1) 代金券或优惠券 The Scrip or the Discount Coupon

代金券是商业单位伴随广告或产品的外包装送给顾客的一种标有价格的凭证,但其价值只能在代价券责任者指定的商店里实现。

The scrip refers to tokens with prices sent to the customers usually accompanied with business ads or external packing, but its value can only be realized in the store appointed by the owner of the scrip.

2) 买赠或附加交易 Buying and Granting or Additional Trading

附加交易是一种短期的降价手法,其具体做法是在交易中向顾客给付一定数量的免费的同种商品。这种方法的常见的商业语言是"买几送几"。例如在北京的"必胜客"店,客人如果在店堂比较清静的特定时间里用餐,根据不同的用餐量,顾客可以得到不同的免费饮料。

Additional trading is a means of short-term lowering the price, whose specific practice is to give a certain amount and same kind of free products to customers. The commonly-used business language is "buy one and get one free". For example, in Pizza Hut in Beijing, if guests have a meal in a specified restaurant during a period of quieter time, they will get different free beverages according to different quantities of meal.

3) 折扣或打折 Discount or On Sale

折扣即在销售商品时对商品的价格打折扣,折扣的幅度一般从 5%至 50%不等。但其幅度过大或过小均会引起顾客产生怀疑其促销活动真实性的心理。

Discount refers to reducing the price of the goods when selling goods, discounts range from five percent to fifty percent. But either the range is too big or too small will arouse the doubt about the reality of the promotion.

4) 回扣或退费优待 Preferential Treatment for Kickback or Refund

通常回扣的标志会附在产品的包装上或是直接印在产品的包装上,例如酒类的回扣标志一般都套在瓶口。消费者购买了有回扣标志的商品后,需要将此回扣标签寄回给制造商,然后再由制造商按签上的回扣金额数量寄发支票给消费者。

Generally speaking, the symbol of kickback is attached to the package of the product or directly printed on the packages, for example, the kickback symbol of liquor goods is often in the bottle mouth. After buying the goods with the kickback symbol, customers need to mail the mark back to the producer, and then the producer will sent the cheque according to the amount of kickback to customers.

5) 有奖销售 Prize-giving Sales

有奖销售是采用发奖券或号码中奖的办法,即顾客在购买时不仅可以得到产品,还有额外的收获,以此刺激顾客的购买欲望。

Prize-giving sales is a way of giving the lottery tickets or the numbers for winning, namely, when customers are buying, they can not only get products, but also have the chance to get additional gains, thus stimulating customers' desire.

6) 赠送样品 Free Samples

样品赠送可以有选择地赠送,也可无选择地赠送,如在商店或闹市地区或附在其他商品中较广泛地赠送等。这是介绍、推销新产品的一种方式,但因其费用较高,对高值商品不宜采用。

Free samples may be sent selectively or indiscriminately. For instance, free samples attached to other goods presented extensively in stores or downtown areas. It is a way of introducing and promoting new goods, but it is not suitable for high value goods to adopt because of higher costs.

7) 现场演示 Spot Presentation

现场演示,就是通过在现场表演、展示商品与服务的方法去进行推广。现场演示可以大量节约介绍产品的邮寄广告的费用,并使顾客身临其境,得到感性认识。

Spot presentation is to carry out promotion by spot performance, goods and service demonstration. Spot presentation can save the cost of introducing products and mailing advertisement, and make customers feel immersive and get perceptual knowledge.

8) 竞赛 Competition

竞赛的方法有多种,常用的是智力和知识方面的竞赛,其内容多数都是与销售产品的公司或其产品有关的问题。竞赛的奖品一般为实物,但也有以免费旅游来表示奖励的。竞赛的地点也可有多种,如在闹市街头、商店门口、会议厅等,有的企业还通过在电视台举办游戏性质的节目,并通过在电视节目中发放本企业的产品作为奖品来进行。

There are many kinds of competitions, and the most commonly-used competitions are intelligence competition and knowledge competition, most of whose contents are related to goods and the company that is selling it. The prize of the competition is the material objects in general, but sometimes it can be the form of traveling for free. Competitions can be held in many places, such as on the street of downtown areas, at the gate of a store or in a meeting room. Some enterprises also use TV stations to host the program of game and distribute their products as prizes.

9) 廉价包装 Cheap Packaging

工商企业可以采用简单包装、小包装换成大包装、除去精美包装等方式，达到降低费用及商品降价的目的，用以更多地吸引"经济型"顾客。此外，企业还可利用多用途包装、系列包装等，以不断吸引顾客，提高其重复购买率。

An industrial and commercial enterprise can adopt the way of simple packaging, replacing big packages with small package, removing elegant packing, etc. to realize the aim of reducing costs and lowering goods prices so as to attract more "economic" customers. Besides, the enterprise can also make use of multi-purpose packaging, series packaging to attract customers constantly and improve their repurchase rate.

10) 商业贴花 Business Appliques

消费者每购买单位商品就可获得一张贴花，待收集到一定数量的贴花时，就可换取商品或奖品。

Every time when a consumer buys unit goods, he will get an applique, and when appliques are assembled to a certain amount, he can exchange them for goods or prizes.

2. 针对中间商的营业推广策略 Sales Promotion Strategy to the Middle Man

此类策略可吸引和激励中间商扩大经营本企业的产品与服务，密切协作关系。其策略有以下几种。

It can attract and stimulate the middle man to extensively operate its products and services, and cultivate an intimate cooperative relationship. The strategies are as follows.

1) 商业折让 Business Allowance

商业折让是指生产企业在零售商向公众发放了代金券的有效期内，向发放这些代金券的零售商出售产品时进行折让，对其进行相应的补偿。

During the effective period when the retailer is giving out the tokens to the public, the manufacturing enterprise will give retailers the allowance and the corresponding compensation when the retailer is selling goods.

2) 批量折让 Bulk Discount

批量折让是指生产企业与中间商之间或批发商与零售商之间，按购买货物数量的多少，给予一定量的免费的同种商品。例如，购买十箱某种商品即无偿赠送一箱的做法，就是批量折让。

Bulk discount refers to granting some free goods to the middle man by the manufacturing enterprise or to the retailer by the wholesaler according to the amount of the purchased goods. For example, purchasing every ten boxes of goods deserves one box for free, which is called bulk discount.

3) 商业折扣 Business Discount

商业折扣是指企业与中间商之间或批发商与零售商之间的交易中，给予购买方一定比例的价格折扣，这种折扣因为是分销渠道内部的折扣，所以称为商业折扣。

It is certain percentage of price discount granted to the middleman by the enterprise or to the retailer by the wholesaler. Because this kind of discount is in the channel of distribution, it can be called business discount.

4) 费用补贴 Allowance for Expenses

费用补贴是生产企业针对零售商在配合本企业进行广告、店堂商品陈列等促销活动时，以及中间商自己从生产企业的仓库将产品直运至销售地时，对其给予一定的费用补贴。

It refers to certain expenses allowances granted by the manufacturing enterprise to retailers for their expenditures when it carries out advertisements, commodity display and such kind of promotional activities, and to the middleman when it transports goods from a storehouse to sales places.

5) 产品展销会、交易会 Exhibitions and Trade Fairs

企业通过举办或参与展销会、交易会、订货会等广泛的营业推广活动，展示自己的产品，显示自身的经济实力和贸易水平，从而与有关客户洽谈业务，最终按展示的样品达成交易。

The enterprise displays its own products, showing its own economic strength and trading level by holding or taking part in the exhibitions, trade fairs, purchasing meetings and such extensive sales promotion activities so to have business negotiations with related clients and make a deal of the eventually displayed samples.

6) 经销奖励 Rewards of Distribution

经销奖励是指对经销本企业产品有突出成绩的中间商给予奖励。例如，采用现金、实物奖励或提供免费旅游等形式激励经销商，以达到促销的目的。

It is a means of granting rewards to the middleman who has made the outstanding achievement. For example, cash, reward of material objects or providing the travel for free are all good means to stimulate the agent to realize the promotional aims.

7) 演示 Demonstration

演示是指企业安排经销者对产品进行特殊的现场表演或示范及提供咨询服务。

It refer to the special spot display, demonstration and providing consultation service by sellers whom the enterprise arranged.

3. 针对推销人员的营业推广策略 Sales Promotion Strategies Aiming at Salesmen

这类策略旨在鼓励推销人员热情推销产品或处理老产品，或促使他们积极开拓市场。可采用的方式有：销售竞赛，如有奖销售，比例分成；免费提供人员培训、技术指导等。

There are some ways to encourage salesmen to promote the products or deal with old products at lower prices. The adoptable ways are: sales contests, such as prize-giving sales, paying on the basis of certain percentage; providing personal training and technical guidance for free and so on.

四、营业推广策略实施程序 The Implementation Procedures of Sales Promotion Strategies

(一)确定营业推广目标 Defining the Goals of Sales Promotion

营业推广目标要根据目标市场类型来确定。对于消费者,目标包括鼓励消费者更多地使用和促使其大批量购买;对零售商,目标包括吸引零售商经营新的商品和维持较高水平的存货,鼓励他们购买过季商品等;对于销售队伍,目标包括鼓励他们支持一种新产品或新型号,激励他们寻找更多的潜在顾客和刺激他们推销过季商品。

The goals of sales promotion should be established according to the types of targeted markets and promotional aims. For consumers, the goals include encouraging the consumers to use more and urging them to purchase a lot; for retailers, the goals include attracting retailers to sell new products to sustain a high level of storage, and encouraging them to purchase out-of-season goods etc.; for the sales force, it includes encouraging them to support a kind of new products or new model, stimulating them to look for potential customers and triggering them to sell out-of-season goods.

(二)选择营业推广类型和活动方式 Choosing the Type of Sales Promotion and Their Ways

企业根据营业推广对象的不同可以选择不同的活动方式。

The enterprise can choose different ways according to different objects.

(三)制订营业推广方案 Working Out the Scheme of Sales Promotion

在制定营业推广方案时,必须对以下问题做出决策:刺激大小、刺激对象、刺激期限、送达方式、时机选择、预算及分配。

When working out the plans of sales promotion, policies must be made for the following questions: the degree of stimulation; the objects of stimulation; the deadline of stimulation; the way of transferring; the choice of opportunity; budgets and distribution.

(四)预试、实施和控制方案 Pre-examining, Carrying Out and Controlling the Schemes

营业推广方案制订后一般要经过试验才能予以实施。通过试验以明确选择的销售工具是否适当、刺激规模是否最佳、实施的方法效率是否最高等。对于每一项营业推广工作都应该确定实施和控制计划。

After working out the scheme of sales promotion, it must be examined before carrying it out. Whether the choice of the tools is appropriate, whether the scale of stimulation is the best and whether the efficiency of implementation method is high, all of these should be defined through experiments. The plan of implementation and control should be defined for every sales promotion task.

(五)营业推广效果评价 To Evaluate the Sales Promotion Effects

企业应该对每一次营业推广的结果都进行细致科学的评价，以便为后来的活动提供参考。常用的评价方法有两种：一种方法是通过邀请部分消费者以评价或打分的形式了解自己想问的问题；另一种方法是在有限的地区范畴内做试用性的测试并进行前后对比分析。

The meticulous and scientific evaluation should be carried out for each sales promotion, so as to provide reference for later activities. There are two kinds of evaluation: one is to learn of the questions by inviting some of consumers to evaluate or give scores; the other is to do the examination by trying out and to make the comparison and analysis in the limited regional category.

本 章 小 结
Summary

促销是企业通过人员和非人员的方式，沟通企业与消费者之间的信息，引发、刺激消费者的购买欲望，使其产生购买行为的全部活动的总称。促销方式具体分为人员推销、广告宣传、公共关系、营业推广四种方式。促销策略是四种促销方式的单项运用和综合运用。企业在制定、选择促销策略时，应综合考虑不同产品的特点、营销目标、企业内部条件等因素，以便达到最佳的促销效果。人员推销策略是指企业根据外部环境变化和内部资源条件建立和管理销售队伍的系统工程的策略。为了增加利润，企业应在人员推销上分配较多的资源，并对营销人员制定奖惩办法，最大限度地调动营销人员的积极性和潜能。广告策略是实现广告活动目标的措施与手段。它是根据企业内外的环境、条件、广告目的而制定的决策方案。公共关系策略就是企业通过一系列活动的运作来树立并维护企业的公共形象，传递企业文化，建立企业与社会间的沟通桥梁，有目的、有计划地影响公众心理，从而使企业处于一个良好的社会环境当中的具体的措施和办法，其策略有宣传性公关策略、交际性公关策略、服务性公关策略、社会性公关策略、征询性公关策略等。营业推广策略是指企业在某一特定时期内，采用特殊的方法和手段对购买者实行强烈的刺激，以达到促进企业销售量迅速增长的一种促销策略。营业推广策略包括对消费者进行营业推广、对中间商进行营业推广、对推销人员进行营业推广三种策略类型，每种策略类型又有多种形式。各种促销策略的实施应遵循一定的程序。

Promotion refers to the overall term of activities, during which there is exchanged information between the enterprise and consumers to trigger and stimulate consumers' desire for purchasing and generate the buying behavior. There are four types of promotion strategies: personal promotion, ads promotion, PR promotion and sales promotion. Promotional strategy is a single movement and comprehensive application of the four promotion strategies. When the enterprise is making and choosing promotional strategies, the characteristics of different products, promotional aims, the enterprise's internal conditions and such elements should be taken into account. Personal promotion is a systematic engineering strategy to set up and manage the sales staff according to the changes of external conditions and internal resources situations. In order to increase profits, the enterprise should distribute more resources to personal promotion, make the plan of rewards and punishments for sales staff, and arouse enthusiasm and potential of salesmen. The ads strategy is the measures and means of realizing the aims of ads. which is a scheme of decision made according to the enterprise's internal and external environment, conditions and aims. PR strategies are the concrete measures and means to establish and maintain public image of the enterprise, transmit the enterprise's culture, build a communicative bridge between the enterprise and the society, influence the public's thinking with purpose and plan so to as place the enterprise in a good social environment. Its strategies include advertising PR strategies, communicative PR strategies, service PR strategies, social PR strategies and consultative PR strategies. Sales promotion is a kind of promotional strategy adopted by the enterprise to employ some kind of particular means and measures to strongly stimulate consumers so as to promote the enterprise's sales volume. Sales promotion strategies include three types: the promotion to the consumers, the promotion to the middle man and the promotion to the salesman.

思 考 题
Questions

1. 什么是促销？促销的作用有哪些？影响促销组合的因素有哪些？

What is promotion? What are the roles played by promotion? What are the elements that influence promotion mix?

2. 简述推销人员的主要推销步骤。

Please briefly state salesmen's major steps of promotion.

3. 什么是广告媒体？如何选择广告媒体？

What is ads media? How to choose ads media?

4. 什么是公共关系？它的基本特征有哪些？

What is public relations? What are the basic features of public relations?

5. 什么是营业推广？营业推广的方式有哪些？

What is sales promotion? What are the main ways of sales promotion?

第十章 营销素养和社会责任
Marketing Ethics and Social Responsibility

【学习目标】
1. 营销人员的营销素养以及如何提高营销人员的营销素养;
2. 社会对于营销的批评;
3. 营销中的社会责任的三个层次;
4. 如何实施对社会负有责任的市场营销。

Learning Objectives

1. Marketing ethics of salesmen and how to improve salesmen's marketing ethics;
2. Criticism for marketing by the society;
3. Three levels of social responsibilities in marketing;
4. How to carry out marketing with social responsibility.

第一节 加强营销素养
Reinforce Marketing Ethics

菲利普·科特勒在其名著《营销管理》中引用了一项调查结果:27%的销售人员创造了52%的销售额。实践证明,销售人员才是决定销售业绩高低的关键。"销售最重要的要素是人。"从销售人员个人角度看,决定其业绩高低的因素有其基本素质、观念、能力等。有人把能力和素质混为一谈,其实二者是不同的。能力可以在短期内培养,而素质则无法在短期内培养出来。

Philip Kotler quoted the result of a survey in his famous book *Marketing Management*, "27% salesmen created 52% of sales". It has been proved that salesmen are the key to the amount of sales. "The most important element of promotion is men". From the view of sales staff, the elements that determine their performance are their basic qualities, ideas and abilities. Some people may confuse ability with qualities. Actually these two concepts are different. Abilities can be cultivated in a short period, whereas qualities can not be cultivated in a short time.

一、营销人员必备的营销素养 Salesmen's Requisite Marketing Ethics

(一)具备现代营销理念 Philosophy of Modern Marketing

营销人员需要清晰地了解现代营销的正确发展方向,保持清醒的头脑,具有前瞻性的思维方式。现代市场营销观念的核心是以消费者为中心,认为市场需求引起供给,每个企业必须依照消费者的需要与愿望组织商品的生产与销售。几十年来,这种观念已被公认,

第十章 营销素养和社会责任
Marketing Ethics and Social Responsibility

在实际的营销活动中也倍受企业家的青睐。然而,随着消费需求的多元性、多变性和求异性特征的出现,需求表现出了模糊不定的"无主流化"趋势,许多企业对市场需求及走向常常感觉捕捉不准,适应需求的难度加大。另外,完全强调按消费者的购买欲望与需要组织生产,在一定程度上会压抑产品创新,而创新正是经营成功的关键所在。为此,在当代激烈的商战中,一些企业对现代市场营销实践经验进行了总结,提出了创造需求的新观念,其核心是市场营销活动不仅仅在于适应、刺激需求,还在于能否生产出对产品的需要。由此出现了关系营销、绿色营销、文化营销、整体营销等新观念。营销人员必须根据企业及外部环境的变化,找到适合自己的营销理念,以适应越来越激烈的竞争形势,从而使其所在的企业适应未来的发展趋势。

Salesmen should clearly know of the correct development direction of modern marketing, keep a calm head and possess the prospective way of thinking. The core of modern marketing philosophy is consumer-centered, which means that market requirements cause supply and every enterprise must organize goods production and promotion according to consumers' needs and wishes. Over the last decades, this philosophy has been generally accepted and is popular with entrepreneurs in real marketing activities. But with the advent of consumption diversity, variability and difference, these requirements show the fuzzy and variable trends of "no mainstream", and many enterprises can not correctly catch the market needs and tendency, so it is increasingly hard to adapt to requirements. In addition, organizing production according to consumers' buying desires and needs will depress product creation to some extent, but creation is the key to the success of marketing. Therefore, in the modern drastic business campaign, some enterprises summarize the practical experience of the modern marketing and propose the new idea of creating "needs", whose core is that marketing activities not only lie in adapting and stimulating needs, but also lie in whether it can produce the needs for products. Thus relationship marketing, green marketing, cultural marketing, whole marketing and other new ideas appeared. Salesmen have to find a marketing idea which is suitable for them according to external changes of the enterprise to adapt to the increasingly drastic situations so as to make their own enterprise adapt to the future development.

(二)良好的品德 Good Morals

营销活动是一项塑造形象、建立声誉的崇高事业。它要求从业人员必须具有高尚的道德情操,诚实严谨、恪尽职守的工作态度和廉洁奉公、公道正派的工作作风。"胆大而不急躁,迅速而不轻佻,爱动而不粗浮,服从上司而不阿谀奉承,身居职守而不刚愎自用,胜而不骄,喜功而不自炫,自重而不自傲,豪爽而不欺人,刚强而不执拗,谦虚而不假装",这应该成为营销人员共同的职业操守。

Marketing campaign is an honorable cause to establish image and reputation. It requires that employees possess noble moral sentiments, honesty and seriousness, devoted working attitude and uncorrupted and decent working style. "Bold but not impatient, quick but not flirty, energetic but not coarse, obedient to the superior but not flattering, responsible but not self-willed, victorious but not conceited, utilitarian but not self-blatant, self-dignified but not arrogant, generous but not cheating, tough but not stubborn, and modesty but not pretentious", these are all the professional qualities of marketing salesmen.

(三)知识渊博、持续学习、勤于思考 Being Knowledgeable, Continue to Learn and Being Diligent in Thinking

市场营销以消费者需求为出发点，强调企业整体营销活动，不仅重视生产后的推销宣传，也重视生产前的调研工作，所以要求营销人员具有完善的知识结构。作为一个营销人员，首先要精通本专业的知识，包括商品、心理、市场、营销、管理、法律、公关、广告、财务、物价、人际关系等知识；其次要具备广泛的兴趣和爱好，包括体育、音乐、美术等领域，扩大自身的知识面。

Marketing is to stress the overall marketing activities on the basis of consumers. Importance should be attached not only to promotional ads after production, but also to the research work before the production, so it is required to possess the perfect structure of knowledge for salesmen. First, one should master the professional knowledge, including the knowledge of goods, psychology, markets, marketing, management, laws, public relations, ads, finance, price, and interpersonal relationships and so on; in addition, they should possess extensive interests and hobbies, which includes the fields of PE, music and art, etc., to expand one's own scope of knowledge.

当今信息时代，知识更新、淘汰的周期非常短，营销人员只有不断学习，提高自身的综合素质，才可能满足市场瞬息万变的需要。因此，优秀的营销人员需要保持旺盛的学习热情，见贤思齐，勤勉不懈，持续学习，不断更新业务知识，深入了解社会、行业、客户，掌握更为先进的营销方法与技巧。

In the information era, the cycle of knowledge renewing and eliminating is short. Only when the salesmen continue to learn and improve their comprehensive qualities can they satisfy the changeable needs of the market. Therefore, an outstanding salesman needs to keep strong enthusiasm for learning, emulates those better than himself, works hard constantly, always renews professional knowledge, thoroughly knows the society, industry and clients, and masters advanced marketing methods and skills.

合格的营销人员会处处留心市场动态，注意观察、分析、归纳、总结，善于发现每一个有用的信息，并且思维敏捷，对周围的细小变化都能很快作出反应，从而改进工作方法，提高工作效率。在营销过程中，营销人员必须能吃苦耐劳，做到脑勤、嘴勤、腿勤，无论对方是不是客户都要热情地介绍产品，态度诚恳地回答对方的提问。

Qualified salesmen will always notice market dynamics and watch out for observations, analysis and summarizing, are good at find out useful information, have a quick response to the minimal changes nearby and to improve the working methods and promote working efficiency. During the marketing process, salesmen must can endure the hardships and stand hard work and must be diligent in thinking, speaking and selling. Whether the other party is an client, he/she should answer his or her questions with an sincere attitude.

(四)良好的心理素质 Good Psychological Quality

心理素质渗透在人们的各种活动中，影响着人们的行为方式和活动质量。营销工作充满酸甜苦辣，这就要求营销人员必须具备良好的心理素质，胜不骄，败不馁。优秀的营销人员会始终保持浓厚的职业兴趣，以持久的热情从事营销活动，探索营销成功之路；同时他们具有充分的自信心，遇到挫折和障碍时，能够自我激励，始终坚信：精诚所至，金石为开。另外，在营销过程中可能会遇到千奇百怪的人和事，因此，营销人员一定要随机应变，灵活应对。

Psychological quality permeates in all kinds of human activities and influences human's behavior and activity qualities. Marketing jobs are full of joys and sorrows of life, which requires that marketing staff possess good psychological qualities and be humble in victory and gracious in defeat. Excellent marketing staff will always keep the professional interest, engage in marketing activities with prolonged enthusiasm and exploit the successful way of marketing. When they encounter frustration and barriers, they will have confidence and be able to encourage themselves. They still believe that no difficulty is insurmountable if one sets one's mind on it. In addition, during the process of marketing, they may encounter all kinds of persons and matters, so marketing staff have to adapt themselves to changing circumstances and handle things flexibly.

(五)良好的团队合作精神 Team Spirit

团队合作精神反映的是一个人与别人合作的精神和能力。一个优秀的营销人员总是具有强烈的合作意识，注意团队成员之间相互依存、同舟共济、互敬互重、彼此宽容、尊重个性、待人真诚、信守承诺，利益和成就共享、责任共担。

Team spirit reflects the spirit and ability of a person's cooperating with others. An excellent salesman always shows the strong cooperative sense, focusing on mutual dependence, staying together and helping each other, respecting each other, being tolerant to each other, respecting individuality, treating others sincerely, keeping promises, and sharing and taking mutual benefits and achievements.

(六)具备营销人员必备的基本能力 Essential Abilities of Marketing Staff

营销人员要具备以下能力：知识能力(了解行业、产品、消费等方面知识)、调研能力(如区域市场考察、评估能力)、判断能力(如在设立经销商时总要优中选优，要具备判断客户素质的能力)、表达能力(能把事情说清楚)、推销能力(如百事销售人员在为经销商实施助销过程中，为批发商拿订单)、谈判能力(如与大卖场冲突谈判，以及矛盾化解)、管理能力(如管理经销商)、服务能力(简单责任事故处理，如因产品质量引发的客户投诉)、结算能力(如货款管理、商业信用、财务能力等)、适应能力(如因经常调整销售区域，销售员要具备适应能力)、进阶能力(不断学习，提升能力)等。

Marketing staff should have the following abilities: the ability to learn (knowing the industry, products, consumption, etc.), the ability to investigate and survey (such as inspection and assessment), the ability to express (state something clearly), the ability to promote (for example, the marketing staff of Pepsi take the orders when they carry out promotion), the ability to negotiate (such as conflict negotiation in the shopping mall and resolution of conflicts), the ability to manage (such as the ability to manage dealers), the ability to serve (the ability to deal with incidents, such as clients' complaints caused by the quality of products), the ability to settle accounts (such as the management of paying for goods), adaptability (Salesman should possess adaptability as they adjust sales areas frequently.), the ability to move forward (the ability to constantly learn and promote) and so on.

二、营销人员提高业务素养的途径 Ways of Promoting Salesmen's Professional Quality

(一)岗前培训 Pre-job Training

企业应对新招聘的营销人员首先进行上岗前的业务素质培训，这样，一方面可以使新的营销人员通过系统的业务技术培训很快适应工作岗位；另一方面，通过建立岗前培训制度，使企业能够科学地对培训费用进行定额预算管理，有效地防止费用定额的忽高忽低现象，节省培训费用。

The enterprise should first organize professional training for newly employed salesmen before they take up their quarters. In doing so, on the one hand, the newly employed salesmen could quickly adapt themselves to the job after systematic professional training; on the other hand, through the system of pre-job training, the enterprise could scientifically manage the budget of the training quota, effectively prevent the training quota from going up and down and save the expenditure of training.

(二)在职脱产学习 Block Release Learning

企业对有发展前途的营销人员可以实行脱产培训制度，将其派送到高等院校或科研机构进修学习，使其成为真正的推销专业人才，以便在今后的工作中发挥更大的作用，或者作为他们晋升提职的依据。因此，在知识经济时代到来之际，企业和高等学校联手培养推销专门人才已经势在必行，而且这种需求会越来越大。

The enterprise can carry out the block release training for promising salesmen. Sending them to colleges or to scientific research institutions to study further is a good way to enable them to become real promotional talents, so as to play a greater role in the future job or becoming a basis of their promotion. Therefore, with the advent of the era of knowledge-driven economy, it is imperative for colleges combining to cultivate sales professionals, and there will be ever-growing requirements.

(三)自我训练 Self-training

这种方法适用于所有的营销人员。它是建立在营销人员自觉意识基础之上的，其目的是使有进取心的营销人员成为最优秀者。自我训练与营销人员的日常生活和工作过程联系密切，营销人员通过把公司的价值观念、行为准则和职业道德规范落实到日常生活和工作中去，并利用时间进行锻炼与进修的方法，逐步把自己培养成一个思想、业务和身体素质都过硬的优秀的营销人员。

This method is applicable to all salesmen. It is established on the basis of salesmen's self-awareness, with the aim of making enterprising salesmen the most excellent persons. Self-training is closely related to salesmen's daily life and work. It is the way to implement the company's values, standards of behavior and the code of professional ethics to the daily life and work, and the way to make use of the time to exercise and further education, which can train oneself as an excellent salesman with the qualifications of minds, profession and physical fitness.

第二节 实施对社会负责的市场营销
Marketing with Social Responsibility

市场营销观念是顾客满意与企业获得利润双赢的哲学，在一只看不见的手的操纵下，引导经济满足千百万顾客不断变化的需求。但并非所有的营销人员都认同这一概念，事实上有些商家的营销行为受到了社会的批评，那么，企业如何通过主动承担社会责任和遵守营销道德来获得社会的认可，是值得深思的问题。

The marketing concept is the philosophy of mutual profits between the enterprise and the customer, under the manipulation of the invisible hand, it can lead economy to satisfy the needs of millions of customers. But it does not mean all the salesmen agree on this conception, in fact, there are some merchants whose marketing behavior have been criticized, then, the question of how the enterprise gain the social recognition by actively taking on the social responsibilities and obeying the marketing moral deserves deep consideration.

一、社会对于营销的批评 Social Criticism of Marketing

由于经济利益的驱动，许多商家的营销伤害了消费者、社会及其他商家。从而引起了社会对营销的批评。

Because of the drive of economic benefits, business marketing of many enterprise hurts consumers, society and other businesses, then, thus leading to the social criticism of marketing.

在伤害消费者方面社会对营销的批评如下：由于高成本的分销、高成本的广告和促销，以及加价过度导致的定价过高；由于欺骗性定价、欺骗性促销和欺骗性包装导致的欺诈行为；由于销售人员说服顾客购买一些本来不想购买的产品而导致的强制买卖；商家提供许多质量不合格并且服务不到位的产品而使消费者买到了假冒伪劣产品或不安全的产品；有些生产商对产品实行有计划的淘汰，使产品在仍有需求时就出局；对穷人提供的服务恶劣而形成经济上的歧视现象，等等。

In the aspect of consumers, social criticism of marketing is as follows: the high pricing because of the distribution of high costs, the ads and promotion of high costs and excessively raising a price; the fraud leading to cheating pricing, deceptive promotion and fraudulent packaging; the forced sale formed by salesmen's persuading the customers to buy what they don't want; counterfeit and shoddy products and unsafe products bought by customers because of the business providing unqualified products and poor service; the eliminating of products before it is really weeded out because of the merchants' planned weeding out of the products; some phenomena of economic discrimination by providing poor service to the poor.

社会对营销的批评集中在伤害社会方面：营销体系过分重视物质上的拥有，对社会基本的价值观和社会责任感造成了极大的冲击，从而形成整个社会的不健康的价值导向。营销导致社会公共产品太少，过量销售私有产品而牺牲了有益于公众的公有产品；营销还导致文化污染，大量有关物质主义、性、权势以及地位等方面的广告侵入，污染着人们的心灵；在大市场营销观念的引导下，一些企业行使着太大的政治权力，他们对政治及立法的影响力可能变得过大。

Social criticism of marketing mainly focuses on the harm to society: marketing system attached more importance to the material possessions, which had a huge impact on the basic social values and responsibilities, so the unhealthy value guidance for the whole society formed. Marketing results in the social public product being so little, selling excessively personal products but sacrifice public products which are beneficial to the public; marketing also leaded to the cultural pollution, a large amount of ads are now interrupting the information on materialism, sex, violence which pollutes people's soul; under the guidance of marketing concept, some enterprises are now making use of political power and their influence on politics and legislation will become more serious.

社会对营销的批评集中在伤害其他商家方面：营销形成竞争对手之间的兼并、造成进入壁垒以及不公平竞争。

Social criticism of marketing focuses on the aspects of hurting other businesses: marketing forms the merger among rivals and results in the entry barrier and unfair competition.

二、营销中的社会责任 Social Responsibility in Marketing

营销活动中的社会责任包括三个层次：企业的利润责任、利益相关者责任、社会化责任，企业必须平衡好这三方面的责任关系，才能在营销中得到各方面的认可，从而使企业得以可持续发展。

There are three levels of social responsibilities in marketing activities: the responsibility of business profit, the responsibility of stakeholders and the responsibility of socialization. Enterprises have to balance the relationship among the three aspects, so as to get the recognition from all directions and make itself develop sustainably.

企业的利润责任是一个组织最基本的责任，即为其所有者赚取最大化利润的责任。事实上，所有的企业都已决定承担企业责任、扮演一个更积极的战略性角色。正如沃尔玛首席执行官李·斯科特(Lee Scott)所说："我们曾认为我们光待在阿肯色州的本顿维尔就可以处理好顾客和社区关系，世界不会来进行干预。"利润责任是企业存在的动力和营销活动的根源。

第十章 营销素养和社会责任
Marketing Ethics and Social Responsibility

The responsibility of business profit is the most fundamental one that is to help the owners gain the maximum profit. Actually, all the business have decided to take on the business responsibility and play a more active and strategic role. As Lee Scott, CEO of Wal-mart, said, "We've believed that only we stay in Bentonville, Arkansas can we deal with the relationship between customers and their community, the world will not intervene." Responsibility of business profit is the power of the business to exist and the root of marketing activity.

企业的利益相关者是指对其目标实现具有较强影响、与企业利益具有较强关联度的群体，主要包括顾客、雇员、供应商和分销商等。这些群体的利益与企业密切相关，并对企业的目标实现有直接的因果关系。家得宝前任总经理罗伯特·纳尔德里(Robert Nardelli)表示："事物变得越来越相互依存，构成要素也愈加广泛。"所以一个企业只有承担起这部分责任，能够在为所有者赚取利润的同时，兼顾对利益相关者所负的责任，实现利益相关者的利益，企业才能正常经营，才能更好地为所有者创造利润。

Stakeholders of the enterprise refers to the group which has a great influence on the realization of its aim and strong relevancy with business profits, mainly including customers, employees, suppliers and distributors. The benefit of these groups is closely related to the business and it has the direct causal relationship with the realization of the business aim. The former general manager of Home Depot, Robert Nardelli denoted, "Things depend more and more on each other, and their components are more extensive." Thus, only when the enterprise takes this part of responsibilities, gives consideration to the responsibilities of stakeholders and realize the profit of them at the same time of making profit for the owner, will the enterprise operate normally and provide the owner with profit.

企业的社会化责任是由于近几年的环境保护主义和消费者保护主义运动才发展出的一个概念。它强调企业在完成利润责任和相关者责任的同时，还要承担起保护生态环境和社会公众的社会化责任。许多力量正驱使企业实践更高层次的社会责任，包括：逐渐提升的顾客期望、演变中的员工目标和抱负、更严格的政府规定和压力、在社会标准中不断开发投资者的利益、严格的媒体监督以及不断变化的商业采购方法。2006年，阿尔·戈尔(Al Gore)的纪录片《被忽视的真相》(An Inconvenient Truth)获得了商业性成功，这表明公众变得更关心环境问题了。甚至香蕉生产商奇基塔(Chiquita)，这个曾经因剥削农民工、污染水源、破坏雨林而声誉极差的公司，也已经提升了工人的地位。并且，更为引人注目的是，奇基塔公司还减少了杀虫剂的使用，减少了侵蚀物和化学品的溢出，甚至在农场中实施了一个较大的循环利用项目。

The social responsibility of the enterprise is a newly developed idea due to the movement of environmentalism and consumerism in recent years. It stresses that the enterprise should take on the social responsibility of preserving the ecological environment and the public at the same time when an enterprise accomplishes the profit responsibility and stakeholder responsibility. Much power is forcing the enterprise to practice a higher level of social responsibility, including the gradually improved expectations of customers, employees' evolving aims and ambitions, the more strict government regulations and stress, investors' constantly developed benefit, the mass media's severe supervision and ever-changing way of business purchase. In 2006, Al Gore's documentary *An Inconvenient Truth* won the commercial success, which indicated that the public is becoming more concerned about environmental problems. Even the banana manufacturer—Chiquita who had a bad reputation of exploiting the peasant-worker, polluting water and damaging the rainforest have promoted the position of workers. It is more conspicuous that the company of Chiquita had reduced the use of pesticides, the overflow of chemicals, and even carried out a bigger project of cyclic utilization on farm.

三、实施对社会负责的营销 Implement the Marketing Responsible for the Society

有效的营销必须和强烈的伦理观、价值观和社会责任感相称。但不是所有人都对社会责任价值观持有如此的正面态度。1776 年，亚当·斯密声明："我压根不理解那些自称为了公众利益的人能得到什么好处。"著名经济学家米尔顿·弗里德曼断言公司的这种社会新行动"在本质上是破坏性的"，因为这暗中破坏了企业追逐利润的目的，浪费了股东的钱。还有一些批评家担心在一些领域的重大商业投资，比如研发，会因太注重社会责任而蒙受损害。

The effective marketing should accord with the strong sense of ethics, values and social responsibility. But not all the people hold positive attitude toward the value of social responsibility. In 1776, Adam Smith demonstrated, "I don't understand at all what advantages the so-called 'for the public weal' persons will get." The famous economist Milton Friedman asserted that the new activity of the company is "devastating in itself", because it furtively disrupted the company's aim of profit-seeking and wasted shareholder's money. There are also some critics who are still worrying about the major business investment in some fields, for example, research and development, which will suffer because of attaching more importance to social responsibility.

但这些批评家只是极少数的。许多人现在相信，使顾客、员工和其他利益相关者感到满意，并取得商业成功，是与采用和实施高标准的商业和营销行为紧密相连的。企业发现，如果一个企业被认为具有社会责任，那么其中一个好处就是能够吸引员工，特别是那些年轻人，他们乐意为自己喜欢的公司工作。世界上最令人钦佩，并日益成功的企业都遵循这样一个守则——为大家的利益服务，而不仅仅只考虑公司本身的利益。

But these critics are in tiny minority. Many people are believing that to make customers, staff and other stakeholders feel satisfied and gain the business success is closely related to the adapted and implemented business and selling behavior of high level. The enterprise found that if an enterprise were considered to have social responsibility, then one of the advantages were to attract its staff, especially the young, to be willing to work for their company. The most admirable and increasingly successful enterprises all follow such codes—to serve others' benefit, not only consider the company's own benefit.

企业的市场营销应支持营销体系长期的最佳业绩，以下五种营销观念可以帮助企业实现这样的目标：消费者导向的市场营销、创新导向的市场营销、价值导向的市场营销、使命感导向的市场营销、社会营销。

The enterprise's marketing should support the long-term best performance of marketing system. The following five marketing ideas can help the enterprise realize such aims: consumer-oriented marketing, innovation-oriented marketing, value-oriented marketing, and the sense of mission-guided marketing and social marketing.

消费者导向的市场营销是指企业应从顾客的观点来看待并组织自己的市场营销活动。它应致力于感受、服务及满足特定顾客的需求。企业只有为顾客创造价值，才能从顾客那里获取价值作为回报。

The consumer-oriented marketing means that the enterprise should regard and organize marketing activity from the customer's point of view. It should work on feeling, serving and meeting the consumers' desire. Only when the enterprise creates value for the customers should it get the value from customers in return.

创新性市场营销要求企业不断寻求真正的产品和营销改进。企业如果忽略新的较好的经营方法，最终会使顾客投向另一个找到较好的经营方法的企业。

Innovation-oriented marketing demands the enterprise to pursue the real product unceasingly and promote its marketing. If the enterprise omits the latest and better way of marketing, it will force customers to turn to a better way of operation of the enterprise.

顾客价值营销是指企业应将大部分资源放在为顾客创造价值的营销投资上，营销人员的许多工作可能在短期内使销售额增加，但比起真正改善产品质量、特色或便利性来讲，增加的价值很少，这就要求不断改善消费者从企业获得的价值，以建立长期的消费者忠诚关系。

Customers' value-oriented marketing means to place most of the resources on the marketing investment which can create value for customers. Much of salesmen's work will increase the sales volume in a short period, but compared with the true quality, characteristics and convince improvement of product, its value increased a little. It requires that they improve the value the customers get from the enterprise to establish the long-term loyal relationship with customers.

使命感导向的市场营销意味着企业应以广泛的社会观点而非狭窄的产品观点来阐述其使命。当企业明确了其社会使命时，员工会对自己的工作感到愉悦并有明确的努力方向。

The sense of mission guided marketing means that the enterprise should illustrate its mission with extensive social point of view rather than with the confined view of product. When the social mission is defined by the enterprise, the staff will be pleased with their work and have a definite direction to strive for.

社会营销意味着不仅要考虑消费者需求和企业需要，还要考虑消费者和社会的长期利益。企业应当明白，如果忽视后两者利益，将会给消费者和社会带来伤害。

Social marketing not only means considering consumers' needs and the needs of the enterprise, but also considering consumers and the long-term social benefits. The enterprise should understand that if the benefit of the latter two were neglected, it would hurt consumers and the society.

本 章 小 结
Summary

营销人员必备的营销素养包括具备现代营销理念、良好的品德、知识渊博、持续学习、勤于思考、良好的心理素质、良好的团队合作精神及必备的基本能力。营销人员可以通过岗前培训、在职脱产学习、自我训练提高自身的业务素养。

The essential marketing attainments which marketing personnel should possess include modern marketing concept, good morals, a wide range of knowledge, further study, thinking diligently, good psychological qualities, team spirit and the basic requisite abilities. Marketing personnel can improve their business attainments through pre-job training, releasing from their work to study and training themselves.

由于经济利益的驱动,许多商家的营销伤害了消费者、社会和其他商家,从而引起了社会对营销的批评。营销活动中的社会责任包括三个层次:企业的利润责任、利益相关者责任、社会化责任,企业必须平衡好这三方面的责任关系,才能在营销中得到各方向的认可,从而使企业得以可持续发展。有效的营销必须和强烈的伦理观、价值观和社会责任感相称。

Due to the drive of economic benefits, marketing of many enterprises hurt consumers, society and other enterprises, thus resulting in social criticism of marketing. Social responsibilities of marketing activities include three levels: the benefits of an enterprise, the responsibilities of the stakeholder and social responsibilities. Only when the enterprise balances the three levels of responsibilities well, will it get the recognition form all aspects and have the sustainable development. Effective marketing has to be commensurate to the strong sense of ethics, values and social responsibilities.

思 考 题
Questions

1. 营销人员应具备哪些营销素养?
What qualities should marketing personnel possess?
2. 如何实施对社会负责任的市场营销?
How to carry out marketing responsibility for the society?

参 考 文 献

[1] 陈丽燕，王忠政. 市场营销学[M]. 上海：上海财经大学出版社，2013.
[2] 韩枫，陈丽燕. 市场营销学[M]. 哈尔滨：哈尔滨工业大学出版社，2011.
[3] 吴健安. 营销管理. [M]. 2版. 北京：高等教育出版社，2010.
[4] 郭国庆. 市场营销学通论[M]. 4版. 北京：中国人民大学出版社，2011.
[5] 陈伟，李拓晨，徐长冬. 现代市场营销学[M]. 北京：清华大学出版社，2012.
[6] 邱小平. 市场调研与预测[M]. 北京：机械工业出版社，2012.
[7] 许以洪，刘玉芳. 市场营销学[M]. 北京：机械工业出版社，2012.
[8] 叶敏. 市场营销原理与实务[M]. 北京：北京邮电大学出版社，2011.
[9] 吴谨，林怡，许罗丹. 市场营销学[M]. 北京：机械工业出版社，2011.
[10] 池丽华，朱文敏. 市场营销学[M]. 上海：立信会计出版社，2011.
[11] 王德胜，南志庆. 市场营销学[M]. 北京：经济科学出版社，2011.
[12] 张再谦，苏巧娜. 市场营销学[M]. 3版. 北京：中国商业出版社，2011.
[13] 王中亮. 市场营销学[M]. 上海：立信会计出版社，2011.
[14] 万后芬. 市场营销学[M]. 武汉：华中科技大学出版社，2011.
[15] 董大海. 营销管理[M]. 北京：清华大学出版社，2010.
[16] 李世杰，于飞. 市场调查与预测[M]. 北京：清华大学出版社，2010.
[17] 连漪. 市场营销管理——理论、方法与实务[M]. 2版. 北京：国防工业出版社，2010.
[18] 史光启. 中国市场营销与管理规则[M]. 北京：清华大学出版社，2010.
[19] 穆健康. 市场营销学[M]. 长春：东北师范大学出版社，2010.
[20] 乔均. 市场营销学[M]. 北京：清华大学出版社，2010.
[21] 邓剑平. 调查与预测：理论、实务、案例、实训[M]. 北京：高等教育出版社，2010.
[22] 魏炳麒. 市场营销调查与预测[M]. 大连：东北财经大学出版社，2010.
[23] 卫海英. 市场营销学[M]. 北京：经济科学出版社，2009.
[24] 徐彤宝，王光娟. 市场营销学[M]. 长春：吉林大学出版社，2009.
[25] 柯惠新，丁立宏. 市场调查[M]. 北京：高等教育出版社，2009.
[26] 李晏野. 市场营销学[M]. 北京：高等教育出版社，2009.
[27] 吴世经. 市场营销学[M]. 4版. 成都：西南财经大学出版社，2009.
[28] 王德章，周游. 市场营销学[M]. 北京：高等教育出版社，2009.
[29] 张先云. 市场营销学[M]. 北京：机械工业出版社，2009.
[30] 杨洪涛. 现代市场营销学[M]. 北京：机械工业出版社，2009.
[31] 罗农. 市场营销学[M]. 北京：清华大学出版社，2008.
[32] 陆娟，乔娟. 市场营销学[M]. 北京：清华大学出版社，2008.
[33] 吴健安. 市场营销学[M]. 3版. 北京：高等教育出版社，2007.
[34] 郭国庆. 市场营销学通论[M]. 北京：中国人民大学出版社，2007.
[35] 法拉尔(Cate Farrall)，林斯利(Marianne Lindsley). 剑桥市场营销英语(*Professional English in Use Marketing*)[M]. 北京：人民邮电出版社，2010.
[36] 徐小贞，彭朝林. 国际市场营销(英文版) [M]. 北京：高等教育出版社，2011.
[37] 李菲. 英汉汉英市场营销词汇手册[M]. 上海：上海外语教育出版社，2012.

[38] 加里·阿姆斯特朗,菲利普·科特勒. 市场营销学[M]. 7版. 何志毅,赵占波译. 北京:中国人民大学出版社,2009.

[39] 菲利普·科特勒,加里·阿姆斯特朗,洪瑞云. 市场营销原理[M]. 亚洲版. 何志毅译. 北京:机械工业出版社,2010.

[40] 迈克尔·R. 所罗门. 消费者行为学[M]. 卢泰宏,杨晓燕译. 北京:中国人民大学出版社,2010.

[41] 格雷厄姆·胡利,约翰·桑德斯,奈杰尔·皮尔西. 营销战略与竞争定位[M]. 3版. 楼尊,王国新译. 北京:中国人民大学出版社,2008.

[42] K. 道格拉斯·霍夫曼,约翰·E. G. 贝特森. 服务营销精要——概念、战略和案例[M]. 中文改编版. 范秀成译. 北京:北京大学出版社,2008.

[43] 菲利普·科特勒,加里·阿姆斯特朗. 市场营销原理[M]. 北京:清华大学出版社,2011.

[44] 菲利普·科特勒. 营销管理[M]. 11版. 上海:上海人民出版社,2008.

[45] 菲利普·科特勒,加里·阿姆斯特朗. 市场营销原理(*Principles of Marketing*)[M]. 北京:清华大学出版社,2008.

[46] J. 保罗·彼得(J. Paul Peter),詹姆斯·H. 唐纳利(James H. Donnelly. Jr). 市场营销专业英语教程(*A Preface to Marketing Management*)[M]. 北京:中国人民大学出版社,2009.

[47] 达娜-尼科莱塔·拉斯库(Dana-Nicoleta Lascu). 国际市场营销学(International Marketing) [M]. 马连福,赵颖,高楠译. 北京:机械工业出版社,2010.

[48] 菲利普·凯特奥拉,玛丽·吉利,约翰·格雷厄. 国际营销(英文版) [M]. 16版. 崔新健改编. 北京:中国人民大学出版社,2013.